DUEL for the CROWN

Affirmed, Alydar, and Racing's Greatest Rivalry

LINDA CARROLL and DAVID ROSNER

ECLIPSE
PRESS

Essex, Connecticut

For Affirmed, Alydar,
and all the other noble Thoroughbreds
who have raced into our hearts

ECLIPSE
PRESS

An imprint of Globe Pequot, the trade division of
The Rowman & Littlefield Publishing Group, Inc.
4501 Forbes Blvd., Ste. 200
Lanham, MD 20706
www.rowman.com

Distributed by NATIONAL BOOK NETWORK

British Library Cataloguing in Publication Information available

Library of Congress Cataloging-in-Publication Data available

ISBN 978-1-4930-8019-9 (paperback)
ISBN 978-1-4930-8020-5 (epub)

♾™ The paper used in this publication meets the minimum requirements of American National
Standard for Information Sciences—Permanence of Paper for Printed Library Materials, ANSI/
NISO Z39.48-1992.

CONTENTS

INTRODUCTION. 1

PROLOGUE: Both the King's Horses 5

PART I: Genesis
CHAPTER 1: Seeds of Greatness 9
CHAPTER 2: Dynasty. .27
CHAPTER 3: The Takeover Artist 59
CHAPTER 4: From the Ashes 79

PART II: Ascendance
CHAPTER 5: Born to Run 101
CHAPTER 6: The Casey Stengel of Horse Whisperers. 117
CHAPTER 7: The Beginning of a Beautiful Rivalry 133
CHAPTER 8: The Kid. 143
CHAPTER 9: The Battle Joined 163
CHAPTER 10: Collision Course 183

PART III: Coronation
CHAPTER 11: Dream Derby 199
CHAPTER 12: Affirmation 221
CHAPTER 13: Dueling for the Crown Jewel 231
CHAPTER 14: Crowning Glory 245
CHAPTER 15: The Anticlimax 261

EPILOGUE: Where Have You Gone, Affirmed and Alydar? 271

APPENDIX I: Affirmed vs. Alydar: The Showdowns 287

APPENDIX II: Charting the Classics: The 1978 Triple Crown 293

APPENDIX III: Dueling Careers: Racing Records of the Rivals 297

APPENDIX IV: Family Trees: Pedigree Charts of the Rivals 301

APPENDIX V: Tale of the Tape: How They Measured Up 305

ACKNOWLEDGMENTS. 307

SOURCES 311

INDEX 319

ABOUT THE AUTHORS 329

INTRODUCTION

IN THE THREE CENTURIES SINCE THE NOBLE THOROUGHBRED FLASHED into our consciousness, we have marveled at the majesty of fabled race-horses from Eclipse to Man o' War to Secretariat. But more than any singular superhorse, what really captivates us and captures our imagination are the match races and the matchless rivalries, for nothing tests the heart of a champion more than a worthy foe whose own pluck brings out the best in both. By that measure, no twinned rivals could ever surpass a peerless pair of chestnut colts who remain as inseparably linked in lore as they were on the racetrack. You simply cannot mention one without the alliteratively named other: Affirmed and Alydar.

Theirs is an unrivaled rivalry that not only ennobled the pastime known as "The Sport of Kings," but also transcended horse racing to hold an entire nation spellbound throughout their epic trilogy of Triple Crown duels. Around water coolers and water troughs in that magical spring of 1978, casual followers and confirmed railbirds alike could compare it only to the fiercest rivalry ever waged by two-legged athletes: the three-fight blood feud pitting Muhammad Ali against Joe Frazier for boxing's heavyweight crown just a few years earlier.

These equine heavyweights squared off a staggering ten times in a span of fourteen months, and although Affirmed won the lion's share of their confrontations, five were photo finishes decided by the blink of a shutter. After dueling four furious miles through the hardest-fought of all Triple Crown campaigns, Affirmed and Alydar were separated by a combined margin of under half a second. The Kentucky Derby may be hyped as "the most exciting two minutes in sports," but the pair's electrifying stretch showdowns kept only intensifying through both remaining jewels, the Preakness and Belmont Stakes. To cap it all off with the coveted Triple

Crown on the line, Affirmed would have to outfight Alydar every hoofbeat of the way in what is widely deemed the greatest horse race ever run. The rivalry's breathtaking climax marked their Belmont stretch duel as a cultural touchstone and put an exclamation point on horse racing's last golden age.

*   *   *

The intertwined saga of Affirmed and Alydar is a study in contrasts as stark as David and Goliath. If Alydar and his human connections personify racing royalty, Affirmed and his crew embody all the underdog outsiders who've had to claw their way into the winner's circle.

Alydar was born into Bluegrass aristocracy as the royally bred pride of Kentucky's Calumet Farm, the Thoroughbred dynasty that had reigned over The Sport of Kings in the same way the New York Yankees dominated the national pastime. Lucille Markey, the blue-blood heiress embraced as racing's grand dame in her eighties, saw in Alydar a last chance to rescue her beloved Calumet. Desperate to restore her storied stable's faded glory, she entrusted her strapping savior to a promising young trainer with a venerable pedigree of his own: John Veitch, himself a Lexington-born son of a Hall of Famer.

Affirmed, by contrast, was foaled and raised down in Florida, far removed from the sport's old-money Kentucky home, at an upstart farm fueled by the new-money millions of a controversial Wall Street financier turned nouveau breeder. Lou Wolfson, an immigrant junkman's son who pulled himself out of poverty as a pioneering corporate raider, saw in Affirmed a chance at redemption after a conviction for securities violations sent him to prison. He entrusted his lanky longshot to a charismatic trainer who like himself was a consummate outsider: Laz Barrera, a Cuban immigrant who climbed to the top from backstretch obscurity through his uncanny ability to coax and charm the most out of his horses.

With so much riding on both homebreds, the choice of jockeys epitomized the differing strategies employed by the opposing teams of rivals locked in a battle of wits and wills: Steve Cauthen, a child prodigy like none the sports world had ever seen, versus the wily veteran who had mentored him, Jorge Velasquez. For all Cauthen's precocious fame as the first racing figure ever feted as *Sports Illustrated*'s Sportsman of the Year, the teen sensation had yet to prove himself in the pressure cooker of any Triple Crown race. As celebrated as "The Kid" was when he began riding Affirmed as a seventeen-year-old phenom ranked the top athlete of 1977, the real stars of 1978 would be the entwined pair of three-year-old colts racing as a team down the stretch and into history—forever together as they took their human connections and countless armchair jockeys along for the ride and the rivalry.

Despite their similar chestnut coloring and their shared bloodlines as descendants of the great Native Dancer, Affirmed and Alydar boasted the kind of clashing styles and complementary personalities that fuel the most enduring rivalries. Off the track, the refined Affirmed was as relaxed and easygoing as the regal Alydar was macho and aggressive. On the track, their contrasting styles forged the equine equivalent of Ali the Boxer versus Frazier the Slugger. Affirmed, lithe and quick like Ali, was the classic frontrunner, gliding with the grace of a deer and the tactical speed and stamina to fend off any challenge, while Alydar, brawny and bullish like Frazier, was the classic closer, relentlessly stalking his nemesis and gearing up to unleash his come-from-behind knockout punch. Their classic confrontation was so close that it would always come down to one gritty champion's indomitable will to win.

*   *   *

Of all the fierce rivals joined together in the annals of sport—from Ali-Frazier and Louis-Schmeling to Army-Navy and Yankees-Bosox—no one-two combination is more tightly bound by a hyphen than Affirmed-Alydar. This alliterative exacta featured the perfect symbiotic relationship, each horse bringing out the best in the other. Which, of course, is the essence of any athletic competition—and, by extension, any compelling rivalry. Imagine Ali without Frazier, Chamberlain without Russell, Magic without Bird, Evert without Navratilova, Federer without Nadal, Nicklaus without Palmer, DiMaggio without Williams, Affirmed without Alydar.

The legend of Affirmed simply couldn't be written without Alydar, for it was the heat of their pitched battles that stamped the victor as one of the most tenacious and courageous warriors ever to grace a racetrack. No matter which horse you backed with your bets and cheers, both of these archrivals and their humans taught us the virtue of heart: Affirmed embodying the resolve to prevail against long odds, Alydar the resilience to persevere in the face of heartbreaking loss.

The passage of time has only elevated their bond to mythic proportions, transcending the Triple Crown and The Sport of Kings itself. On an

ESPN television show counting down the twenty best sports rivalries of all time, Affirmed versus Alydar ranked fifteenth—the only members of their species to crack a list predictably topped by Ali versus Frazier and Yankees versus Red Sox.

When the first edition of *Duel for the Crown* was published in 2014, thirty-five years had elapsed since their rousing Belmont stretch duel produced what everyone was then calling "the last Triple Crown winner"—history's longest such interregnum by fully a decade. In that edition, we concluded, "Everyone agrees that there will probably be another Triple Crown winner someday, but there will never be another rivalry quite like Affirmed and Alydar."

Now that the drought is finally over—with American Pharoah ending it in 2015 and Justify joining him three years later in sport's most exclusive club—this revised and updated edition of *Duel for the Crown* shows why we can double down on that declaration about a rivalry that's as peerless as it is timeless. For, of the thirteen Thoroughbreds to have now won the Triple Crown, only one has ever had to prove his mettle and earn his immortality by outdueling such a formidable foe over and over and over again.

PROLOGUE

Both the King's Horses

THE TWO CHESTNUT COLTS THUNDER DOWN THE HOMESTRETCH, GALLOP-
ing side by side and head to head, like a matched team. Gracefully skimming
along on the rail, Affirmed—streamlined and elegant, his coat gleaming in
the late-afternoon sun like burnished bronze—controls the pace, a frontrunner who simply hates to be headed. Breathing down his neck and eating
up ground on the outside with each powerful stride, Alydar—bigger, burlier,
and brawnier, his muscles rippling through a coat that glistens a rich dark
chocolate against Affirmed's butterscotch—presses relentlessly while gearing up to unleash his fearsome closing kick.

As they charge deep into Saratoga Race Course's historic homestretch,
there is much riding on this stakes race that annually represents the proving
ground for horse racing's brightest young hopefuls. The very name of the
race—the Hopeful Stakes—evokes the dream shared by everyone who has
ever bred or bought a Thoroughbred in pursuit of the sport's holy grail, the
Kentucky Derby. As the most prestigious race for two-year-olds at America's oldest and grandest racetrack, the Hopeful boasts a storied tradition
as the debutante ball introducing the public to a who's who of budding
legends—from Man o' War to Native Dancer to Secretariat to . . .

Of the 28,946 Thoroughbreds foaled throughout North America in
1975, Alydar had been anointed the chosen one from the moment he hit
the Kentucky bluegrass running. As the prince of Calumet Farm, heir to
revive the dynasty that had for decades reigned over The Sport of Kings,
Alydar was practically fitted for the Triple Crown from the time of his royal
birth. Affirmed may have shared rich bloodlines with him, both of them
descendants of Native Dancer, but Alydar was the one most clearly bred for

greatness. The 1977 Hopeful Stakes would be his first big step on the trail leading to the 1978 Kentucky Derby.

But now, with Alydar and Affirmed locked in a pitched duel down the Saratoga stretch, it suddenly dawns on everyone that there is not just one Derby horse in this year's crop—but rather there are two of them. Through the final furlong, as the other hopefuls disappear in their wake, Affirmed has the lead by a head. His jockey, teen sensation Steve Cauthen, taps him up to ask for a little more speed. The acceleration is more powerful than anything Cauthen has ever felt before. The jockey glances to his right and is amazed to see Alydar surging along with them. Alydar challenges, but Affirmed digs in and won't let him pass. Cauthen realizes right then that this is a special horse, one that will heroically fight to protect his lead. At that moment, Affirmed's rider already knows something that Alydar and everyone else are about to find out: the race and the rivalry are only just beginning. The battle has been joined.

As their eyes lock in the deep stretch, neither Affirmed nor Alydar could know that the image staring back would ultimately define each horse's legend and legacy. Nor could they know that this instant would signal the genesis of a rivalry that would propel them together into the 1978 Triple Crown campaign—and beyond, into immortality.

PART I

GENESIS

Raise a Native (Keeneland Library Meadors Collection)

CHAPTER 1

Seeds of Greatness

RAISE A NATIVE—THE SIRE OF ALYDAR, THE GRANDSIRE OF AFFIRMED, and the most influential stud horse of his generation—came within a snip of being gelded before he could even get to the starting gate, let alone the breeding shed. That's how close the story of his two greatest descendants came to ending before it could begin.

From the moment he was foaled early in 1961, Raise a Native was the kind of strapping specimen that Thoroughbred empires get built around. Bounding to his feet quicker than most foals, he was soon out zipping around the rolling bluegrass pastures of central Kentucky and showing off his catlike agility amid bursts of stunning speed. Veteran horsemen at racing's preeminent breeding farms marveled at how, even as a baby, he had "the look of eagles."

More important, he had the look of his sire: Native Dancer, the legendary gray colt who flashed through America's consciousness in the early 1950s as the first equine TV star. At the dawn of the golden age of television, "The Gray Ghost" stood out on newfangled black-and-white TV screens not only for how his striking dapple-gray coat contrasted with all the indistinguishable browns of his foes, but also for how he overpowered them down the stretch. What captured the viewer's imagination was the electrifying way Native Dancer won all but one of his twenty-two career starts, lagging way behind until the stretch turn and then thundering past his rivals as if they were moving in slow motion.

Raise a Native, aside from his chestnut color, was the spitting image of his famous father, with the promise of the same lightning speed, raw power, and massive size. Small wonder that, when he was auctioned at the 1961 Keeneland Fall Sale, Raise a Native commanded $22,000—the most anyone had ever bid on a weanling. Within nine months, he would be brought to auction once again, his new owner hoping to turn a quick profit on his exceptional looks, his value having grown in direct proportion to his developing musculature.

The colt was just the kind of prospect Louis Wolfson was shopping for as he built up his fledgling stable. An impoverished immigrant's son who had parlayed a Florida junkyard into an industrial empire, Wolfson became rich as a Wall Street financier and infamous as a takeover artist astutely waging proxy fights over America's corporate giants. Credited with inventing the hostile tender offer, he was branded by *Time* magazine as one of America's first corporate raiders.

Wolfson was well into his forties when he was advised by his doctor to find a relaxing pastime to relieve the stress of high finance and, given his longtime interest in watching and betting on Thoroughbreds, he decided to try his hand at owning and breeding them. Although he started modestly by purchasing a dozen middling horses in 1958, he soon threw himself into the racing game with the same wheeler-dealer fervor he'd honed in his boardroom battles.

By the following year, Wolfson had unleashed a bold assault on the Thoroughbred establishment every bit as audacious as his hostile takeover bids. The more the racing elite dismissed him as a novice too naive to realize how many generations of bloodlines and sweat were needed to build a winning stable, the more he relished the challenge. Any self-made millionaire fearless enough to take on the likes of Montgomery Ward and American Motors wasn't about to be cowed by Kentucky's Thoroughbred institutions—not even mighty Calumet Farm, the racing and breeding dynasty sprawling over a thousand acres of prime Lexington bluegrass.

On his mission to show up the skeptics, Wolfson's first real order of business was to recruit a trainer capable of instantly putting his new Florida-based stable on the map. He reached out to Burley Parke, a masterful trainer who at fifty-four was already nine relaxing years into retirement at his own California ranch. Renowned as "The Futurity King," Parke had earned his nickname because of his uncanny eye and unsurpassed talent for bringing along young stock, having schooled a remarkable nine futurity stakes two-year-old champions. When Wolfson tried to coax him out of retirement to work the same wonders for his nascent Harbor View Farm stable, the erstwhile trainer politely demurred. Wolfson persisted with the same powers of persuasion that had forged many a Wall Street deal, finally luring Parke with an unheard-of $100,000 guaranteed salary—more than twelve times what the standard trainer's fee of 10 percent would have been worth based on Harbor View's paltry 1959 winnings of $80,161.

In his first year on the job, Parke saddled fifty-four winners and earned $679,865 in purses—making Wolfson's three-year-old stable the nation's third-leading money winner of 1960, behind only the aristocratic empires of Cornelius Vanderbilt Whitney and Harry F. Guggenheim. As unprecedented as Wolfson's rocket-like rise was, he was impatient to push to the next level. He craved that one yearling that could win the Kentucky Derby as a three-year-old and then become the foundation sire on which a breeding empire could be built. That's the dream Wolfson was chasing when he sent Parke to Saratoga, New York, in August 1962.

No sooner had Parke arrived at the annual Saratoga Yearling Sale than a copper-colored colt with superb conformation caught his eye. He immediately raced to the phone to call his boss. Picking up the receiver in his office, Wolfson was surprised by the breathless enthusiasm emanating from the phone. Taciturn and reserved by nature, the soft-spoken Parke was not given to hyperbole. But now, he was positively gushing about a Native Dancer son muscled like a gladiator and polished like a shiny new penny. The trainer raved about Raise a Native's striking good looks, his surprisingly mature body, his huge and powerful hindquarters, and, to top it all off, his impressive pedigree. To be sure, Parke didn't have to say anything about the colt's sire because everyone knew everything there was to know about Native Dancer, a cultural icon so famous that *TV Guide* ranked him the second-biggest television attraction behind only Ed Sullivan. Parke did, however, have plenty to report about the colt's dam: a modest stakes-winning sprinter named Raise You, from whom Raise a Native inherited not only his chestnut coat but also a dose of pure speed. All of which made Raise a Native the most coveted of the ten Native Dancer yearlings parading through the plush auction ring that summer.

Parke told Wolfson that this horse, seemingly born on the steps of the throne, was exactly what they'd been searching for. What he needed to know was how high he could bid.

"Spend what you need to," Wolfson replied without missing a beat.

The bidding was fast and furious. When the hammer finally fell at $39,000 (more than three times the Saratoga Yearling Sale's record average), Wolfson had the star he needed to build his farm around.

One thing Parke couldn't see in the auction ring would become painfully obvious as soon as the robust colt bounded off the van at Harbor View Farm in Ocala, Florida. Raise a Native, it turned out, had inherited something beyond physical brilliance from his famous father: a temperamental disposition. On and off the track, Native Dancer had always done just as he pleased. And now, Raise a Native was proving he was all that and more: rambunctious, headstrong, stubborn. Right from the start, he seemed determined to test Parke's renowned patience. No matter how unruly his horses were, Parke had always remained unflappable and unwavering, all the while getting even the most stubborn student to submit to his will. The question was, could Parke perform the same kind of magic with Wolfson's unruly yearling?

Each morning upon his arrival at Hialeah Park's backside barn, the trainer would be reminded just how much of a challenge he faced. It would start the moment Raise a Native's groom brought out the tack. As soon as the colt spotted the saddle, his eyes would roll back until the whites were showing, his nostrils would flare, and all his muscles would begin to quiver. He would be bouncing around so much that it took a herculean effort just to get the saddle on his back, let alone girthed up. All this even before he could be led out to the track to begin his workday. Almost all the Harbor View exercise riders refused to even mount the volatile, uncontrollable colt. Only a wet-behind-the-ears seventeen-year-old was brave enough to agree to get on him and face the bronc rides disguised as workouts.

Parke was becoming more and more exasperated with each passing day. Having tried every trick he knew, he was beginning to wonder if it was time for the strategy of last resort: castration. He worried that if they didn't geld the colt, Raise a Native would never be calm enough to load into a starting gate, much less run a race.

One day, he called Wolfson to explain the situation. "I'm afraid we may need to geld this colt to settle him down," Parke said quietly. "It may be the only way to get him trained."

Wolfson took a deep breath, shrugging in resignation. As much as he wanted a Kentucky Derby winner, what he really desired was a colt that would later make his mark in the breeding shed. But if the horse couldn't be made to run on the track, no one would want to breed to him anyway. Finally, Wolfson let out a sigh and said, "OK, Burley, do what you need to do."

Even with Wolfson's permission, Parke was hesitant. He feared that castration might be a huge mistake, robbing future generations of an influential sire. So he decided to postpone the decision until the next time he saw Wolfson in person.

On a beautiful Saturday morning in January 1963, Wolfson, as was his weekly ritual, packed up his three sons and headed over to Hialeah Park to watch his horses work. He was especially interested in seeing Raise a Native. By the time he arrived, the colt was already saddled and making his way from the shedrow to the track. Raise a Native seemed on his best behavior prancing down the bridle path on his way to be schooled by Parke at the starting gate. If the inquisitive colt seemed to be paying more attention to the flock of flamingos in the infield than to his rider's commands, at least he was being so uncharacteristically well behaved that the exercise boy, for a change, managed to stay in the saddle the whole way without getting thrown. Upon reaching the starting gate, however, Raise a Native, as if on cue, played one of his favorite tricks. He dropped to the ground, rolled onto his side, and lay motionless. This time, Parke was ready. He jumped off his stable pony and ran over to an attending groom to grab a bucket of ice-cold water, which he promptly dumped over the prone colt's head. Startled, Raise a Native jumped up and shook his head violently, sending a spray of droplets over everyone around him. He stood quietly while Parke lifted the exercise boy back into the saddle, then he meekly walked over to the starting gate. The colt knew he had finally met his match.

The battle won, Parke could now focus on getting Raise a Native ready not for a vet appointment but for a post time. From that moment on, the teacher had an apt, attentive pupil to train for the two-year-old prodigy's highly anticipated maiden race.

Barely a month later, debuting in a three-furlong "baby race" at Hialeah, Raise a Native started to fulfill his promise right from the bell, flying over the three-eighths of a mile to win by a full six lengths. He was then shipped to New York, where he would take up residence on Belmont Park's backside in preparation for his next big step up. It didn't take long for his early morning works to start drawing attention from the New York beat reporters.

One day that spring, the dean of American turf writers, Charles Hatton, was sitting in his aerie above the Belmont press box watching the morning works as usual when he glimpsed a powerful chestnut flying by. Hatton immediately started pounding out the colt's public introduction on his battered Royal typewriter: "Raise a Native worked down the Belmont backstretch this morning. The trees swayed."

If the trees were swaying at Belmont, they were positively bending over at nearby Aqueduct Racetrack once Raise a Native made his New York racing debut there. Over the next few months, he handily won three straight races in track-record times, each performance more spectacular than the previous. The last two, both Aqueduct stakes races, made him something of a phenomenon. Fans started flocking to "The Big A," crowding around the paddock to catch a glimpse of this rising-star son of Native Dancer now making a name for himself.

Even the most hardened horsemen were becoming gushing fans. "In all the years I have been training horses, Raise a Native is the best two-year-old I've ever seen race," marveled Hirsch Jacobs, the seasoned trainer who had saddled more winners than anyone else in history. "I believe he will be one of our all-time greats."

As it was, Raise a Native was already being compared to his own sire, to Citation, even to the incomparable Man o' War. Joe Hirsch, Hatton's respected colleague at the *Morning Telegraph*, reached all the way back to the nineteenth century's most fabled champion, calling Raise a Native "the second coming of Hindoo."

To the understated Parke, it was enough that Raise a Native was "the greatest young horse I've ever trained." The only remaining question was whether the colt possessed the stamina to stay the Kentucky Derby's mile and a quarter, especially given that his sprinter's style emulated that of his pacesetting dam more than that of his fast-closing sire. Though he had sped to four wins without ever seeing a horse in front of him, he still hadn't gone longer than five and a half furlongs. As part of Parke's plan to answer the nagging doubts incrementally, he took Raise a Native to New Jersey that summer for the Sapling Stakes, a step up at six furlongs.

Prepping for the race, the unthinkable happened. At the end of a fast morning work at Monmouth Park the day before the stakes, the prohibitive favorite pulled up lame with a bowed tendon. He limped off the track,

Native Dancer after winning the 1953 American Derby (Keeneland Library Morgan Collection)

barely able to take any weight on his left foreleg. Parke called Wolfson with the bad news: Raise a Native bowed a tendon and would never race again.

Crestfallen as he was, Wolfson didn't second-guess his trainer or curse his own bad luck. He just said, "Burley, are you going to be OK?" The two continued on for a while, each consoling the other over the premature retirement of what they both considered to be the horse of a lifetime. Just before hanging up, Wolfson injected some words of hope. "Don't worry," he said. "One of these days, we'll grab on to another one."

*   *   *

Little did Wolfson know that Raise a Native would make that happen, too.

The dreams left unfulfilled on the racetrack, where Raise a Native had streaked like a shooting star, would have to blossom in the breeding shed if they were to become a reality. Although his meteoric career flamed out almost as quickly as he ran, Raise a Native had shown enough brilliance to still be in high demand as a stud horse. Because of his precocious talent and the early maturity that made this two-year-old look twice his age, breeders from Kentucky to England were lining up for his services even though he had yet to produce a single foal. They flooded storied Spendthrift Farm, where he'd been sent to stand at stud, with more than a hundred applications to buy breedings at $5,000 a pop.

When Raise a Native's first foal crop hit the ground running in 1965, that stud fee would seem like a bargain. His foals were uniformly attractive and well conformed. He was stamping them with his good looks and his athletic ability, no matter what mare they were out of. Four would eventually become stakes winners, chief among them Wolfson's own Exclusive Native.

Exclusive Native was a striking chestnut out of Wolfson's foundation dam, Exclusive, herself a moderate runner who turned out to be an exceptional broodmare with five stakes winners to her credit. It didn't take long to see that the sleek colt had inherited the signature speed of his sire line. He won his first three starts as a two-year-old, including the Sanford Stakes at Saratoga, but lost his next four before sustaining a slight cannon-bone fracture that sidelined him until the following summer. He returned to win the Arlington Classic, but was injured again in his next start on the same Monmouth Park track where his sire's career had ended. As with Raise a Native, Wolfson had no choice but to retire his foundation sire's son to stud. That broke Wolfson's heart because Exclusive Native had earned his own special place there as the first Harbor View homebred to shine on the track.

Despite all of Harbor View's trips to the winner's circle and Wolfson's ranking among the nation's leading owners and breeders, he wasn't able to enjoy his success as much as he might have. For most of the decade, the U.S. Securities and Exchange Commission had been coming after him for alleged securities violations. In 1966, just as Raise a Native's second foal crop hit the ground, Wolfson was indicted for selling unregistered stock. A year later, he was convicted and sentenced to a year in federal prison.

The conviction almost ended his career in racing. To pay his overwhelming legal fees, Wolfson had to sell off most of his horses, many at fire-sale prices. Exclusive was sold outright as Wolfson dissolved his entire broodmare band. Raise a Native was sold for a record $2.6 million to a syndicate of breeders organized by Spendthrift. Wolfson did hang on to two shares each in Raise a Native and Exclusive Native, entitling him to two breedings a year per stallion if he ever got back into racing. But with the loss of his foundation stock, Wolfson's racing dreams seemed just as far gone.

On the eve of the 1969 Kentucky Derby, Wolfson entered the minimum-security federal penitentiary in Florida's Panhandle. Trading in his usual custom-tailored suit for a dull-gray uniform, inmate number 3362 would watch that spring's Triple Crown races on a black-and-white TV in the prison's dayroom with a gaggle of thieves, con artists, bootleggers, and draft dodgers. It was bittersweet to see a familiar-looking chestnut become Raise a Native's most successful son on the track. Majestic Prince, the aptly named pride of Raise a Native's second foal crop, bore all the usual signatures of the sire line: a coppery coat, that strapping build, the lightning speed. Bred by Spendthrift and sold as a yearling for a record $250,000, Majestic Prince was proof positive that Raise a Native could be just as effective at stud as he'd been on the track. After winning the Derby by a neck and the Preakness Stakes by a head, Majestic Prince ran the Belmont Stakes despite a tendon injury and was soundly beaten by the rival he'd outdueled for both previous Triple Crown jewels, Arts and Letters. Watching the race that ended Majestic Prince's career from prison, Wolfson couldn't escape the feeling of déjà vu, struck anew by the Raise a Native curse of unsoundness. He would keep that in mind if he ever got back into breeding.

Released from prison after serving nine months and a day, Wolfson spent the next year deciding whether to rebuild his stable from scratch. Ironically, he was listed as the nation's leading breeder in 1970 and '71, thanks to the racing stock he had bred but largely had to sell off. When Wolfson finally decided that he wanted to use racing to redeem himself and to restore his reputation, he threw himself back into it with his standard drive and a renewed enthusiasm.

This time, he would have by his side a racing insider: his new wife, Patrice, the only daughter of the legendary trainer Hirsch Jacobs. Theirs was a marriage of opposites, the perfect union of a real-life racing princess who had been born to the sport and an upstart outsider who had bought his way into it. The marriage of blood and money established the foundation for a great Thoroughbred partnership, one that would lead directly to the mating of Affirmed's sire and dam.

The newlyweds wasted no time getting down to matchmaking. Wolfson was particularly glad that he had held on to two shares apiece in Raise a Native and Exclusive Native. In the wake of Majestic Prince's star turn, Raise a Native's stock had skyrocketed. He was now deemed the top stud at the nation's top stud farm. Exclusive Native was also making a name for himself at Spendthrift, with a bay colt from his first foal crop, Our Native, having taken third behind Secretariat and Sham in the 1973 Kentucky Derby and Preakness.

For the following year, Wolfson planned to send two mares to Raise a Native and two to Exclusive Native up at Spendthrift. He had recently purchased a mare named Won't Tell You, in foal to Raise a Native, for a modest $18,000. Beyond the forthcoming Raise a Native foal, Won't Tell You had the advantage of being closely related to Our Native's dam, both of them sired by the versatile champion Crafty Admiral. That in itself might have made her a good choice for Exclusive Native, but Patrice had noticed that both Exclusive Native and Won't Tell You shared a common ancestor—the brilliant French distance runner and sire Teddy—just a few generations back. She thought that by doubling up on Teddy, they might produce a strong horse possessing plenty of stamina. Beyond the solid pedigree, Won't Tell You had proven a sturdy and durable, if not particularly fast, racehorse. She may not exactly have burned up the track—running $5,000 claiming races, winning rarely, and earning a total of just $21,000—but she had survived her twenty-six career starts without injury to retire sound. Although Won't Tell You had yet to produce a stakes contender, Patrice had a hunch it was just a matter of finding the right sire to nick with her bloodlines.

So what if it looked like an ill-arranged marriage of royalty and a commoner? The Wolfsons made the match and booked Won't Tell You to Exclusive Native for the 1974 breeding season.

* * *

Just as Raise a Native had before him, Exclusive Native made himself right at home in Spendthrift Farm's lush bluegrass paddocks, plush stallion barn, and, of course, bustling breeding shed. From the time each was vanned to the Thoroughbred capital of Lexington, Kentucky, home became the 6,100 rolling acres of prime bluegrass that made up America's largest horse farm—and, more to the point, America's leading horse factory.

To Leslie Combs II, the horse trader who had founded Spendthrift Farm on just 127 acres in 1937 and then transformed Thoroughbred breeding from a genteel pastime into a dog-eat-dog business, they were fields of dreams. Notorious as "the master salesman of the century," Combs wasn't just peddling horseflesh—he was selling lottery tickets to the winner's circle and generations of proven bloodlines. He did it with all the charm of a politician, introducing himself in his thick Bourbon drawl as "good ol' Cousin Leslie" and throwing lavish soirees for well-heeled clientele that ranged from Fred Astaire to Elizabeth Arden, from Lord Derby to Captain Guggenheim, from Louis B. Mayer to Louis Wolfson.

If the fourteen-room colonial mansion where Cousin Leslie served mint juleps to his wealthy clients was like the second coming of Tara, it was nothing compared to the Southern hospitality he offered to the farm's richest stallions. Designed like no other stallion barn, it was a large, low-slung, U-shaped building constructed of sandstone and steel, with sixteen spacious stalls fanning around a grass courtyard adorned with multicolored flowers and manicured shrubs.

Dubbed the "Nashua Motel," it was built in the late 1950s to create a proper home for Nashua right after Combs made him history's first million-dollar stallion. Combs had bought the 1955 Horse of the Year at auction for a record $1.25 million and put together a group of investors to split the cost by divvying up the breeding rights into thirty-two shares. That popularized the syndication of stallions—a practice Combs had innovated after World War II when he'd sold a few friends some breeding shares to spread around the risk in a horse he'd just bought—and propelled it into the space age.

For years after the big bay was retired to stand at Spendthrift, he remained the king of the eponymous Nashua Motel, reigning from his prime stall at one end of the U-shaped stallion barn. But now he was no longer the top stud. That distinction belonged to the chestnut stallion occupying the stall directly across the courtyard at the other end of the U: Raise a Native, whose $2.6 million syndication had made him the richest stud. In a nearby stall was his son Exclusive Native, himself syndicated for a cool $1.9 million. Each time one of them got a phone call in the stallion barn, it meant he was being summoned for another expensive date.

On a cool day in March 1974, the phone rang for Exclusive Native. A few minutes later, his groom led him from his stall, both hands gripping the lead rope. Neck curled and nostrils flared, the muscular stallion jigged impatiently next to the man as they made their way down the path. It didn't take long for them to cover the fifty yards to the breeding shed where so many champion racehorses had gotten their start.

A cottage-sized white building with green trim, sloping roof, and large sliding doors at either end, the unassuming shed didn't look like the kind of place that could launch stakes winners worth millions. Visitors whimsically referred to it as "the bedroom," but the men who ran it with the efficiency of a factory assembly line never called it anything but "the breeding shed." With an eight-man crew that operated like a precision drill team, the average time for a breeding was six minutes (the record of three minutes having been set during one hectic hour and a half when thirty mares were bred to thirty stallions). During the peak season from mid-February to late June, the breeding shed stayed open seven days a week, night and day. Its interior was lined with thick green foam-filled mats that looked like they'd been borrowed from a high school gym. Covering one full wall above the mats, brass nameplates immortalized all the stakes winners conceived there— including Exclusive Native himself.

Exclusive Native and his handler passed through the open front door, the stud shank jingling as the stallion tossed his head in anticipation of his latest blind date. Won't Tell You stood in the center of the shed awaiting his arrival, her handler stroking her neck to keep her calm. Before she'd been brought in through the back door, Won't Tell You had had a conversation with the farm's teaser stallion to determine whether she was hormonally "hot" enough to be receptive to the stud horse himself. As the teaser sniffed her all over, nuzzling and nipping, she'd squatted submissively, tail lifted high, exposing herself. She was ready. One of the crewmen had wrapped a gauze strip around the top of her tail, cleaned her with warm water, then led her to the breeding shed.

As soon as Exclusive Native spotted the mare, his penis dropped and started to enlarge. A crewman plunged a handful of cotton into a steel bucket that was emblazoned EXCLUSIVE NATIVE and filled with warm water. Grasping the stallion's swollen member, the man gently washed it, taking care to stand clear of any cow-kicking hooves. Once the stallion was ready, his groom led him over to Won't Tell You. Two crewmen quickly positioned themselves on opposite sides of her haunches, one holding her tail out of the way, the other ready to help guide the stallion in if necessary.

Once Exclusive Native got the signal from his handler, he immediately reared up and mounted Won't Tell You, grabbing on to her shoulders with his front legs and resting his muzzle on her neck. After a few primal thrusts, his tail flagged. He slid off and was led out the front door, his posture now docile.

In the few seconds it had taken, all the months of the Wolfsons' painstaking planning had been consummated. Now it would be a waiting game:

Spendthrift Farm's stallion barn in 1962 (Keeneland Library Meadors Collection)

waiting the thirty days to see if the mare took and was pregnant, waiting the eleven months for a foal to grow inside her, waiting the two years to see if the baby had what it took to be a racehorse.

* * *

Less than a month later, Raise a Native was peacefully munching hay in his stall at the Nashua Motel when yet another phone call came from the breeding shed. If Exclusive Native's mating had represented a match between a prince and a commoner, Raise a Native's was to be a royal wedding fit for a king and a queen. He was being summoned by blue-blood racing royalty to breed to the foundation dam of Calumet Farm, the most dominant dynasty ever to rule over The Sport of Kings.

Calumet was, to put it simply, Camelot.

To anyone passing through Lexington in the heart of Bluegrass Country, Calumet Farm—just a gallop down the road from Spendthrift—must have looked like horse heaven. It covered 1,038 lush emerald acres of rolling bluegrass and sloping meadows, crisscrossed with sixty-four miles of freshly painted white plank fences, dotted with thirty-seven white barns and sheds trimmed in devil's red, anchored by a colonial mansion and matching colonial stallion barn, all of it connected by six miles of snaking country lanes shaded by towering oaks and sycamores.

Beyond its breathtaking physical beauty, Calumet Farm was a state of mind. An authentic American institution, it was the epitome of Bluegrass heritage and racing tradition. The mere mention of the word "Calumet" conjured up images of regal Kentucky Derby champions draped in garlands of roses and of joyous owners graciously accepting trophy upon trophy in winner's circles across America.

Reigning over it all was Lucille Markey, queen of Calumet, matriarch of the dynasty, grande dame of racing. Her first husband, Warren Wright, had built the stable from scratch in the early 1930s and brought it to national prominence in 1941 when a flaming chestnut homebred named Whirlaway captured the Triple Crown and the public imagination. By the time Citation repeated the feat in 1948 and became racing's first equine millionaire, Calumet Farm had become a household name across America.

No stable ever dominated racing as Calumet Farm did from 1941 to 1961. Calumet led the nation in race earnings twelve of those years, topped the breeders' list fourteen times, and won the Kentucky Derby an amazing seven times—all the while carrying The Sport of Kings through its golden age as America's true national pastime.

Calumet was to racing what the New York Yankees were to baseball—one of the greatest dynasties the sports world had ever seen. The devil's-red and deep-blue silks of Calumet became as fashionably familiar across America as navy-blue Yankee pinstripes. Frustrated horsemen at rival stables—echoing baseball's rallying cry of "Break up the Yankees"—would actually mutter, "Break up Calumet."

In the end, Calumet would break up all on its own. Upon Warren Wright's death in 1950, his widow, Lucille, inherited enough good stock to lead the breeders' earnings list for seven straight years as if fulfilling a Calumet birthright. The problem was that the stable's best bloodlines were petering out and a gradual decline in the farm's fortunes seemed inevitable. Calumet's collapse, however, was so sudden as to be shocking. The nation's leading money winner in 1961, Calumet plummeted out of the top ten the very next year. By the mid-1970s, the farm was in free fall, its devil's-red and blue silks fading almost completely from view. By 1974, annual race earnings had plunged from its record-smashing $1.4 million in 1947 to just $117,109.

Through it all, Lucille Markey never lost heart. She was sure that somehow Calumet could recover and even recapture its old glory. But she also knew she was getting on in years, her eightieth birthday fast approaching, her carefully coiffed white hair making her the very image of the grand Southern matriarch. If she was going to find a way to restore Calumet to its rightful place, it was now or never.

The Calumet dynasty had been built on an old racing maxim: "Breed the best to the best and hope for the best." But with the loss of its top stallion, the farm no longer had the best to breed to the best. The only saving grace was that it did still have its great mare lines. In particular, there was the line descended from Blue Delight, a multiple stakes winner who was the source of several generations of swift fillies culminating in Sweet Tooth. A lop-eared and levelheaded bay, Sweet Tooth had modest success on the track, winning ten of forty-one races and placing second in a stakes for two-year-olds, before being retired to Calumet's broodmare band. After Sweet Tooth foaled a good-looking filly in 1973, Markey became hopeful that if she bred the mare to the right stallion, she'd have Calumet's next star.

The only question was which stallion to breed her to. With nothing of note in Calumet's own barn, Markey was now relying on outside stallions. Six years earlier, she had bought two breeding shares in Raise a Native. The first of those for 1974 would go to Sweet Tooth. All she had to do was hop on a van and ride the twelve picturesque miles from Calumet to Spendthrift Farm.

*   *   *

Raise a Native's date with Sweet Tooth went much like his son Exclusive Native's tryst with Won't Tell You had gone a month earlier in the very same breeding shed. It was, however, more intense.

By now, Raise a Native had grown into himself, nearly 16.3 hands and massive. Ripped like a bodybuilder, with exceptional bone, he was far heavier than the more elegant Exclusive Native. He was also much harder to handle, not just because of his powerful build but also because of his dominant nature. He was far more aggressive than his son, both in the breeding shed and on the way to it. He would jog boisterously at the side of his handler, sometimes bouncing around so much that he'd crowd the man off the walkway. Once in the breeding shed, he was all business. The stud crew called him "the six-second horse"—a nod to the four seconds he shaved off his son's record time in accomplishing the deed. That speed and efficiency, along with his exceptional fertility, made him a stallion manager's dream.

On this particular day at Spendthrift, Raise a Native, as usual, needed just one six-second mounting of the Calumet mare to get the job done. Like his son had before him, Raise a Native, eyes glazed, left the breeding shed contentedly and, for now at least, docile.

Both stallions had planted their seeds. Of the more than fifty thousand mares bred that year, only about forty thousand would manage to conceive, of which only thirty thousand would produce foals the next year, of which maybe ten thousand would ever get to the racetrack, of which just eleven would make it to Churchill Downs for the 1978 Kentucky Derby. Given those astronomical odds against producing a single great champion, what was the likelihood that history's fiercest rivals would both be conceived in the same breeding shed within a month of each other?

The Wolfsons, playing a longshot hunch by breeding the top stallion's son with their own modest mare, recognized that a horse like Affirmed comes along more by magic than by plan. In contrast, Markey, playing the percentages by crossing the top stallion with her own royal family's foundation dam, had great expectations that her plan would produce a horse just like Alydar.

Either way, the stakes could not have been higher. For Lou Wolfson, it meant nothing less than personal redemption. For Lucille Markey, it was a last chance to restore the glory that had once been Calumet's—from the dynastic racing tradition to the mythical aura that had made it Camelot.

Warren and Lucille Wright at Saratoga in 1940 (Keeneland Library Cook Collection)

CHAPTER 2

Dynasty

THE CALUMET DYNASTY HAD ITS BEGINNINGS FAR FROM THE LUSH BLUE-grass pastures of Kentucky—in a cramped rented room in downtown Chicago that served as a combination laboratory, office, and bedroom for an ambitious baking powder salesman cum entrepreneur named William Monroe Wright.

Wright got his start peddling baking powder door-to-door in the 1870s in his native Ohio. Soon, his charm and persistence rocketed him up the corporate ladder at the Royal Baking Powder Company, then the nation's leading producer of an ingredient as essential to American housewives of the latter nineteenth century as flour and butter.

But Wright was an independent sort, and at age thirty-seven, restless and dissatisfied with a middle-management position, he took a big gamble: he quit his job and sank his entire life savings of $3,500 into the quest to find a better baking powder.

Perhaps the urge to take that big risk and the desire to create something new burbled up from deep within Wright's DNA. The imagination and inventiveness spurring him on appeared to be shared by members of his wider family. At the same time as he was tackling baking powder, two of his Ohio cousins, Orville and Wilbur Wright, were embarking on a path that would make the Wright surname the most famous in aviation history.

Following his own dream in 1888, William Wright moved his wife and young son into a four-hundred-square-foot loft room that would double as their home and, on the other side of a curtain partition, his new company's makeshift lab. After a year of trial and error, he discovered that by adding egg whites to the traditional formulation he could make a double-acting baking powder. The key chemical in traditional single-acting baking powder, calcium phosphate, reacts at room temperature to produce bubbles that plump up batter. By adding the sodium aluminum phosphate found in egg whites, Wright created a more powerful leavening agent because this new compound would spark a second rise once the batter reached the right temperature in the oven or on the stovetop.

Wright hoped that seemingly simple innovation would turn out to be the recipe for success, but first he would need a company name that would resonate with prospective customers. He struck on a name that would be familiar to his target market of Midwestern housewives since it adorned many local landmarks and was rooted deep in the region's heritage: Calumet. That was what the French called the Native American peace pipe offered to Père Marquette when the Jesuit missionary explored the Illinois Territory back in the seventeenth century. In keeping with that history, cans of Calumet Baking Powder would prominently feature what would become the company's trademark: the profile of an Indian chief in full headdress.

Manufacturing his new product by night and selling it by day, Wright soon turned Calumet into a staple in kitchens across the Midwest. Within three years, he had enough business to expand his operations from the cramped rented room to a three-story factory on Chicago's west side.

By the turn of the century, sales were surging, but Wright found himself restless once again and losing interest in the day-to-day management of the company. With the success of the business allowing him more leisure time, he started to indulge in a passion he had inherited from his father: a love for fast trotting horses. In an era when far more Americans still traveled by horse and buggy than the newfangled contraption known as the automobile, Wright was hardly alone in his fascination with trotters. It was a time when harness racing reigned supreme—dwarfing Thoroughbred racing, not to mention baseball, boxing, and all other spectator sports—and the Standardbred was the most popular breed in America. Wright loved "talking horse" with other Standardbred enthusiasts, and as his interest in racing deepened, he let more of the management of the Calumet Baking Powder Company fall to his only child, Warren.

Though Warren Wright was just in his mid-twenties at the time, he'd already built a long, albeit eclectic, résumé. When he was barely in his teens—and fed up with the austerity his father had mandated during the year spent experimenting with baking powder formulations—Warren left home and took a job as an assistant cowhand at a Texas ranch owned by a family friend. After just a year, his mother demanded he return home where she could keep a closer eye on him. Not easily deterred, he got himself a paper route in Chicago. When that didn't bring in enough cash, he came up with a novel way to augment his sales: he would chase after horse-drawn trolleys, hop aboard while they were in motion to avoid paying the fare, and hawk his newspapers to riders between stops. When his mother found out, she put an end to that job too, fearing for his safety. At fifteen, he finally found a position that would mollify his mother and that was more suited to his own persistent nature: bill collector for a wholesale grocery firm. He excelled at it, and within two years he was able to persuade his father that the family business could use his talents in the same capacity. By 1900, Warren had taken over day-to-day management of the Calumet Baking Powder Company and was running the office with the efficiency of a quality-control engineer.

Short, stout, and bespectacled, the soft-spoken young man seemed shy and unassuming at first glance. But he ruled the company with the firmness of a field general. Although friends fondly referred to him as "Napoleon" and "the little giant," his employees didn't find his manner or management style endearing. They never knew where they stood with him. His moods could be mercurial: one minute charming, the next cold and impassive. Salesmen bridled as he verified the charges on their expense accounts for accuracy and honesty, "raising hell," as one put it, when the numbers didn't add up. His attention to detail, from the sales quotas to the performance evaluations he instituted, was in sharp contrast with the relaxed way his father had been running the company for years.

The elder Wright was affable and unassuming, as comfortable gabbing with his secretary as with his top executives. But Warren made everyone uncomfortable, especially those passing by his office who could sense his intense blue eyes watching over everything. One former Calumet salesman recalled, "The old man would be sitting there kidding with everyone in the office, then Warren would walk in and you could hear a pin drop."

Father-son battles became commonplace, as the pair clashed over the direction the company should be taking. William was satisfied with the way things were: he wanted to sit back and enjoy the profits from the company he had built. Warren craved more: he wanted to plow the profits back into the company so he could make it bigger and better. Ambitious as ever, he moved production into larger and larger factories, expanded sales into more and more territories, and advocated branching out into subsidiary enterprises.

Through the first decade of the twentieth century, he was able to take ever-increasing control of the company as his father's horse habit grew. By now, William had gone from just talking horses to buying them. Needing a home for his new purchases, he bought an estate in horse country outside Chicago and named his new venture after his company: Calumet Farm.

It wasn't long before he became more preoccupied with Calumet the farm than Calumet the company. Taking advantage of William's preoccupation with horse racing, Warren assumed even more control over the company's direction. In 1914, Warren formally succeeded his father as president and promptly put all his expansion plans into high gear. Not content with simply selling more baking powder, Warren bought a chemical plant to supply the raw ingredients, a printing company to make the familiar Indian-head labels, and a factory to manufacture the cans that would contain the product.

That vertical integration coupled with his micromanagement of all facets of the business, from the scrutiny of every penny spent to the efficiency standards and monitoring systems he implemented in the factories, streamlined the company and facilitated his true mission, which was to corner the baking powder market. He mounted aggressive advertising and guerrilla marketing campaigns, going so far as to use smear tactics to suggest that competing products contained ingredients that were unhealthy if not downright dangerous. All of Wright's efforts combined to put Calumet well on its way to becoming a household name in kitchens across America.

While Warren was busy poring over the company spreadsheets and lording over the boardroom, his father was dreaming of the day when the Calumet name would be as synonymous with harness racing as it was with baking. That wouldn't happen overnight.

William's first foray into horse breeding was truly seat-of-the-pants. He had bought a speedy two-year-old named Glendora G, but unfortunately the filly went lame within a year, ending her racing career before it could begin. Left with limited options, Wright decided to breed her to the stallion next door. Never mind that no one on his new farm knew much about horses or breeding. When the time came for Glendora's blind date at the neighboring farm, delivery of the filly was entrusted to Wright's driver, a man who knew far more about automobiles than horses. With one hand on the steering wheel and the other grasping the end of Glendora's lead strap, the driver roared down the road with the filly in tow. Half a mile later, she trotted up the driveway of the stud farm, drenched with sweat and nostrils flaring. Before she could even catch her breath, Glendora was bred and, in 1916, she produced a leggy bay colt Wright named Peter Manning after a friend of his.

The colt was so quirky and unruly that Wright decided to geld him. When finally deemed ready for fast company, Peter Manning was shipped to Lexington, Kentucky, where he caught the eye of a well-known trainer. After taking him out for a test drive, the trainer convinced his biggest client to make an offer on the big-strided gelding. The next day, at the urging of friends, Wright sold Peter Manning for $21,000, the largest sum that had ever been paid for a three-year-old gelding. It was a decision that would become one of Wright's biggest regrets.

At the time, though, Wright had a lot on his mind. His health had been deteriorating, to the point where doctors feared he would not survive. He decided to sell off his farm and most of his horses. Even his foundation mare, Glendora G, went at the fire-sale price of $80. It would take a series of seven major surgeries to restore his health—and rekindle his passion for the trotters.

Wright had watched from afar as Peter Manning won race after race for his new owner, ultimately shattering the world record for the mile in 1922 with a time that would remain unchallenged for sixteen years. Though he was sorry he'd sold the speedy gelding, Wright took immense pride in having created such a superstar. Bitten by the breeding bug, he wanted to prove that the record-breaking gelding wasn't just a fluke and that he could produce many more just like him.

First, he would need a new farm to start over again. During his numerous visits to Kentucky over the years to look at stallions and young stock, he had been impressed with the lusher land, the warmer climate, and the more relaxed Southern lifestyle. In 1924, the seventy-three-year-old Wright lighted upon the perfect property in Lexington: Fairland Farm, already a famous Standardbred nursery known for its natural beauty, the excellence of its bluegrass, the gently undulating ground that promoted good drainage, and the copious ancient hardwood trees that afforded ample shade for mares and foals. What made Fairland Farm even more appealing was the availability of several adjacent tracts of land, bringing his total acquisition to 407 acres. His new venture would bear the name of his erstwhile one: Calumet Farm.

Along with the $2 million he spent for the property, Wright purchased Fairland Farm's foundation sire, Belwin, for a record $50,000. A few weeks later, he also bought his new stallion's harem, the seventeen broodmares that had built Belwin's reputation as the most influential sire of his age. The seventeen new mares joined Wright's other recent purchases—including Glendora G, whom he'd tracked down after a long search and bought back—to form a broodmare band that was unequaled in America. For Wright, money was no object when it came to building his Standardbred empire. In just five years, he would spend more on the farm and the bloodstock than any other breeder ever had in such short order.

No matter how much Wright spent, his new old-money Kentucky neighbors scorned him as a carpetbagger with unrealistic aspirations. They would laugh behind his back when he'd assert that his goal was "improvement of the breed." As for Calumet, they dismissed it as nothing more than an "old man's plaything." None of that made any difference to a septuagenarian pursuing his dream with the energy and enthusiasm of a teenager chasing after his first love.

Wright was so absorbed by this new venture, spending hours on end planning future matings to build his racing stable, that he had barely a moment to think about Calumet Baking Powder. On those rare occasions when he dropped by the company headquarters, he'd head right to Warren's office and begin to talk horse, anxious to share Calumet Farm's latest conquests. He'd regale his son with tales of high-priced horse purchases and of Calumet trotters traveling from city to city to compete on the Grand Circuit, the series of championship harness races famous throughout North America as "The Ragin' Grand." As Warren listened, all he could think about was how much money this extravagant horse habit was siphoning from the company's coffers. Inevitably, he would explode. His voice booming through the closed door of his office, he would rail at his father for wasting company funds on a frivolous pastime.

For his part, William couldn't understand what the fuss was about. After all, their company was flush. Not only had Calumet become the world's leading manufacturer of baking powder, but it was selling two and a half times more than all its competitors combined. The Calumet Baking

Powder brand was now a bona fide American institution, its Indian-head label a fixture in virtually every kitchen, restaurant, and home economics class the land over.

By 1928, the company William had started with $3,500 was worth a cool $32 million. That's the price tag its chief suitor put on it. The Postum Cereal Company, waging a series of major acquisitions that would transform it into America's dominant manufacturer of packaged grocery goods, desperately wanted to add Calumet Baking Powder to a shopping list that boasted everything from Jell-O to Maxwell House coffee to Birds Eye frozen foods. Postum, which within a year would be known the world over as the General Foods Corporation, made Warren Wright an offer he couldn't refuse. Warren made the deal, drew up the papers, and went to Calumet Farm to get his father's signature. William blanched, stunned that his son had gone behind his back and made a deal for something the old man saw as *his* baby. For the next week, the two fiercely battled over the future of the company. In the end, Warren prevailed and William signed the sales agreement.

It turned out to be a stunningly prescient move. Within a year, the stock market crash had plunged the nation into the Great Depression, and the Wrights, having sold the Calumet Baking Powder Company at the height of the boom for a whopping $32 million, emerged as one of the richest families in America.

William Wright was enjoying the spoils of his windfall. As the vast majority of Americans were trying to claw their way out of the Depression, he was plowing millions of dollars into Calumet Farm. He more than doubled its size, ultimately expanding to 1,200 acres. In addition to remodeling and enlarging the handsome brick mansion that came with the property, he built an opulent stallion barn renowned as the finest in Kentucky, scores of superb stables to shelter the rest of his growing herd, and miles of well-groomed roads and white plank fences crisscrossing the farm. He was even more extravagant when it came to buying up bloodstock. In a few short years, he had expanded his broodmare band to more than two hundred and had made Calumet by far the largest and most expensively stocked breeding establishment in North America.

All of that was done in the pursuit of one goal: to breed a horse that could win trotting's most coveted prize. The Hambletonian Stake was the richest and most prestigious harness race in the world. Wright had, in fact, been instrumental in devising that annual championship for the best three-year-old trotter—the Kentucky Derby of harness racing. To win the Hambletonian would be the ultimate validation for Wright as both breeder and owner. For years, it proved to be an elusive goal. Finally, in 1931, a bay colt he had bred stunned everyone by making the Hambletonian the first win of his career.

In an ironic twist of fate, Wright didn't see Calumet Butler capture the big prize. He had suffered a stroke three months earlier and, on the day his greatest wish was fulfilled, he lay in a coma back at his farm in Kentucky. At the ceremony following the race in Goshen, New York, Dick McMahon, Wright's farm manager and Calumet Butler's driver, accepted the championship cup with tears in his eyes. "Ever since he founded Calumet Farm, it has been Mr. Wright's ambition to breed there a colt that would win the Hambletonian Stake under our colors," McMahon said, his voice cracking. "Now he has done it and this is the happiest day of my life, but the pitiful thing about it is that Mr. Wright will never know."

Two weeks later, William Wright died without ever having regained consciousness.

*   *   *

Upon his father's death, Warren Wright inherited the bulk of a $60 million estate—including Calumet Farm and all 550 horses on it.

Though Warren wasn't particularly enamored of trotters, which he dismissed as slow and boring, he did share his father's passion for horse racing. What he loved was the heart-pounding rush of Thoroughbreds, the exhilarating sight of the fastest breed hurtling flat out down the stretch. Warren was already beginning to dabble in Thoroughbreds at the same time as his father was building America's premier Standardbred stable. At first, trips to the track were just a chance for Warren and his wife, Lucille, to spend a pleasant afternoon watching the races and hobnobbing with high society. Flat racing by this time had become more glamorous, and the track was a place for the rich and famous, dressed to the nines, to see and be seen.

As time went on, Warren's interest in racing was fanned by his growing friendship with fellow tycoon John D. Hertz, the founder of the eponymous car rental empire and an avid Thoroughbred breeder and owner. Warren and Lucille accompanied Hertz to the 1928 Kentucky Derby and got so caught up in the excitement that they bet $25,000 on their friend's Reigh Count.

As the horses thundered down the homestretch, Lucille jumped up and unconsciously began to pound on the back of the man in the box in front of her while cheering Reigh Count on. For his part, Warren couldn't imagine anything more thrilling than the sight of his friend's horse drawing away to a three-length victory and of his friend striding into the winner's circle to accept the Kentucky Derby Gold Cup.

When his father died, leaving a huge inheritance, Warren was primed and ready to take the plunge. Barely a month after William Wright's death, Warren went on a shopping spree that would give the next incarnation of Calumet Farm its start. At the 1931 Saratoga Yearling Sale, he purchased his first three Thoroughbreds for a total of $13,000. Two months later, he traveled to Lexington for the Keeneland Fall Sale and, with Hertz at his side whispering advice and placing the actual bids, Wright added eleven more—all of them broodmares—to his rapidly expanding Thoroughbred stable. While the first three yearlings were shipped to Hertz's trainer in Chicago to prepare them for racing the following year as two-year-olds, the broodmares were simply sent four miles down the Versailles Pike to join the Standardbreds at Calumet Farm.

To make room at Calumet for his new purchases, Wright began to take apart, horse by horse, the Standardbred empire his father had built. By early 1933, only 152 of his father's 550 trotters remained on the farm, which now housed his first 46 Thoroughbred acquisitions. By that summer, all but one of the remaining Standardbreds had been auctioned off. The only one he kept was his father's favorite mare, now well into her retirement at thirty-four.

Though his father had had great success with trotters, Warren saw them as a bad investment. As a businessman, he recognized that it was impossible to make a profit in harness racing. "My father did better than anyone else," he said, "but except for enjoyment, he was just throwing money away."

To Wright's way of thinking, it was Thoroughbreds that offered the real possibility of making money. Thoroughbred racing was now enjoying a surge in popularity at the very time sports were starting to evolve from leisurely pastimes to big business. The opportunity presented by that recent phenomenon in what had become America's fastest-growing sport was not lost on Wright.

Back when his father was getting into trotters just after the turn of the century, Thoroughbred racing had been reeling. At the height of the temperance movement, antigambling reformers had forced many states to outlaw betting—a ban that virtually destroyed flat racing throughout the nation. Spurred by a series of race-fixing scandals involving unsavory bookmakers and drugged favorites, the antigambling crusaders took dead aim at the 1908 Kentucky Derby by outlawing the only form of wagering then allowed at Churchill Downs. In desperation, Churchill Downs responded by exploiting a loophole in Louisville's antigambling law to introduce pari-mutuel wagering—a European practice in which all bets were placed in a centralized pool from which odds could be calculated and payouts shared among the winning ticket holders after the track's commission was deducted. Though the replacement of bookmakers with pari-mutuel machines may have put a tourniquet on racing in Kentucky, it couldn't stanch the bleeding elsewhere. At the time, only twenty-five racetracks remained operational in a nation that had boasted more than three hundred of them just a decade earlier. Within a few years, the antigambling wave would sweep Thoroughbred racing out of every state save Kentucky and Maryland—leaving trotters as the only alternative for enthusiasts interested in simply seeing horses compete for the pure sport of it. Even after states started lifting their gambling bans in the teens and embracing pari-mutuel wagering as the wedge through which flat racing could be revived, that couldn't reverse the precipitous decline in attendance, purses, and bloodstock prices that forced many stables to fold and some of the bigger ones to move abroad.

Not until the end of World War I, when a new era of prosperity and optimism sparked the cultural revolution known as the Roaring Twenties, would a confluence of forces rescue American racing from extinction. Of all the sports and entertainment diversions drawn into the vortex of the live-for-today hedonism defining that decade of decadence, none benefited more than horse racing. Not only did Thoroughbreds far surpass trotters and reclaim supremacy as The Sport of Kings, but they also enabled horse racing to once again rival baseball and boxing as the king of sports.

Leading the charge of athletic titans into the Roaring Twenties was a strapping chestnut colt whose name would become as synonymous with that so-called Golden Age of Sports as the two sluggers famed for making baseball and boxing the most popular of spectator spectacles. Just as Babe Ruth did with his towering home runs and Jack Dempsey did with his pulverizing knockout punches, Man o' War captured the nation's imagination with an incomparable twenty-eight-foot stride that left rivals and speed records ravaged in his wake. Dominating one race by an incredible hundred lengths and whipping the first-ever Triple Crown winner by a stunning seven lengths in a 1920 match race as captivating as Dempsey's heavy-weight title fights, the Thoroughbred aptly nicknamed "Big Red" was, in the words of the eminent turf writer Joe Palmer, "as near to a living flame as horses get." A savior carrying horse racing out of the darkness on his broad back, Man o' War drew record crowds wherever he ran and millions more visitors to the Lexington farm where he stood from his retirement until his nationally broadcast funeral. Burnishing his legend as the greatest racehorse who ever lived, Man o' War's supreme legacy may have been making his sport not just respectable but also glamorous.

That was the fashionable setting that called to the Wrights and other Chicago socialites. Society columns devoted much ink in describing Wright and his elegant young wife at the races. Accompanying photos would catch Warren chatting with the city's rich and mighty, nattily attired in a double-breasted suit, a boater or a homburg hat covering his close-cropped white hair. At his side would be the lanky beauty Lucille, sporting a chic designer dress with the dark curls of a debutante wave just peeking out from beneath a flapper cloche or a wide-brimmed hat. The Wrights looked and felt at home in their owner friends' boxes, catching up on the latest society gossip between races.

Like Wright's friend Hertz, these horse owners were wealthy magnates who indulged in racing not as businessmen but as sportsmen. It wasn't called The Sport of Kings for nothing—only those with king-sized bank accounts could afford it. Like Wright's father had done with trotters, these Thoroughbred owners weren't in it to make a profit. But Wright never did anything just for the fun of it.

To be sure, he had heard the old racing axiom: "If you want to make a small fortune with horses, start with a large one." But with his business sense, he was convinced that he could do something few others accomplished or even aspired to: make money racing.

One look at the rising purses told him it was possible. In 1930, the Triple Crown winner Gallant Fox emerged as the first horse ever to earn over $300,000 during a single season. That's ten times more than Calumet Butler earned the following year, when he won harness racing's biggest prize for Wright's father. No wonder Wright thought the future was in Thoroughbreds.

But it would be a lot more difficult to put Calumet Farm in the black than Wright imagined. In 1932, the debut of the Calumet racing colors which had been appropriated from the baking powder label—devil's-red jockey silks with blue bars on the sleeve, blue collar, and blue cap—was anything but splashy. For the whole year, Calumet won just one race and a total of $1,150. The following year, the growing stable managed nineteen wins yet still earned only $22,055 in a season during which Wright had shelled out $180,000 for broodmares alone. Although Calumet's annual winnings continued to trend upward through the 1930s, Wright was nowhere near breaking even. The savvy business mogul who had boasted of having "made a fortune saving money" was now pouring $200,000 a year into his new farm and stable—with scant revenue to show for it.

Wright couldn't understand what was going wrong. He had bought the best broodmares money could buy and bred them to the best stallions available. And he thought he had just the right horseman caring for them. Along with the farm, he had also inherited his father's trainer, Dick McMahon, the crusty old handler who drove Calumet Butler to his Hambletonian win. Though McMahon's expertise was only with trotters, Wright figured that there couldn't be much difference between Standardbreds and Thoroughbreds, so he let McMahon stay on as farm manager. McMahon kept things the way they had always been at Calumet and other top Standardbred farms. He continued to turn mares and weanlings out in the fields 24/7 with only three-sided loafing sheds to provide shelter from the howling winter winds, supplementing pasture forage with a small portion of hay and grain that was fed from long community troughs in the sheds. Problem was, when Wright would stop by the farm, his Thoroughbreds looked ribby and dull-coated.

Wright pored over farm journals, scribbling notes on the newest horse remedies and additives. He bought the latest fad vitamins and patented supplements. Before long, every horse on the farm was getting seven different pills and powders with their feed. But none of that worked. The horses he bred still looked unthrifty and were performing poorly on the track. Worse, they were breaking down with alarming regularity under the increasing workloads that were supposed to make them race better.

For years, Wright had blamed the trainers that he hired and fired with stunning regularity. In what became a rite of fall, Wright would replace his trainer at the end of each season in the hope that the latest hire would be the one to saddle a Kentucky Derby winner. But every spring, his hopes would be dashed. His frustration peaked when his prized three-year-old, Bull Lea, went into the 1938 Kentucky Derby as the second favorite only to lug home a humiliating eighth. Wright was so discouraged at Calumet's performances and prospects that he confided to Lucille that he was seriously considering selling off his racing interests.

One day the following spring, as he was chatting up one of his stablehands, Wright could no longer hide his exasperation. "I have the best mares in the country—everyone tells me that—but I can't raise a good horse," he grumbled. "What's the matter?" The stablehand, who had previously worked at one of the nation's top Thoroughbred farms, decided to take a chance and give his boss a dose of reality. He told Wright that mares and weanlings at other Thoroughbred farms were always brought into the barns at night and fed ample helpings of oats and hay in individual stalls. The man had been horrified at the way Calumet's horses were being cared for. He explained that horsemen familiar with both breeds would commonly say, "You can turn a Standardbred and a Thoroughbred out all winter on the same rations, and in the spring the Standardbred will be fat and healthy and the Thoroughbred will be skinny and poor."

The longer Wright listened, the redder his face got. He stomped over to McMahon's office to chew him out. Slamming the door behind him, Wright yelled, "You don't know how to run a farm!" Just like that, McMahon was out of a job and Wright took over active management of Calumet.

Upon taking the reins, Wright resolved to reverse the first failure he had ever experienced and redoubled his efforts to build a Thoroughbred empire. He poured millions more into sprucing up the farm itself: building a sumptuous new barn with a handpicked pine-plank interior trimmed in chrome, converting some of his father's loafing sheds into actual barns that could be closed up in inclement weather to shelter mares and weanlings, installing a six-furlong training track and cavernous training barns. But the most significant upgrade would involve not bricks and mortar but flesh and blood: he needed to find a trainer masterful enough to judge and develop talent.

*   *   *

One steamy afternoon in that summer of 1939, Wright watched in dismay from his owner's box at Chicago's Arlington Park as one of his best horses got trounced by a longshot hay burner. Barely able to contain his fury after the race, he blurted out, "Any trainer who can beat my horse with that pig is the best trainer in the world!" Glancing down at his program, Wright immediately recognized the trainer's name. As coincidence would have it, this was the very trainer who had guided a sore-footed unknown named Lawrin to an upset win over Wright's favored Bull Lea in the previous year's Kentucky Derby.

In the instant it took to make that connection, Wright set his sights on the trainer he now viewed as the future savior of Calumet Farm: Ben Jones, a rough-and-tumble Missouri cowboy known simply as "Plain Ben."

Lawrin's stunning upset win in the 1938 Derby had burnished the fifty-five-year-old trainer's reputation as a wily horseman—said by some to be "half horse" himself—and put him on Wright's radar. Since Jones was in the longtime employ of another stable, Wright would have to bide his time. Early in 1939, Wright heard a rumor that Jones was thinking of quitting. So when the trainer once again upset one of Calumet's stars that summer day at Arlington Park, Wright figured it was time to make his move.

Wright made a beeline to the clubhouse box where Plain Ben, easy to spot in his trademark white Stetson and black cowboy boots, sat watching the races. "Phone me this evening at the Drake Hotel," Wright said simply and left. On the telephone, he invited Jones to dine with him the next morning. When they met up in the luxury hotel's opulent dining room, they made a striking picture: the tall, powerfully built cowboy with the bulldog jaw towering over the stout businessman. At breakfast, there would be no small talk between the plainspoken horseman and the punctilious millionaire.

"Ben, I want you to train my horses," Wright said straightaway.

"Mr. Wright," Jones responded, "I'm afraid your horses aren't good enough."

Startled, Wright shot back, "Well, by George, if I'm not raising them good enough, I'll buy them for you."

Ever the aggressive negotiator, Wright then made a lowball offer to Jones: an $8,000 annual salary and 5 percent of the horses' winnings. Jones insisted on $15,000 a year and the standard 10 percent commission. Unable to come to terms, the two men parted, Jones heading home to Missouri to mull it over. He had to weigh the appeal of working for a rich farm like Calumet against the stable's chronic underachievement and Wright's penchant for firing trainers at the drop of a race.

The longer Jones spent mulling it over, the more impatient and nervous Lucille Wright got, fearing that some other stable would snap the trainer up before these two bullheaded men could come to an agreement. So she reached for the telephone, hoping she could push things along.

"Mr. Jones, we have never met," she said, introducing herself. "Things look sad right now, but we are serious about racing. Please come to Churchill Downs and talk to me."

"When do you want me there?" Jones said without missing a beat.

"Yesterday," Lucille replied firmly.

A few days later, Jones showed up at Churchill Downs for their meeting. As Lucille reached out to shake his hand, he immediately whipped off his Stetson, slipped it under his arm, and bowed slightly. Standing in the shadow of the racing mecca's signature Twin Spires, neither the mistress of Calumet nor the object of her desire could escape the powerful symbolism.

"I know all about you," Lucille said, "and the one thing I want more than anything else is to win the Kentucky Derby."

Plain Ben Jones (Keeneland Library Meadors Collection)

Plain Ben leaned down, kissed her on the cheek, and said simply, "That's what I want—and we will get it."

*   *   *

Soon after his arrival at Calumet later that summer of 1939, Jones checked out the yearlings in the stable to see which ones would make the best prospects to race as two-year-olds. Of the twenty youngsters romping in the farm's pastures, only one, a rugged little colt with powerful hindquarters and a long and luxuriant tail, could catch Jones's eye. This was the homebred son of top European sire Blenheim II—an Epsom Derby winner Wright bought a quarter interest in for $60,000 from the Aga Khan three years earlier—and a well-bred though temperamental Calumet mare named Dustwhirl. By the time he was two, the colt had matured into everything Jones expected—and then some. With his flaming-red tail practically scraping the ground, the smallish chestnut went by the nickname "Mr. Longtail," the given name Whirlaway, and every epithet his exasperated trainer could think of calling him.

High-strung and hard to handle, Whirlaway tried Jones's patience right from the start. To be sure, the colt could gallop tirelessly, running hard in his morning works without losing any of his edge. The problem was getting him calm enough to race. He was wild and wild-eyed, ever in motion, jumping and rearing at the mere sight of his tack. It took several men just to saddle him.

If he was rank and knuckleheaded off the track, he was completely crazy on it. That was clear right from his racing debut in a five-furlong sprint for maiden two-year-olds during the spring of 1940. He was all over the track, mainly on the outside rail, and though he did manage to win by a nose on sheer talent, that erratic racing style would become as much a trademark as his long tail. In race after maddening race, he displayed a zany habit of veering wide off the stretch turn and drifting out from the inside rail to the middle of track, often bolting straight toward the outside rail. His antics inspired newspapermen to throw a thesaurus full of pejorative adjectives at him, ranging from "willful" and "unmanageable" to "dimwitted" and "nitwitted." Not that Jones could argue with them. "Dumbest horse I've ever trained," he'd growl, shaking his head.

Thus began Jones's mission to cure Whirlaway of his temperamental behaviors, not to mention his addled habit of careening out in the stretch.

That summer Jones made taming "my problem child" his own personal project, devoting his full time and attention to Whirlaway while letting his son Jimmy, as the stable's assistant trainer, handle all of Calumet's other racehorses. Every day, from before dawn to quitting time, would be dedicated to trying to instill some horse sense into this head case. Riding alongside Whirlaway on his own white stable pony, Plain Ben—part horse whisperer, part psychoanalyst—employed a kind of aversion therapy to desensitize the colt to all the scary sights that caused him to shy at the racetrack. Jones would spend hours on end in the hot summer sun trying, under calm and reassuring conditions, to get Whirlaway past the issues that haunted him on the track. One day would be spent simply standing at the starting gate to cure his penchant to startle at the sound of the bell; the next day would be spent just saddling him over and over again; another day would be spent acclimating him to the inside rail as groups of horses galloped by; and so it went. Though the tedious repetition eventually quieted some of the quirky behaviors, nothing seemed to cure Whirlaway's habit of veering out in the stretch.

Only his sublime speed and explosive kick enabled the colt to compensate and overtake everyone to win seven of his nineteen starts as a two-year-old. But against stiffening competition, the problem would be harder to overcome in the three-year-old prep races leading up to the 1941 Kentucky Derby. Making matters worse, Whirlaway was off his form early that spring. In an effort to restore the colt's old snap and spirit, Jones wanted to lay him off for a couple of weeks of rest and relaxation. Problem was, Wright had other ideas. Desperately wanting to win the prestigious Flamingo Stakes, he was pressuring Jones to run his precious "Whirly" in Hialeah Park's marquee race. Jones was used to deflecting Wright's heavy-handed micromanagement, having angrily thrown away the vitamin supplements his boss insisted he give the horses and instead stubbornly sticking to a straight diet of oats, hay, and grass. So when now faced with Wright's insistence on running the Flamingo, Jones decided to invent a slight foreleg injury to buy Whirlaway time to rest and regain his strength.

As soon as the colt was sufficiently recharged, Jones entered him in a sprint to sharpen him both physically and mentally. Wright was on a fishing trip aboard a friend's yacht in the Florida Keys when the morning papers were delivered and he spotted Whirlaway's name in the Tropical Park entries for a five-and-a-half-furlong allowance race. Enraged, he immediately put to shore in a motor launch and jumped into the limousine he had waiting for him at the dock to whisk him to the Miami track. Once there, he rushed to his owner's box, where he found Jones sitting and watching the races before Whirlaway's, and began railing at the trainer.

"This is a mile-and-a-quarter horse, not a five-and-a-half-furlong horse!" Wright yelled. "I want him scratched!"

"I'm not going to scratch him!" Jones shot back, jumping to his feet and towering over his angry boss. "This is my way of training, and I think he should run. He needs this race."

The heated argument continued to escalate right up to post time, the faces of both men becoming redder with each passing barb. Still angry, they stopped arguing just long enough to watch Whirlaway capture the sprint in his usual rousing style—coming from way off the pace, veering out in the stretch, then catching up in the very last stride to win. Not until many of Wright's friends had stopped by to congratulate him would he cool off enough to speak with his trainer. Finally, he took Jones aside and said sheepishly, "I'm never going to train another horse. From now on, you are doing the training. Use your own judgment, and do what you think is best."

If only taming Whirlaway were as easy as handling his owner. With each passing prep race, Whirlaway's Kentucky Derby hopes faded further. In the most important test of his career, the Blue Grass Stakes, he veered so far out on Keeneland's stretch turn that he transformed a sure win into a six-length loss. When the same thing happened in the Derby Trial at Churchill Downs four days before the main event, Calumet's Derby dream was turning into a nightmare and Whirlaway himself was turning into a national punchline.

Not even the eminent Grantland Rice, the Man o' War of sportswriters, could resist needling the frustrated Jones. "They tell me your horse is a halfwit," Rice quipped.

"I don't know about that," Jones replied dryly, "but he's making a halfwit out of me!"

Clearly at his wit's end, Jones decided to take a big gamble after the Derby Trial by changing jockeys just days before "The Run for the Roses." He needed a rider who was strong enough to keep Whirlaway from veering out in the stretch but who at the same time had a light enough touch to keep from hanging on the colt's notoriously sensitive mouth. Only one jockey had both the strong body and the soft hands to fit that bill: Eddie

Arcaro, who was already a decade into an incomparable career that would stamp him as "The Master." Arcaro had ridden some eight thousand horses, including Lawrin to his Derby upset for Jones, but never anything like the unpredictable mount he would be introduced to at Churchill Downs a couple of days before the big race.

During the morning works that day, Jones stationed himself astride his fat white pony right off the stretch turn, just a few feet out from the inside rail, and ordered Arcaro to ride Whirlaway through the narrow hole between the two obstacles. As Arcaro breezed Whirlaway around the turn, he couldn't for the life of him see how there would be enough room to squeeze between the rail and the trainer's mount. The jockey finally shook his head and thought, "If that old man's game enough to sit there, I'm game enough to run him down!"

Even though Arcaro managed to expertly steer Whirlaway through the opening on the inside rail at the very spot where the colt would always bear wide, Jones was still taking no chances. On Derby Day, in the paddock right before the race, he suddenly yanked out a pocketknife and muttered, "I'll fix that stupid sonuvabitch." As Arcaro blanched in fear for his mount's safety, Jones used the blade to cut away the inside cup of the blinkers Whirlaway had been wearing to improve his focus. "That should keep him from bolting," Jones said emphatically. The makeshift one-eyed blinker, with a leather cup blocking peripheral vision of the right eye and nothing obstructing the left, would encourage the colt to focus on the inside rail while discouraging him from veering to the outside since horses usually won't run where they can't see. As he led Whirlaway out for the post parade, Jones had one last trick up his sleeve. "Eddie," he said in his final instructions to the jockey, "don't take the lead until you're headin' for home. This horse can pass any livin' horse. Just wait for the straight part of the track, 'cause when he's got horses to pass, he won't run wide."

As the eleven starters paraded onto the track to the strains of "My Old Kentucky Home," all eyes in the largest crowd ever to see a horse race—the first to crack a hundred thousand spectators—fixed on the flaming chestnut they had made the slight betting favorite as well as the usual big fan favorite. No one was surprised to see Whirlaway break slow from the gate and settle in at the back of the field, biding his time down the backstretch. Skimming the far turn, Arcaro expertly started threading Whirlaway between horses with a quarter of a mile to go as the crowd roar crescendoed in anticipation.

The jockey positioned his mount in fourth place and, following Jones's pre-race instructions to the letter, continued to coast around the bend. Whipping off the turn between the bunched horses, Arcaro finally let him rip. Hitting the homestretch straight as a flaming arrow this time, Whirlaway unleashed a cyclonic burst of speed to shoot past the frontrunners as if they were standing still. His long tail billowing behind him like a banner flapping in the wind, he accelerated through the stretch to open eight lengths of daylight and shatter the track record for a mile and a quarter with a mark that would last for over two decades.

The only spectator at Churchill Downs who didn't see Whirlaway's thrilling triumph was the one who'd actually named him: Lucille Wright. She had arrived at the Wrights' trackside box dressed for the occasion in Calumet's colors—resplendent in red shoes, a navy-blue suit, a red blouse starred in blue and white, and a small blue hat ornamented with a red veil and red crocheted ball hatpins—and eager to cheer on her Whirly. But as soon as he broke from the starting gate, she closed her eyes and tucked her head into her husband's shoulder. She spent the entire race that way, every few seconds nervously asking Warren, "How's he doing? How's he doing?" Not until Warren and the deafening crowd let her know that Whirly had indeed won did she finally open her eyes. When she did, Warren saw they were brimming with tears of joy.

In that moment, the Wrights' dream had finally been realized. No sooner had Warren accepted the Kentucky Derby Gold Cup and the record $61,275 first prize in the winner's circle than he set his sights on the Triple Crown. With an instant replay in the Preakness Stakes, Whirlaway unleashed his patented burst from dead last to win commandingly by over five lengths. Then, with a chance to become only the fifth horse to win the Triple Crown, he turned the Belmont Stakes into a front-running romp, his waving tail likened to a mocking banner that teased his vanquished foes. Sweeping the Triple Crown in such stirring style, Whirlaway emerged as a national sensation and Calumet the toast of the racing world. After ten years of red ink, Calumet Farm had finally made it into the black, thanks largely to Mr. Longtail's 1941 winnings of $272,386. That year Calumet led the nation with $471,091 in winnings, shattering the record for annual earnings by almost $150,000 and more than tripling what Wright's stable had ever won before. Now that Calumet had finally reached the pinnacle, the big question was whether it had staying power.

Whirlaway running away with the 1941 Kentucky Derby (Keeneland Library Morgan Collection)

* * *

Whirlaway went on to become the first horse ever to win more than half a million dollars, breaking Seabiscuit's record, before a leg injury forced his retirement in 1943. The two-time reigning Horse of the Year received a hero's welcome at Calumet, where he would stand at stud and remain the fondest of favorites with the Wrights.

For all the esteem in which they held their Whirly, though, he was not the most important horse gracing Calumet's pastures. That distinction would belong to the big brown colt who had so disappointed Warren Wright in the 1938 Kentucky Derby: Bull Lea.

When Wright had purchased him for a mere $14,000 at the 1936 Saratoga Yearling Sale, it wasn't with a plan to make Bull Lea into a herd sire. The colt turned out to be a decent though hardly special runner, winning only ten of twenty-seven starts and $94,825, before a bowed tendon forced his retirement the following year. His breeding prospects weren't expected to be any better than his racing performances had been. In the beginning, his services were hardly in demand, even at the modest stud fee of $500. A few breeding seasons to him sold for just $250 and others were given away for free, yet he still failed to have a full book his first year at stud.

That would all change after his first foal crop hit the track running as two-year-olds in 1943. Though hardly known as a stayer when he was on the track, Bull Lea, through some sort of genetic fluke, was siring horses that could run all day. The parade of Bull Lea champions would begin flowing as if they were coming off a conveyor belt.

His first foal crop alone boasted two all-time greats: Armed, an ornery little brown gelding who succeeded Whirlaway as history's richest racehorse with $817,475 in winnings, and Twilight Tear, a big bay who became the first filly ever selected Horse of the Year. In 1947, the season Armed trounced 1946 Triple Crown winner Assault in a $100,000 match race to secure his own Horse of the Year honors, Calumet became the first stable to break the million-dollar barrier in annual earnings. With a record one hundred trips to the winner's circle that year, horses carrying the devil's red won a mind-boggling $1,402,436 to more than double its own national earnings mark.

By the time Bull Lea's fifth foal crop yielded the greatest racehorse this side of Man o' War, there simply was no catching Calumet.

The first time Plain Ben laid eyes on that bumper crop of 1945, as he leaned on the fence grading the farm's four dozen yearlings on conformation and movement, two bay colts stood out. One was a mahogany bay named Coaltown but better known around the farm as "The Goose" for the way he snaked out his long, thin neck while running. The other was a rangy blood bay named after the Medals of Honor awarded to America's World War II heroes: Citation. If there wasn't much in Jones's grades to distinguish between the two bays that day, it wasn't long before Citation raced to the fore.

Even before Citation's three-year-old campaign could begin in earnest, no less an expert than Sunny Jim Fitzsimmons, the esteemed trainer of Triple Crown winners Gallant Fox and Omaha, had already anointed "Big Cy" the greatest racehorse of all time. "Better than any horse I ever saw," he declared, "and I saw Man o' War."

One horseman who remained unconvinced was Eddie Arcaro, the peerless jockey tapped to ride Citation in the 1948 Kentucky Derby. Of Calumet's two Derby entries, Arcaro actually preferred Coaltown, the pert sprinter, to Citation, the versatile champion notorious for running only as fast as needed to win.

A couple of days before the Derby, Arcaro grabbed Jones's arm in the hotel lobby and pulled him off to the side. "Tell me the truth," the jockey said, "can Citation beat Coaltown at a mile and a quarter?"

The trainer's reply was short and pointed. "Citation can beat Coaltown doing anything."

In the paddock just before the post parade, Arcaro was still having second thoughts when he nervously turned to Jones and asked, "Gee, Ben, are you sure I'm on the right one?"

"You're on the right one," Jones snapped with an air of finality as he grabbed the jockey's left shin and hoisted him up into the saddle.

Right out of the gate on the sloppy Churchill Downs track, Arcaro would have one more pang of doubt as Coaltown sped to the lead and kept pouring it on, showering Citation with mud balls down the backstretch while opening up seven lengths on the field. Well aware that Citation was lazy and inclined to loaf, Arcaro urged him forward with a cluck, and the colt shot into high gear. Like a greyhound running down a rabbit, Citation caught Coaltown coming around the stretch turn and then darted past his stablemate as they hit the straightaway. Citation was still opening up daylight when he crossed under the wire three and a half lengths in front.

It was the closest any horse would get to Citation that spring. He dominated the Triple Crown campaign with speed and stamina to burn, capturing the Preakness by five and a half lengths and the Belmont by eight. Running his streak of stakes wins to a record fifteen in a row, he sealed his near-unanimous selection as 1948 Horse of the Year. He would go on to become the first horse ever to earn a million dollars, dominating all comers over every distance from five-furlong sprints to two-mile marathons.

In debates from barrooms to backstretches over history's greatest racehorse, Citation would be rivaled only by Man o' War. When it came to comparing stables, of course, there was no debate.

No stable ever dominated racing as Calumet Farm did in the 1940s. From 1941 to 1949, Calumet boasted two Triple Crown winners, four Kentucky Derby champions, and five Horse of the Year honorees. The stable led the nation in race earnings for seven of those nine years, smashing the million-dollar mark each of the last three. For that, Wright could thank Bull Lea.

Of all the bets Wright made on breeding stock, the $14,000 he had paid for Bull Lea turned out to be the best investment since the $3,500 his father put up to start the Calumet Baking Powder Company—as America's prepotent sire produced progeny that would win more than $13.5 million on the racetrack. With Bull Lea affording Calumet Farm a production line evoking the baking powder empire's conveyor belts, Wright had the entire farm and stable running with the well-oiled efficiency of his old company.

Citation working out at Santa Anita (Keeneland Library Cook Collection)

Thus had Wright achieved everything he'd ever imagined. Just as he had taken Calumet the company to the pinnacle, so had he built Calumet the farm into a Thoroughbred dynasty that was not only generating huge profits but was also thoroughly dominating The Sport of Kings.

*   *   *

As Calumet grew more powerful and dominant in the late 1940s, Warren Wright was becoming increasingly frail and sickly. Lucille could see that her septuagenarian husband was having trouble, and she winced as she watched him struggling to keep up his daily routine at the farm.

By 1946, Warren, too, was beginning to see that his life was changing and that there was no fending off the ravages of aging. He started to think about his legacy and what would happen to the glorious empire he'd spent two decades building. One day, he sat down with Lucille and asked if she would want to keep Calumet after he was gone. When she asserted that she would, he started to methodically teach her everything she would need to know to run the farm as he had. He told her he'd written in his will that the farm would go to her to do with as she saw fit. Keep it as long as you enjoy it, he said, but "if it causes you any heartaches, sell it."

There was a lot for Lucille to learn. Though she had always ridden—one of her earliest memories was of being plopped on a horse before she'd even started walking—she hadn't any interest in racing until she married Warren. But even as Warren was throwing all his energy into building his Thoroughbred empire, Lucille stayed mostly in the background, leaving the management of the farm and racing stable completely to him.

In the early years, when Warren was poring over pedigrees and searching for the finest mares to breed to his stallions, Lucille's main contribution was to come up with catchy names for the resulting foals. That turned out to be a good thing since Warren's attempts had been pedestrian, albeit family-centric, naming Calumet's first two racehorses Lucille Wright and Warren Jr. Lucille seemed to have a flair for picking punchy names. When Dustwhirl started to produce, for instance, Lucille decided to give the mare her due by naming the first four babies Dust By, Whirlette, Whirl Right, and, most famously, Whirlaway. Dustwhirl's final foal would be named Good Ending.

Back when Warren first realized he needed to spend more time at Calumet to make sure things were done "the Wright way," Lucille jumped at the chance to make the move from Chicago. She had been born in Maysville, Kentucky, so this was a sort of homecoming for her. It was rumored that her ancestors traced all the way back to early Kentucky settler days and that her father had fought in the Civil War. That pedigree made it all the easier for the Wrights to fit in with Kentucky blue-blood society. While Lexington locals felt William Wright's fortune had a sort of unseemly newness to it, the family's greenbacks had lost a bit of their crispness by the time Warren and Lucille moved to Kentucky, making them look a lot more like "old money."

Once they'd settled in on the farm, Lucille got back to her riding. As a young girl whose father forbade her from riding alone out of safety concerns, she had nevertheless done it when he wasn't looking, standing on a tree stump, coaxing one of his horses over, and jumping on for a gallop. Always a daredevil and tomboy at heart, she grew up to be confident in the saddle, never balking when one of her Calumet mounts seemed a bit wild. Warren sometimes would blanch as he watched her riding through some rank horse's antics. He feared that one of those Wild West moments was going to leave his wife injured. Finally, he put his foot down. "One day I was riding a mare that was a real buzz saw and Mr. Wright grounded me for good," Lucille later recalled.

When Warren started to feel his age, he brought Lucille in on the nuts and bolts of Calumet's management. She learned how to read a pedigree and a race record—and what to look for in potential matches for the farm's stallions. Warren figured Lucille had enough horse sense to be able to learn the ropes with a little coaching. "Mr. Wright always had faith in me as a horsewoman," she would say years later. "At first I didn't agree with him, but I kept deeply interested and learning. After a while, I didn't want to be just an owner and a fan. I wanted to be the best. Mr. Wright always said to aim high. He wasn't starting horses to finish second or third. He always went for first."

By 1948, Warren's health had deteriorated to the point that he was in and out of the hospital. In the fall of 1950, he was admitted to a New York City hospital not knowing whether he'd ever be able to come back to the farm he loved. For the next four months, Lucille stayed with him, sleeping in a chair next to his hospital bed at night. When he died at the age of seventy-five on December 28, 1950, reporters quickly started asking what was going to become of the farm. The day after he died, Lucille told everyone, through their thirty-year-old son, Warren Jr., that Calumet would continue and it would be run as it always had been. When Warren's will was read, Lucille learned that she had inherited, along with the farm, the bulk of the Wright family fortune.

Lucille chose to grieve in private, staying away from the racetrack even on occasions that featured memorials to her late husband. It wasn't until a full year after his death that she decided it was time to go back to living her life. She sold the palatial Palm Beach estate that she and Warren had always enjoyed during the racing season at Hialeah. She bought a lavish Spanish-style stucco mansion in the affluent Bel Air district of Los Angeles, dyed her hair blond, and decided to spend her winters on the West Coast. The rest of the time would be spent in Lexington. "I'm back in harness, running Calumet as I think Warren would have wished it," she told a reporter. "I think I'm probably better qualified than anyone else. For eighteen years, I watched Calumet develop from a hobby that neither of us knew much about to the leading money stable of the country for seven of the past nine years."

Lucille started showing up at the track once again, appearing elegantly clad, her blond hair in a fashionable do. It wasn't long before friends started looking for a new mate for the beautiful—and very rich—widow. One of the eligible bachelors they chose was a thrice-divorced raconteur who couldn't have been more different from her Warren. Whereas Warren appeared aloof and austere, Gene Markey was a charmer, a bon vivant, a man about Holly-wood famed for squiring a bevy of beautiful movie stars. Whereas Warren was short and stout, Markey was tall, dashing, and debonair, his round face punctuated by bushy flyaway eyebrows that arched impishly as he held court. With a flair for the dramatic and a gift for gab, Markey loved to tell stories—be it at the society soirees he enlivened with his Dartmouth-honed repartee, in the juicy romance novels he authored from experience, or in the risqué screenplays he scripted before the Motion Picture Production Code enforced morality. When he was a producer and associate producer at 20th Century Fox in the late 1930s, his movies, ironically, included the popular Shirley Temple vehicles *Wee Willie Winkie* and *The Little Princess*.

For all his film credits, Markey was best known for the glamorous trio of stunning movie stars he married during what he half-jokingly called "my turbulent days." In the 1930s alone, he wed two leading ladies cele-brated for their exotic beauty, first Joan Bennett and then Hedy Lamarr. No sooner had he been divorced for the second time than World War II abruptly altered the course of his life. Markey, who had joined the Naval Reserve after seeing combat as an Army lieutenant in World War I, was called to active duty in the wake of Pearl Harbor. Earning Navy promotions to the rank of commander and then commodore, he served as assistant intelligence officer on Fleet Admiral Bull Halsey's staff at Guadalcanal and won the Bronze Star (for leading a reconnaissance mission in the Solomon Islands) along with the Legion of Merit and a Commendation Medal.

After the war, while serving as special assistant to Secretary of the Navy James Forrestal, Markey wasted no time resuming his courtship of Holly-wood glamour girls. Given that he was never considered conventionally hand-some and was starting to become portly, a 1946 *Washington Times-Herald* headline asked, "Other Men Say: What's Gene Markey Got That We Haven't Got?" The article chronicled how Markey had "become the most sought after unattached man in the cinema firmament, so sprinkled with far handsomer, richer male stars." It was accompanied by a photo of Rudolph Valentino with a caption that read, "Not so hot—by comparison. Though all American wom-anhood swooned over him in his day, Rudolph Valentino was no Markey."

Myrna Loy, who that year became the third movie star to marry Markey, would provide this answer to the riddle posed by the newspaper's headline: "Gene could charm the birds off trees, although birds were never his particu-lar quarry—women were, the richer and more beautiful the better, and I never knew one who could resist him. He could make a scrubwoman think she was a queen and a queen think she was the queen of queens."

A year or so after Markey's 1950 divorce from Myrna Loy, he was introduced to Lucille Wright, the queen of Calumet, by mutual friends in the Bel Air society set. Asked to escort Lucille to a formal dinner, Markey went home resolved to learn more about his latest quarry. He did his research that night, querying her old friends about her likes and habits. One of the things he discovered was that her childhood nickname was "Zookie." On their next date, as the pair stepped out of the Bel Air house where they'd just had dinner, Markey put his arm around her shoulders, leaned in, and whispered in her ear, "What now, Zookie?" Like so many women before her, Lucille was smitten.

Markey courted her with a flourish, and the couple began spending more and more time together. By the end of the summer of 1952, they announced their engagement. The news shocked many of Lucille's Chicago friends who never thought she'd remarry after all those years with Warren. Some, though, said they expected it, having noticed how devoted Markey had become. After two false starts, the couple was finally married early that fall in New York City by a justice of the peace.

Gene Markey's arrival in Bluegrass Country would transform Calumet Farm, almost overnight, from a social wallflower into the belle of the ball. With his presence adding a touch of glitter and glamour, Calumet's imprint expanded beyond the sports section to the lifestyle pages. The stuffy dinner parties that the Wrights had occasionally hosted gave way to the Hollywood-style bashes that the Markeys would routinely throw for Gene's A-list pals. Frequent houseguests ranged from Hollywood royalty, like his close friends John Wayne and Douglas Fairbanks Jr., to real royalty, like the international playboy and racehorse owner Prince Aly Khan.

Be it formal dinners or wild parties that lasted from dusk till dawn, Markey played the consummate host. He'd often relieve the butler and mix drinks for the guests himself. He took special pride in his "Passion Punch," a potent concoction he'd perfected while stationed in the South Pacific containing three different types of rum sweetened with an assortment of exotic fruit juices. By the second round, even the most experienced of tipplers were woozy and wobbly. With Markey at center stage, Calumet could give Leslie Combs's Spendthrift Farm, the neighboring Thoroughbred empire celebrated as much for its lavish parties as its peerless breeding operation, a run for its money. It wasn't long before Combs, the horse trader famed as "the prince of the Thoroughbred party circuit" for wining and dining well-heeled investors, took a shine to Markey and his Hollywood cronies. Though lacking the manor-born Southern hospitality and thick Bourbon accent that made "good ol' Cousin Leslie" a master salesman, Markey was accepted—and assimilated—into Bluegrass high society far more readily than any of the Wrights had been. "No duck ever took to water as I have taken to Kentucky," Markey liked to say.

For all his newly minted good-ol'-boy charm, Markey commanded—and demanded—respect. Everyone was instructed to address him by his naval rank—first as "Commodore" and later, following his retroactive promotion to rear admiral, as "Admiral." Even after officially retiring from the Navy in 1956, he would proudly insist on always being called "Admiral Markey" and would throw away any mail addressed to a "Mr. Markey" without even opening it.

To encourage her new husband's desire to resume writing, Lucille decided to build him a log cabin as a studio not far from the main residence. She transported an authentic eighteenth-century log cabin from western Kentucky and furnished it with such pioneer period pieces as a butter churn, a hanging fireplace kettle, and Kentucky rifles. There, scrawling in longhand at an antique pine desk, Markey would pen novels ranging from *Kentucky Pride*, a rip-snorting adventure romance about life in Lexington after the Civil War, to *Women, Women, Everywhere*, a comic pulp about "the world's most experienced lover" based at least partly on his own playboy past. Whiling away the hours in the cottage he dubbed his "chicken coop," kicking back in his comfy moccasins while a flock of hens clucked just outside his window, he was the very image of a country squire.

For Lucille, who proclaimed she "never knew what love was" until she wed Markey, theirs was a true storybook marriage. Having the first time around married a man twenty-one years her senior, she could now enjoy the companionship of one her own age. If Warren Wright had proved a master at making money, Gene Markey excelled at spending it and enjoying it. As a wedding present, Lucille gave her second husband, along with a large sum as "spending money," matching Rolls-Royces—one to chauffeur him around Lexington and the other to accompany the couple wherever they traveled.

It was the road Rolls-Royce that would run up the miles on the odometer, since the globetrotting Markeys spent only a few months of the year at Calumet. The rest of the time they passed following their horses on the track during the fashionable Saratoga and Hialeah race meets—summering at their Saratoga Springs home, wintering at their Miami Beach estate on exclusive La Gorce Island. Lucille, who had accompanied Warren to Europe just once in thirty years of marriage, joined the Admiral on frequent trips abroad. They would sometimes spend fully half the year, from spring till fall, jet-setting around Europe. Despite the omnipresence of their racehorses among the favorites, it wasn't out of the ordinary for the Markeys to miss the Kentucky Derby itself while vacationing in England or France.

When they were at home in Lexington, the Admiral made a daily habit of sauntering down to Calumet's training track at dawn, clad in his morning coat and ascot, to watch their young racehorses work and to share his thoughts with Plain Ben and Jimmy Jones. Lucille, whose main contribution throughout Warren's reign had been naming the horses that would carry the devil's red, ceded much of that responsibility to Gene while holding all other farm decision-making for herself. Eschewing Warren's trademark micromanagement style, she was content to leave the racing stable in the capable hands of the father-son team renowned as "the Jones Boys."

Despite a changing of the guard—with Lucille having succeeded Warren at the farm's helm and the aging Plain Ben having assumed the title of the stable's general manager while promoting Jimmy to trainer of record—it was still business as usual for Calumet. In 1952, a rugged Bull Lea son named Hill Gail ran away with Calumet's record-breaking fifth Kentucky Derby Gold Cup. The stable continued to top the earnings list with annual purses exceeding $1 million, and Bull Lea reigned supreme as the nation's leading sire with offspring winning more than $1.5 million a year. But, with Calumet's fortunes so tied to Bull Lea's, all that was about to change dramatically.

*   *   *

For two decades, Calumet Farm had owed much of its glory to the foundation sire upon whom Warren Wright had built history's most dominant dynasty. Soon after Bull Lea had transitioned from the racing stable to the breeding shed, Ben Jones had given Wright two pieces of advice regarding Calumet's prodigious progenitor. First, Jones cautioned, don't breed Bull Lea to many of the outside mares lined up on a waiting list overflowing at $5,000 a pop: "That would be like owning a hammer and hitting yourself on the head with it." And as for Calumet's surpassing band of broodmares, Jones's advice was even more succinct: "Breed 'em all to Bull Lea."

The problem was, all of Bull Lea's sons turned out as unsuccessful at stud as they had been unbeatable on the track. The very offspring that had stamped Bull Lea such a prize stud—his résumé boasting a Triple Crown winner, three Kentucky Derby winners, and fifty-eight stakes winners— would themselves fail to live up to expectations in the breeding shed. By the time everyone realized just how poorly Bull Lea's sons were producing, too many breeding seasons of top Calumet mares had been wasted on those highly touted young stallions.

As Bull Lea aged into his twenties with no heirs apparent, Lucille compounded the problem with her refusal to buy new stallions, insisting that Calumet continue to rely on its homebreds. Making matters worse, she began selling off many of the dams that Warren had assembled into racing's best broodmare band. With each passing year, the dependable Calumet bloodlines were getting thinner and thinner.

If the devil's red no longer seemed quite as daunting in the starting gate or as ubiquitous in the winner's circle by the mid-1950s, only a dynasty like Calumet could keep running so well on fumes and on automatic pilot. When Iron Liege and Tim Tam gave Calumet back-to-back Kentucky Derby wins in 1957 and '58, the Markeys missed it all while vacationing in Europe. It wouldn't be long before the Markeys' absentee ownership caught up with them: Calumet's dominance was fading in direct proportion to its breeding prospects. At a time when expenses were so high that the horses carrying the devil's red had to win at least $600,000 a year just for Calumet to break even, the stable's colors came to symbolize red ink. By 1959, after three straight years leading the nation with about $1 million in purses, Calumet's annual earnings had dropped below $500,000 for the first time since World War II and the number of trips to the winner's circle had dipped below fifty for the first time since the simultaneous prewar arrivals of Ben Jones and Whirlaway.

Much like the red ink on the ledger, the writing was on the wall. The seeds of the inevitable decline of the dynasty had been sown. Even as Lucille Markey continued to reign as Bluegrass aristocracy and to bolster her stature as racing's grande dame, Calumet was contracting and its winnings were plummeting.

All of which was opening the door for a new breed of owner—for, specifically, an outsider like Louis Wolfson.

Lou Wolfson, leading Roving Minstrel in 1960 (Keeneland Library Morgan Collection)

CHAPTER 3

The Takeover Artist

IN MANY WAYS, LOUIS WOLFSON WAS A TYPICAL IMMIGRANT'S SON: HARD-working, competitive almost to a fault, and determined to prove he was just as good as, if not better than, peers with pedigrees that traced back to the *Mayflower*. Born in 1912 as the third of Morris Wolfson's eight children, Louis learned early on what it was like to be poor and resolved that one day he would find a way to make a better life for himself and his family.

His father, having fled Lithuania as a teen in 1896 to escape con-scription into the Russian army as well as the anti-Semitic wave of pogroms sweeping through Eastern Europe, had come to the New World with nothing but the clothes on his back. Morris Wolfson started out as a street peddler and then, when he'd saved enough money to buy a cart and horse, supported his growing family as a ragman, finding value in other people's junk. By the time Lou was in his teens, his father had bought a junkyard in Jacksonville, Florida, but the family was still struggling to make ends meet.

Lou had barely reached high school when he decided that his paper route wasn't bringing in enough money to supplement the family's meager income. His older brother Sam came up with the bold idea of turning Lou into a prizefighter to cash in on the youngster's powerful build, athletic prowess, and natural scrappiness. Along with a modicum of prize money, there was a potential bonanza in the form of coins traditionally tossed into the ring by appreciative fans at the end of each fight. Never mind that neither brother had any boxing experience. Sam promptly perused some training manuals, gave Lou a crash course in the manly art of self-defense, and began booking bouts. Well aware that their father's Old World values would never countenance such a pugilistic pastime, Sam figured the best way to keep it a secret was to give Lou a nom de guerre: "Kid Wolf."

It didn't take long for Kid Wolf to begin making a name for himself, winning enough fights to earn a coveted invitation to box on the undercard at Jacksonville's prestigious Arcade Theatre. Stepping into the ring for the big fight, the brothers Wolfson surveyed the throng packed into the ornate movie palace and couldn't help fantasizing about the windfall of coins sure to hail down on the victor. As if he needed any more motivation, Lou peppered his opponent with punches right from the opening bell. At the end of the first round, Sam happened to glance into the crowd at ringside and spotted a familiar face. As soon as Lou got back to his corner between rounds, Sam leaned into his ear and blurted, "Finish this guy off. Pop's in the crowd!" At the sound of the bell for the second round, Lou rushed in for the knockout, unleashing a devastating uppercut that rocketed his foe into the air and onto the canvas. No sooner was the vanquished victim counted out than a torrent of coins started showering the ring. The brothers, careful to keep their backs to the crowd and their faces hidden, bolted without even pausing to pick up any of the victor's spoils, leaving behind Kid Wolf's biggest payday and considering that a small price to pay for avoiding the wrath of Pop.

Later that night, as they tiptoed into the house thinking they were home free, they were startled to glimpse Pop standing in the shadows with a leather belt dangling from his hand. With a stern rebuke and lecture on the importance of education, Pop did what no fighter could: knocked out Kid Wolf's boxing pursuit and, in the process, kicked off Lou Wolfson's football career.

Lou was now concentrating all his energies on the gridiron at Jacksonville's Andrew Jackson High School, where he developed into an All-Southern end and earned a full scholarship from the University of Georgia. To a broad-shouldered teen who often confided to friends that he had "to make some money," football had become the ticket to the American Dream. His plan was to become an All-American college star, graduate to a pro football career, then settle into a coaching position.

That's the dream Lou was chasing his sophomore year when he got into his first big game. On the kickoff opening the second half, he took all the adrenaline he'd pent up as a substitute on the Georgia bench and unleashed it on the unsuspecting Yale ballcarrier, All-American running back Albie Booth. As Booth fielded the kickoff and began snaking his way through a thicket of would-be tacklers, Lou took dead aim with his sturdy six-foot-two frame on the slight five-foot-six fireball. Lou hit him with such force that his own left shoulder jammed back in its socket, dislocating the joint. Doctors repaired the damage with surgery that included a steel plate, but the dislocated shoulder would never heal right and Lou's football-playing days were over.

Though he stayed in school and returned to the Georgia campus for his junior year, academic life was not for him. His grades had never been that good, and he found the lessons taught in his classes to be boring. At the end of that year, he dropped out of college and went home to Jacksonville, the scrapyard, and the family business.

*   *   *

In the spring of 1931, M. Wolfson & Company, like so many small businesses, was reeling, crippled by the Great Depression. It didn't take long for Lou Wolfson to see that the family concern was in trouble: there was next to no market for scrap metal. Only Japanese buyers were still purchasing metal, and every junkyard in the nation was competing for their business. Lou knew he needed to find a new way to help his family get ahead. Noticing that oil and gas were starting to take off, the ambitious young man figured that this might be the opportunity he was looking for. Fuels being extracted in Texas needed to be shipped across the nation, and energy companies were already starting to build pipelines. Lou soon convinced his dad and brother Sam to join in a new venture: Florida Pipe and Supply. As seed money, the Wolfsons drew $5,000 against family life insurance policies and added a $5,000 loan from an old friend.

Wolfson attacked business challenges with the same ferocity he showed on the football field and in the boxing ring. Though college may have bored him, his math skills, when it came to practical problems, were superb. Perhaps the biggest advantage he had, though, was the years spent observing the way his father discovered value in what others cast off as junk.

The ability to quickly assess the worth of other people's discards was what brought the family company its first big windfall. One day in 1932 as he was driving back from a party with a friend, he spotted piles of pipe and plumbing fixtures strewn along the road near an abandoned building site. The materials had been meant for a development that millionaire merchant and philanthropist J. C. Penney had planned to construct to house retiring clergy. When the Depression hit, Penney had forsaken the project, leaving behind the building supplies, including the pipe and plumbing fixtures.

Wolfson quickly tallied in his head the retail value of those supplies and, seeing a possible financial coup, approached Penney's son and slyly offered to remove all of the "junk" free of charge. For his part, the younger Penney figured the materials must be worth a little something—though he was happy at the prospect of having the site cleaned up at no charge. Penney countered that Wolfson could haul everything off the site for $275. Wolfson jumped at the opportunity and over the next year he sold the salvaged pipe and supplies piecemeal for a total of $100,000. That big score gave him an adrenaline rush that brought back memories of the gridiron.

As it turned out, that was just the beginning for Florida Pipe and Supply. Within a few years, the country would start to pull itself out of the Depression. Building began to pick up again, with much of the new growth financed by federal dollars. Along with civilian projects like housing developments, the government was starting to build up its military might. The winds of war were blowing throughout the world, and it didn't take a crystal ball to predict that the United States could soon become embroiled too. In anticipation, new airfields and other installations were ordered up along the Florida coast, which turned out to be a boon to construction companies like the Wolfsons'.

By the time America had actually entered World War II, Florida Pipe and Supply was doing $4.5 million of business a year, most of it in government contracts. Though his brothers had enlisted, Lou was home helping his dad run the company, having been rejected by the Army as 4F because of a bad kidney and his injured shoulder, which still popped out of joint every time he raised his hand. Lou felt bad about having to sit out the war and tried to compensate for it in a variety of ways. If he ran across a distraught soldier bidding farewell to his wife at a train station, for instance, Lou would slip a $100 bill into an envelope and hand it to a porter to give to the unsuspecting couple.

When the war ended, the family decided to liquidate their company, which left them $2.5 million to divvy up. Not a bad return on a $10,000 investment. With no company to run, Lou Wolfson started to cast about for another project that might hold the promise of turning a big profit fast. His attention soon lighted on two Florida shipyards that had come up for sale, one privately held and a much larger one owned by the federal government. Though Wolfson had little interest in the smaller one, its purchase allowed him to say he was an active shipbuilder—one of the main qualifications the government had stipulated for anyone submitting bids on its yard.

Wolfson toured the government's yard and then came up with a bid that turned out to be just $27,000 more than the second-highest offer and, amazingly, just $292 more than the government's own secret appraisal of what the buildings and land were worth. Critics sniped that it was beyond belief that Louis Wolfson could have come so close to the appraisal without help. One congressman went so far as to snidely suggest that Wolfson must have had "mental telepathy." Though the purchase sparked two government investigations, no one was ever able to find anything wrong with what he had done. In the end, both shipyards paid off handsomely, making millions, a portion of which he shared with his workers.

By now, Wolfson had honed his prospecting skills, having learned how to dig deep into a company's books to see if there was gold hiding beneath the surface. One of his first "mining" successes was Capital Transit, the company that ran all the trolleys and buses in Washington, D.C. Over the years, Capital Transit executives had stockpiled nearly $7 million in surpluses, a fact that quickly caught his eye. While stashing away those profits, the company had been stingy with its dividends. As a result, its share price fell since no one wanted to own a stodgy stock that didn't pay much in dividends.

By the time Capital Transit came to Wolfson's attention in 1949, the stock price had plummeted so far that the value of all the shares taken together represented just one-sixth of the actual worth of the company's assets. Once he recognized the company's true value, the astute businessman bought up enough stock to give him control. He immediately raised the dividends the company paid out, and that, once again, brought him under the scrutinizing eyes of Congress. In the face of politicians criticizing him for "raiding" the company's coffers, he countered that, with unions fighting to protect workers and with management battling to hang on to its big salaries and perks, there was no one besides him to look out for the shareholders.

While stockholders may have viewed him as a hero, the Washington press was slamming the controversial entrepreneur. He was dubbed "The Undertaker" by detractors who saw him as a sleazy takeover artist in the business of capturing wounded companies and then, after draining all their assets, leaving them to wither and die insolvent. The *Washington Post* labeled him "the most hated man in Washington" and branded his tactics "a harkback to the robber baron days of the last century."

By the time he'd sold off his shares, he was a lot richer, but he may have inadvertently sown the seeds of his own undoing. He'd made some very powerful enemies in Washington, some of whom would come back to haunt him more than a decade later. At the time, though, he had no inkling of what was to come. He was riding high and had developed a taste for the adrenaline rush that came from financial conquest. In many ways, the war to win control over a company was like the battles fought on the football field, and Wolfson enjoyed the exhilaration he felt after each victory.

No matter how much money he accumulated, he was always aware of his place in the world and of his responsibilities to everyone around him. He once explained to a reporter how that affected his actions: "I always wanted to be a champion in everything I did. And to be a champion in business takes more brains and guts and hard work than any other job. If a man is a champion in business and if at the same time he is humble and has a feeling of compassion for his fellow man, he can do a lot of good in the world."

For Wolfson, that meant giving some of the money he made to those who were less fortunate. He gave to charity; he set up the Wolfson Family Foundation to grant money to worthy causes. He also gave on a smaller scale, which meant he was always a soft touch for individuals with a pet project and little money to fund it. When he heard about an elderly woman trying to build a small church all by herself, for instance, he handed his chauffeur $5,000 and told him to see that the church got built.

It wasn't just the everyday folk who turned to Wolfson for help. A host of famous friends sought his financial advice and aid. Frank Sinatra, who would introduce Wolfson as "my Italian pal Luigi," sought his help in the early 1950s when the singer was out of work and in despair. He was hardly alone. There were Hollywood stars like Marilyn Monroe and Debbie Reynolds, sports heroes like Joe DiMaggio, and power brokers including senators, congressmen, and governors.

Still, Wolfson's main focus remained company takeovers. At about the same time as he was making his bid for Capital Transit, he'd orchestrated the takeover of a medium-sized construction and engineering company named Merritt-Chapman & Scott. With Wolfson at the helm, the company thrived and profits skyrocketed more than fourfold in just four years. As time went on, he continued to collect companies. If it turned out that a newly acquired enterprise had a future, he tucked it into the Merritt-Chapman fold; if it looked cash-rich with no prospects, he liquidated what he could and dumped it. By 1954 Merritt-Chapman had diverse holdings, ranging from a paint manufacturer to ironworks to ship- and dredge-building companies. It had, in fact, become America's first conglomerate. "You name it, we build it," he liked to quip.

His tremendous financial successes intrigued the press. In 1954 alone, such major magazines as *Life* and the *Saturday Evening Post* ran lengthy profiles on the wealthy financier, the latter's headline introducing millions of readers to "Florida's Fabulous Junkman." Photos in those magazine spreads showed a forty-two-year-old Louis Wolfson, strikingly handsome, his close-cropped curls still dark, his blue eyes intense. What couldn't be seen in the photos was his charisma. He radiated a warmth that drew people to him. When he entered a room, the conversational buzz would drop off and people would stare for a moment to take him in before resuming their chatter.

Another man might have enjoyed the adulation, but Wolfson never liked attention. Shy and private by nature, he would go to parties when he felt it was necessary but would hang back from the bevies of conversationalists, standing against a wall, surreptitiously checking his watch from time to time to see when it might be OK to leave. Whenever he could, he'd bring his wife, Florence, and spend most of his time talking only to her. His social discomfort led some to see him as distant and aloof, but those who knew him well said he was anything but.

Though he had offices in Jacksonville, he preferred to work at home at his $600,000 Miami Beach estate, which allowed him to spend more time with Florence and the kids. In a modestly furnished office on the first floor of the opulent family home snuggled up against Biscayne Bay, Lou would spend the day fielding dozens of long-distance calls and poring through the financial records of companies that intrigued him. Though others might have found the corporate spreadsheets dull, he enjoyed working with numbers, and the exercise seemed to soothe and relax him.

*   *   *

Louis Wolfson's next target was so big that it would thrust him into national prominence: Montgomery Ward. Like Capital Transit, Montgomery Ward was cash-rich. Its eighty-one-year-old chairman, Sewell Avery, had squirreled away more than $300 million in cash assets fearing that another Great Depression was just over the horizon. Avery's rainy-day fund had prompted some on Wall Street to derisively dub the mail-order monolith "Ward's Bank and Trust Company." From Wolfson's perspective, this was a big company stalling out under stagnant and incompetent leadership. Though Ward's profits had risen after the war by 21 percent, those of its closest competitor, Sears, had soared 230 percent.

In the summer of 1954, Wolfson and his inner circle started to quietly buy up Ward shares, gearing up for a proxy fight. But Avery fought back with far more vigor than Wolfson had anticipated. Ward's chairman took out newspaper ads and gave interviews decrying Wolfson as a raider and a liquidator who was interested in using proxy fights only to pry open the company's treasure chest to enrich himself. Avery's smear campaign highlighted every instance in which a government agency had investigated Wolfson's business activities. Ultimately, said Avery, Wolfson was looking for money to fund future takeovers. Wolfson was wounded by Avery's bitter barbs, but could do little about them. In the end, Wolfson wasn't able to take over the management of Ward. But he could take some consolation in having toppled Avery and in the company's adoption of many of the ideas Wolfson had suggested. Though he stayed on the company's board for a year, Wolfson eventually lost interest and sold off all his stock.

It was a turning point for Lou Wolfson. With the accumulation of companies and wealth, his focus changed from making more and more money to grander plans of social change and legacy building. The signs were clear. When he was offered a $60,000 bonus by Merritt-Chapman's directors, he refused it and asked that it be distributed among the hourly workers. When one of his other companies suggested he take an annual salary of $100,000, he turned that down too. "When I started out, I wanted to make money," he explained. "I wanted to make sure my wife and four kids would never have to worry about money as long as they lived. But you can make so much money that it doesn't matter anymore."

Wolfson was beginning to view himself as a catalyst of change. He saw American businesses becoming less innovative and more mired in mediocrity. He wanted to shake up management, not just at Montgomery Ward but at companies across the nation. It was a bold ambition—one that didn't sit well with the executives at America's major corporations. They didn't like change. They didn't relish the prospect of having to worry about this overreaching son of an immigrant waiting for them to make the mistake that would allow him to take over their companies and oust them from their cushy jobs. As they watched the Ward saga play out, many wondered if there might be a way to put this upstart back in his place.

There was other fallout from the Ward proxy fight: Lou Wolfson's public image had taken a big hit. Many newspapers had sided with Avery and his board, portraying Wolfson as a corporate pirate out to steal and liquidate. Until the Ward battle heated up, most Americans hadn't paid much attention to Wolfson and his conquests. But with Montgomery Ward, Wolfson was trying to take over an American institution and the press was portraying him as a wolf at the door—or, as *Time* magazine branded him and his ilk, "a corporate raider." It was an appellation that Wolfson hated.

It seemed that everywhere he turned, his notoriety was bringing more and more unwelcome attention. The Montgomery Ward proxy fight turned his business life into a running soap opera with weekly installments in *Time* and his personal life into fodder for the emerging genre of supermarket tabloids. *Confidential*, the *Time* of scandal sheets, ran an exposé implying an affair with Hedy Lamarr, the Hollywood sex goddess who, long after her divorce from Gene Markey, frequently sunbathed with the vacationing Wolfson family at the Beverly Hills Hotel. Shy and private as he was, Wolfson bridled at the gossip mongering now that he had landed directly in the spotlight.

To be sure, the bad publicity was annoying. But more ominous was the rate at which he was accumulating powerful enemies.

* * *

By the mid-1950s, not even his defeat in the Montgomery Ward proxy fight could undermine Wolfson's standing at the forefront of a new breed of corporate colossus. The *New York Times*, in a 1955 spread headlined "Today's Giants in Finance," profiled Louis Wolfson alongside half a dozen moguls including Howard Hughes and H. L. Hunt. When *Fortune* magazine published its 1957 compilation of the seventy-six wealthiest Americans, there—listed among all the assorted Rockefellers, Mellons, and Du Ponts—was Wolfson, his worth estimated at between $75 million and $100 million. Other sources placed his personal net worth north of $250 million. More than that, he controlled an industrial empire valued at $400 million.

His vast wealth notwithstanding, things were already starting to go sour for Wolfson. Men he had trusted and put in positions of power at Merritt-Chapman were caught making shady deals. But the real turning point, as far as the American public was concerned, came when Wolfson tried to divest himself of his holdings in American Motors.

Wolfson had considered trying to take the company over and had, along with family members and associates, bought up a large amount of stock. When he eventually lost interest in the company, he asked one of his partners, Elkin Gerbert, to sell off the stock. Gerbert did him one better, opting to sell the stock short, which meant that Wolfson and his associates were not only selling the stock they owned but also "borrowing" more than one hundred thousand shares to sell. Gerbert was banking on the stock price of American Motors dropping. Had things worked out as planned, meaning the price fell, the Wolfson group would have later replaced the "borrowed" shares with ones that cost less to purchase, yielding a profit on the difference. But the stock soon started to climb, and within a short time it had gone from $10 a share to $12.

That's when things took a turn that would bring Wolfson onto the Securities and Exchange Commission's radar. A trusted associate named Alex Rittmaster leaked a story to the *New York Times* that made Wolfson look like a crook. Rittmaster told the *Times* that he knew for a fact that Wolfson, thinking that American Motors' stock was going down, was therefore selling off everything. When investigators at the SEC saw the *Times* story, they started looking into Wolfson's finances and quickly discovered the short sales. They charged Wolfson with trying to manipulate the market by planting misleading information. Though he was able to settle the matter with no admission of wrongdoing, the whole affair added to the stress that was starting to take a toll on the financier's heart.

His doctor, hoping to get him to relax, suggested he take up a hobby to distract him from the pressures of his financial empire. To Wolfson, sports seemed the natural choice. Over the years, he had made a number of unsuccessful attempts to purchase big-league professional sports franchises, from baseball's Brooklyn Dodgers and Washington Senators to football's Washington Redskins and Baltimore Colts. Now he tried a new tack: he would build his own sports empire from scratch.

* * *

For years, tracing back to the late 1940s, Lou Wolfson had enjoyed occasionally going to the racetrack. At first, the primary appeal was simply the adrenaline rush of betting, which he indulged in heavily by any standard. A natural risk taker who thought nothing of throwing away $5,000 shooting dice, he could drop even more money at the track, where he would bet as much as $1,000 a race.

As time went on, though, he began to realize "there was considerably more to racing than just betting." He started taking trips to Kentucky so he could visit the big Bluegrass breeding farms. At Spendthrift, he marveled at the million-dollar stallion Nashua; at Claiborne, he was struck by Nashua's famously temperamental and influential sire, Nasrullah. As much as he appreciated the horses, what most impressed him were the stud farms themselves, the two venerable institutions most responsible for transforming Thoroughbred breeding into big business. While making the rounds of farms and racetracks, he became particularly intrigued by the old horsemen he met—from Hall of Fame trainers like Sunny Jim Fitzsimmons and Max Hirsch to owners like Albert Warner, each in his seventies or eighties. "All of these men are devoted to racing, and it seems to have kept them youthful in spirit," he observed. "The lesson wasn't wasted."

So, at the age of forty-six, Wolfson embraced racing as the perfect vehicle to keep his spirit young and his heart healthy. Never content to do anything halfway, he resolved to go all in and start a big-time stable that could compete with the nation's elite farms. The racing establishment didn't take long to offer up an opinion. Racing stables, the skeptics intoned, weren't built overnight; they were forged over the course of many decades by old-money millionaires with pedigrees as rich as the centuries-old bloodlines of the Thoroughbreds themselves. Did this upstart outsider really think he could just come in and instantly be competitive with Thoroughbred racing empires that boasted storied names like Calumet, Brookmeade, Greentree? He was, the naysayers scoffed, too young, too green, too unlearned. Worse, they sneered, he was too brash, too impetuous, too audacious.

But Wolfson was sure that in horse racing, just as in business, he could find the fast track to the winner's circle. "I've been a winner in everything I've ever attempted, and firmly believe that money well spent plus brains can equal success even in this very tough business," he reasoned. "I heard all those it-can't-be-done stories in my business career too, yet we managed to do quite a few of them. So racing became a challenge, and I like challenges."

He bought his first racehorses early in 1958 from a friend, a former Miami restaurant owner named Charlie Block. That summer, when Block and his veteran trainer, A. G. Robertson, left for the Keeneland Yearling Sale, Wolfson handed them $125,000 and told them to spend it however they saw fit. Block and Robertson used $114,000 of Wolfson's seed money to buy four yearlings for him. With Robertson signing on to train Wolfson's racehorses as well as Block's at Hialeah Park, the start-up stable needed only a name to race under. Wolfson chose one that referenced his Bal Harbour home overlooking Biscayne Bay: Harbor View Farm. As for the stable's colors, he designed Harbor View's silks after the large flock of flamingos that famously waded in Hialeah's infield lake: flamingo pink accented with black sleeves.

By the end of his rookie year in racing, his fledgling stable of four nondescript horses had combined to win a total of six races and a paltry $20,110. For 1959, the stable's first full calendar year in operation, Harbor View horses won eighteen races and a modest $80,161—a big improvement, but a long way from breaking even. The silver lining was that Wolfson had cut his gambling from $1,000 a race to no more than $100 or $200 and now bet only on his own horses—so, as he liked to joke, "I saved a lot of money buying my first horse." The problem was, he was losing a million a year just trying to get the stable off the ground. To take it to the next level, Wolfson realized he needed a top trainer.

He sought a recommendation from fellow Florida-based horse owner Fred Hooper, a self-made millionaire like himself who had won the 1945 Kentucky Derby with the very first Thoroughbred he'd ever purchased. Hooper recommended his own trainer, Ivan Parke, who declined Wolfson's proposition but suggested an alternative: his older brother Burley.

Burley Parke had started race riding as a young boy on his rancher father's Quarter Horses at local Idaho county fairs and soon moved on to Thoroughbreds at bush tracks out West. He was only sixteen when he broke through to become the nation's second-leading jockey for 1921, but that good fortune would be short-lived as the family curse of weight gain soon forced him out of the saddle. Of the six Parke brothers who transitioned from riding Thoroughbreds to saddling them, Burley would have the most success—as a Hall of Fame trainer with a knack for bringing along young racehorses.

In the late 1940s, Charles Howard hired him to run the Northern California racing stable made famous a decade earlier by Seabiscuit. That's where Parke would bolster his legend by taming a temperamental four-year-old Howard purchased from the Aga Khan as an afterthought in a package deal: Noor, an Irish-bred product of Nasrullah's first foal crop who had inherited every bit of his sire's nasty temper but had yet to show much on the track.

A mild-mannered and soft-spoken man by nature, Parke brought to his work a patience he'd learned from listening to his charges. Spending months simply observing how Noor related to the humans who cared for him, the wiry little trainer realized that the big black colt calmed down when those around him were gentle and quiet. So instead of bullying him into behaving better, Parke started sweet-talking Noor. "I don't permit any person in my employ to speak harshly to Noor or to snap commands at him," Parke told all his stablehands. "He resents it and he shows it." Gradually, Parke convinced Noor to focus his energy on battling his competitors rather than his handlers. The proof of Parke's velvet-glove treatment became clear when Noor returned to the track in 1950 from an injury-induced year's hiatus. Through that winter and spring, Noor shocked the racing world by outdueling Citation—the pride of Calumet since winning the 1948 Triple Crown—in four straight showdowns, the last two in world-record time. When Noor was retired to stud at the end of an eventful year punctuated by the death of Howard, Parke likewise decided it was time to quit at the top of his game.

A self-described "Idaho farm boy," Parke was just forty-five when he settled into a quiet retirement at his fifty-five-acre fruit ranch in Northern California. He was nearly a decade into retirement, enjoying the quiet life of fishing and hunting along with farming, when Wolfson came calling in 1959. Though Parke had steadfastly resisted all offers to return to racing, Wolfson lured him back the same way he'd built Harbor View's stable: by opening his checkbook and acquiring the best money could buy.

Of the first four yearlings that Wolfson had bought at the Keeneland auction the previous year, Parke took an instant liking to a big chestnut colt purchased from Spendthrift's Leslie Combs. Wolfson named the colt Francis S. after his pal Frank Sinatra, and Parke promptly developed him into a leading three-year-old contender during the prep season for the 1960 Kentucky Derby. Francis S. handily won the Wood Memorial, but a throat infection sidelined him from the Triple Crown classics. By the time he came back strong to win his second stakes that July, Harbor View was no longer a stranger to the winner's circle.

In 1960, the stable's first full season under Parke, his horses carried the flamingo-pink colors to fifty-four wins, more than even Calumet had each of the two previous years. More impressive, they won a hefty $679,865 to rank third nationally in earnings, behind only C. V. Whitney's stable and Harry F. Guggenheim's Cain Hoy Stable.

That fall, at Parke's recommendation, Wolfson bought a Count Fleet grandson named Roving Minstrel for $100,000. Just a few weeks later, Roving Minstrel made that purchase price back by outracing the nation's top two-year-olds to win the Champagne Stakes at Belmont and to establish himself as the Winter Book favorite for the 1961 Kentucky Derby. With Harbor View riding high that New Year's, Wolfson could toast not only the stunning success of 1960 but also the brighter promise of '61.

Never before had a novice owner rocketed to the top so quickly. If it shocked the racing world, it came as no surprise to Wolfson—or anyone who had followed his earlier assaults in the fields of business and high finance. From his perspective, the explanation was simple: he saw no difference between running a racing stable and running a conglomerate like

Merritt-Chapman. In racing as in business, his management philosophy relied on delegating authority: while Parke was working wonders at Hialeah with Harbor View's racehorses, Combs was laying the foundation for Wolfson's breeding operation.

Wolfson's long-range breeding strategy to produce a homebred champion depended on accumulating a strong broodmare band. Of the ten to fifteen well-bred fillies that Combs picked out for him each year, Wolfson would buy three or four as potential broodmares, keeping the best producers and culling the others. Within three years, Wolfson's mare band had grown to thirty-two, all housed at Spendthrift. He'd bought a stallion imported from England and had purchased breedings to the likes of Swaps and Royal Charger as well as shares in Spendthrift-syndicated studs like Nashua and Gallant Man. The more time Combs spent planning breedings with his new friend, the less surprised Kentucky's "Great Syndicator" was by the Floridian's fast climb. Combs was impressed with his friend's thirst for knowledge and willingness to pay top dollar to buy the best stock. Wolfson certainly spent with a lavish hand: more than $3 million over his first three years alone. That's how he bought his way into the upper echelon at Hialeah Park.

On the backside at Hialeah, Harbor View headquartered its stable in Barn A on "Millionaire's Row" right alongside Calumet, Brookmeade, Greentree, Cain Hoy, and all the other blue-blood institutions that had achieved their eminence through decades of painstaking effort. Harbor View, led by that brash young newcomer Lou Wolfson, was an outlier no more. No less a hardened horseman than Calumet trainer Jimmy Jones summed it up for everyone: "He doesn't brag on his horses when they win, and he doesn't cry on them when they lose. He backs his opinions with his money, and he's been right more often than wrong. He'll be around, and at the top, for a long time."

As if to confirm that he was indeed in it for the long haul, Wolfson set down roots by building a farm of his own. Convinced that a good horse could be bred and raised anywhere, he eschewed the august Thoroughbred hubs of Kentucky, Virginia, Maryland. Ever the maverick outsider, he instead made his stand in a place where horse farms had only just begun to spring up: the new frontier of Florida.

It wasn't until 1943 that a highway construction magnate named Carl Rose—having discovered that calcium-rich limestone under the soil in north-central Florida was good for building not only strong roads but also strong bones—established Ocala's first Thoroughbred farm on 20,000 acres he had bought at just $5 per. With its abundant sunshine and temperatures much less oppressive than Miami's, Ocala offered something that Kentucky's Bluegrass Country and all the other horse heavens lacked: a tropical environment in which Thoroughbreds could be trained 365 days a year.

The conducive climate and nutritious grass notwithstanding, horsemen still weren't exactly racing to follow Rose's lead. There were all of three horse farms in north-central Florida in 1956 when a Maryland breeder named Joe O'Farrell bought one of them, renamed it Ocala Stud, and proceeded to ignite a Thoroughbred boom in the Sunshine State. The 993-acre farm that O'Farrell took over had produced the colt who that spring became the first Florida-bred horse ever to win the Kentucky Derby: Needles, so named because of the numerous injections he required to survive pneumonia as a sickly foal. But O'Farrell knew it would take more than one homebred champion to put Ocala's fertile soil and tropical climate on the Thoroughbred map. So he devised a gimmick that would revolutionize commercial breeding and, in the process, transform Ocala into a breeding center to rival Lexington, Kentucky. Rather than simply breeding Thoroughbreds and selling them as untried yearlings, he innovated the practice of first breaking and training homebreds before auctioning them off as two-year-olds that were "ready to run." With the 1957 advent of his "Hialeah sales of Florida-bred two-year-olds already in training," O'Farrell established the Sunshine State as a worldwide leader in this newfangled auction of ready-to-race Thoroughbreds.

This practice provided the perfect answer for Florida, with its growing winter market facilitated by wealthy snowbirds. Establishment Kentucky breeders, criticizing the practice for pushing yearlings and two-year-olds to run too hard before their bones were mature enough to handle such intense training, dismissed it as a gimmick that prized salesmanship over horsemanship. "They've got all those rich people down there with nothing to do," Combs scoffed from up in Lexington, "so they sell them a horse."

Ocala, then a sleepy little outpost with a population of thirteen thousand, also attracted a new breed of ambitious owner: horsemen who did not belong to the Eastern establishment and found Bluegrass Country too difficult, if not impossible, to break into. Ocala opened doors for racing neophytes who felt unwelcome by the close-knit high society of Kentucky breeders—outsiders just like the business moguls Jack Dreyfus, William McKnight, and, of course, Louis Wolfson. Much like his immigrant father before him, Wolfson viewed Florida as a land of opportunity, its Bahia grass proving just as nutritious as Kentucky's famed bluegrass. At the urging of O'Farrell, who was fast emerging as the nation's leading commercial breeder, Wolfson was at the forefront of a stampede that would make Florida a breeding center second only to Kentucky in producing stakes winners and stamp Ocala as bona fide horse country.

In September 1960, Wolfson purchased 478 acres in Ocala. He named the open-air spread Harbor View Farm—never mind that it was three hundred miles north of his Bal Harbour view of the bay—and commenced construction on barns and a training track. Harbor View was now officially on the map.

While Harbor View Farm was being readied for occupancy, Wolfson's stable pointed toward the 1961 Kentucky Derby with renewed vigor and a Winter Book favorite in Roving Minstrel. The high-strung bay was primed to take his first step in the Derby prep season as the favorite in Hialeah's marquee Flamingo Stakes. But a month before the race, Roving Minstrel reared in the walking ring in front of Barn A, flipped over backward, and struck his head hard on the ground, fracturing his skull. Surgery could not save him, and he died the next day from a cerebral hemorrhage. Wolfson began the search for his star's successor, and he soon acquired a turf specialist named Wolfram who would help keep the stable's winnings at half a million dollars a year.

More than anything, what Wolfson coveted was the elusive champion that could not only dominate on the track but also pass on fast bloodlines as a prepotent sire. From the moment Parke spotted Raise a Native in the auction ring at the 1962 Saratoga Yearling Sale, Wolfson was sure he had found his first can't-miss champion. More than that, he was sure he'd found a foundation stallion upon which to build a Calumet-style empire.

In short, a Bull Lea of his own. But those hopes were dashed when injury cut short Raise a Native's promising career as a two-year-old in 1963. "When you lose a horse like Raise a Native, it's a terrible blow," Wolfson sighed. "About the best you can do is hope that something else in your stable can be a suitable substitute."

Of all the potential substitutes in Wolfson's stable, the easiest to overlook might have been a compact bay named Roman Brother. At the January 1963 Hialeah sale of two-year-olds in training, Wolfson had paid just $23,500—about half what Raise a Native commanded five months earlier—for this O'Farrell-bred colt most horsemen dismissed as way too small at barely 15 hands and 889 pounds. Dwarfed in every way by his celebrated stablemate Raise a Native, Roman Brother presented a bigger challenge than merely his slight build: he was, as his Harbor View handlers referred to him, "a mean little devil." Raise a Native may have barely escaped the castration that was contemplated to settle down his infamous temperament, but the same was not true of Roman Brother. The colt had to be gelded in order for Parke to have any chance to tame him for the racetrack. While Raise a Native was blowing away the competition and track records in the spring of 1963, Roman Brother had run just one maiden race.

Emerging from the shadows in the wake of Raise a Native's forced retirement, Roman Brother made a nickname for himself as "Mighty Mite"—running away with the Champagne Stakes that fall, placing second in the 1964 Belmont Stakes, and capturing the 1965 Horse of the Year title. That made Roman Brother the first Horse of the Year ever to earn that honor after being bought at public auction. The little gelding ran his purse winnings to $943,473, falling just shy of becoming history's sixth equine millionaire. Not a bad return on Wolfson's $23,500 investment. In fact, it was considered the biggest sales bargain in racing. The financier known as "The Junkman" had once again seen value where others hadn't—a trait sure to serve him as well on the racetrack as it had in the junkyard and the boardroom.

With Roman Brother leading the way, Harbor View established itself as racing's second-leading money winner in 1964, behind only the Phipps dynasty's Wheatley Stable. In 1965, Wolfson was so close to the title and so fiercely determined to win it that, on the last day of the year at Tropical Park and Santa Anita, he started buying up race favorites from other stables in the morning to win while sporting Harbor View's flamingo-pink colors in the afternoon. The tactic didn't win him any fans among rival horsemen or, for that matter, the earnings title itself—as Harbor View fell $5,325 shy with $889,921 in annual winnings. But the eleventh-hour shopping spree did remind everyone of the great lengths to which he would go to secure a championship.

Just seven years after crashing the party, Lou Wolfson had Harbor View poised to take over racing's top spot. The future of his stable looked brighter than the blue skies over his Florida farm. But unbeknownst to Wolfson, the ominous storm clouds that had been building on the horizon were now careening toward him.

Calumet Farm's filly barn in 1961 (Keeneland Library Meadors Collection)

CHAPTER 4

From the Ashes

Lou Wolfson's high-profile battles for Montgomery Ward and American Motors had put him in the crosshairs of powerful enemies who saw this upstart financial wizard as a serious threat to the status quo. Nervous CEOs and government officials, aiming to put the takeover genie back in its bottle, hoped the Securities and Exchange Commission might provide the ammunition. Wolfson had popped up on the SEC's radar with the American Motors stock debacle. That episode sparked the agency's interest in him, and by the mid-1960s investigators were scrutinizing stock deals involving Merritt-Chapman and a much smaller company named Continental Enterprises, Inc.

Back in the 1950s, when Wolfson had purchased Continental, it consisted mainly of a chain of movie theaters. Over the years, he had tucked other small companies into its fold. Then, in the early 1960s, he decided to liquidate some of the stock and, over a two-year period, he and one of his associates, Elkin Gerbert, sold 633,000 shares in the company. The legal catch, which Wolfson said he knew nothing about, was that Continental had not been registered with the SEC. While companies can sell some stock without registering with the SEC, an obscure rule in the Securities Act of 1933 details how many shares can be sold and to whom. The whole point of the 1933 act was to prevent stock buyers from being scammed. When a firm registers with the SEC, it must provide a description of its assets, business, and the stock to be offered for sale. It must also provide the SEC with information on the management of the company and supply financial statements certified by independent accountants. The SEC doesn't make any recommendations based on the information supplied by individual firms; it just makes the data available to the public. Companies aren't required to register, but if they don't, the 1933 act places limitations on sales of the stock.

While Wolfson was never accused of fraud or deceptive practices, he was indicted in 1966 for "willfully violating" the federal securities laws by selling more than the 1 percent of the company's stock allowed by the act. In describing Wolfson's situation at the time, *New York Times* business reporter Terry Robards called the case "the first serious test, in a criminal context, of a little known rule in the Securities Act of 1933." In general, brokers and CEOs alike had been blissfully ignorant of the rule up until the Wolfson case. "Because of the misunderstanding about the rule and its exemptions, it has often been breached," Robards reported. "Furthermore, brokerage houses, to which the rule directly pertains, had been lax in their compliance procedures in some cases."

What really grabbed people's attention was the SEC's decision to hand its investigation over to the Justice Department to prosecute criminally rather than following up on its own with a civil case. Wolfson was perplexed by the choice, telling reporters that he wasn't aware of the 1933 act and therefore couldn't have willfully violated it. And certainly, he hadn't tried to cover up the sales. "I didn't use any fictitious names in selling the stock," he said. "No Swiss banks." Besides, Wolfson said, he'd reported every sale on his income tax returns.

Wolfson couldn't understand why the prosecution was coming after him with such ferocity. This was the kind of case where ignorance should have been a defense: to convict, the prosecution would have to prove that he knew the law and broke it on purpose. Wolfson said he had depended on subordinates to keep track of everything. "I'm not a detail man," he explained. His lawyers argued that it was up to his stockbrokers to inform their client about the SEC rules.

Neither those arguments nor the parade of celebrity character witnesses, ranging from Joe DiMaggio to Ed Sullivan, could sway the jury. On September 29, 1967, Wolfson was convicted on all nineteen counts, sentenced to one year in prison, and fined $100,000.

Just a month after the indictment in the Continental affair, federal prosecutors had dragged Wolfson back into court in a second case, this time alleging unscrupulous dealings with Merritt-Chapman stock. After four months of testimony, the judge, the same Edmund L. Palmieri who had presided over the Continental case, concluded that there was not enough evidence to prove Wolfson had committed fraud. But that wasn't the end of the matter since Palmieri allowed the case to go forward, instructing the jury to only consider charges of perjury and obstruction of justice. After a seven-week trial that ended on August 8, 1968, Wolfson was convicted on all counts. Palmieri once again handed down a sentence that included a fine and jail time. Wolfson was told that he would have to pay $32,000 and that he would spend eighteen months in prison, a sentence that would start when he had finished his jail time for the Continental case. His lawyers fought back and tried to get both verdicts overturned.

At the time, though, the legal machinations were the least of Wolfson's worries. He'd had a heart attack in 1966. And while his lawyers battled for him in court, his attention was taken up almost exclusively by the breast cancer that had descended upon his wife, Florence. It was an aggressive cancer, and Lou wanted to spend as much time with her as possible before the inevitable occurred.

Eventually his lawyers were able to get the Merritt-Chapman verdict overturned on appeal, and although the government retried the case twice more, it was never able to get a jury to convict Wolfson. The conviction in the Continental case stood, however. And on April 25, Wolfson entered Eglin Federal Prison Camp, a minimum-security penitentiary in Florida's Panhandle.

Wolfson would spend the rest of his life futilely trying to clear his name. Decades later, legal and business experts would decry his conviction. Henry Manne, former dean of the George Mason University School of Law, would characterize it as "a completely trumped-up securities violation case heralded by the managerial establishment." Business historian Robert Sobel put it this way: "From the vantage point of a quarter-century later, it seems clear that Wolfson had no criminal intent, that the government had come after him with guns blazing, determined to rid the business scene of a dangerous raider."

The fallout from Wolfson's convictions didn't stop with him. In May 1969, right after he began serving his sentence, *Life* magazine ran a story reporting a financial link between Wolfson and Supreme Court Justice Abe Fortas. Back in 1966, Fortas had been paid a $20,000 fee to advise the Wolfson Family Foundation on how to divvy up funds between charitable and educational projects. Fortas had returned the money the same year, but just the whiff of a connection between him and the recently incarcerated financier was enough to bring down a sitting Supreme Court justice. After declaring that he hadn't done anything wrong, Fortas resigned days after the *Life* story hit the stands.

With Wolfson serving jail time, there could be no racing for Harbor View. States like Maryland would not allow anyone convicted of a felony to have a license until the sentence was served. Further, Wolfson was cash-poor, most of his money tied up in the firms he held stock in, and he now had to pay back the $14.5 million in loans he'd taken out to finance his defense. His Harbor View stable would have to be liquidated, with all of his racing-age stock dispersed at public auction. His sons Steve and Gary paid a total of $1,655,000 for the youngsters they planned to race in their own Happy Valley Farm colors. They also hung on to some of Harbor View's better broodmares. All in all, more than three hundred horses were sold, some at fire-sale prices. The only things of value that Wolfson couldn't bring himself to part with were his two shares apiece in Raise a Native and Exclusive Native.

For all intents and purposes, Wolfson was out of racing, and Harbor View Farm's colors disappeared from the racetrack and the public consciousness.

*   *   *

Calumet Farm may not have disappeared from the racing scene like Harbor View Farm, but the depth and suddenness of its descent were even more stunning.

The year 1961 would turn out to be a watershed: the last gasp of the Calumet dynasty and the Camelot mythology. Horses carrying the devil's red and blue did manage to win sixty-two races and $759,856 to lead all stables in annual earnings, but Calumet's era of dynastic dominance was clearly coming to an end. Not only did those earnings represent barely half the haul of Calumet's heyday in the late 1940s, but it wasn't even enough to put the farm in the black for 1961.

Earlier that year, as if to foreshadow Calumet's impending crash, Plain Ben Jones died of a heart attack at seventy-eight. Though Plain Ben had long since handed over the reins to his son, Jimmy Jones simply could never outrun the long shadow cast by a father then hailed as the greatest trainer of all time, the only one to have saddled six Kentucky Derby winners. Racing insiders considered Plain Ben's death more than merely symbolic, suggesting that the success Jimmy enjoyed was due in large part to coaching from his dad, who had continued to live in the Calumet trainer's cottage long after his retirement.

Almost overnight, Calumet plummeted not only from the top spot but clear out of the top ten on the earnings list. In 1962, after a twenty-year reign in which the stable had ruled horse racing like no other dynasty ever had dominated any sport, Calumet won just thirty races and $337,667. The next year was even bleaker, its horses earning only $168,543 and failing to win a single stakes race.

Jimmy Jones, normally as garrulous as his father was taciturn, was finding it harder to keep up appearances as the affable trainer who passed his days at the track sharing his gift of folksy Midwestern gab with any horsemen, railbirds, and celebrities who happened by. Always exuding a slightly manic air with a perfectionist's attention to detail, the short, chunky trainer now found his patience taxed, his round face reddening at each mounting frustration. When tasks weren't performed to his satisfaction, he would snap at stablehands, "There's a right way to do things—and then there's the Calumet way!"

Which is the same thing he felt like reminding Lucille Markey. "Mrs. Markey thought Calumet could win without continuing to work at it," Jones would grouse with a shake of his head. The cheapening of what had been such a rich product, he confided, turned his stomach. It reached the point where he took his concerns directly to Lucille. Just as Plain Ben had once butted heads with Warren Wright over the original master's micromanagement that bordered on meddling, Jimmy Jones now found himself often challenging Lucille over the current mistress's thriftiness that bordered on chintziness.

Calumet's champion bloodlines, he warned her, were petering out. For years, he had publicly fretted that her breeding stock was dominated too much by Bull Lea and argued that Calumet desperately needed to outcross. Jones beseeched Lucille to find a stallion worthy to succeed Bull Lea as Calumet's foundation sire. Aging through his twenties, Bull Lea had long since stopped siring champions, his get failing to win a single stakes race after 1961. With Bull Lea's sons having all failed at stud, Jones couldn't understand why Lucille stubbornly insisted on continuing to rely on her unproductive homebred stallions. "Breeding farms must have good stallions," he admonished. "Without one, you don't have much going for you."

Even more vexing to Jones was Lucille's culling of the surpassing broodmare band around which Warren had meticulously built the Calumet dynasty. The band, once pregnant with upward of eighty choice broodmares, was now shrinking steadily. Not only had Lucille stopped buying broodmares for the farm because of rapidly inflating prices, but she was also following her friend Leslie Combs's advice that her band was too large and needed to be thinned out. It was a measure of what she would sell off that many of the suggested culls were good enough to wind up as productive broodmares at Combs's own Spendthrift Farm. At a time when the number of Thoroughbred foals registered in North America had more than doubled since Calumet's heyday, Lucille further reduced its chances by culling her broodmare band and thus her annual foal crop. Where once Calumet was producing four dozen babies a year out of a North American foal crop of five thousand, now the stable had less than half as many to choose from out of an annual North American foal crop that had exploded to eighteen thousand.

With Lucille as reluctant to do the math as she was to spend money for new bloodstock, Jones lobbied her hard to revive the broodmare band.

"We've got to heat it up again, get some new, hot blood," he pleaded with her.

"We have plenty of horses," she replied tersely, "and don't need more."

Exasperated, Jones finally blurted out a warning: "You are going out of business."

For Jones, it was the last straw. He was, he snapped, "fed up." It was clear that the mistress of Calumet did not hold him in anywhere near the same esteem as she had his father, and even clearer that she wasn't about to provide him with the horses he believed were needed. He was just fifty-seven when he quit abruptly early in the fall of 1964, formally retiring from his Hall of Fame training career and leaving to become Monmouth Park's racing director.

After a quarter-century of stability in the hands of the Jones Boys, Calumet's racing stock was handed over to a journeyman trainer named George Poole. This was the beginning of what soon became a revolving door at Calumet's stable—four different trainers in one four-year span. Each successive trainer would encounter the very problem that Jimmy Jones had warned Lucille Markey about: the trickling out of Calumet's bloodlines to the point where rival horsemen scoffed that all that remained in the barn was "a bunch of crows."

On June 16, 1964, symbolizing the extinction of the Calumet dynasty, Bull Lea died at the age of twenty-nine, leaving behind a legacy as the most successful stallion America had yet produced. The dark brown colt Wright had bought for just $14,000 would win $94,825 on the racetrack and then sire progeny that would win more than $13.5 million.

Upon his death, a large statue of Bull Lea was placed in Calumet's immaculately manicured equine cemetery shaded by dogwoods and landscaped with flowers matching the stable's devil's-red and blue colors. The bronzed Bull Lea, bullishly built and square-headed, stood regally atop a white marble pedestal, overlooking his own gravesite and those of Calumet's champions, many of whom he had sired. Arrayed in a semicircle before Bull Lea were gray marble headstones memorializing his most famous progeny—his sons lying to his left, his daughters to his right. Up until Calumet closed its wrought-iron gates to visitors in the late 1960s, the equine cemetery remained the farm's top tourist attraction. It also served as a fitting memorial to a bygone era, the only place where Calumet could still elicit awe, if only as a haunting reminder of the ghosts of dynasty past.

Like the farm's equine cemetery, its Trophy Room, centrally located behind the grand staircase on the ground floor of the main residence, represented the most tangible remains of the Calumet legacy, another bittersweet reminder of faded glory. The Admiral and Lucille Markey continued to proudly entertain guests in the large pine room lined from floor to ceiling with the stable's gold and silver trophies. When Ben Jones arrived, there had been all of ten trophies on display; by the time he died, there were nearly fifty times that many in every conceivable shape from cups and bowls to plates and urns. They may have been appraised at millions of dollars, but they would remain priceless to Lucille. They shone on as polished reminders of a golden age that seemed more distant with each passing year, their luster fading with each succeeding disappointment on the track.

As the 1960s trudged on with one humiliating loss after another, Lucille could only take joy in Calumet's glorious past. Calumet had not even qualified a Kentucky Derby starter since Tim Tam's 1958 triumph at Churchill Downs—a decade-long drought that would have dragged on if not for a powerful great-grandson of Bull Lea named Forward Pass.

The betting favorite for the 1968 Derby, Forward Pass was overtaken in the stretch by Dancer's Image and lost by a length and a half. Hours after Dancer's Image celebrated in the winner's circle, however, his postrace urinalysis came up positive for Butazolidin, an anti-inflammatory drug commonly known as "Bute" that was administered to him early Derby week to treat a swollen fore ankle. Three days afterward, Kentucky racing stewards disqualified Dancer's Image for a drug that was then legal in training but not in races there and declared runner-up Forward Pass the official Derby winner. It marked the first time the Kentucky Derby was ever decided on a disqualification, the most hollow victory in racing's most hallowed spectacle. How telling that Calumet had reclaimed the spotlight by default without even returning to the winner's circle, its eighth Derby win extending its own unchallenged record in the most unsatisfying fashion. There would be no blanket of roses draped over the big bay's withers and no Kentucky Derby Gold Cup presented to his connections; there was only a tarnished title and controversy that would dog them throughout the Triple Crown campaign—and beyond.

By overpowering Dancer's Image in their Preakness rematch and romping home by six lengths, Forward Pass set up a controversial Belmont Stakes bid to become the first Triple Crown winner in the twenty years since Citation had proved himself the pride of Calumet. As if to save racing from the awkwardness of the asterisk that would have accompanied his name like a scarlet letter, Forward Pass surrendered the lead in the Belmont stretch and placed second by a length and a half to a longshot named Stage Door Johnny.

Thanks to Forward Pass's bizarre spring campaign, Calumet managed a return to the top ten in annual earnings, ranking third among all stables in 1968. The Run for the Roses may be hailed as "the most exciting two minutes in sports," but the battle over history's most controversial Kentucky Derby would drag on in court for five years before Calumet finally collected the $122,600 winner's share. Throughout the protracted legal battle, Lucille vowed never to run another horse in Kentucky if the courts didn't affirm Forward Pass's Derby win. It was perhaps the clearest measure of how desperately she was clinging to Calumet's faded glory.

That flash of glory in the bittersweet spring of 1968 proved to be just a solitary spike. With both Markeys growing too infirm to devote much energy to the farm's operation, Calumet's slide resumed. In 1970, the stable won only nineteen races—the fewest since 1933, its first full year of operation. In 1974, it won only thirteen races and $117,109 in purses—the smallest haul since 1939.

Through it all, Lucille insisted that Calumet's reputation remain paramount. To this epitome of the grand Southern lady, nothing was more important than keeping up appearances. If she scrimped on the bloodstock in the barns and fields, she spared no expense to keep Calumet's thousand acres looking like a picture postcard at a time when sustaining the farm and stable cost over a million dollars a year. She vowed to continue spending $10,000 a year on paint alone to keep the farm's white plank fences looking as bright as freshly fallen snow. She decreed that all the white barns trimmed in devil's red continue looking as pristine as when Warren would routinely run his index finger along their chrome trimmings to make sure there was no dust.

To Lucille, nothing was more important than preserving the reputation of Calumet Farm—and of the family. And nothing demonstrated that better than her strained relationship with her only son, Warren Wright Jr. After her first husband's will left the farm to her rather than to a thirty-year-old scion who had shown no aptitude for being able to run such an enterprise, Lucille became increasingly exasperated by how Warren Jr.'s behavior embarrassed the Wright and Calumet names: his drinking, his spendthrift habits, his failure to pay bills on time. The final ignominy occurred in the mid-1950s when Lucille confronted her ne'er-do-well son over raging rumors that his wife, Bertha, was carrying on an affair and demanded that he either leave the marriage or move out of the refurbished Calumet farmhouse the couple shared with their three children. After Warren chose to leave, never to return home, the continuing scandal made him the laughingstock of Lexington and widened the rift with his mother. So icy was their relationship that she allowed him to visit only by appointment and, upon his 1961 conviction for income tax evasion, never wrote him in prison or had much contact with him afterward.

It galled Lucille that Warren Sr.'s will had established a trust that, upon her death, would leave control of Calumet Farm to Warren Jr. and his family. But since she couldn't change that, she could only focus on continuing the Calumet tradition by resurrecting the phoenix from the ashes.

If 1974 represented a nadir for Calumet, it also presaged something of a rebirth. That would be a big year for Lucille's prize broodmare Sweet

Tooth, the homebred daughter of Bull Lea grandkids On-and-On and Plum Cake. In early March, Sweet Tooth foaled Our Mims, a big bay filly resulting from an outcross with the respected French sire Herbager, who was standing at Claiborne Farm. A month later, Sweet Tooth was bred to Raise a Native at Spendthrift Farm, where he stood in syndication. Sweet Tooth's maiden mating with Raise a Native two years earlier had produced a good-looking chestnut named Hopefully On. Although Hopefully On would ultimately win just three races and $20,800 in his short career on the track, Lucille, with two breeding shares in Raise a Native, was betting on a nick with Sweet Tooth. Entrusting the very future of Calumet on her best-bred mare, Lucille hung her hopes for one last shot of old glory on Sweet Tooth's latest progeny: first Our Mims and then, especially, the baby that Sweet Tooth was now carrying, a colt who within three years would achieve fame as Alydar.

*   *   *

If Calumet and Lucille Markey were praying for a revival, Harbor View and Lou Wolfson would need nothing short of a resurrection.

Upon his release from prison on January 26, 1970, two days shy of his fifty-eighth birthday, Wolfson was at loose ends and effectively out of the racing game. He was preoccupied with redeeming his name, defending his honor, and effecting judicial and penal reform. Insisting he was a victim of selective prosecution, he would spend $2 million waging an unsuccessful campaign to prove his innocence.

Less than a month after his release from prison, Wolfson was saddened by news that would change everything: Hirsch Jacobs, the winningest trainer of all time, had died of a cerebral hemorrhage at the age of sixty-five.

Over the years, Wolfson had grown close to the beloved horseman, had looked up to him as a mentor, and had become a trusted family friend of the horse-loving Jacobses—from Hirsch and his wife, Ethel, to their daughter, Patrice, and their sons, John and Tommy. For years in the 1950s and '60s, Wolfson occupied the owner's box at Aqueduct directly behind Hirsch Jacobs's, and the two men loved to talk pedigrees between races. In Jacobs, Wolfson had found a kindred spirit. Like Wolfson, Jacobs was an impoverished Jewish immigrant's son who transformed himself from the ultimate outsider into a self-made success by finding and realizing value in other people's discards. Just as Wolfson had in the business world, Jacobs personified the rags-to-riches rise in the racing game.

Far from the Bluegrass pastures and Midwestern plains where trainers were typically raised, Jacobs had grown up poor on the streets of Brooklyn, one of ten children of an immigrant tailor. Dropping out of school at thirteen to bring home money as a steamfitter, he found his true calling when his partner in a rooftop pigeon loft, where they raised and raced their well-bred homing pigeons for sport and prize money, introduced him to the racetrack and then persuaded him to try his hand training a cheap Thoroughbred. Right from the start, Jacobs displayed a knack for training horses and was already saddling winners by the time he was twenty-two. The upstart dubbed "The Pigeon Man" soon caught the eye of Isidor Bieber, a Runyonesque ticket hustler and high roller who suggested they team up to form a racing stable. Bieber would provide the bulk of the bankroll and Jacobs all the horse sense and training savvy.

Lacking the resources of the Bluegrass blue bloods, the two city slickers needed an affordable way to compete with the racing aristocracy on the brink of the Great Depression. Their strategy was to buy cheap, unsound nags out of claiming races—the lowest-level competitions in which any horse entered can be bought, or "claimed," beforehand by any interested party at a predetermined price—for Jacobs to magically turn into winners. Upon taking possession right after a claiming race, Jacobs would quickly diagnose the sorry specimen's problem: lameness, poor conditioning, emotional issues. Then he would proceed to work his magic with a combination of equine psychoanalysis and home remedies, which ran the gamut from special mudpacks and compresses to vinegar and even the white iodine he might have just used to cure a troublesome corn on his own foot.

Damon Runyon himself, for whom Jacobs trained a few claimers, swore his longtime friend could talk to horses in that soft, soothing voice of his. "I have eavesdropped on him around the stables many a time and heard him soft-soaping those equine characters," Runyon revealed in his newspaper column. "He generally wins their confidence and learns all their troubles. I do not say that they up and tell him, understand. No, I do not say that, because it is something I cannot prove, inasmuch as Hirsch Jacobs himself denies there is any open banter between him and his horses. But if they do not tell him, who does?"

It didn't take long for Jacobs's unorthodox methods to pay off. In 1933, he saddled 116 winners to lead all trainers nationally for the first time in a category he would dominate for over a decade. Three years after that breakthrough, he saddled a record-smashing 177 winners. Year after year, Jacobs and Bieber would continue to acquire cheap claimers and run them, as one rival scoffed acidly, "like a fleet of taxicabs." The more Jacobs dominated the ordinary races that filled out daily cards with horses the high-society stables had discarded, the more jealousy and resentment he elicited from an inbred racing aristocracy. Over and over, they dismissed him as nothing more than a "claiming trainer."

Then came the cheap claimer that would change everything.

In the spring of 1943, Jacobs was hanging around the Belmont Park paddock one day when a two-year-old chestnut happened to catch his keen eye, an average-looking colt named Stymie. Even though Stymie had finished both of his career starts way out of the money, Jacobs turned to Bieber and said, "I've got a feeling about that colt. I like the way he walks. He's a proud little thing." Perusing the entries a few days later, Jacobs noticed Stymie's name listed in a claiming race at Belmont. Jacobs raced down to the track and got there just in time to claim Stymie for a mere $1,500.

From the moment he snapped a lead shank on Stymie right after the colt's plodding seventh-place finish, Jacobs realized what a headstrong, tough, and disagreeable animal he had purchased. It didn't take long for the trainer to conclude that the best way to both calm and condition the horse was to race him relentlessly. The stubborn colt would run in ten more claiming races for Jacobs, without any takers, before finally winning anything— and then only a $3,300 claimer. From that humble beginning, Stymie began to improve steadily if slowly through his two- and three-year-old seasons.

Then, almost overnight, Stymie blossomed into "the Cinderella horse," the ugly-duckling claimer maturing at age four into a majestic champion. Running with his head held high in a proud carriage reminiscent of his great-grandsire Man o' War, Stymie perfected his charge-from-behind style to earn 1945 champion honors in the handicap division. The next year, he won enough to lift his trainer to the top of the annual money list for the first time with $560,077 in stable earnings. Now whenever talk at the track got around to training geniuses, Hirsch Jacobs was suddenly being mentioned in the same breath as Calumet's resident master, Plain Ben Jones.

Likewise was Stymie himself now traveling in fast company that included Calumet's golden gelding, Armed, and the 1946 Triple Crown winner, Assault. Stymie may have lacked his two rivals' speed and versatility—being a one-dimensional plodder who needed a long distance and a fast pace in front to set up his rousing come-from-behind stretch runs—but he proved himself the toughest and sturdiest campaigner of them all, pounding out 141 miles of hard racing under backbreaking weight handicaps.

That blue-collar work ethic earned Stymie fame as "the people's horse." Like Jacobs a commoner in The Sport of Kings, Stymie was the hero of all the $2 bettors who lived vicariously through the little claimer who could. He was already the biggest equine celebrity since Seabiscuit when he overtook Armed in 1947 to become history's richest racehorse. The following year, showing the wear and tear of 131 career races, Stymie was finally retired at age eight with earnings of $918,485—a record that would last three years before being broken by none other than Citation.

Stymie's earnings stake enabled Jacobs and Bieber to purchase a 283-acre horse farm in northern Maryland and boldly branch out into the breeding end of racing. They gratefully named the farm Stymie Manor. Thanks to Stymie's rags-to-riches fairy tale, the claiming trainer graduated to the breeding business where, he quipped, "all you need is money, money, and more money." If he lacked the kind of money enjoyed by all the millionaire sportsmen who could afford to breed Thoroughbreds and race them as an expensive hobby, he compensated with the horse sense that enabled him to spend it wisely and parlay it into a bloodstock empire of his own. The key to breeding, he concluded, was written in the pedigrees: "just good families."

To Jacobs, horse racing was all about families—both equine and human. Three years after his 1933 wedding, he began running his horses in the salmon-pink and emerald-green racing silks registered to his young wife, Ethel. She would remain the owner of record for most of the horses her husband bred and trained right up until their only daughter was old enough to join them in the family business.

Patrice, born in 1937 and named after Damon Runyon's second wife, grew up in the sheltering warmth of her family's ten-room redbrick Georgian colonial in the tony Queens neighborhood of Forest Hills Gardens, just a short ride from the Aqueduct, Belmont, and Jamaica racetracks. She was educated by nuns at the request of her Catholic mother and with the consent of her Jewish father, who routinely deflected his wife's attempts to convert him but let his children be brought up as Roman Catholics.

Like her two brothers, Patrice inherited her father's fierce passion for horses. As she grew old enough to accompany him to the races, Dad did his best to insulate her from the railbirds, touts, and assorted riffraff that populated the racetrack from the backside barns to the betting windows. She became a familiar figure in the owner's box and in the winner's circle, often on her father's arm. But she continued to lead a very cloistered life, always found in the company of her parents. "Dad doesn't allow me to hang around the barns too much while we are at Belmont and Aqueduct," she once told a reporter, "but at Saratoga, I get out there with him and the horses on a pony!"

When she went off to Virginia's Marymount College, she would spend her weekends not at football games with her classmates but trackside at Pimlico, Laurel, or Bowie. Upon graduation, she moved back with her parents, writing the occasional article for the *Morning Telegraph* and dabbling in painting. Now in her early twenties, petite with her chestnut curls bobbed short, she was, in the words of *Sports Illustrated*, "as animated and pretty as Debbie Reynolds."

As time went on, Patrice spent more and more of her days around the barns on the backside. It didn't take long for her father to see that she had a special way with horses. In her presence, even the most fiery steed would become more calm and relaxed.

Every year, Jacobs would let her pick a horse or two from his stable as her own, to run in her name and in the same pink and green silks as her mother's. Patrice's first horse was just an old show jumper who clearly wasn't cut out for racing. The next winter, her father offered her a choice between a couple of his homebred two-year-olds. She picked a skinny, gawky brown colt named Hail To Reason. From the moment Patrice selected him, Hail To Reason became, as one turf writer noted, "Miss Jacobs' special pet." Apparently, the feeling was mutual. Hail To Reason would see Patrice walking toward him, prick up his ears, and nuzzle her as soon as she got within reach. She would whisper to him and he would immediately let down. She could often be seen sitting in a chair at the entrance of his stall reading a book while he quietly hung over her shoulder.

A growthy, rangy two-year-old who needed six races to break his maiden, Hail To Reason matured to win nine of eighteen starts that season, setting a Saratoga track record to capture the 1960 Hopeful Stakes by ten lengths and thus stamp himself a favorite for the following year's Kentucky Derby. He had already clinched the 1960 juvenile championship when, during a galloping workout one Sunday morning that September, he stepped on a thrown horseshoe and fractured both sesamoid bones in his left foreleg. "Diabolical fate," Hirsch Jacobs muttered over and over as his son John, serving as his assistant trainer, held the colt's ankle off the ground while they waited for the horse ambulance to arrive.

"Mr. Jacobs," the ambulance driver said as soon as he surveyed the scene, "are you going to destroy him here or after we get him back to the barn?"

Jacobs shook his head and snapped, "I'm not going to destroy him, if I have to put that leg back on myself!"

Since there were no vets at Aqueduct that early on a Sunday morning, it was left to Jacobs to roll a plaster cast on the damaged fetlock and keep the colt calm without the benefit of tranquilizers. John called home and tearfully told his mother, "Hail's broken down and he'll never race again." When Ethel relayed the news to her daughter, Patrice started to cry and couldn't stop for days. When they visited the barn, Patrice dropped beside her prostrate horse and cradled his head in her lap. "My dreams," she would later say, "were shattered." With Hail To Reason teetering between life and death for a month, Jacobs would be credited with saving him and nursing him back to health to stand at stud.

If Jacobs could find any consolation in the forced retirement of "the greatest horse I ever had," it was that he already had another promising weanling in the barn. The dark brown homebred, named Affectionately, would go on to become the champion two-year-old filly of 1962 and the second female ever to earn half a million dollars.

With Affectionately leading the way, Jacobs ascended to the top spot on the breeders' list in 1964 for the first time with $1,301,677 in annual winnings. The next year, he not only repeated as the nation's leading breeder (his $1,994,649 in annual winnings second only to Calumet's 1952 record of $2,060,590), but also topped the trainers' list (his $1,331,628 in winnings second only to Ben Jones's 1947 record of $1,334,805). That double feat placed Jacobs at the very pinnacle of his profession.

In many ways, however, he was still an outsider. It remained out of the question for him to join the Jockey Club, that elite circle of patrician Anglo-Saxons who for generations ruled the racing industry like their own private fiefdom. Instead, Jacobs threw his weight behind the Horsemen's Benevolent and Protective Association in the late 1960s when it challenged the sovereignty of the Jockey Club and the New York Racing Association, joining the HBPA's board to fight for the rights of backside workers. When Aqueduct was polarized by a horsemen's strike, Jacobs called the dispute "a classic case of the blue bloods against the Italians and Jews." For all his wealth and success, Jacobs remained a champion of the little man, from the minimum-wage stableboy to the $2 bettor.

Such principled stands constituted yet another reason Lou Wolfson was so drawn to Jacobs. The two men shared a mutual respect and admiration, not to mention parallel life arcs right out of a Horatio Alger story. Just as Wolfson could look at a spreadsheet and see potential in companies where others couldn't, so had Jacobs succeeded by looking at conformation or pedigree and seeing potential in horses where others couldn't. Wolfson could spend hours on end listening to Jacobs passing on breeding tips. Patrice, too, would sit for hours by her father's side, soaking up his breeding wisdom "like a sponge."

Short, chunky, and invariably dressed in a conservative brown suit, Jacobs loved talking horse in his owner's box at Aqueduct, the scruffy old Queens racetrack where he based his stable. Though reserved and unassuming by nature, he was known to always greet everyone he saw with a smiling "Hiya."

In the summer of 1966, the sixty-two-year-old horseman was enjoying his hard-earned accession to the peak when he suddenly suffered a stroke. His son John, two years Patrice's senior, took over as the stable's day-to-day trainer. Although Hirsch came back the next year to remain active as a trainer on a limited basis, the mild stroke forced him to lessen the burden on his family by dismantling two-thirds of the Bieber-Jacobs Stable under doctor's orders. The horses they sold off for a total of $4 million brought higher averages at auction than those in the prestigious Keeneland Sales, some of the fiercest bidding ironically done by the very blue bloods who looked down upon the outsider who had built his empire on cheap claimers that the millionaires wouldn't have wasted their bluegrass on.

Jacobs was now a millionaire in his own right. The nation's leading breeder for four straight years, he was hailed as the most successful trainer of all time, having saddled far more winners than any horseman ever had before him on his way to raising his record-smashing total to 3,596 with over $15 million in earnings. The only thing he hadn't accomplished in his Hall of Fame career, it seemed, was winning the Kentucky Derby or, for that matter, either of the other jewels in the Triple Crown series.

Then came the horse that offered his best hope for ending that drought: a well-bred colt named Personality. It was poetic justice that Personality stemmed from the mating of his two favorite homebreds, Hail To Reason and Affectionately. So excited was Jacobs by Affectionately's first foal that the normally low-key horseman never missed an opportunity to whip out his wallet like a proud father and show off a baby picture of "the best horse I've ever bred."

By the time Personality embarked on his three-year-old campaign in 1970, though, Jacobs had been hospitalized with an arterial blockage that hampered blood flow to the brain. He was gravely ill that February when his children, visiting him in the Miami Heart Institute, handed him a photo of Personality losing a sprint at Hialeah the previous week. "Papa, we'll win a big one with him," Patrice said reassuringly, "just you wait and see." Hirsch nodded and then studied the picture of his prize bay, staring at it for the longest time with furrowed brow as if something was amiss. Finally, he pointed at Personality's head and, though he was having difficulty speaking, asked softly, "No blinkers?" When John confirmed that the colt was indeed not wearing blinkers, Hirsch went back to studying the photo. Finally, he looked up at his training protégé and whispered, "Do better—blinkers."

Four days later, Hirsch Jacobs lapsed into a coma and passed away. Wearing blinkers from then on, Personality won the Wood Memorial at Aqueduct to stamp himself a Kentucky Derby favorite and, after a disappointing eighth on the first Saturday in May at Churchill Downs, captured the Preakness Stakes by a neck. Posthumously, Hirsch Jacobs had finally won a Triple Crown race, and done so with a homebred who was en route to becoming his first Horse of the Year honoree.

Patrice was devastated by her father's death. She was thirty-two, wealthy, and attractive, but she was too grief-stricken to even want a social life. She turned for support to Lou Wolfson, the longtime family friend who had lost his wife of thirty-two years, Florence, to cancer just two years earlier. As Lou consoled Patrice, they bonded in their shared grief.

They had first met, when she was twenty-one and he forty-six, at Saratoga, where their families occupied adjacent boxes at the historic racetrack and stayed at the same grand resort hotel throughout the fashionable August meet. With each succeeding summer, the two families spent increasingly more time socializing together in Saratoga Springs, and Lou named one of his first racehorses Royal Patrice in her honor. For her part, Patrice felt an immediate connection with Lou. She would tell people he was so much like her father that she felt like Lou was a member of the family. He likewise developed "a deep feeling and love for the family" and now, a decade later, wanted to support them through this difficult time.

In the wake of Hirsch Jacobs's death, his son John, who had served as his trusted assistant for more than a decade, carried on his legacy as the chief trainer, guiding Personality to the Preakness win and homebred stablemate High Echelon to a Belmont Stakes win three weeks later. While John continued to run the stable through that bittersweet season, plans were in motion to sell off all the horses by the end of the year under the terms of the Bieber-Jacobs partnership agreement.

While in the process of liquidating the bloodstock, Patrice and her mother realized there were some homebreds they couldn't bear to part with. In particular were two mares registered to Ethel: Affectionately and Straight Deal, a Hail To Reason daughter honored as 1967's champion distaff handicapper. Patrice mentioned their predicament to Lou. "I'll tell you what," he offered, "I'll buy out Bieber's interest in Affectionately and Straight Deal, because I know what they mean to you and I don't want them to go somewhere away from you." When Patrice demurred, Lou insisted, "There's such sentiment there. Take Affectionately and Straight Deal out of the sale."

Even after Lou entered into a partnership with Ethel on the two mares, he had no plans to rebuild his own stable. On the contrary, throughout 1971 he repeatedly rebuffed Patrice's coaxing to get back into racing. He felt he needed to spend his time trying to clear his name and working on the social issues—like prison reform—that had become so important to him during his nine months at Eglin. But Patrice could see what a toll those lofty goals were taking. The more time he spent trying to change the world and to restore his good name, the more frustrated and disillusioned he got. She worried that if something didn't change, he would never be happy again. She was sure that racing could be the key to turning things around, and that if he could be convinced to at least get back into breeding, he might be pulled out of that dark place he'd fallen into.

In the end, her persistence and persuasiveness paid off. Her enthusiasm started to rub off on him, and he began to pay more attention to the plans she was suggesting for the horses they owned in partnership. He watched with interest as she drew up charts like her father had before her. And in the process, his own interests in breeding and racing were rekindled.

Now Patrice and Lou were bonding not just out of their shared grief, but more and more out of a shared passion for racehorses—not to mention a growing recognition that they had very similar tastes in just about everything from music to movies. Soon the two shy, quiet people were cocooning together. And on December 30, 1972, they were married in Miami.

Their union incorporated some of the Bieber-Jacobs bloodstock with that of the old Harbor View. Of the horses Lou had sold off to his sons Steve and Gary before going to prison, he bought back twenty-four mares to restock Harbor View Farm. His growing broodmare band would at times number more than a hundred. What's more, he still had his breeding shares in both Raise a Native and Exclusive Native—the investments that he wouldn't let go in the liquidation. Having led the nation's breeders list in 1970 and '71, ironically thanks to horses that had been sold in the 1960s liquidation, he was finally back in the breeding business.

He resolved to rebuild Harbor View almost from scratch with his new partner, Patrice. She became not only a lifelong companion but a trusted adviser in breeding matters. Theirs was a partnership of two horse lovers who both preached the breeding gospel according to Hirsch Jacobs.

That philosophy had informed Lou's decision to buy a ten-year-old retired racehorse named Won't Tell You at the Keeneland Sale early in 1972 for $18,000, a very modest price for a mare who was in foal to Raise a Native. On the track, Won't Tell You had been nothing special, winning only five claiming races in twenty-three starts. But what piqued Wolfson's interest in Won't Tell You was her sire, Crafty Admiral, the durable and versatile champion handicapper of 1952 who was linebred to Teddy three generations back on the top side and four generations back on the bottom side. Lou never passed up a chance to buy up Crafty Admiral mares, whose inherited sturdiness might offset Raise a Native's inherent unsoundness. The 1972 Raise a Native foal that Won't Tell You was carrying would turn out to be a disappointment, a future claimer named Century Gold. But that couldn't deter the Wolfsons from breeding her again—first to Raise a Native's son Native Heritage in 1972 and then, after a year in which she was barren, to Raise a Native's son Exclusive Native in 1974. The Wolfsons chose to breed her to Raise a Native sons because Patrice had noticed that the cross would afford the opportunity to linebreed to the sire her father loved, Teddy.

Getting back into breeding was one thing, but racing again was quite another. It took Lou over a year following his release from prison to decide he wanted to reapply for the racing licenses that had expired. Once he finally committed to getting back into racing, he did so with his typical drive and a newfound enthusiasm. He had begun dipping his toe into the shallow end in 1971 when New York, Maryland, and Florida all granted him racing licenses. By 1974, the year Won't Tell You was bred to Exclusive Native, Lou was all in and the Wolfsons were becoming a fixture around the racetrack, a strikingly handsome couple who would hold hands and gaze lovingly at each other.

That 1975 foal crop would signal the return of both Wolfsons to the racing game. Patrice felt reinvigorated as a new bride whose heart was warmed "seeing my husband start to blossom, to enjoy going to the races again." As they eagerly awaited the birth of those foals in the winter and spring of 1975, Patrice considered it "really like a rebirth"—for her because she thought she'd "lost practically everything in the horse business" when her father died and for Lou because he felt the same thing when he was imprisoned. That foaling season, of birth and rebirth, couldn't come soon enough.

PART II

ASCENDANCE

Alydar with John Veitch on a flight to Lexington (Jim Raftery/Livingston Collection)

CHAPTER 5

Born to Run

ON FEBRUARY 21, 1975, WON'T TELL YOU DELIVERED A BRIGHT CHEST-nut colt whose elegant face was emblazoned with an irregularly shaped star that flowed into a narrowing strip. His broad forehead tapered down to a fine muzzle, giving him an intelligent look. The colt was leggy, refined, and well balanced. Though his dam's pedigree predicted a sturdy and resilient foal, it was otherwise unremarkable and certainly not in the same league as some of the other broodmares foaling out that spring at Harbor View Farm. So there would be no phone call to announce the little chestnut's birth, like there would be when Straight Deal, the mare that Lou and Patrice Wolfson owned in partnership with her mother, foaled. For the next several months, the colt and his dam would be turned out with the other babies and broodmares where he would learn to play and socialize. Once he was weaned, he would spend his days in a pasture with the twenty-odd other colts born that spring.

When the Wolfsons stopped by in the fall to check out the young horses, Lou and Patrice walked over to the colt's field. They paused, elbows resting on the fence, to watch the youngsters play. For some reason, the bright chestnut colt caught Patrice's eye. She wasn't sure why she was drawn to him. Though relatively tall, he was among the scrawniest of the bunch. As she stared out across the field, the colt spotted her and stopped his play. Breaking away from his pasture mates, he trotted over, and when he reached the fence where Patrice was standing, the little guy pushed his nose forward, nuzzled her, and then stuck his head in her arms. Patrice was startled, but instantly charmed. She scrutinized the lanky baby and wondered what it was about him that had called out to her. He lifted his head up and stared directly into her eyes, and she knew. "My heavens," she thought, "he looks like Stymie." She looked into the colt's eyes and said, "You know, you look just like Stymie." Then she gripped his halter and turned his head so she could read the nameplate, which was emblazoned WON'T TELL YOU since the babies who hadn't been named yet wore their dam's name on their halters. "So that's who you are," she said to the colt. After a few minutes he turned away and trotted back to his companions, and the moment was over. Lou, who had been watching silently the whole time, smiled to see once again that mysterious connection his wife seemed to make with certain animals.

Although there still wasn't anything to make the Wolfsons think this colt could be a future star on the track, he had made an impression on Patrice and she would remember to check in on him each time she and Lou visited the farm.

*   *   *

A month after Won't Tell You foaled her colt, Sweet Tooth was getting ready to drop hers.

As a heavy rain pelted down and lightning crackled through the dark Kentucky sky, Sweet Tooth had been brought into her stall in Calumet Farm's foaling barn where she was being closely watched. It was clear that she was close and that the baby would come soon. By 9:30 P.M., the thunderstorms had passed and the temperature had settled into the seasonable sixties. All was quiet in the barn, except for the steady crunching sounds as the mares chewed their hay and the occasional snort as they cleared the dust from their nostrils. By 10:30, Sweet Tooth had begun to move around, looking vaguely uncomfortable. Now there was no doubt that tonight would be the night. As time passed, the mare looked more and more uncomfortable. Then with a gushing sound, her water broke. Within minutes she dropped down, and two small front feet appeared, followed by a tiny head. By 11:20, a big chestnut colt lay at her side. His dark brown coat was marked only with a small splash of white between his eyes and discreet low white socks on his left front and right hind legs.

The next morning Melvin Cinnamon, the farm manager, recorded the birth and its particulars in the foal register. "Wonderful, fine-looking big colt," he wrote, noting that the birth had taken place at 11:20 P.M. on March 23, 1975. Right from the start, Cinnamon and everyone else on the farm were convinced that this brash and bouncy specimen was going to be a star. Even the colt seemed to know it. He had a self-possessed and regal air from the moment he gathered his long, spiderlike legs beneath him and wobbled up to survey his world.

At Calumet, though, there would be no special treatment even for a star like Sweet Tooth's new foal. When he was weaned, he was turned out to run and play with all the other colts born that year. This was the only way, the Markeys felt, for babies to learn how to handle themselves and to become the warriors that would later battle it out on the track. As Lucille and the Admiral watched the young horses racing through Calumet's huge fields, they knew they had some special babies. By the time Sweet Tooth dropped this 1975 Raise a Native colt, the Markeys already were seeing great promise in her 1974 filly by the French stallion Herbager. There was no question that both the filly and the colt had unlimited potential—but the Markeys were worried that their current trainer, Reggie Cornell, might ruin them before they ever had a chance to make their mark.

Cornell was the fourth trainer that had tried unsuccessfully to fill the boots of the Jones Boys. For Lucille, it brought back unpleasant memories of the time before Plain Ben Jones took the reins at Calumet when Warren had been so frustrated he practically sold off all the horses. Now, just as then, colts and fillies would start their training at Calumet full of promise and potential, but when they reached the track, the injuries would start to pile up. Pretty soon they'd be back at the farm recuperating without ever having started, let alone won, a race.

The Markeys began casting about, looking for someone with the talent to bring along their precious young prospects. They asked their farm manager if he had any suggestions. As it turned out, Cinnamon did have someone in mind: a young trainer named John Veitch.

*   *   *

John Veitch was just thirty at the time and younger than any trainer Calumet had ever hired, but he came from venerable racing lines, just as Sweet Tooth's colt did. He was the son of Hall of Fame trainer Sylvester Veitch, who in turn was the son of leading steeplechase rider Silas Veitch. Syl Veitch, following in his own father's footsteps, had gotten his start riding and then training steeplechasers before finally switching to flat racing in his late twenties. During his nearly two decades training at Cornelius Van-derbilt Whitney's stable, Veitch saddled four champions, including Pha-lanx, the 1947 Belmont Stakes winner, and Counterpoint, who was voted 1951 Horse of the Year after handily capturing the Belmont. When Whit-ney divorced and bolted for California in 1958, Veitch decided he would rather find a new employer than move to a state he detested. Snapped up by George D. Widener, Veitch continued to turn out winners, including another champion. Following Widener's death in 1971, Veitch opened his own public stable, which he had been running ever since. "What else would I do? Go crazy? Jump off a bridge?" he shrugged, explaining his decision to start his own stable in his sixties. Racing, simply put, was in his blood, and his bloodlines.

Though John Veitch had been out on his own for just two years, he already had considerable experience working as an assistant trainer at the racing stables of both Widener and Paul Mellon, apprenticing first with his father and then with Elliott Burch, the head trainer at Mellon's Rokeby Stables. What really made the younger Veitch appealing to the Markeys was his experience working for a single big client; in other words, he knew how to be a private trainer. By the 1970s, public trainers—those who div-vied their time between a bevy of clients—had become the fashion, with few still opting to devote all their attention to just one farm.

Born in Lexington, Kentucky, John Veitch had been around horses and horse racing all his life. Even as a young child, he had accompanied his father to the track, hanging out with the grooms and exercise boys while Syl Veitch worked. An inquisitive and intelligent boy, John soaked up whatever he saw, learning every detail of horse care from proper mucking of stalls to the construction of a spider bandage that would fit perfectly over an injured knee. Sometimes he was asked to help out, and that set the lessons more permanently. The time with his father's workers was entertaining and interesting but, being the only child at the track, the boy longed for some buddies. He had always been drawn to animals of all kinds, and eventually he came to look at the horses as his friends. He would spend hours on end communing with the horses that liked to be treated as pets, steering clear of the ones he had been told could be dangerous. He learned which ones would let him come into the stall when they were lying down, which ones would allow him to lie down next to them and rest his head on their necks. The more time he spent with them, the more he came to understand their body language and the subtle changes in facial expressions. While back at the Whitney farm on Long Island, he'd learned to ride, taking lessons with C. V. Whitney's son Searle. The two would gallop their Connemara ponies from estate to estate. All in all, it was an idyllic existence.

By the time the boy turned nine, his parents started to worry about his schoolwork. The family was traveling from track to track, which meant the boy could never adjust to any one school, and it wasn't helping his grades. Their solution, to his dismay, was to pack him off to military school. A shy child, he felt out of place and longed for those magical hours spent with the grooms and exercise boys. Most of all, he missed the time spent communing with his horse friends. Though he did discover eventually that there were other boys at the school from racing families, he never quite settled in. Eventually his parents found a place in Garden City, Long Island, and from then on, that became the boy's home and where he attended high school. No more traveling with Dad, but no military school either. When he was old enough, he started helping his father at the track during the summers and on school vacations. One of his big thrills was riding with the horses being shipped from Belmont Park to Hialeah in a boxcar. The cars were specially designed to move horses, divided into three sections, each with stalls for eight horses. Each section had two sets of four stalls facing one another, with an aisleway in between where the hay was stacked and barrels of drinking water were stored. Two to three men would ride in each section to care for the eight horses. For a teenager, it was a great adventure.

Increasingly immersed in the racing life, the boy wanted to start his career as a trainer right after finishing high school, but his dad wouldn't hear of it. Syl Veitch told his son that college was important, even for a racehorse trainer. "It will help you deal with the owners," Syl had said. So the boy went off to Bradley University in Peoria, Illinois, once again separated from the horses and the racing life. In college he was drawn to history and literature, some poets calling out to him loud enough that he memorized whole stanzas of his favorite poems and pages from his favorite novels. Still, he remained impatient to get back to his one true love.

Once he graduated from college, Veitch started working as an assistant trainer to his father at the Widener farm. When he felt he'd learned all he could there, he struck out on his own, apprenticing as an assistant trainer to Burch at Rokeby. From his father and Burch, he learned there were many ways to bring a horse along—and to listen to what each individual horse was trying to tell him. Some were quick learners; some were slow. Some were precocious; some were late developers. He learned to fit the training to the horse, instead of the horse to the training—and that you could ruin a good horse by taking the wrong approach. After several years, he wanted to start his own stable, but his father advised him to wait a little longer. "They'll expect more of you because you are my son," Syl Veitch had said. So the boy, now a man, continued to work, and to learn, as an assistant.

By 1974, he felt he was ready to go out on his own. He left Rokeby and started up a small racing stable based at Belmont Park. Even then, though, John Veitch had big dreams. One evening that summer, as the trim, balding young trainer whiled away the hours in a nearby bar with turf writer Bill Nack, the two began to talk about their lives and their ambitions.

"John," Nack said, "if you could choose one job at the racetrack, what would it be?"

The twenty-eight-year-old Veitch smiled and thought it over for a bit. "I'd like to see what I could do with a big stable of well-bred horses," he said finally. "I think I'd like the chance to train horses for Calumet Farm."

It seemed like a pipe dream. At the time, Veitch was just beginning his career and wasn't getting very far very fast. By the fall of 1975, he was still struggling to make ends meet. He'd had only two or three owners at a time, each of whom had three to five horses in training. He'd been doing moderately well, but had no real stars in the barn. To save on living expenses, he'd moved into a tiny unheated room in an old boiler building at the track. The cinder-block walls and concrete floor were painted a drab gray, and the only fixtures were a toilet and a sink. Veitch shivered through that autumn sleeping on a foldout bed, consoling himself with the thought that he was at least close to his horses. He could easily do his 8 P.M. check to make sure everything was OK—and didn't have to pay someone to do the 4 A.M. feeding.

One exceptionally cold December evening when Veitch was curled up with a new history book trying to ignore the frigid temperatures in his little room, the phone rang. He put down the book and trudged over to grab the receiver.

"John Veitch," he announced.

"Hi, it's Melvin Cinnamon," the voice on the phone answered. "How are you?"

Veitch and Cinnamon had known each other for years, but it had been a long time since they'd talked. They chatted for a while about Veitch's dad and their families. Then Cinnamon said, "Mrs. Markey isn't happy with Reggie Cornell and she's looking to make a change. She's looking for a new head trainer and would like to know if you'd be interested in interviewing for the position."

Veitch was stunned, and paused for a moment to process this sudden and unexpected possibility of good fortune. Though Calumet was nowhere near as powerful as it had been in the 1940s, '50s, and '60s, it was still Calumet Farm.

"I'd be more than interested," Veitch said finally.

"Good. I'll be in touch."

After the two men hung up, Veitch sat for a bit wondering how serious the offer actually was—and when he might hear back.

The months passed. December turned into January, then February, then March. By that time, Veitch was sure that the Markeys had decided to keep Cornell—or had found someone with more experience to hire. Then in April, Cinnamon called again, this time asking if Veitch could make time to fly down to Florida and have dinner with him on the night of the thirteenth. The next day, the two of them would have lunch with Mrs. Markey and the Admiral. Veitch was excited, though nervous, figuring he might have finally landed an interview.

During the dinner with Cinnamon, there was no discussion of the possible job at Calumet. Veitch figured that would come the next day when he visited with the Markeys. The following afternoon over lunch, the four discussed horses and racing. When dessert arrived, the Admiral turned to Cinnamon and said, "I'm sure you've discussed with Mr. Veitch what his salary will be and told him how happy we are to have him on board." Veitch was confused, but waited till after the lunch was over to pull Cinnamon aside to ask what was going on.

"Melvin, what's this about?" he queried. "I thought this was going to be kind of an interview where they were going to sound me out."

"They had already made the decision that you would be their next trainer," Cinnamon responded. "It was just a matter of timing. Tomorrow we're going out to Hialeah and we're going to inform Mr. Cornell that he's no longer Calumet's trainer."

Just like that, John Veitch went from barely scraping by as a public trainer with a handful of horses to earning more than $30,000 a year and running the most famous racing stable in the country.

At Hialeah the next day, Veitch felt sorry for Cornell but ecstatic about his own change in fortune—until he had a good look at the horses. Though the colts and fillies were well-bred, they were for the most part overworked and fat. Many had the kind of soft-tissue injuries that you'd expect to see in older, heavily raced horses. They didn't look at all like the shiny new cars Veitch had expected to find. Instead, they were like rental cars that had been driven hard. The biggest disappointment was Turn To Turia, a half-brother to Forward Pass. Cornell had assured the Markeys that the colt would be ready for the 1976 Kentucky Derby. But as Veitch surveyed the horse's legs, he realized that Turn To Turia wouldn't be going to the Derby—or any other races that year. The best thing for the colt, Veitch concluded, was to go back to Calumet to rest and recuperate. Veitch steeled himself for the phone call to Lucille, not sure how she'd take all the bad news. But to his surprise and relief, she took it in stride and told him not to worry. Then she suggested that he fly up to Calumet to discuss strategies and to have a look at the young stock.

At the airport in Lexington, Veitch was collected by the Markeys' driver in their trademark silver Rolls-Royce. As the car wended its way up Calumet's long driveway, Veitch was struck by the pastoral beauty of the farm. The dogwoods lining the road were all in bloom and the lush verdant pastures dotted with budding racehorses. When they got to the house, the Markeys' butler, Charles, grabbed the trainer's luggage to take to the upstairs guest room. Later, when Veitch came down to meet the Markeys for a drink before dinner, Charles took him aside and said quietly, "Your man forgot to pack your pajamas, robe, and slippers." Charles said he'd sent off to the store in town for replacements. At first Veitch wasn't sure how to respond, but then, smiling to himself, told the butler, "I appreciate your kindness and I'll have a word with my man when I get home." He knew he'd entered a different world.

That night over dinner, Veitch and the Markeys talked about racehorses and about Calumet's history. The next morning, with a handful of papers detailing the pedigrees of all the farm's horses, Veitch took a tour with Cinnamon and Calumet's resident farm trainer, Ewell Rice. Before they walked out the door, Lucille had told Veitch that she wanted his impressions of all the young prospects.

When they got to the field with the yearling colts, Veitch surveyed the little herd, observing the interactions between the youngsters. It was clear that the muscly dark chestnut with the tiny star was the leader of the group—and also the fastest by far. When the colt took off, all the others bolted after him. "He's sure got charisma," Veitch thought, and then asked who the handsome chestnut was. "That's the Sweet Tooth colt," Cinnamon told him. Though Veitch knew it was too soon to be thinking about it, dreams of the Kentucky Derby started to flutter through his head.

The trip to Calumet had given Veitch renewed hope for the future. But now he had to go back to Hialeah and deal with the disarray that had been left by his predecessor. Veitch sent some of the horses home to rehab injuries and did his best to get the remaining colts and fillies in shape to run. By the end of 1976, Calumet had only $87,725 in winnings to show for the year. Even more galling, its horses won just four races—by far the stable's worst showing since its debut year of 1932. Veitch was disheartened and discouraged, sure that he'd blown his big chance.

When December rolled around and it was time to head back down to Hialeah, he was once again invited to have lunch with the Markeys in their Miami home. The thought of having to discuss a season he saw as marking his complete failure as a trainer made him depressed. During lunch, he turned to Lucille and told her that he was ashamed of his performance and that he would completely understand if they wanted him to resign.

"I feel I let you down," he said with a sigh.

Lucille looked him in the eye and replied, "No, John. I let *you* down. I haven't given you good enough horses. But I want you to know we have some wonderful yearlings coming along and I really hope that things will be better next year."

* * *

The yearlings at Calumet were given their names in the fall. Brass name-plates were ordered up for their leather halters and for their stall doors. When it came to Sweet Tooth's colt, the Markeys wanted something that would allude to his regal heritage, but they were also feeling somewhat whimsical. After kicking around some names, the Admiral finally suggested they call the colt Alydar, a private joke between the couple that played on Lucille's greeting to one of their most aristocratic friends: Prince Aly Khan, whom she often addressed as "Aly, darling."

At Calumet, as at many Thoroughbred farms, fall was also the time when the yearlings started their race training. Much of the early work was done in the stalls, where the babies were introduced first to wearing a bridle and carrying a bit in their mouths. Once they were comfortable with that, a saddle was placed on their backs and the girth tightened. If they were calm about the process, the next step was to let them feel weight on their backs. A groom would give the rider a leg up, and if the horse remained quiet and relaxed, the rider would simply lie belly down across the saddle for a few minutes and then drop back off. After repeating the procedure several times, the groom would lead the yearling around the stall with the rider lying across the saddle. The next day, after being hoisted up, the rider would swing his leg over the saddle and sit for a minute or two. Not all the babies were happy with this new phase of their new lives. Some would hump their backs up as if to buck. Some would wriggle as if this might unload the weight from their backs. But Alydar was the perfect student. It was as if he knew he was growing up and was about to embark on something important.

Once the yearlings were comfortable with being mounted, they were led out of the barn with a rider on board. When they got to Calumet's training track, the grooms let go of their bridles and the riders began to work on steering, pulling on the left rein to get a left turn and the right rein to go right. The next step was to start walking, and then jogging, around the track. When the babies were used to all the new sights and sounds and could relax while jogging around the track, the riders would ask them for a slow and leisurely gallop. In just a few months, their lives would change dramatically. They would leave the familiar barns and track of Calumet to start their new careers as racehorses.

As Veitch watched the Calumet yearlings unload at Hialeah in early December 1976, he felt a mixture of excitement and joyful anticipation, the kind of emotions a child might experience as he walks in on a pile of presents stacked under the Christmas tree. These babies were the future, embodying all of his hopes for the coming year as well as the Markeys' dreams of a renewed Calumet.

Among them was Alydar, the horse that Veitch and everyone at the farm felt might be the key to that new beginning. Veitch took particular note of the big, powerful-looking colt walking down the ramp and was satisfied to see that he seemed to have traveled well. Alydar stood out among the others, attractively put together with the look of an elite athlete. He carried himself as if he knew his heritage, as if he knew just how special he was.

The colt stepped off the ramp quietly, looking around at his new surroundings but too tired to have much of a reaction. The fifteen-hour trip had taken a lot out of all the yearlings. Though they had been trained to ride in the van back at the farm, they had never been on a long trip like the one from Lexington to Miami. The young horses were led off the van by the grooms who would be taking care of them now and walked to the stalls that would be their homes for the rest of winter as real training commenced and their talents were being assessed. For now, though, the yearlings would be allowed to recuperate from their long ride.

During the next three days, they were all body-clipped, their grooms shearing off the shaggy coats that had kept the yearlings warm during the chilly winter nights in Kentucky. They wouldn't need all that hair in Miami, where the days averaged eighty-five and the nights seventy. They were bathed and walked around the backstretch and given time to assess their surroundings. It was a big change for the young horses. They'd spent their entire lives up to that point on the same farm with the same horses. Now there was a new routine and the hustle and bustle of a very busy racetrack. Once the yearlings had acclimated, Veitch started their training. He was a patient man and was careful not to overface the young horses, knowing how easy it would be to push too hard and injure them mentally or physically.

Four days after they arrived at Hialeah, the colts and fillies were tacked up and walked from the stable area down the half-mile sand path that ran between the stands and a line of tall Australian pines to the track. Veitch rode with them on his stable pony, watching carefully to see which ones got along with the rider he'd assigned them and which might need to be switched. For Alydar, Veitch had chosen his best exercise rider, Charlie Rose, and best groom, Clyde Sparks, knowing full well that the Raise a Natives could be strong and strong-minded—and that it was a lot easier to prevent a bad habit from starting than it would be to correct one once it was ingrained.

When they got to the track, they moved along to the stretch area where there was a long chute that was used for the shorter races in the afternoon. It was usually much less crowded there and the babies could be jogged two or three abreast as they got used to the strange new sights and sounds. At the quiet pastoral Calumet, they had been accustomed to being out with only six to eight others, with nary a sound besides the birds and the muffled hoofbeats of their comrades. At Hialeah, they would be sharing the track with two to three hundred horse-and-rider combos jogging and galloping by them—and sometimes at them.

By the beginning of the new year, when they had all turned two years old (per Jockey Club rules stipulating that all Thoroughbreds celebrate their birthdays on January 1 no matter when they were actually born), it was time to start galloping on the track. The gallops were leisurely at first, with the babies taking four minutes to go a mile—twice as long as they'd later be asked to cover the same distance. Veitch would often put seven of his charges on the track at the same time, a pair followed by another pair, followed by a group that was three abreast. He would switch up the order periodically so they'd all get used to the feeling of having horses in front kicking sand up in their faces, to being the horse on the rail, or to being the one on the outside. The idea was to have them exposed to every experience they might encounter in a race before they actually ran one.

After a month or two of those leisurely gallops, some of the babies, Alydar among them, seemed to be coming along much faster than the others. These were the ones that Veitch started breezing, or, in other words, galloping a short distance at a faster pace. At this point, he was looking for speeds of about fifteen seconds per eighth of a mile, or furlong. Later on, he'd want to see them covering a furlong in twelve seconds. The babies still weren't being pushed to their fastest pace, but they were starting to be tested. Alydar, always the perfect student, seemed up to whatever task Veitch threw his way. That made him the kind of horse you had to be careful with because he would give you everything you asked for, even if it came at a cost to him. Each time he watched Alydar breeze, Veitch felt the temptation to let him run full tilt to see what the colt was made of. But that could easily have resulted in an injury, so as much as Veitch wanted to rip the wrapping paper off that very special Christmas present, he forced himself to be patient and to wait.

All the while, the trainer kept track of the minutest details of the two-year-olds' lives—how much they ate, how much they drank, what their manure looked like, how often they passed urine, how well they cooled out after a breeze, whether they were fresh the day after a breeze. If anything changed—if a horse ate or drank more or less than usual, for example—Veitch knew it could be a sign that a problem was developing.

Though there were others with promise in the group that came from Calumet that year, none took to the training regimen like Alydar. The colt seemed to thrive on the work, and the harder it got, the more he liked it. Once Alydar and the others were galloping easily on the track, Veitch began to teach them about the starting gate. First, he would have the riders walk the two-year-olds around the gate. Then, after they were calm in its presence, he would open both the front and back doors and have his exercise boys ride the young horses through the gate forward, then backward. When the babies were comfortable with that, they would be ridden into the gate and the back door would be shut. Next their riders would jog them out, and then they would start galloping them out. Once the colts and fillies had adjusted to that, assistant starters would begin climbing up over them—as they might in a real race. Eventually, both doors would be closed and the two-year-olds would be asked to gallop out as soon as the front door was sprung open. The very last step was to add the bell. If it was all done systematically and calmly, the young horses would not be afraid to get into the gate in a race and would break cleanly at the bell.

By early March, it was clear which two-year-olds would be ready to actually start racing that spring. At the head of the pack was Alydar. He had balked at nothing and seemed to enjoy learning new things. Veitch felt a surge of satisfaction watching the colt glide around the track, his huge strides effortless and smooth.

*   *   *

While Alydar had immediately been recognized as a star, Won't Tell You's colt hadn't made much of an impression on anyone working at Harbor View Farm. The only feature that made the lanky chestnut stand out from the others was his exceedingly mellow nature and his habit of taking long, luxurious naps. The colt loved to sprawl out in his stall and would often drop off into such a deep slumber that scarcely anything would wake him.

At feeding time, all the other horses would be pawing and banging on their feed tubs as the grooms brought out the grain. Not Affirmed. If Affirmed was in the middle of a good snooze, the groom would have to step over him to put the grain in the colt's tub. When Affirmed was done with his nap, he'd slowly stretch his legs, then heave himself up and give a good shake. He'd mosey over to the tub and start munching on his grain. When he was done, he'd lie back down and take another nap.

Though Affirmed may have wriggled his way into Patrice Wolfson's heart, that didn't mean he was going to be a good racehorse—just that he was her pet. Other than the hugs she gave him when she stopped by for a visit, he received no special treatment. Like all the other yearlings at Harbor View, he was started in the fall of 1976.

The farm trainer, Melvin James, started Affirmed out the same way he did with all the other Harbor View babies: first lessons all in the colt's own stall. James tacked him up, and Affirmed barely flicked an ear. James wasn't surprised. Of all the babies born at Harbor View in the spring of 1975, Affirmed was the quietest—and the laziest. The colt actually looked bored with the whole training process. He didn't flinch when the exercise boy bellied up on his back, or when the rider sat upright. He turned easily to the left and right when his rider pulled on the reins. He was just as nonchalant when he was taken out to the small paddock for his first rides outside. In fact, the colt acted like he'd been at this all his life.

When James started running him on the track with pairs of other yearlings, Affirmed always came out in front, but only by a few inches. As the weeks passed, James kept improving the quality of horses he trained the colt with, but the result was always the same: Affirmed out in front, by just a head or a nose.

While some of the others got a bit hot as training progressed, nothing seemed to affect Affirmed's laid-back disposition—or his love of sleep. One day a visitor to the farm came running up to James, worried that there was something wrong with the tall chestnut colt because he'd been lying down for a long time and wouldn't get up. James just smiled and said, "Oh, there's nothing wrong. That's just Affirmed being Affirmed."

Late in 1976, Harbor View's race trainer, Laz Barrera, called from his California headquarters to ask James which yearlings appeared to have the most promise. Then he asked James to pick the five he liked best and to ship them down to Hialeah. That winter, Affirmed was shipped off to Hialeah, where Barrera's brother Willie would start the colt's race training. It didn't take long for Willie to see that this colt had a lot more talent than anyone had guessed. Though Patrice had bonded with Affirmed, no one really thought he'd be a star. In fact, the Wolfsons had been so unimpressed with Won't Tell You's babies, including Affirmed, that they'd sold the mare at the previous fall's Keeneland Sale for a mere $5,500.

Shortly after Affirmed started training on the track, Willie called Lou Wolfson to tell him about the colt. "This is the best horse you've ever had," Willie said.

Lou wasn't convinced. "That mare never threw anything that was any good," he responded. "And remember, I owned Roman Brother."

"This one is better," Willie said simply.

In the end, the Wolfsons decided to give Affirmed a chance and told Willie to ship the lanky chestnut colt up to Laz Barrera's East Coast stable at Belmont Park so the trainer could give the colt a closer look.

Laz Barrera (Keeneland Library Barrett Collection)

CHAPTER 6

The Casey Stengel of Horse Whisperers

FROM HIS BRUSHED-BACK DARK HAIR AND SOULFUL BROWN EYES RIGHT down to his custom-tailored three-piece suit and spit-shined black shoes, Laz Barrera cut a striking figure. His appeal, however, went much deeper than that. Within moments, his warm, affable, and gracious manner would bubble forth. Those who got to know him better found him to be sentimental, romantic, compassionate—and disarmingly funny. To sportswriters and all the readers they introduced him to, he was always the charismatic, charming, clever, captivating, and colorful Cuban.

Laz Barrera was such a colorful character that *Sports Illustrated* dubbed him "the Casey Stengel of the racetracks"—a nod to the engaging way the trainer would hold court much like the old New York Yankee manager beloved for his rambling monologues. Barrera certainly had a way with people as well as horses, regaling reporters with homespun yarns, backstretch philosophy, and sage advice dispensed in his unique mix of broken English, shattered syntax, and amusing malapropisms. He did so in a Cuban accent described by the famed sports columnist Jim Murray as "a cross between Desi Arnaz with hiccups and Ricardo Montalban with a mouthful of mashed potatoes." The fabled trainer Charlie Whittingham spoke for many of their fellow horsemen when he cracked, "You can never tell whether Laz is speaking English with a Spanish accent or Spanish with an English accent."

"A lot of people don't understand my English," Barrera would shrug in response. "If they don't understand me, it doesn't bother me, because my horse understands my English."

Nobody, though, understood him better than Lou Wolfson. Right from their first encounter, Wolfson could see beyond all the style to the substance of the man. He recognized in Laz Barrera many of the same qualities he had admired in Hirsch Jacobs. More so than even second-generation immigrants like Jacobs and Wolfson himself, Barrera was the ultimate outsider: a first-generation immigrant who had paid his dues toiling for decades on the backstretches of his native Cuba and of Mexico before starting all over from the bottom in the United States. That odyssey stamped Barrera as Wolfson's favorite breed of outsider: the underdog who struggled to pull himself up one cheap claimer and one demoralizing disappointment at a time. In this self-made trainer, Wolfson could see the second coming of Hirsch Jacobs. All of which made Barrera, in Wolfson's eyes, "my kind of man."

While no one could resist Barrera's magnetic personality, Wolfson was drawn more to the familiar ring of his rags-to-riches story. With a résumé that read like a Horatio Alger novel translated into Spanish, Barrera seemed to enjoy nothing better than spinning yarns from it in a mash-up of Spanglish and Stengelese. Courtly, courteous, and cooperative, he would spend countless hours fielding reporters' questions and telling stories—until, he'd sigh, "I don't got nothing left in my brains."

The abiding image of Laz Barrera finds him at his backside barn entertaining newspapermen and horsemen alike with animated stories of his long journey from impoverished hot-walker at the age of eight to overnight sensation at the age of fifty-two.

*   *   *

Whenever anyone would ask Barrera what was the secret to his sudden success, his eyes would crinkle. "That's easy," he'd deadpan. "I was born on a racetrack." Then, with a mischievous smile, he'd break into a meandering saga that was the stuff of sportswriters' and screenwriters' dreams.

The son of a part-time Quarter Horse jockey and a French missionary's daughter who worked as a midwife, Lazaro Sosa Barrera was born in 1924 in the Havana suburb of Marianao. If not actually born "on a racetrack" (or, as Murray quipped, "in a house in the middle of the infield"), he did grow up just a horseshoe's toss from the only one in Cuba: Oriental Park, the legendary track built a decade earlier on land that his grandfather once owned and that had become a winter haven for American racehorses before Hialeah Park displaced it as the fashionable destination for the horsey set.

"I was born next to Oriental Park in Cuba and have been on the racetrack all my life," he would say when asked about his beginnings. "I remember the first time I went to a track. I was maybe four or five. It was the Cuban Christmas, and it was celebrated at Oriental Park. The children were given gifts, and a man gave me a new baseball. I never had a new ball before, and I just rubbed it and looked at it like it was something made of magic. Everyone else watched the races, and I played with the ball. In Havana when I was a boy, I loved to play baseball. First I was a catcher. No glove. No chest protector. No mask." Here he would pause and point to a white scar under his now-meaty chin. "A bat," he'd explain. "I couldn't afford the mask. After the bat hit me, I switched to second base."

It wasn't long before he switched to the backstretch. As the ninth of twelve children growing up "very, very poor," Laz followed in the family tradition of getting a job at Oriental Park as soon as he was old enough. He was barely eight when he started working seven days a week as a hot-walker for an up-and-coming American trainer named Hirsch Jacobs, leading sweaty horses along the backstretch until they cooled down after their morning works. He made $3 a week walking hots in the 1930s, keeping just 50 cents for himself and turning the rest over to his mother to help put food on the table for his eight brothers and three sisters.

Over the next several years, Laz worked his way up to groom, and at sixteen took out a trainer's license. He began conditioning horses at Oriental Park, while in his spare time making race picks in the newspaper *El Mundo*. By twenty, he'd saved up enough to put $50 down to buy his first horse, a filly named Donnagal. Unfortunately, he never got the chance to show what he could do with her. "A terrible hurricane hit Cuba that year," he would lament. "Donnagal got all cut up by flying glass and could never run again. The track was destroyed and would have to be rebuilt. I was young with no responsibilities, and I felt it was a good time to try something new. So I set off for Mexico City."

By that time, leaving Cuba had already been a dream of his for a while. "To improve myself," he would explain. "That is the challenge for everybody. If you think you be a deadbeat, you be a deadbeat all your life. You have to dream and work very hard."

To scrounge up the fare for the trip from Havana to Mexico City, he had to sell off a horse he'd just acquired. But getting there wasn't enough. Not long after he arrived empty-handed, the authorities discovered he was a few months shy of the legally required minimum age of twenty-one and they revoked his trainer's license. As soon as he was old enough to reapply, he found a patron through friends. He figured he had lucked out when that owner signed him to a five-year contract to train a small stable of horses at the Hipódromo de las Américas. But that was before he got to know his new boss.

"This owner in Mexico City thought he knew everything," Barrera would say with a roll of his eyes. "The first five horses I ran for him, I win. But the sixth horse gets beat a nose on the wire and this owner gets mad—mad at me, mad at the jockey. This crazy man runs down from the stands and wants to beat up the jockey. I say, 'This is not a man I want to work for.' I quit. I wouldn't train for him anymore and went to the stewards and told them so, too. They said, 'He has you under contract, and if you do not train for him, you cannot train here.' I said, 'The hell with this,' and went to Cleveland, Ohio, and became a jock's agent for Jorge Núñez, and we did good together."

Ever one to make the best of a bad situation, Barrera enjoyed his stay in Cleveland. "I got the chance to see major-league baseball games, and my favorite team was the Yankees. When they would come to town, I'd go into the centerfield bleachers for thirty-five cents. I'd sit behind Joe DiMaggio, and one night when he hit three home runs, I caught one of the balls."

After waiting out his original five-year Mexican contract, Barrera eagerly returned to Mexico City and resumed training horses. Even though races were held only three days a week at the Hipódromo, he racked up enough winners one year to rank second in North America to Willie Molter, the leading U.S. trainer in the late 1940s. Not that things ever came easily to Barrera.

"Training in Mexico was tough," he would recall. "If you didn't do good for an owner right away, you hear the sound of the vans backing up to take the horses away. At one time, I had seventy horses to train and had the best owner in Mexico to work for. He loved me. He would call in the morning and say, 'Laz, please don't eat breakfast before I get there. I want the joy of eating breakfast with you. I'll cook for the grooms and all the help.' He would say that I was working too hard and we should fly to Acapulco to rest. I would tell him the only reason I was tired was because he kept me up all night. We would go to Acapulco and get in great games of dominos and we'd win because I could really play dominos. One night a man pointed a finger at him and said, 'The only reason you win is because that Cuban guy is with you.' My owner just laughed and said, 'Go yourself to Havana and get a man who looks like him. But you will have to go many times to Havana and you will never bring a man back who can play dominos like him.'"

Or train horses like him, apparently. Barrera was already starting to develop a reputation for handling them with care. He wasn't so much a horse whisperer as a horse listener. "What I've tried to do is get to know my horses in the same way I know my friends," he would explain. "Racehorses are all different, but I think of them as human beings. I don't know, are they so different from ballplayers? They are affectionate animals. You get the most out of them if you treat them with affection."

Despite Barrera's knack for getting the most out of them, he couldn't overcome the limitations of toiling in the minor leagues with their lower class of horseflesh. In a sport as capricious as horse racing, being the best in Mexico was a long way from conditioning well-bred Thoroughbreds in the major leagues north of the border.

"Racing is such a strange sport," Barrera would later muse to a bevy of reporters. "In 1951, I flew out of Mexico City with twenty-seven thousand dollars in hundred-dollar bills in sacks. If somebody does this today, they think they are running drugs. I was going to the United States to buy a horse named Crafty Admiral for an owner who wanted the horse returned to Mexico. Crafty Admiral was for sale for twenty-five thousand dollars and had been a good two-year-old in the U.S. We got to Miami and it looked like the sale was all set, but the veterinarian wouldn't OK the deal because he didn't think the horse was sound. I didn't know what to do, but I didn't want the plane to go back empty, so I filled it up with hay and straw and we flew back with no Crafty Admiral. Later he was sold for less than twenty-five thousand dollars and went on to be an excellent horse. If he raced in Mexico, he probably would never have been heard of and he might have broken down." Here Barrera would pause for dramatic effect. "You see, if Crafty Admiral had gone back to Mexico City with me, I would not have Affirmed today," he'd continue, breaking into a sly smile. "There probably wouldn't *be* any Affirmed today—because Crafty Admiral became the sire of Won't Tell You, Affirmed's mother."

Beyond the racetrack, Barrera started carving out a life for himself in Mexico City. Known there as "the Cuban Tyrone Power," he certainly looked the part of the swashbuckling matinee idol, especially when hanging out with the notorious Dominican playboy Porfiro Rubirosa. When the international jet-setter was in town, the pair might be sighted kicking a soccer ball down fashionable streets or testing young bullfighting prospects at a *tienta* with the great Mexican matador Carlos Arruza. Barrera felt so at home in Mexico that it was only a matter of time before he started to settle down and establish roots.

It was at a dance in Mexico City that he first laid eyes on Carmen Miramontes. Thunderstruck, he promptly cut in on her partner and began courting the athletic young woman everyone knew by her childhood nickname of Cha-cha. She was an Olympic diver preparing to represent Mexico in the 1948 London Games, and each dawn on his way to the racetrack for the morning works, Laz would drive past the outdoor pool where she was training and wait just long enough to spot her on the springboard in her red bathing suit. They were married the following year, in the spring of 1949, and wasted little time starting a family. All three of their children—Blanca, Alberto, and Lazaro Jr.—would be born in Mexico.

By the late 1950s, however, Lazaro Sr. began to feel restless. He felt the need to find another opportunity to improve himself and prove himself. He was also feeling depressed. Having recently attended his mother's funeral in Havana, he realized he would probably never return to a homeland swept up in the revolutionary tide that had just brought Fidel Castro to power. "I could see the political situation in Cuba was very bad," Barrera would recall, "people running away."

At about this time, in 1959, a Californian named Hal King, who trained some horses in Mexico City, talked Barrera into going to the United States. "You have so much ability you're wasting your time here," King told him. After much soul-searching, Barrera decided that the time was right to try his luck for a year pursuing bigger stakes in The Land of Opportunity. He would do so "with some nervousness—not necessarily because I was concerned with my own ability, but because of what I was giving up and because I would have to leave my family behind for that year."

Wrenching as it was, Mexico's leading trainer left it all behind—the family and the seventy-horse stable replete with grooms and hot-walkers— to start a one-horse stable alone at Hollywood Park near Los Angeles. "When I arrived in America," he would later recall, "I was practically broke. And I could hardly speak a word of English."

All he had to his name was a cheap claimer named Destructo that he had bought in Mexico for $6,000. "When I decided to come to California, there was only Destructo," he'd say. "I was his owner, his trainer, his groom, his hot-walker, everything." He'd smile fondly. "My best training job was with that six-thousand-dollar claimer who got me to America. I did well with him. He ran third, then he ran second, and then he won, but he was claimed from me." When Destructo was claimed out of that last winning race for $7,000, Barrera suddenly found himself with no horse and no money beyond the sale price and purse. "One win and my stable was wiped out," he'd sigh, shaking his head. "I ran out of horses. I had to start all over."

Just when things were at their bleakest, he caught a break from a fellow trainer he had befriended not long after arriving in California. Bill Winfrey, who had famously trained the great Native Dancer through a near-perfect career, was stabled across from Barrera's now-barren stall at Hollywood Park and had taken a shine to the personable Cuban. Winfrey was planning to take a vacation and was seeking a temporary replacement to train the horses he handled for the high-society sportsman Alfred G. Vanderbilt. Recognizing Barrera as "a talented and thorough horseman who gives attention to every detail," Winfrey asked him to take over the training of eight horses owned by Vanderbilt. Barrera did so well with those loaners that Winfrey, upon his return from vacation, concluded that his friend was wasting his time at Hollywood Park. "New York," Winfrey advised, "is the place for you."

Not long after that, Barrera met the New York–based owner who could make the move possible. Emil Dolce, a Long Island restaurateur who had built a small but profitable stable on claimers, was looking for a new trainer. Barrera took over Dolce's stable on a full-time basis in 1960 and settled down on Long Island with Carmen and the kids.

Among the first horses Barrera trained in New York was Grid Iron Hero, a $7,500 claimer that he turned into a stakes-winning handicapper. Barrera had done such a masterful job with Grid Iron Hero that Lou Wolfson expressed interest in buying the colt from Dolce. Barrera's commission on the sale would have been $20,000—a pittance for Wolfson, but a windfall for the trainer in those days. When Wolfson came around to look at the bay, however, Barrera felt compelled to pull him aside and say, "Mr. Wolfson, I respect you too much to let you waste your money. This horse is not sound." Wolfson thanked Barrera for his candor and made a mental note to keep an eye on the trainer's career.

Several years later, when Burley Parke decided to retire from training, Wolfson remembered the honest Cuban and recruited him to take over Harbor View's stable. By now one of the leading trainers in New York, Barrera was reluctant to leave Dolce out of a sense of loyalty. Wolfson had his heart set on a private trainer to saddle Harbor View's horses exclusively, just as Parke had done for the past several years. With Barrera unavailable, Wolfson hired Parke's younger brother Ivan as Harbor View's trainer. When Ivan Parke retired just as Harbor View was gearing up its revived stable in the early 1970s, Wolfson remembered Barrera and reached out to him once again.

By this time, Barrera had established himself as a trainer known for getting the most out of horses that were generally still a cut below top class. He had been on a roll since winning his first major U.S. stakes race in 1971 with Tinajero, a well-bred gray colt he'd brought over from Puerto Rico for owner Rafael Escudero. On his growing client roster, Escudero was the owner Barrera had become closest with and the one he couldn't bring himself to abandon. "I asked him to train exclusively for Harbor View Farm," Wolfson recalled, "but he told me he had one owner he didn't want to give up. The man had a malignancy. Laz was afraid he might die if he dropped him. I was so impressed with his loyalty and his feeling. I told him to take part of my horses if he wanted them, and he did."

That was in 1974. Barrera had come full circle: the eight-year-old boy once employed as a hot-walker by Hirsch Jacobs was now a fifty-year-old man employed as a trainer by the late horseman's daughter, Patrice, and her husband, Lou Wolfson. Ever since Barrera arrived in New York, there had been no trainer he admired more than Jacobs and none whose advice he heeded more. Whenever one of his horses got relaxed enough to yawn before a race, Barrera couldn't help but smile and recall one of Jacobs's maxims: "If your horse yawns, he will run his best." Now Barrera would get the chance to apply lessons learned from Jacobs to horses owned by Jacobs's daughter. "Absolutely I believe in fate," Barrera declared. "Things like that happen too much not to believe in fate."

As fate would have it, the horse that would propel Barrera from backstretch obscurity to national prominence was almost as much of a surprise sleeper as the one that had done the same thing for Jacobs's career three decades earlier. Bold Forbes—or, as Barrera would always mangle the name, "Bo Forbus"—would become his own personal Stymie.

Of all the horses Barrera was then training for twenty-one different owners, he could tout a couple of Harbor View two-year-olds as Kentucky Derby prospects ahead of this "Bo Forbus." In fact, when Puerto Rican banker Estéban Rodríguez Tizol, the owner who had bought Bold Forbes as a yearling for a modest $15,200, decided to send him to New York from the San Juan track where he was winning routinely in 1975, Barrera had to be coaxed into finding stall space in his crowded barn at Belmont Park.

Upon the brown colt's arrival at Barn 47 as a two-year-old, Barrera was dismayed to find a small, compact sprinter with warm shins that would require careful care. What was worse, Bold Forbes had a bad habit of easing up if no challengers were threatening his lead. Barrera quickly cured that loafing problem by cutting football-shaped holes in the blinkers to give Bold Forbes more peripheral vision of his charging pursuers, but fixing this sprinter's inability to be rated would require much more patience and ingenuity.

Heading into the spring of 1976, Barrera had won a lot of races but never a stakes worth $100,000—what racing folk reverently referred to as a "hundred-grander." He'd come to think of it as a jinx that regularly irked him. That all changed the day Bold Forbes ran off with the Wood Memorial over a mile and an eighth of Aqueduct dirt and thus stamped himself Barrera's first Kentucky Derby entrant.

Not that anyone was giving Bold Forbes any chance against Honest Pleasure, at 2-to-5 the heaviest Derby favorite since Citation in 1948. Bold Forbes was, after all, just a sprinter whose pedigree suggested he could never get the classic distance of a mile and a quarter, especially since his stubborn refusal to be rated meant he would likely burn himself out by the time he reached the stretch at Churchill Downs. Just to make it to the wire, sneered the handicappers, "he'll need a cab at the eighth pole." Addressing those concerns in the morning works leading up to the Derby, Barrera sent Bold Forbes off on a series of leisurely two-mile gallops rather than the fast four- and five-furlong breezes that trainers habitually relied on to sharpen their charges.

As it turned out, that would make all the difference in the 1976 Kentucky Derby. After shooting to the front as if the starting gate were on fire, Bold Forbes would have to summon every ounce of heart and newfound stamina down the stretch to fight off Honest Pleasure's bid for the lead at the sixteenth pole and draw off to win by a length. In the wake of the biggest Derby upset in the twenty-three years since Native Dancer's sole career loss, friends and family lifted Barrera onto their shoulders and carried him into the winner's circle where, tears rolling down his cheeks, he told a national TV audience how thankful he was for the opportunity given him in the United States. "It's still all here if you want to work for it," said the man who had become a naturalized U.S. citizen three years earlier. "Where else could it happen for a Cuban by way of Mexico City who had lost his one and only horse after his first win in a new country?"

The tears had barely dried when he was handed a telegram that read simply MY MAN and was signed simply BILL. Waving that wire from Bill Winfrey, the trainer who had loaned him the horses to revive his career after he'd lost his one and only, Barrera sobbed, "I am so proud of this. This means so much to me. Since I was a little kid in Cuba, the dream of my life was to train the winner of the Kentucky Derby. Oh, how long this road has been."

In a sense, the ride was just beginning. Blasting out of the gate in the Preakness Stakes two Saturdays later, Bold Forbes blazed the fastest three-quarters of a mile in Pimlico's 106-year history before the suicidal pace and a foot injury left him staggering down the lane a well-beaten third. Between the badly gashed coronary band just above his left hind hoof and the marathon distance of the upcoming Belmont Stakes, the handicappers gave him no chance of getting a mile and a half three weeks later without needing a wheelchair at the eighth pole. "Let them talk," Barrera shrugged on the eve of the Belmont, breaking into a mischievous grin. "But remember the fish: the only way the fish die is when he opens his mouth."

Bold Forbes wasted no time shutting up the skeptics in his usual style: breaking first from the gate, opening six lengths on the backstretch, then gamely hanging on to his ever-shrinking lead through Belmont's interminable homestretch to win by a desperate neck. "Never in a million years did I think Bold Forbes would win a mile-and-a-half race," his jockey, Angel Cordero Jr., breathlessly told the national TV audience afterward. "He didn't want to go that far, but Laz got him to do it." The only one more drained than the horse was the trainer, who found himself once again overcome with emotion. "I cried in the winner's circle," Barrera confessed later, "because a man who wins the Belmont and does not cry is not a man."

By wiring the field in both the Derby and the Belmont, a lightly regarded little sprinter let the world in on a secret heretofore known only to the racetrack regulars: Laz Barrera had a way with horses that few other trainers possessed. Like Jacobs, Barrera had a gift for getting temperamental horses like Bold Forbes to relax and even yawn before big races. And like Jacobs, Barrera had a knack for winning horses over and getting them to run right out of their breeding for him.

There is an old racetrack adage: "A good trainer can't make a bad horse win, but a bad trainer can make a good horse lose." After Bold Forbes came within four lengths and a clipped coronet of sweeping the Triple Crown in 1976, this corollary could be heard around the racetrack: "If you've got a cheap horse, there's a dozen guys you can give him to. But if you've got a good horse, there's only one—give him to Laz Barrera."

*   *   *

Every new arrival that came under his shedrow would get what was known as "the Barrera Look," an hourlong examination in which the trainer would simply study the equine specimen without uttering a word. Through his large wire-rimmed glasses, Laz Barrera would observe how the horse was put together, how it moved, how it stood, how it reacted to its surroundings. If he saw anything he thought was off, he would write in a book, "Horse is not happy."

By the time Affirmed finally got the Barrera Look in the spring of 1977, the two-year-old chestnut had already been put through his paces by two of Laz's brothers: first going to Willie at Hialeah Park, then to Luis at Belmont Park. They were the first of many Barreras who would have a hand in the care and conditioning of Affirmed.

Just as Hirsch Jacobs had done, Laz Barrera ran his large stable as a family business. His eight brothers would all become trainers, three of them working for Laz himself. Like Laz, his brothers all got their start with horses on their grandfather's farm and with racehorses at Oriental Park before they turned ten. Some preceded Laz to the United States from Cuba, others followed—but none could boast anywhere near the success he had. Thanks to Bold Forbes's breakthrough 1976 campaign, Laz led all trainers nationally for the first time with $2.4 million in annual purse winnings. That brought his cumulative purses in the twenty-seven years since he immigrated to nearly $20 million.

His burgeoning bank account enabled him to help dozens of relatives flee postrevolutionary Cuba and likewise immigrate to the United States. By 1977, Laz had brought thirty-seven nephews, nieces, and cousins out of Cuba, setting them up with U.S. residences. "Expensive?" he asked rhetorically. "Yes. But what is expensive when you can do something for your family?"

There was no underestimating the importance of family in the Latino culture generally and in the Barrera clan specifically. So it was predestined that Laz's sons would follow him onto the Belmont backside. He had told his wife, "You raise the girls, I raise the boys." His philosophy underscored a cultural machismo: "You know, your sons are the most important thing in your life. Your wife could divorce you. Your daughter, she marries and then she no longer has your name. But your sons, they carry your name all their lives. Nothing can ever change that." Their given names may have been Americanized—Alberto to Albert and Lazaro Jr. to Larry—but their surname remained synonymous with training horses from the time each was old enough to learn at their father's knee on the backside. Albert, the eldest by six years, dropped out of college to become a trainer. Larry graduated from high school in the spring of 1977 to go to work as an assistant trainer for his father at Belmont. In no time, Larry would be put in charge of the horses stabled in California, where Laz would come to base his bicoastal operation at Santa Anita Park.

In addition to his own sons, Laz served as a surrogate father to the jockey who became his preferred rider: Angel Cordero Jr. Laz had known Cordero's father as a jockey in Havana and remembered Junior as a young boy hanging around Oriental Park. Junior was still a naive teenager when he arrived in New York from Puerto Rico in 1962 and his father told Barrera, "You know, this kid has never been away from home, so you're his father now." Barrera took that responsibility to heart, giving the nineteen-year-old his first mounts. Maturing into a fierce competitor known for his swagger on and off the horse, Cordero went on to lead the nation's jockeys in wins for 1968 and, thanks to his masterful rides through Bold Forbes's Triple Crown campaign, in earnings for 1976. After his father died, Cordero took to addressing Laz as "Papa." Similarly, Cordero called Laz's brother "Tío Luis," or Uncle Luis.

When Laz had set up his New York stable in the early 1960s, he brought in Luis, two years his senior, as his top assistant. By putting Luis in charge of the horses stabled in Barn 47 at Belmont, Laz could rest assured that his instructions would be carried out by a trainer he trusted and respected.

From the March day that Affirmed was shipped up from Hialeah with all the other Harbor View horses, Luis was charged with conditioning him and bringing him up for his maiden race. For the next two months, Affirmed, like Alydar, would be putting in morning works at Belmont in preparation. His regular exercise rider, Bernie Gonzalez, would get the mount in Affirmed's first race, taking advantage of the five-pound weight allowance accorded apprentice jockeys. Laz, staying in California until the racing season was over at Santa Anita, planned to arrive after Belmont's spring opening and then to settle into Barn 47 for the season. He wasn't about to change his itinerary to catch Affirmed's maiden race. He would fly in afterward.

* * *

Affirmed was destined to make his racing debut in total obscurity. Two days into a strike by pari-mutuel workers that precluded betting at Belmont Park, the grandstand was a ghost town that Tuesday afternoon of May 24. A total of 5,662 diehard fans would take advantage of the free admission and pass through the turnstiles that day, but only a fraction of those would be able to claim they actually witnessed Affirmed's debut in the fourth race on the card—a maiden sprint of five and a half furlongs with a modest purse of $10,000.

Even among the ten young horses entered in that maiden race for two-year-olds that had yet to win anything—half of whom were first-time starters like him—Affirmed was barely on the radar. Although there was no wagering at the track and the tote boards were strangely dark, the morning-line odds installed Affirmed as a 14-to-1 longshot, the fourth-longest price in an uninspiring field.

That couldn't dampen Patrice Wolfson's enthusiasm for her special pet. That afternoon, Patrice stood on the verdant grass of Belmont's paddock, the walls of the track's ivy-covered clubhouse rising high behind her. As the two-year-olds paraded by, she scanned the walkway looking for her boy, excited as the mother of a kindergartner on the first day of school. Suddenly she spotted Affirmed prancing at the side of his groom as they made their way to the saddling stall where he would be tacked up for the race. She was struck by how beautiful he looked on this day, his neck curling, his chestnut coat glistening in the sun, his caramel-colored mane billowing in the breeze. As the colt and his groom made their way along the path, he started to jig and tossed his head. "He's certainly on his toes today," Patrice thought, and realized that was part of what made him so glorious to look at.

She hung back, opting not to walk over to the stall but instead to watch from across the paddock as Luis Barrera and the jockey's valet saddled Affirmed. She watched as Luis threw Bernie Gonzalez up in the saddle and then as the rider and colt made their way around the parade ring. When they had started for the track, she headed up to the owner's box where Lou sat waiting for her.

She was relieved to see her Affirmed go into the starting gate quietly and excited when he broke well on the lead. She hadn't known what to expect in this first race. While Affirmed was close to her heart, there was no reason to think he'd do anything special on the track. But there he was, leading the pack and steadily drawing away from the other horses. He crossed the wire four and a half lengths in front of a Cordero-ridden horse named Innocuous. Patrice was so delighted that she scarcely noticed that Affirmed's win was greeted by an eerie silence in the near-empty racetrack. Those who were able to get their $2 wagers down at an Off-Track Betting parlor collected a tidy $29. Though his time was a pedestrian 1:06, respected turf writer Joe Hirsch wrote in his *Daily Racing Form* column, "Any colt who can win his first race has accomplished something; when he can win it like Affirmed did, he is something special."

Later that night, Laz Barrera called the Wolfsons at home to ask about the race. "Pa-tree-see-a," he said in that unmistakable accent of his, "what did you think?"

"Oh Laz, he had such nice action," Patrice said. "He looked beautiful."

Laz told her that he was pleased with Affirmed's performance, but that he'd heard the colt was "on his toes."

"I heard he was all over that little girl groom," he said. "She couldn't handle him. We'll have to do something about that."

That would be one of many changes now that Affirmed had caught Laz's attention. In the three weeks until Affirmed raced again, Laz would be on site to take over the hands-on training. There would be a new groom, a new jockey, a newfound respect for the lanky chestnut colt.

And looming ahead was the much-ballyhooed Alydar, the pride of Calumet.

BELMONT PARK, N. Y.
HARBOR VIEW FARM OWNER
L. S. BARRERA TRAINER
INNOCUOUS 2nd

PURSE $20,000

AFFIRMED

MAY 24, 1977
BERNIE GONZALEZ UP
5 1/2 FUR. TIME 1:06
GYMNAST 3rd

Affirmed's first win in his maiden race at Belmont Park (Bob Coglianese)

John Veitch on his stable pony accompanying Alydar to the track (Jim Raftery/Livingston Collection)

CHAPTER 7

The Beginning of a Beautiful Rivalry

John Veitch was getting frustrated. Twice the trainer had signed Alydar up for a maiden race at Belmont Park, and twice the race had been canceled after too many horses had dropped out. Though no one was offering any official explanations, talk on the track was that Alydar's reputation had preceded him: other trainers with youngsters hoping to break their maidens were steering clear of any race that listed the highly touted Calumet colt. Alydar had been putting in impressive works in the mornings, and trainers who had been paying clockers on the side to provide information on the quality of their competition were fully aware of how well the Markeys' budding star was doing.

What really had caught everyone's attention was a superfast work the colt put in earlier that spring under one of the nation's leading jockeys, Jorge Velasquez. Veitch had decided to let Alydar show a little more speed and told Velasquez he wanted the colt to cover five-eighths of a mile in 1:01. "Start off slow and then, on the turn to home, drop him down and let him run," the trainer instructed. Positioning himself on the Belmont stretch, he sat on his pony checking his stopwatch as Alydar drew near. It soon became clear that Alydar, allowed to kick into high gear, was really pouring it on. By Veitch's calculation, the colt was going to do the five furlongs far quicker than the trainer wanted. He waved to Velasquez to slow Alydar down. The jockey was surprised. He couldn't imagine they were going too fast because his mount was galloping so effortlessly, but he did as the trainer requested. When Veitch checked his watch at the end of the work, he did a double take: the colt had covered the distance in just 58⅖ seconds. Soon the track was abuzz with chatter about the blazing work that was sure to scare off all the competition.

Now it was already June, and Veitch knew the colt might grow sour if he didn't start racing soon. Besides, Veitch and the Markeys needed to know whether those impressive morning works could translate into a brilliant performance in the afternoon. Some horses, dubbed "morning glories" by racing folk, never make the transition: they can't handle the stress or they just aren't sufficiently competitive.

Veitch finally opted to enter Alydar in an upcoming stakes race at Belmont. Though the competition was bound to be tougher than it would be in a maiden event, at least the race wouldn't be canceled. The Youthful, a $35,000 stakes race for two-year-olds, was sure to have horses with more experience than Alydar, not to mention some, including Affirmed, that had already broken their maidens. Still, the trainer figured it was worth it to get his colt some experience competing against other youngsters. Besides, he knew he had an extraordinarily talented colt. Why not let him run? If everything went right, there was a chance that Alydar might even win a stakes race on his first trip out.

Because an injury had sidelined Velasquez in late May, Veitch had turned to another veteran jockey, Eddie Maple, to ride some of Alydar's works and the colt's first start. In the days before the Youthful, Veitch continued to work Alydar as he had been, breezing five furlongs one day, walking the next, galloping a mile to a mile and a half the next three days, then blowing out three furlongs the following day. Veitch adjusted the schedule slightly so that he could blow the colt out to sharpen him the day before the five-and-a-half-furlong race.

The temperatures had risen into the low eighties on race day, June 15, as Alydar's groom, Clyde Sparks, began the sequence of steps that would become a prerace ritual for the colt. First Sparks took away Alydar's hay and water. Then he started rubbing the colt's liver-chestnut coat to a brilliant sheen. About half an hour before post time, Sparks slipped the bridle over Alydar's head. The groom led the colt out of the stall and walked toward the paddock area with Veitch striding along behind them. Alydar walked quietly into the saddling stall and stood calmly as Maple's valet started to tack him up. Standing to the colt's left, the valet placed the saddle pad and the saddle cloth, inscribed with a large number 7 marking the post position, on Alydar's broad, muscular back. Then he lifted the jockey's tiny racing saddle on top of them. Veitch, who had moved to the colt's right side, adjusted the saddle's position to where he felt it fit best. After the valet handed him the girth and the overgirth under the colt's belly, Veitch buckled both and checked to make sure they were tight enough—a little loose and the saddle could slip during the race with disastrous consequences. He was pleased to see how calmly and professionally his colt was taking in all these new experiences.

Once Alydar was saddled, the groom led him out to the parade ring, where Veitch hoisted Maple up into the saddle. The trainer had already explained to Maple that the plan was to teach Alydar to be a come-from-behind horse. Knowing that the colt had a strong sprinter influence through Raise a Native, Veitch's goal in training had been to teach Alydar to relax until his jockey asked him to kick into high gear in the homestretch. The colt's aggressive temperament wouldn't allow him to be asked for more than one kick. Based on Alydar's breeding and conformation, Veitch figured the colt might have made a brilliant sprinter, but the Markeys wanted a Kentucky Derby horse and the best the trainer could hope for was one trained to get the distance of the classic races who would explode in the stretch with a single burst of speed—a one-run horse. Before Maple asked Alydar to move off, Veitch gave his instructions: "Let him relax in the beginning, and then drop him off and let him run." He watched as the pair left the ring and made their way to the track. Then he turned away and headed up to Calumet's box to watch the race.

* * *

In Laz Barrera's barn, Affirmed had gone through a similar prerace ritual. The trainer had been as good as his word to Patrice Wolfson and had changed some things up, including the colt's groom. And now in the early afternoon before the Youthful, Affirmed was standing quietly as the new groom, Juan Alaniz, readied him for the race. Alaniz and the colt seemed to click the minute the slight man with close-cropped black hair first entered the stall. There was something gentle and calming about Alaniz's manner. But it was in the prep for the race that Alaniz would really make his mark.

As he slowly and carefully brushed out Affirmed's mane and tail, the colt visibly let down. Once all the hairs had been smoothed and organized, Alaniz began to braid the colt's mane and then the upper part of his tail. Something about the braiding process soothed Affirmed, and in minutes his head started to droop and he almost looked as if he could fall asleep. That mellow mood remained as Alaniz walked him over to the saddling stalls. He seemed like a completely different horse from the one Patrice had watched prancing in the sun, mane waving in the wind, on the way to his maiden race. Now, she thought as she watched him come into the paddock area, he was calm and steady, almost boring to look at. But that relaxation was just what Barrera wanted. And so, even though the trainer thought all that braiding was a little prissy, he allowed it. All through the tacking-up process, the colt remained mellow. He stood quietly as Barrera hoisted up his jockey, this time Angel Cordero Jr.

Jockey and colt made their way out onto the track and then over to the starting gate, where they waited with the others, including Alydar, to be led in. Though Affirmed's betting odds had improved as a result of his first win, he still wasn't the favorite. That honor had been reserved for Alydar. The big, precocious colt everyone thought might be starting on the journey to next year's Derby went to the post at 9-to-5.

When the bell rang, all eleven youngsters broke cleanly, Affirmed settling into second right behind Buck Mountain with Alydar trailing well behind. As Affirmed began to move up on the inside, closing to within a neck of the leader around the turn, Alydar continued to lumber along at the back of the pack. At the top of the stretch, Affirmed kicked into another gear, flew past Buck Mountain, and opened a length and a half. Alydar, finally finding his stride, gradually moved up into fifth place. As the finish line loomed ahead, Wood Native, another Raise a Native grandson, started to put pressure on Affirmed, but the Harbor View colt fought him off to win by a neck. Alydar would finish a discouraging fifth, almost five lengths behind Affirmed.

Patrice was delighted to see her colt win once again. It was still too soon to have any Derby dreams, but she was pleased to see that her favorite boy seemed to have some real racing talent.

For Veitch, the race was a major disappointment. He hadn't known what to expect, but had hoped that his colt might at least be up in front. One consolation, he thought, was that Alydar had gotten some experience

Alydar breaking his maiden in a race at Belmont Park (Bob Coglianese)

and was starting to pick up speed toward the end of the race. Maybe next time he'd be in better position to show off the powerful thrust Veitch had seen in the morning works. The trainer would look for another five-and-a-half-furlong race for the colt to break his maiden in.

It didn't take long. Less than a week later, he entered Alydar in a maiden race—and this time it didn't get canceled. On June 24, the big colt, with Maple again in the irons, lined up with nine other youngsters. Alydar broke alertly, powering to the lead on the turn, gaining ground with every stride until he crossed the wire six and three-quarters lengths in front. Veitch let out a sigh of relief. His colt had redeemed himself, and now the trainer had some good news to report to the Markeys.

* * *

Two weeks later, on July 6, Alydar and Affirmed would once again be entered in the same race. This time it was Belmont's Great American

Stakes, another five-and-a-half-furlong race for two-year-olds. Despite Affirmed's win in the Youthful, Alydar was the favorite at 4-to-5, with Affirmed the third choice at 9-to-2.

When the bell went off, Affirmed banged into the gate, hitting his head and breaking one of his front teeth. That didn't slow him down, though, and he went right to the lead and in seconds was nearly a length ahead with the rest of the field bunched behind him. Alydar, this time, was not going to be left behind. Maple kicked him into high gear on the turn and they moved up quickly from fourth place, skimming along on the outside. By the head of the stretch, the Calumet colt, who had a five-pound weight advantage, was closing rapidly on Affirmed. Within a few strides, Alydar surged ahead and began opening the gap. By the time he hit the finish line, Alydar was in full throttle and three and a half lengths ahead of second-place Affirmed— and only three-fifths of a second off the track record.

Veitch was jubilant and convinced that Alydar had finally come into his own. The trainer figured he had everything in order and could now start mapping out his colt's road to the Derby.

For his part, Barrera wasn't at all happy with what he'd just seen. As soon as the race ended, the trainer turned to the Wolfsons and told them he wanted to take Affirmed out to the West Coast to run in the Juvenile Championship at Hollywood Park. He wanted a chance to build up Affirmed's confidence and, with Alydar around, that might be tough. "We've got to get him away from that big monster," he told Patrice and Lou.

So Affirmed was shipped out to California and entered in the Juvenile, a step up at six furlongs. Cordero was tied up on the East Coast, so Barrera asked Laffit Pincay Jr.'s agent if the five-time national champion would be available to ride the race—and also to ride one of the morning works so the jockey could get an idea of what the colt was like. On the morning of the work, Barrera instructed Pincay to breeze the colt five furlongs. As they galloped along, it seemed to Pincay that the colt was distracted—ears flicking first this way, then that—and not working particularly hard. When they came to a stop, Pincay rode over to where Barrera was standing, stopwatch in hand.

"Do you know how fast you went?" Barrera quizzed the jockey.

"Oh, I think it was probably around one-oh-one," Pincay responded.

"No," Barrera said. "It was fifty-eight seconds."

Pincay was stunned. The colt had felt like he was just lumbering along. "Boy, this horse can run!" the jockey said.

In the Juvenile, on July 23, Affirmed broke well and immediately took the lead. The 2-to-5 favorite flew through the first quarter in 21⅗ seconds and the half in 44⅖, leaving the field way behind. By the time he hit the finish line, he was seven lengths ahead, having sped through the six furlongs in 1:09⅕. Barrera was happy. His colt seemed to be more relaxed with every race. It was time to fly east, this time for the Saratoga meet where Affirmed would run in the Sanford Stakes on August 17 as a prep for the Hopeful Stakes, the venerable track's most prestigious race for two-year-olds, where in all likelihood he would meet Alydar once again.

After the Great American victory, Veitch decided to send Alydar to the Tremont Stakes at Belmont on July 27. Once again Alydar was the favorite, with the only other real competition coming from a Woody Stephens–trained colt named Believe It and the sprinter Jet Diplomacy. As the horses broke, Jet Diplomacy took the lead, with Believe It close behind. While the two colts dueled for the lead, Alydar lurked back in the pack, waiting until the final furlong to make his move. With a sudden burst of speed, he flew by both of them, winning the six-furlong race by a length and a quarter in 1:10.

Just a week later, Alydar stole the show at the Sapling Stakes at Monmouth Park on the Jersey Shore. Although Veitch had been pleased with Alydar's performance in the Tremont, Eddie Maple had complained that the colt had a tendency to look around while going down the track. Veitch mulled over the possibility of adding blinkers because he felt it might help the colt focus better when the jockey asked him to move out. Just a couple of hours before the race, Veitch made his decision: Alydar would wear blinkers that would only partially obscure his peripheral vision.

The big colt looked splendid as he headed toward the starting gate. When the horses sprang out at the bell, a relaxed Alydar settled into third place. This time he started moving up fast, and at the far turn he was already second and closing. With an explosive burst of speed in the stretch, he flew into the lead and pulled away to win decisively by two and a half lengths, having run the six furlongs in 1:10⅗. Now, Veitch was confident that his colt was ready for the Hopeful.

At about the same time, 225 miles north at Saratoga, Alydar's half-sister Our Mims was winning the Alabama Stakes for three-year-old fillies. It marked the first time in Calumet's long history that the stable had won two $100,000 races on the same day, evoking the glory days when Citation and Coaltown would routinely capture stakes on the same afternoon. Racing enthusiasts were now predicting a rebirth for Calumet. Some were even starting to compare Alydar's performances to those of Citation as a two-year-old. It was a heady time for John Veitch.

*   *   *

At the beginning of August, the Wolfsons headed up to Saratoga, where they rented a house near the racetrack. They would be there for the month, enjoying the town's old-time feel. Each morning they would head over to the backside of the track, and Patrice would give Affirmed his cuddle and tell him how wonderful he was. When Affirmed arrived at Saratoga, Patrice had been concerned because his knee had been banged up. But Laz Barrera assured her that it was a minor injury and the colt would recover in a couple of days. Affirmed's works went well in the mornings, and Barrera entered him in the Sanford. There was just one problem: Barrera hadn't settled on a jockey.

He turned first to Angel Cordero, remaining faithful to the East Coast star who had ridden Affirmed in both of his Belmont stakes races. "That's your horse," Barrera told the jockey. But Cordero opted instead to ride Darby Creek Road, convinced that the winner of the Saratoga Special Stakes had a better chance to emerge as a Derby contender.

Barrera turned next to Laffit Pincay, the West Coast star who had substituted for Cordero in Affirmed's lone California race. Pincay thought Affirmed had the makings of a star, and he wanted to ride him in the Hopeful. But his agent, George O'Bryan, said the Sanford was such a small race that Pincay shouldn't forsake his regular West Coast clientele to fly east for a minor midweek stakes. "We can always get Affirmed back later," O'Bryan assured him. "We don't have to ride him this time. We can ride him next time in the Hopeful."

"Is Laz OK with that?" Pincay asked.

"Yes," the agent replied. "I said, 'How about if we skip the Sanford and run the Hopeful?' He said, 'OK.'"

Clearly, something got lost in the translation, because Barrera was tired of playing musical jockeys. Shaking his head, he bristled, "Now I got one of the best horses in America, and I don't want to keep changing riders. I say, anybody ride him now rides him forever."

He would find that "forever" jockey in a once-in-a-lifetime wunderkind who was taking the racing world by storm: Steve Cauthen.

Steve Cauthen (Keeneland Library Mochon Collection)

CHAPTER 8

The Kid

THE KID WAS A NATURAL-BORN HORSEMAN.

Bred as well as any foal dropped in the Bluegrass, Stephen Mark Cauthen was born there on May 1, 1960—coincidentally during Kentucky Derby week—to a mother who trained racehorses and a father who shod them. If his robust birth weight of seven pounds twelve ounces hardly hinted that he could grow up small enough to someday be a jockey, it soon became clear that young Steve Cauthen was indeed a natural in the saddle.

He was still in diapers at the tender age of one when his father first hoisted him onto a horse to get him out of the way of some cattle. He was just two years old when he began to ride ponies, without a trace of fear. He was barely three when he attended his first Kentucky Derby at the same age the horses do, romping on the grass along the Churchill Downs backstretch and watching in wide-eyed wonder as rising star Braulio Baeza rode Chateaugay to a rousing upset.

By the time he turned five, Steve Cauthen had already shown an affinity for horses and had become an accomplished rider in his own right. That was the year Tex and Myra Cauthen had finally settled the family down once and for all in Bluegrass Country, affording their precocious son forty acres of farmland to gallop across. To get to their new farm in the northern Kentucky hamlet of Walton just twenty miles south of Steve's birthplace, the Cauthens had traveled a circuitous five-year route through whatever Southern racetracks provided work for a family of self-described "racetrackers." Tex, who still went by Ronald Cauthen when he got his start as a thirteen-year-old cowboy breaking wild horses, had ridden out of Texas at fifteen to become a nomadic racetracker—first as an exercise boy and stablehand, then as a hard-luck trainer, and finally as a blacksmith. It was at a track that he met Myra Bischoff. The petite blonde, who had grown up in a racing family on a Thoroughbred farm near Walton, was holding a horse Tex was shoeing for her father. The connection was as deep as it was instantaneous. The couple soon married, forging a life together while bouncing around Southern and Northeastern tracks where Tex would shoe horses for up to $18 a pop and Myra would train off and on.

The arrival of their firstborn a year later didn't change that itinerant lifestyle, so Steve was practically weaned on backstretches throughout the South and Midwest. It wasn't until he reached school age and a kid brother was born that his parents decided it was time to put down roots in the Bluegrass. There, centrally located sixty miles north of Lexington and twenty miles south of Cincinnati, Tex could count on regular farrier work on the Kentucky-Ohio racing circuit while Steve could hone his riding skills, galloping pell-mell across the pastures of their modest farm.

Not long after the Cauthens settled into their plain wooden farmhouse, word started filtering to Latonia, the small Kentucky track where Tex was building a reputation as a skilled shoer, about "something unbelievable" happening down the road in the tiny town of Walton. One skeptical racing official was curious enough to drive the seven miles from Latonia to check it out. "I saw this tiny kid handling a Thoroughbred in full gallop, sitting over him like a regular exercise rider," he marveled. "I never forgot the name Steve Cauthen after that. You don't forget a kid five years old who looks like that on a horse."

That was also the age at which the youngster's weight began to level off. As a six-year-old, he tipped the scales at forty pounds, only ten more than he had weighed when he was eight months old. Even though he was smaller than the other first graders, any notion of growing up to become a jockey couldn't yet compete with every boy's dream of being a major-league ballplayer or an NFL quarterback. Riding was just something he did for fun.

When he wasn't galloping the family's handful of cheap Thoroughbreds around the farm, young Steve was tagging along with his father at the racetrack. On school days, he would wake up hours before class so he could accompany Dad to Latonia for the farrier's daily 5 A.M. rounds. One morning while Tex was shoeing a horse elsewhere on the backside, Steve was hanging around the stall of an old stakes winner named Slade, a stallion so high-spirited and ill-tempered that all the stablehands feared going near him.

"Hey, Steve," the horse's trainer, Lonnie Abshire, called out with a grin, "you got your riding boots on?"

"Yup," replied the kid, already a horseman of few words.

"You want to ride this dude?"

"Yup."

"OK, put the tack on him, boys! You sure you can do it, Steve?"

"Yup."

When Abshire abruptly called an end to the escapade, explaining that he couldn't rightly put a seven-year-old on the meanest stallion at Latonia, Steve excitedly begged the trainer to, please, let him ride Slade. Finally, Abshire relented and reluctantly lifted the boy into the saddle. As the young rider walked the horse around the barn, Slade was tossing his head, snorting defiantly, baring his teeth. Fearing for the rider's safety, the trainer glanced up at Steve and couldn't believe his own eyes: the kid was actually laughing at the horse. Dismounting as nonchalantly as most children hop off a school bus, the second grader simply shrugged. "I understand how kids might be scared of some things in their lives," he would later explain, "but it never did occur to me to be scared of a horse."

Fearless and unflappable, he was already demonstrating an uncanny connection with the beasts. He was only eight when his parents gave him his first horse, along with a lecture on the responsibility that went with ownership. From his parents, he learned how to care for and properly groom his new prize. Soon his father started teaching him how to start yearlings under saddle. Tex was impressed with Steve's ability to calm even the spookiest colts and with the boy's amazing sense of balance, which allowed him to stick with yearlings that might have ducked out from under a less talented rider. At local 4-H horse shows, Steve won more than his share of ribbons for riding. He seemed to be drawn to anything related to horses. By the same token, all the coming-of-age rituals that appealed to his schoolmates—going to the movies, listening to records, hanging out at dances—left him bored. He wanted more, and he knew where he could find it.

One day when he was all of twelve years old, he went to his father and made a proclamation: "Dad, I want to be a race rider."

Formulating a response on the spot, Tex Cauthen realized it was time to sit his son down and tell him the facts of race riding. His own riding hopes had faded when he shot up late in adolescence, ultimately to five foot nine and 150 pounds. In his travails as a blacksmith, he had seen too many jockeys killing themselves to make weight with starvation diets, vomiting rituals, sweatbox marathons. If he was the exact opposite of those stereotypical Little League parents living vicariously through their children, he also wasn't about to dash his own son's dreams. So when Steve announced his aspiration to become a jockey, Dad was ready with a facts-of-life talk that was at once pragmatic and supportive.

"I think it's a good idea and I'll help you," Tex started, pausing for emphasis, "on two conditions."

When the boy's soulful brown eyes inquisitively wondered what those stipulations were, his father went on to lay them out. "First, don't ever let it swell your head or change you as a person. And second, promise that you'll give it up if you start to grow too big. The minute you have to start starving yourself to make riding weight, you'll have to look for something else to do with your life."

Steve nodded. The ground rules thus established, Tex had a game plan ready to offer. "If you're going to try it, you might as well try to be the best," he said. "There are a lot of fine points that some riders learn very late in their careers or never learn at all. I can show you some of them, and what I can't show you, some of my friends probably can. Just pay attention. And be ready to work at it."

If the seventh grader was merely an average student in the classrooms where he daydreamed about horses, he was determined to be an honors student in this crash course his father would teach at the farm and at the track.

To school him on the basics, Tex got films of nearly a hundred races at nearby Latonia and at River Downs just across the Ohio River in Cincinnati—the bush tracks where he spent most of his workdays—and, each evening after dinner, he would take them up to Steve's room. Turning the boy's bedroom into a classroom, they screened those patrol films over and over on a borrowed projector, running them backward and forward so Steve could dissect the jockeys' moves, techniques, and strategies. They paid closest attention to the top jockey at River Downs, Larry Snyder, since he had won the most races in North America one year while riding low to cut down on wind resistance—a style that Steve decided to emulate.

The bulk of the homeschooling took place out behind the farmhouse in the red barn where Tex introduced his son to the fundamentals of holding the reins and the whip. That's where Steve would practice the art of wielding the whip—not on a horse's flank, but on the side of a bale of hay. He would routinely wake up at 4 A.M., trudge out to the barn in the pitch dark, and climb two ladders to the cramped hayloft. There, he would sit astride a bale of hay and, for two hours in the predawn silence, grab hold of the reins hanging off a post and practice his whipping technique with a stick, repeatedly passing the makeshift crop from hand to hand and snapping it down onto the side of the bale with an expeditious flick of the wrist. Alone in the barn, he learned to tag the horse precisely within an eighth of an inch of his target—in the process chopping up bale after bale of the hay his father had bought for $2.50 apiece.

The kid would become so engrossed while slapping away that one time he was startled to glimpse his father standing behind him in the hayloft. "What are you watching?" Steve asked. "Am I doing something wrong?"

"Nope," Tex replied. "I was just wondering if you'll ever be worth all these bales of hay you're beating to pieces."

"Sure hope so," Steve said without missing a beat of the stick.

The education of a jockey became most intensive when summer school was in session and Steve could spend every day at the racetrack. He got a summer job at River Downs, where he would muck stalls, walk hots, and soak up every nuance of the jockey's craft from dawn till dusk. Almost every day, he would spend long hours standing near the starting gate, studying the techniques of various riders and the reactions of various horses in the noisy steel contraption. One summer, he spent every morning in the clockers' stand on the backstretch with the men who timed the daily works, developing a clock in his own head so accurate that he could judge without a stopwatch precisely how fast each horse was galloping within a fifth of a second. Then he'd watch the afternoon races from the starters' stand near the inside rail, learning to anticipate the break from the gate and to navigate those first chaotic strides of a race.

Mentally, he already felt prepared to handle whatever a thousand-pound Thoroughbred could throw at a ninety-pound jockey while hurtling forty miles per hour through traffic. Physically, however, he was still just a wispy teenager with a cherubic, pale, cowlick-draped face that made him look even younger than his tender years. Once he had declared his ambition to become a jockey, his father advised him to lift weights to increase strength. A competitive all-around athlete who grew up playing baseball, football, and basketball until his peers got too big for him, he added yoga to his morning regimen to make his arms and legs supple enough for the demands of the sport he felt offered the most level playing field to a diminutive farm boy.

Three days after celebrating his fourteenth birthday, he made the pilgrimage to Churchill Downs to attend the Kentucky Derby, this time watching the race not as just another fan but as a student studying each jockey's every move. Scrutinizing Angel Cordero's triumphant trip aboard Cannonade in that 1974 Derby, Steve Cauthen vowed to someday capture the sport's marquee race himself.

Soon enough, he started to demonstrate his own riding proficiency on the track, if only as an exercise boy galloping and breezing horses in the mornings before hitching a ride to junior high in time for the homeroom bell. On the backstretch at Latonia, he began to build a reputation for being able to handle the big, tough, headstrong horses that were running off with bigger, tougher, stronger exercise riders. That was a by-product of his unique ability to relate to horses—something he attributed to having been raised "to be a horseman, not just a jockey."

Until he reached the legal age to become an apprentice jockey, sixteen, he would have to bide his time. During his sophomore year at Walton-Verona High School, where he was hitting the books hard enough to get A's and B's as part of a deal with his father, he would tell friends that he'd soon be dropping out to become "the best race rider in the world." Even when they responded by teasingly calling him "Super-jock," he'd keep right on proclaiming his ambition—not with the cocky bravado of the stereotypical jockey, but with the quiet confidence of a shy, easygoing kid determined to break the mold.

On May 1, 1976, he fittingly celebrated his sixteenth birthday at Churchill Downs, watching Cordero ride Bold Forbes to a stunning upset over Honest Pleasure in the Kentucky Derby. The excitement always attendant on Derby Day was heightened this time by the sweet significance of turning sixteen—for this was the day Cauthen finally became eligible for his jockey's license. "I thought this day would never get here," he told his parents later that evening at a birthday dinner. "I'm ready to start, Dad. I'm ready to ride."

*   *   *

Eleven days after the Derby, Steve Cauthen was back at Churchill Downs getting ready to ride his long-awaited first race as a jockey. He calmly walked into the storied paddock trying to appear as bold as any five-foot, ninety-two-pound sixteen-year-old possibly could on the headiest day of his young life. His first professional mount was a $5,000 claimer named King of Swat, who went to the post for the day's opening race a 136-to-1 longshot. Cauthen got him out of the gate well and positioned him near the lead, but the sprinter predictably ran out of gas in the stretch and lugged home sixteen lengths off the pace, dead last.

Five days after his inauspicious debut, Cauthen readily returned to the familiar surroundings of River Downs, a minor-league track where the competition was softer than on the hallowed ground of Churchill Downs. Making this more of a homecoming, he was riding the featured race on a gelding owned by his mother and trained by her brother, his Uncle Tommy. Lagging in last place fifteen lengths out of it on the turn, Cauthen tagged Red Pipe with the whip just as he had practiced on the hay bales, and the stretch runner responded by charging home to win by a length and a half. In the tenth start of his young career, the rookie rider had broken his maiden.

Just a week and a half later, on May 27, he rode his fifth winner—a milestone for any rider because it officially starts the one-year clock on the weight allowance enjoyed by apprentice jockeys. That handicap, enabling a horse to carry lighter weight under an apprentice than a veteran jockey, is designed to compensate for beginner's inexperience and the resulting difficulty getting mounts from trainers. When they first start out, fledgling apprentices are given a ten-pound weight allowance—denoted on the racing charts by three asterisks, known as "bugs"—until they win five times. Then the handicap drops to seven pounds—marked by two bugs—until they ride another thirty winners. At that point, it drops to five pounds—marked by a single bug—until the one-year clock expires and successful apprentices graduate from "bug boys" to full-fledged "journeyman jockeys."

Cauthen needed barely two months of his River Downs apprenticeship to dispense with all but his single bug, riding 26 winners in the track's spring meet and a record 94 through its summer meet. By summer's end, his combined 120 winners in seventy days had shattered the track record for a full season despite his having ridden only a fraction of it.

Ready to take the next step up in class, he moved on to the stiffer competition of Arlington Park in Chicago. Ted Atkinson, a Hall of Fame jockey who had been the first ever to win over a million dollars in a single year, was working as a steward there when Tex Cauthen asked him to point out any flaws in Steve's riding style. Atkinson had to look hard for several days before he could find one, and even then it was only that the apprentice needed more race experience to hone his judgment in positioning his mount and anticipating openings. Otherwise, Atkinson reported back, "he's the finished product now."

During his three weeks at Arlington, Cauthen won forty races to finish third in the jockey standings, fourteen behind leader Larry Snyder, the very rider he had studied all those nights on film up in his bedroom. As the Chicago racing season moved crosstown to Hawthorne for a month, with Cauthen winning twenty-seven races to Snyder's thirty-two, observers could see how well the rookie was mastering the veteran's low riding style.

Crouching far forward with his back parallel to the horse's neck and his head buried in its mane, Cauthen would ride so low that spectators without binoculars sometimes thought he had fallen off his mount. Opposing jockeys thought the same thing when they would glance back and fail to see him crouched down behind the horse's head. He rode so level and so still that racetrackers joked about how you could serve drinks on his back at the quarter pole without spilling a drop before the finish line. He seemed one with the horse.

With his smooth style and silky touch, Steve Cauthen was being called the coolest apprentice to burst on the scene since seventeen-year-old Willie Shoemaker began his record run of 8,833 winners in 1949. Even more daunting than being labeled "the next Willie Shoemaker" was being hailed "the embryo Arcaro" and compared to the incomparable jockey revered as The Master, Eddie Arcaro himself. Cauthen possessed what Atkinson termed "the Arcaro seat," meaning that he was always perfectly balanced on his mount whether crouching low over the withers or perched high in the irons. What's more, Cauthen possessed the Arcaro feel, meaning that his hands, notably outsized, were as soft as they were strong, sensitive enough to perceive through the reins clues about a horse's status at a given moment and then to communicate tactical commands back to his mount. That, more than anything, defined Cauthen's magic touch. He was at his most sublime when hand-riding down the stretch: his hands, tucked in behind his mount's ears with reins and whip gripped by his long fingers, pumping back and forth to urge the horse on, two athletes flowing in perfect rhythm to the wire. As if all that physical prowess, tactical skill, and natural instinct weren't enough, he also possessed an intangible that none of the greats who had it before him could articulate: an inexplicable ability to inspire racehorses, to calm the most skittish of them, to get the very best from every one of his mounts.

For all his precocious poise, however, he was still just a babe in the backwoods, a virtual unknown outside the Cincinnati and Chicago tracks where he was progressing like a minor-league ballplayer from Single A to Double A to Triple A. The prince of the bug boys had a long way to go before he could ever be accepted as a bona fide "race rider," the term the hardboots reserved for only the best of major-league jockeys. Before he could challenge the era's star race riders like Willie Shoemaker, Angel Cordero, Laffit Pincay, and Jorge Velasquez, Steve Cauthen had many more baby steps to take.

For the next steppingstone in his painstakingly plotted progression, Cauthen returned from Illinois to Kentucky for the fall meet at Churchill Downs and rode twenty-four winners in three weeks. One day, Churchill's leading jockey, Don Brumfield, came back from winning a stakes race at Aqueduct and mentioned to Cauthen that there was no standout apprentice up in New York. "Take a shot up there," the veteran advised. "I think you'll do real good there."

Tex Cauthen agreed that his son was ready to try the big time in New York, to test himself on the major-league racing circuit that boasted the best horses, the best jockeys, and the best purses. All he needed was a big-time jockey agent to book the mounts for him from trainers notoriously reluctant to entrust their best horses to green apprentices.

Tex had begun shopping for one a few months earlier, recognizing that a well-connected agent is worth every penny of his 25 percent commission on a jockey's earnings. Eddie Campbell, the local jockey agent who had been securing Steve's mounts at River Downs, recommended the one regarded as the best not only in New York but in all of America: Lenny Goodman, a fast-talking Brooklynite who over three decades had built a reputation for smoking expensive cigars, for sporting Brooks Brothers suits and Gucci shoes, and for representing only star race riders at the top of their game. For the past twelve years, he had lined up mounts for Braulio Baeza, the steely nerved Hall of Famer who had reigned as a five-time national champion but was now battling weight problems and depression. Though agents are allowed to represent two jockeys at a time, one journeyman and one apprentice, Goodman had not deigned to manage a bug boy in a quarter of a century. But with Baeza sidelined by his weight and verging on retirement, Goodman seemed primed to make an exception in pursuit of his next meal ticket.

So the Cauthens flew to upstate New York during Saratoga's August meet on a mission to find the high-powered jockey agent who was being recruited by over a dozen established riders. At the quaint old track, Tex spotted Lenny Goodman smoking his trademark cigar outside the racing secretary's office and introduced himself. "My son Steve is riding two horses here today," Tex said. "He's the leading rider at River Downs, and I was hoping you might look at him and see what you think."

Goodman unfolded his copy of the *Daily Racing Form* and studied the bug boy's two mounts. "These are terrible horses," he said, returning his gaze to Tex. "He's got no shot to win. But I'll take a look at him."

Watching this unknown rookie finish next to last in both races, Goodman could nevertheless see the talent—the fearlessness, the patience, the balance, the skill in switching the whip. "I like your kid," he told Tex after the audition. "But we got a problem here. He's sixteen, a baby. I don't want some racetrack hustlers latching on to him and getting him broads and telling him he's the greatest thing since Arcaro. They could ruin him in record time."

Tex assured Goodman that his levelheaded son exercised as much mature horse sense off the track as he exhibited on it. What's more, Tex went on, a family friend who trained horses in New York, Chuck Taliaffero, and his wife would welcome Steve into the stability of their home in Floral Park, Long Island, near Belmont. Goodman rolled the cigar around his mouth in contemplation. "Fine," he said at last. "When you can work out the arrangements and you want to come to New York, just call me."

Two months later, after Steve finished up his successful steppingstone at Churchill Downs, Tex made the call. "Send him up here," Goodman responded. "Let's get started."

* * *

If Steve Cauthen's reputation hadn't preceded him to New York in late November 1976, the country boy wasted no time making a name for himself in the big city. After losing on his first four mounts the day he made his Aqueduct debut, he threaded a longshot mare named Illiterate through an opening down the stretch to win the featured race by a neck over a favorite ridden by Cordero. From the moment the tote board lit up at $61.20 for a $2 bet, Cauthen exploded on the big time like a supernova. Burning up the track through a December cold snap, the hot apprentice proved he belonged by capturing one in every five races—the best winning percentage of any jockey for Aqueduct's fall meet. In one seventeen-race stretch, he brought home twelve winners. Over one two-day span, he became the only jockey ever to win six straight New York races and then captured his first stakes, outriding Cordero and Velasquez on a 19-to-1 longshot that had been struggling in claimers.

No rider had ever made a grander entrance on the center stage known as New York's "Big Wheel." In just twenty-one days at The Big A before the track's 1976 season adjourned for Christmas, Cauthen won an eye-opening 29 races and $375,000 in purses—bringing his year-end total to 240 winners and $1,244,423, of which the rookie earned the standard 10 percent jockey's share.

Beyond the races and the money, he had won over the toughest fans in all of sports: the hard-bitten New York railbirds notorious for judging jockeys most critically and most profanely. Before each race, horseplayers at The Big A and at Off-Track Betting parlors throughout the city would scour the *Racing Form* looking for his asterisked name while asking aloud, "Who's the kid riding in the next race?" And then minutes later as his mount turned for home and invariably made a well-timed move, they would chorus, "Here comes the kid!"

Before long, that became his nickname: "The Kid." It may not have been as catchy as "Stevie Wonder" or the other appellations bestowed on him, but it was the nickname that best suited his personality and riding style for its understatement and efficiency. The Kid was rewriting not only the record book but also the lexicon, with vanquished jockeys and horse-players said to have been "Cauthenized." While a New York accent could be forgiven for mispronouncing Cauthen as "Caw-thin" rather than the correct "Coth-in," it was easier for everyone—from the inveterate railbirds to the veteran riders in the jocks' room—to simply call him by his nickname.

When racing resumed at Aqueduct right after New Year's, The Kid was no longer just a jockey, just a prodigy, just a sensation. He was now a full-blown phenomenon.

The Kid was larger than life, if not larger than five foot one and ninety-five pounds. Not only had he become the biggest story in the insular world of horse racing, but he was in the process of transcending the sport like no two-legged athlete ever had. A breath of fresh air and athletic purity lifting a Runyonesque pastime out of its smoke-filled shadows, he single-handedly transformed a utilitarian racetrack—all cold steel and concrete dotted with piles of dirty snow—into a golden mecca. Newspaper, magazine, and television reporters flocked to the frozen Queens track hard by JFK Airport to chronicle the storybook legend of the Kentucky farm boy who looked ages younger than his sixteen years but rode like a grizzled old master.

Suddenly, everyone wanted a piece of him—from the morning shows to the evening news to *The Tonight Show*. "I want to get Steve Cauthen on; we're trying," Johnny Carson deadpanned in his *Tonight Show* monologue. "He's the only jockey in the world you can bet on to win, place, or break out. If he keeps going from the finish line to the winner's circle as often as he does, the racetracks will have to hire crossing guards."

Nothing captured that wholesome youthfulness better than The Kid's first *Sports Illustrated* cover: a baby-faced boy next door with a sweet smile and clean-cut chestnut hair swept low across his brow, his pale complexion clashing with the splashy green and yellow silks he was wearing. The cover line beside his winning smile said it all: THE CAUTHEN PHENOMENON.

Here was a prodigy like none the sports world had ever seen. Never before had an athlete so very young made such a meteoric rise to dominate an entire professional sport. Old-timers had to reach back fully four decades for a comparison to "Rapid Robert" Feller, who was a seventeen-year-old farm boy when his blinding fastball started setting major-league strikeout records. The Cauthen Phenomenon evoked closer comparisons to Nadia Comaneci, who as a fourteen-year-old pixie just the previous summer led the Romanian gymnastics team to Olympic gold and became history's youngest all-around champion. No sooner had she dazzled the world with her unprecedented perfect 10 than Cauthen began redefining greatness in another sport favoring diminutive athletes. That he was so slight and frail-looking made his prodigious performance all the more astonishing. And with each succeeding winner he rode, the legend only kept growing.

The Year of The Kid, as 1977 was destined to become, got off to a blazing start with Cauthen winning twenty-three races in one spectacular week, breaking Cordero's record not only for New York State but also for the entire country. During that record run, Cauthen astoundingly won almost half his starts and came in the money three-quarters of the time. The following Saturday, he won six races in a single afternoon to tie the New York State record shared by Cordero, Velasquez, and Shoemaker—a feat he would become the first jockey ever to repeat. By mid-February, Cauthen already had surpassed the million-dollar mark in purse winnings faster than anyone ever had in a calendar year. As the brutal winter thawed into spring, he was on pace to win nine hundred races and $6 million by year's end—incomprehensible numbers that would smash the all-time national records.

The Cauthen Phenomenon could be quantified on the tote board by how his mere presence in the irons transformed a "live longshot" into what the handicappers call a "false favorite." With horseplayers betting the odds down on all his mounts, the payouts from his winners were petering out like oil from a field that had been drilled by too many prospectors. But not even that could stop bettors from backing his mounts. In the least predictable of all sports, Cauthen was the closest thing there was to a sure thing. So horseplayers were happy to put their money not on the horse, but rather on the jockey.

That flew in the face of the age-old racetrack axiom, "Jockeys don't win races—horses do." Though a smart ride can help a horse almost as much as a flawed one can hurt, a jockey is ultimately only as good as his mount. Even if fully 90 percent of the winning equation comes from the horse, as racetrackers suggest in explaining the jockey's 10 percent share of the purse, Cauthen's contribution could still make the difference between finishing first or out of the money. So while Lenny Goodman initially had to hard-sell horsemen to get his little-known client mounts back in the fall, now the agent had his pick of the best horses from trainers who were finding the wunderkind's talent and weight advantage to be an irresistible combination.

The pace was dizzying both on and off the track. After dominating Aqueduct from Monday through Saturday against the East Coast's top jockeys (Cordero, Velasquez, et al.), he would hop a flight to California for Sunday showdowns at Santa Anita against the West's top guns (Shoemaker, Pincay, et al.), and then grab the red-eye back to New York in time for Monday's first race at The Big A. While proving himself on both coasts in the nation's two most important winter meets, he somehow found time to make command performances at racetracks that lured him to points in between with unheard-of appearance fees. While fans had always flocked to tracks to catch fleeting glimpses of every superhorse from Man o' War to Secretariat, this was the first time they were drawn expressly to see a two-legged superstar. Everywhere he rode on a "Steve Cauthen Day," the guest of honor inflated attendance by thousands just as he deflated the odds on his mounts.

All of which made him a transcendent celebrity appealing both to grownups who had never been to a racetrack or placed so much as a $2 Derby bet and to young girls who inundated him with fan mail requesting his photo as if he were a rock star. Other jockeys surely would have relished the kind of attention he was drawing, particularly the ones who'd stride out of the jocks' room before each race brandishing their whips like swords. But not Cauthen, who'd quietly and calmly file out with all the nonchalance of a kid spilling out of homeroom and heading to his first-period class rather than to the paddock. To him, the swarm of reporters awaiting his arrival in the jocks' room every morning was an occupational hazard to be tolerated with perfunctory politeness. Shy and humble, he answered questions like he rode races: with no wasted motion or wasted words. Inquiring minds wanted to know everything about him: what he ate ("Whatever I want"), how much he dated girls ("Maybe one a month"), what time he went to bed (9 P.M. in order to get to the track by 6 A.M. for the morning works), what he read (the *Racing Form* and textbooks for the English and American History correspondence courses he was taking toward his high school diploma).

At the very time a fellow sixteen-year-old named Wayne Gretzky—already the most eagerly anticipated child prodigy in the history of any big-league sport—was still playing junior hockey, The Kid had the teen idol market cornered. He recorded an album titled *And Steve Cauthen Sings Too*—a rare failure widely panned for what *People* magazine called his "frail, reedy voice," but that at least proved he was human. More telling, he was entertaining bids from publishers for his authorized biography, which would be authored by respected sportswriter Pete Axthelm and titled—what else?—*The Kid*. It was on one of his Sunday jaunts to Santa Anita that Cauthen had met Swifty Lazar, the high-powered literary and showbiz agent who represented everyone from Humphrey Bogart to Ernest Hemingway to Richard Nixon. Lazar, who at five foot three was himself a jockey-sized horse owner, wasted no time signing and promoting The Kid. "He's one of a kind," raved Lazar. "When will we see another like him? He's going to tell his life story at *sixteen*. The endorsement offers pour in daily, they're in the millions. He's got dignity, poise, perception. Ninety-five pounds on a horse. On the rail, through horses. Fearless. Good-looking."

*   *   *

On May 1, 1977, The Kid celebrated his seventeenth birthday—still too young to vote, to drink, even to place a bet on a horse in New York State. But the boy, who had not even begun to shave, was about to grow up in a hurry.

On May 27, the prince of the bug boys was scheduled to graduate from his apprenticeship. Although he had already proved himself by winning his share of stakes races—in which apprentices must forfeit their bug and get no weight advantage over journeyman jockeys—the skeptics maintained that his dominance would disappear along with his five-pound allowance.

The hardboots also warned about another rite of passage that the apprentice had yet to face, what Arcaro considered the final initiation into that exclusive club of genuine race riders. "Let's not put Steve Cauthen on a pedestal yet," Arcaro cautioned from the highest perch. "The hazards of racing lie ahead. If he rides long enough, he's going to have spills, and you never know how he will react. Some jockeys can't take the physical shocks of injuries. Don't start telling me how great a jock is until he's broken his collarbone about five times."

On May 23, as New York's Big Wheel turned from the asphalt jungle to the leafy suburbs for the opening day of Belmont Park's spring meet, Cauthen would be put to that test. Bay Streak, his mount in the fourth race, suddenly snapped a front leg just as he was turning into the stretch on the lead and went down. The young jockey was thrown to the turf and trampled instantly by Velasquez's onrushing mount in a gruesome three-horse spill that resulted in both of their horses being destroyed. Barely conscious when he was carted off the grass, Cauthen was hospitalized with a severe concussion, a broken arm, two fractured fingers, some cracked ribs, lacerations requiring twenty-five stitches—and the psychological scar of his first serious spill.

Two days later, a swarm of microphones and cameras surrounded him as he was leaving the hospital's pediatric wing in a wheelchair, a slouching figure looking tinier than ever with his mother by his side, a cast on his right arm, and stitches and purplish bruises on his boyish face.

"What happened?" one of the reporters pressed him.

"Horse snapped a leg," he mumbled as he was wheeled out of the hospital lobby, succinct as ever.

Recuperating weeks faster than doctors had ordered, he returned to Belmont Park a month to the day after the spill, raring to show that he hadn't lost his magic touch or his steely nerve. Immediately met by a media mob even bigger than the indomitable Seattle Slew had drawn there twelve days earlier for his Belmont Stakes triumph and Triple Crown coronation, Cauthen shrugged off any suggestion that he might be gun-shy by cracking, "I've been falling on my head since I was two."

As befit his storybook career, he then got right up on a horse with the cosmically fitting name of Little Miracle—a four-year-old Harbor View homebred who happened to be Affirmed's half-brother, another chestnut son of Won't Tell You and grandson of Raise a Native. And as so often happens in fairy tales, Cauthen went on to drive Little Miracle through a tight opening between horses in the stretch and win his comeback race going away. Then he calmly handled the horde of cameras, microphones, and notebooks that stalked him into the teeming winner's circle. When two rival TV crews jockeying for position got into a pitched battle over camera locations, the bemused object of all this attention admonished the combatants. "Be patient," Cauthen lectured, "it's a virtue."

Just three days later, The Kid would come of age once and for all when he lost his bug, which had been extended by the spill's injuries until after he could resume riding. For the past year, while he was shattering all apprenticeship records with 524 winners and $4.3 million in purse earnings, rivals had complained that giving him a five-pound weight allowance was like "a license to steal," akin to granting major-league baseball hit king Pete Rose four strikes every at-bat. "Let's see how it goes," Cordero challenged, "when he loses his bug, when he's riding in tough competition all summer, when maybe he goes a few days without a winner."

Now that the weight allowance was gone, the big test would be whether Cauthen could prove that he didn't really need the advantage considered to be worth a length in most races, that he could keep beating journeyman jockeys on equal terms, that he could continue getting the quality mounts that trainers had been giving him. Many a hot apprentice before him had flashed like a shooting star, disappearing as fast as his bug. For a cautionary tale, Cauthen had only to look at George Martens, who had outpolled him to win the 1976 Eclipse Award as the nation's top apprentice but was already sinking into obscurity his first year as a journeyman jockey. Now Cauthen was determined to prove he wouldn't wind up with the same fate.

In his first start as a full-fledged journeyman jockey, well aware that every trainer would be scrutinizing his every move that day at Belmont, Cauthen rode a claimer named Crab Grass around four horses in the stretch to win going away. Then he proceeded to win the next two races on the program handily with the same patented here-comes-the-kid stretch runs. After Cauthen hopped off his third straight winner, having passed his biggest test and silenced the skeptics, Lenny Goodman could be seen lighting up one of his victory cigars. "Tell all the people who've been wondering,"

Goodman cracked with a smirk, "that the kid and I won't have to look for a new line of work for a while."

The loss of the bug notwithstanding, Goodman continued to line up classy mounts and The Kid kept winning on them. As an apprentice, Cauthen had won one in every four races. Now, as a journeyman, he was winning once every five times out—and still running away with the jockey standings. No one could deny now that he was indeed a bona fide race rider. More important, it was clear that he would have no trouble continuing to get mounts, continuing to get the classy horses from the top trainers.

Among those trainers lining up for his services was Laz Barrera.

*   *   *

One frigid morning early the previous December, Barrera had been taking care of business as usual in his Belmont Park barn—home of the nation's top stable led by 1976 Kentucky Derby winner Bold Forbes—when he spotted Lenny Goodman headed in his direction with a big cigar clenched in his teeth and a young boy at his side wearing a camel-hair newsboy cap, looking like two characters out of a Dickens novel. "Oh," the trainer thought, "some friend of Lenny's must have sent his little kid to see Bold Forbes."

Barrera reached out to shake the agent's hand, smiled, and said benevolently, "I'd be glad to meet this little kid—"

"No," Goodman cut in, "this isn't just somebody's kid. This is my new rider."

"Hoo, Lenny, you gonna go to jail for this," Barrera laughed. "This kid looks like he's twelve."

Steve Cauthen was now on the personal radar of the trainer who had burst into national prominence the same year as the boy wonder had. That winter, Barrera began keeping a close eye on Cauthen's races. The trainer liked what he saw: not just a jockey, but a true horseman. Horses may not have remembered what Cauthen looked like, but they certainly recognized who he was the minute he hopped up on their backs. He was a finesse rider whose cues were so subtle that you couldn't see them, only their results. He got his mounts to do whatever he wanted without ever getting into a battle. All of which made him Barrera's kind of rider.

The following May 24, the day Cauthen's harrowing spill was splashed across banner headlines as the lead story of every sports section in New York, his name also appeared in agate type in the Belmont entries for that afternoon's fourth race—as the jockey slated to ride Affirmed in the two-year-old's maiden outing. As fate would have it, Cauthen spent that day hospitalized while Affirmed's ride went to another apprentice: the colt's regular exercise rider, Bernie Gonzalez. With Cauthen still convalescing three weeks later, Affirmed's second ride went to Cordero, a longtime Barrera favorite who had ridden Bold Forbes to glory a year earlier. Cordero would ride Affirmed twice in a row, then Pincay would substitute when the colt was shipped to California for his fourth race. Now that both of those established stars had opted not to ride Affirmed in the Sanford Stakes at Saratoga, Barrera decided to offer the mount to a jockey who might stay in the irons "forever."

Cauthen, who had by this time been riding regularly for the trainer, made perfect sense. "I know Cauthen is young, but I take a chance," Barrera said. "It is very important to have the same guy ride your good horse all the time. When you take a rider off to use another, it drives the horse crazy." When Barrera approached Goodman, the agent didn't hesitate to agree to the "forever" commitment.

For his part, Cauthen jumped at the opportunity. Not only would he be riding for Barrera, one of the top trainers, but he'd be doing it in a stakes race.

Having conquered Aqueduct and then Belmont, Cauthen was ready to step up to the third spoke of New York State's Big Wheel: Saratoga, America's oldest and quaintest racetrack as well as host to racing's most prestigious meet. Unlike those other big tracks, Saratoga's cozy ambience put the fans and jockeys in intimately close contact. The path from the jocks' room to the paddock took riders right through the crowds, allowing fans to see the jockeys up close and to maybe even get autographs. That tradition posed a unique conundrum for a celebrity like Cauthen, who was besieged by autograph seekers wherever he walked on the hallowed grounds. He would pause to sign as many autographs as he could, but sometimes he would have to keep walking and focus on the ride to come. Despite the efforts of the Pinkerton guard accompanying him through the crush, fans would occasionally grab at him, hang on to his silks, even trip him. He would run this gauntlet before and after up to nine races a day, which was a little like a major-league ballplayer meeting the public and signing autographs between every inning.

Early in Saratoga's 114th annual meet, the teen phenom reached a milestone in the Whitney Stakes, one of America's most prestigious races for older handicappers, by riding Nearly on Time to an easy front-running win over a field that featured Forego, the three-time reigning Horse of the Year. It was Cauthen's three hundredth New York winner of 1977, breaking the record that Velasquez had set the previous year over a full twelve months.

A few days later, Cauthen met the horse who would carry him into posterity.

Leading up to the Sanford, Barrera asked Cauthen to ride several works on Affirmed so the jockey could get a feel for the horse. Cauthen liked the way the colt looked and moved. But it didn't take long for him to get an introduction to Affirmed's lazy side. The colt would gallop in the morning, but he wasn't going to do anything he didn't need to do. He'd just lumber along at a reasonable clip.

On the day of the race, the Wolfsons visited with Affirmed in the morning as was their custom, Patrice giving the colt a big hug and telling him just how wonderful he was. When afternoon came, they walked over to the paddock to watch the colt being saddled. When Barrera boosted Cauthen up, Patrice was struck by how young and unfinished both the colt and the jockey looked. "They look like babies," she thought.

As Cauthen and Affirmed headed off to the track, the Wolfsons walked up to their box, which was located just behind the one Patrice's mother had been occupying for years. Part of what made Saratoga so enjoyable for Patrice was the proximity of extended family. It was one place she could share the big moments with her mother, just over the back of a box seat.

At the bell, Affirmed broke alertly with Cauthen but galloped at a relaxed pace, allowing two others—Tilt Up, who had gone off as the co-favorite with Affirmed, and the sprinter Jet Diplomacy—to set the early fractions. Halfway around the turn, Affirmed started to lug out, but Cauthen was able to bring him back in the stretch and then asked him to get serious. The colt perked up and turned it on, flying by the leaders down the middle of the track to win by two and three-quarters lengths. His time for the six furlongs, 1:09⅗, was only a fraction off the stakes record. While it wasn't exactly like being on a rocket ship, Cauthen was impressed. "This is a really neat little horse," he said to himself.

Pleased with the outcome, Barrera figured he'd finally found his "forever" jockey. He asked Cauthen to ride the colt again the following week—in the Hopeful Stakes.

Affirmed and Steve Cauthen at Saratoga (Bob Coglianese)

CHAPTER 9

The Battle Joined

THE VENERATED SPORTSWRITER RED SMITH ONCE FAMOUSLY OFFERED these directions to Saratoga Race Course: "From New York City, you drive north for about 175 miles, turn left on Union Avenue and go back 100 years." With the Victorian charm of its old wooden clubhouse, its quaint candy-striped awnings, and its cozy elm-shaded paddock, Saratoga transports everyone back to a bygone era when blue-blooded swells fashionably came to the races in horse-drawn carriages. The oldest and most storied sporting venue in America, the timeless track had opened during the bloodiest throes of the Civil War—in August 1863, just a month after the Battle of Gettysburg—and then got stuck in a time warp of straw boaters and Dixieland bands.

For all the tradition and nostalgia steeping its hallowed grounds, however, the spotlight during Saratoga's racing season has forever focused not on the past but firmly on the future. By night, the rich and famous bid millions in the nation's premier yearling sale to buy horseflesh and hopes; and by day, at the track where they rub shoulders with $2 horseplayers in a curious mingling of high society and low culture, all binoculars are on the lookout for that special two-year-old capable of inspiring Derby dreams. It's no coincidence that the grand finale of Saratoga's annual summer meet is not its marquee stakes for established stars, but rather its most prestigious featured race for two-year-old hopefuls. This is the only stakes race not named after a horse, a person, a place, or a thing. Instead, it is named for a feeling, for the passion shared by anyone who has ever bred or bought a young Thoroughbred racehorse: the Hopeful.

On the last Saturday in August 1977, as the dawn broke over the spa town and the morning mist hung over the track and shrouded the Victorian spires of its creaky wooden grandstand, no one had higher hopes than John Veitch.

The Calumet trainer had been very much looking forward to the seventy-third running of the Hopeful Stakes. Over the past several months, Alydar had grown a little taller and had put on even more muscle. The colt had won the Sapling decisively and was looking strong in his morning works. Even more in his favor was the fact that the Hopeful would be a step up at six and a half furlongs. That extra half a furlong might work to Alydar's advantage. Veitch had always expected his big colt's performance to improve with increasing distance. Now, on the morning of the race, the trainer figured he had done all he could to prepare his blossoming star for the big time.

For Affirmed, the Hopeful represented a step up not only in distance, but also in class. This was his first foray into the top tier of stakes races: Grade I, the highest level of events designated for superior racing stock. Alydar had already broken through to win a Grade I stakes race with the Sapling. Now Affirmed, fresh off his win in the Grade II Sanford, was ready to join Alydar in taking their first big step on the road to the Kentucky Derby, the grandest Grade I stakes race of them all. The star-studded roster of future legends that had proclaimed their coming of age by winning the Hopeful as two-year-olds boasted the likes of Man o' War, Whirlaway, Native Dancer, Nashua, and, just five years earlier, Secretariat. Not even those who breathlessly touted Alydar as the second coming of Secretariat were quite ready to put him in that fast company just yet. If handicapping horses is considered a fool's game, nowhere is that more true than with the green two-year-olds who are the least predictable of all. By the time the bettors had spoken, Alydar was sent to the post as the even-money favorite, with Affirmed the 5-to-2 second choice.

Patrice Wolfson watched, with trepidation, as Steve Cauthen rode Affirmed onto the track with the four other colts in the post parade. This was the first time he would face Alydar since the Great American, and though her colt had improved greatly since then, the racing world was abuzz with talk of the Calumet star and how he was already a sure Derby contender.

Aside from their chestnut color, the two colts couldn't have looked more different as they took their positions in the starting gate. To Patrice, it seemed as if Affirmed, who always had looked a little light, had gotten even smaller as he lowered himself, head down, awaiting the bell. In contrast, Alydar looked huge in the gate, standing alert on the inside post position, puffing himself up.

At the break, Alydar swerved into Tilt Up, who in turn bumped Darby Creek Road. Jockey Eddie Maple had no choice but to settle Alydar into his usual spot at the back of the pack, while Affirmed broke cleanly to the lead on the outside. The pace was fast enough that Cauthen chose to rate Affirmed and let Tilt Up and Darby Creek Road pass going into the back-stretch, content to just stay close and bide his time around the turn. Correctly figuring that Alydar was about to challenge the frontrunners coming off the turn, Cauthen asked Affirmed to gradually pick up the pace and start making a move of his own. As they thundered down the stretch, Cauthen was struck by how Affirmed "looked the leader in the eye and just went on." With an eighth of a mile to go, Affirmed blew past Tilt Up, Alydar in hot pursuit. The two chestnuts powered away from the field as a team: Affirmed keeping a head just in front, Alydar driving hard on the far outside. With a sixteenth to go, Cauthen tapped Affirmed on the shoulder and felt the colt surge forward "like he was shot out of a cannon." Glancing over, the jockey was stunned to see Alydar and Maple accelerating right along with them. But Affirmed dug in and inched away from his rival to win by half a length in a stakes-record 1:15⅖, less than half a second off the track record.

As he made his way to the winner's circle, Cauthen reflected on what had just happened. The "rocket ship" acceleration he had felt on Affirmed was like nothing he'd ever experienced on any of his previous two thousand mounts. He knew he'd found a "special" horse. "I'm never giving up this horse," he said to himself as they hit the winner's circle.

Waiting for them there was a beaming Patrice. She was ecstatic that her boy had won, but what made this triumph resonate even more deeply was the memory of how her Hail To Reason had romped off with the same race seventeen years earlier. This was such a heartfelt moment that she really pushed for her husband to join her in the winner's circle for the first time. Lou resisted for a bit because he didn't like being the center of attention, but eventually she prevailed. She took his concession as a sign both of his love for her and of his admiration for what their little horse had just accomplished. Affirmed had proven that he could hold his own and that he had heart. Patrice and Lou both realized now that he might be a very special horse.

Laz Barrera, too, thought he might have a budding star. Until now, Affirmed had been so anonymous that even his own trainer kept confusing him with a three-year-old stablemate named Affiliate. "All the time I find myself entering Affiliate in a stakes race that Affirmed belongs in, or writing down 'Affirmed' when I mean 'Affiliate,'" he complained. For that, he could blame Patrice's penchant for naming horses after her mother's beloved Affectionately. Watching Affirmed leave the winner's circle after the Hopeful, Barrera told a reporter, "Steve Cauthen rode this horse like he was born on him. Affiliate was named the outstanding two-year-old of the Hollywood Park meeting and now, with this win, he has to be the best two-year-old anywhere." Barrera paused, catching himself, and shook his head. "Dammit," he sighed, "this isn't Affiliate—it's Affirmed!"

*　　*　　*

If Affirmed had just gone a long way toward finally making a name for himself, he still needed to prove that the Hopeful upset wasn't just a fluke. He would have to wait only two weeks to get the chance—in a rematch with Alydar in the Futurity Stakes at Belmont Park. This time, having won two of their three meetings in what was already being hyped by turf writers as a real rivalry, Affirmed would go to the post as the favorite, at 6-to-5.

With Alydar the second betting choice at 3-to-2, an underdog for the first time in his seven career starts, John Veitch was feeling the pressure. The only consolation the trainer could take from the Hopeful defeat was that Saratoga had also been the setting for the only loss of Man o' War's storied career—to a fellow two-year-old aptly named Upset. But that didn't soothe any of his disappointment or angst. When Veitch reviewed the Hopeful with Maple, the jockey voiced his concern about Alydar's refusal to switch leads in his races despite the fact that he always did so when asked in the morning. Maple was concerned that Alydar would tire if he spent the entire race on one lead. With the Belmont Futurity representing another step up at seven furlongs, the jockey was especially eager to fix the problem before it became a bigger issue as the races on the road to the Derby incrementally lengthened.

"This horse is not going to run as good as he can without switching leads," Maple warned Veitch.

The trainer dismissively countered that there was plenty of time to work on the problem before the Derby. "He'll switch the first Saturday in May," Veitch said curtly.

Veitch was far more concerned with the second Saturday in September. For the Belmont Futurity, as in their last showdown, the two rivals had scared away all but three other competitors. This time, however, the contest was being billed as a match race right from the start, with Alydar drawing the inside post position 1 and Affirmed right next to him in 2.

"Don't worry about being on the lead," Barrera told Cauthen while hoisting the jockey into the saddle. "Wait for number one."

Following the trainer's instructions and his own patient riding style, Cauthen rated Affirmed after breaking sharply and tucked him into second up the backstretch behind the longshot Rough Sea, with Maple steadily moving Alydar from his usual last-place start up to third. Heading into the turn, Cauthen decided to send Affirmed to the lead on the rail. Maple responded instantly by making a move of his own, easing Alydar off the rail and roaring up alongside Affirmed. As they swung through the turn, the two colts battled for the lead—Affirmed driving on the inside, Alydar glued to his right shoulder, the rest of the field fading behind in their wake. At the top of the homestretch, Alydar poked his head in front. But Affirmed would have none of it and dug in. He accelerated, drew even, and then pushed his head back in front. Thundering down the stretch, the colts dueled for the lead, Alydar surging, then Affirmed answering as the finish line loomed closer. In one last desperate attempt, Alydar lunged for the line. The two colts crossed under the wire together, eleven lengths clear of their closest pursuer, and it took a photo finish to determine that Affirmed had held on to beat Alydar by a scant nose.

Patrice Wolfson felt a warm glow of pride and happiness as she and Lou made their way down from their box to the track. To Patrice's surprise, Lou, overcome by the moment, stepped up to their colt, took the lead shank from the groom, and proudly led Affirmed into the winner's circle. For the first time, the Wolfsons were allowing themselves to think that maybe, just maybe, they had a Derby horse. Affirmed and Cauthen were each celebrating a personal milestone: the first career victory in a $100,000 race. "Affirmed never gave up, even though he was headed," Cauthen marveled.

"He's a fighter," Barrera agreed. "I wasn't worried when he was headed because he runs best with a horse alongside him. The other horse is a fighter, too. They were like Joe Frazier and Muhammad Ali."

The race was a huge blow to John Veitch, who felt like a prizefighter reeling from a one-two combination. Having lost two straight showdowns to Affirmed and three of their four meetings, the trainer needed a counterpunch. He was still sure he had the best two-year-old in America, but he couldn't figure out what was wrong. Though he had tried just about everything he'd learned over the years, his colt was still coming up short. As Veitch mulled it over, he realized there was one option he hadn't yet explored: a jockey change. Perhaps with a stronger and more aggressive rider, Alydar might be able to summon that little bit of extra drive he would need to turn the tables on Affirmed.

Veitch reached out to a jockey who already knew Alydar well: Jorge Velasquez.

*   *   *

Back in Panama, Jorge Velasquez had grown up dirt poor in Chepo, a small farming town thirty miles northeast of Panama City. With his parents having separated before he was a year old, the boy was raised by his father's sister, Francisca, in a house with dirt floors, bamboo walls, and a thatched roof. Jorge was barely eight when he started working full-time in the fields, picking beans and tomatoes for up to a dollar a day. When he got a job four years later as a delivery boy for a bakery that paid him not in cash but in bread, it was the first time he could remember not going to sleep hungry. He had just turned thirteen when a friend suggested that he use his diminutive size—five foot three and one hundred pounds—as a ticket out of poverty by becoming a jockey.

When he told his family about the idea of taking up a perilous sport that was notoriously rougher in Panama than in America, his Aunt Francisca—the adoptive mother to whom he'd grown very close—hit him over the head with a pot. Undaunted, young Jorge resolved to ride races "as a way to get my family out of poverty." He moved to Panama City and worked a few months in his father's butcher shop before finally landing a job with a trainer at the tiny country's lone racetrack, the Hipódromo Presidente Remón. On the backside of the Panama City track, Jorge spent long days working for nothing but the experience—and devoting himself to learning the jockey's trade.

The government had just set up a jockey school at the track as part of its vocational training program, and Jorge immediately signed up. Running the school was an old ex-jockey named Bolivar Moreno, who would conduct classes in the stables for about a dozen boys. "He's a good teacher," Jorge decided, breaking into a smile, "but he'd be better if he have horses." In this novel jockey school without horses, Moreno would have his pupils sit astride barrels, holding makeshift reins and putting their feet in makeshift stirrups all fashioned out of rope. On those barrels, Jorge and his classmates learned the basics of their chosen craft—how to keep low, how to use the whip, how to hand-ride, and all the other necessary techniques in a curriculum that Moreno based on Eddie Arcaro's five-part 1957 *Sports Illustrated* series titled "The Art of Race Riding." Once the students had gotten the hang of it, they would ride simulated races on their barrels during which the professor would bark instructions like a track announcer: "We're going into the gate now . . . It's going to be three-quarters of a mile . . . Now you're breaking out of there . . . Rate the first part . . . And sprint the last quarter."

While awaiting the opportunity to try out those lessons in a real race, all the students worked long hours on the backside—mucking stalls, walking hots, grooming and feeding horses. Since they received no pay for all their labors, Jorge had to make ends meet by pitching pennies, eventually becoming so skilled that he could win two or three dollars a day. After the trainer he worked for gave him a broken-down racehorse to ride and care for, Jorge went from barn to barn panhandling hay and oats for the big bay with the bad leg. "He got leftovers," Jorge would later recall, "but I learned to ride on that horse." Hungry in every sense of the word and determined to get ahead, Jorge and the other aspiring jockeys all hustled trainers for a chance to gallop horses in the mornings. Not that any amount of exercise rides could prepare them for the trial by fire that was racing in Panama, a throwback to America's Wild West ride-'em-cowboy days before patrol cameras and eagle-eyed stewards began scrutinizing races for jockey infractions.

Upon turning sixteen, Jorge Velasquez was finally old enough to get his apprentice jockey's license. But he had such trouble getting any mounts at the Hipódromo that he considered quitting and crawling home to Aunt

Francisca in Chepo. When he finally did convince a trainer to give him a shot, Velasquez demonstrated in his first race just how green he was. Early in the race, his mount was dawdling so much that a passing jockey glanced over, noticed loosely flapping reins, and actually yelled at him, "Boy, pick up the reins!" Velasquez shortened his reins, connecting with his mount's mouth for the first time. The horse grabbed the bit and took off. That was exactly the kind of on-the-job training Velasquez needed, though in future races he would have to do it without any professional courtesy from opposing jockeys.

Panama was notorious for being a brutally tough training ground. The only break an apprentice like Velasquez got was that every few days the card included one race restricted only to rookies—although, as it turned out, those events were the roughest of all, pitting the jockey school graduates against one another in showdowns to weed out all but the wiliest and hungriest. From that Darwinian crucible, it was Velasquez who emerged as the track's sensation of 1963, breaking all of Braulio Baeza's apprentice records.

Just before Velasquez had arrived at the track for its jockey school two years earlier, Baeza had left to ride in the United States—the latest in a growing line of Panamanian jockeys to flourish in The Land of Opportunity. In the mid-1950s, Manny Ycaza had paved the way for the Panamanian invasion with a flourish, captivating American railbirds with a flashy charisma, a fiery temper, and a reckless style that earned him not only numerous stakes wins but also record suspensions for rough riding. Baeza introduced Americans to the exact opposite type of Panamanian rider, from his stately ramrod-straight erectness in the saddle during the post parade to his icy-cool countenance and his smooth, rhythmic style as he rode to the top of the U.S. racing charts. After he had been hired by the venerable Florida owner Fred Hooper and left for America's greener pastures in 1960, Baeza became the role model Velasquez emulated for his dignified character: quiet, businesslike, compassionate.

Velasquez also copied Baeza's success on the track, riding 347 winners in three years during Panama's short 150-day racing seasons and making $500 a week. Having survived that trial by fire, he longed for the chance to try his luck and skill in the United States, where the homegrown jockeys as a group lacked the burning desire that drove the young Panamanians' hunger for wealth and fame.

In the summer of 1965, Ramon Navarro, the Panamanian trainer who had first tipped Hooper on Baeza, did the same for Velasquez. Hooper imported Velasquez to the United States and set him up as a contract rider based in New Jersey. Only nineteen, Velasquez wasted little time establishing himself as the dominant jockey on the Jersey racing circuit. In 1966, his first full season there, he won 300 races to rank second among all jockeys in North America and then proclaimed to his agent, "I want to be the leading rider of America." True to his desire, he then went out and racked up 438 winners to top the 1967 list. Though Velasquez longed to prove himself against stiffer competition, Hooper insisted that his jockey continue to ride in New Jersey. The day after their three-year contract expired, Velasquez packed up his tack and headed for New York to test himself against the best.

It didn't take long for Jorge Velasquez to make a name for himself on New York's Big Wheel. He instantly developed a reputation for winning photo finishes. "The secret to the photo finish," he explained, "is to have the nerves to wait until the last sixteenth of a mile. Patience, patience. Wait, wait. Every rider knows where the finish line is, but the trick is to give your horse that *push* exactly at the right time—just when he hits the line. You give him the last push, you give him his head, and he drops it down on the wire. The horse with his head down crossing the finish line usually gets the picture."

During his first full season in New York, Velasquez was in the picture enough to lead all jockeys nationally on the 1969 money list with $2,542,315 in purse earnings—surpassing the five-time reigning champion, Braulio Baeza himself. It's telling that the next year Velasquez would be supplanted by yet another countryman: Laffit Pincay Jr., who would go on to top the money list the following four years, eventually break Willie Shoemaker's all-time record for career winners with 9,530, and have the Panama City jockey school named after him as its most successful graduate. Pincay, like Baeza the son of a jockey, was one day younger than Velasquez, and the two teens had been classmates for a couple of years at the jockey school. Clearly, nothing got lost in the translation of the school's motto from Spanish: "Panama is the cradle of the best jockeys in the world."

As their underdeveloped country of barely a million citizens started to dominate the U.S. jockey standings, Velasquez and Pincay together were now leading the latest tidal wave of the Panamanian invasion. Pincay, who like Velasquez and Baeza before him was imported to the United States by Hooper after a tip from Navarro, would rival Shoemaker for supremacy on the West Coast. At the same time, Velasquez would quietly rival the flashy Angel Cordero for East Coast supremacy.

When Velasquez first came to New York during the summer of 1968, he stayed at Cordero's Queens home for months while acclimating to the culture shock of the Big Apple and the Big Wheel. Comfortably settling in to the lifestyle and Americanizing the pronunciation of Jorge from "Hor-hay" to "George," Velasquez found himself at the top of his game and his profession.

In many circles, he was regarded as the finest craftsman riding in the United States. While other great jockeys each possessed a signature skill—Shoemaker's touch, Pincay's strength, Cordero's aggressiveness—Velasquez personified what horsemen call "a complete rider." He was good at everything, the consummate technician and tactician. Between 1971 and 1976, he reigned as the leading New York rider four times, winning the Triple Tiara for three-year-old fillies aboard Chris Evert in 1974. All of which earned him a place of honor in the jockeys' room at Belmont and Aqueduct: a corner locker that was the equivalent of a senior executive's corner office.

That's where he was, late in the fall of 1976, when a sixteen-year-old apprentice named Steve Cauthen first entered the jocks' room at The Big A and soon received the honor of an end locker catty-cornered from Velasquez's. "In the jockeys' room," Cauthen would recall, "Georgie was in the corner opposite the valet I ended up with; I had Sully, and he had Reno. Georgie took me under his wing right from the beginning. He was always very friendly. There's a camaraderie in the room among pretty much everybody, but there's guys you feel drawn to, and I felt a friendship and closeness with Georgie because he was nice to me. I felt accepted right from day one."

For his part, Velasquez marveled at how maturely the kid he called "Stevie" handled New York's fiercer competition right from the start and how humbly he handled the spotlight that was soon thrust on him during his record-smashing winter. Minutes after Cauthen won a stakes race for the first time just two weeks into his Big Apple introduction, Velasquez and Cordero, the star veterans he most admired, made a mock presentation of helmet and goggles to him for beating their favorites on a longshot. Before long, Cauthen would be demolishing Velasquez's New York record of 299 winners in a year as well as Cordero's national record of $4.7 million in annual purse earnings.

"How can you deny a guy like Stevie?" Velasquez would say with a shrug and a welcoming smile. "You've got to take him under your wing. He respects people and pays attention, and he learns fast. And I was thrilled to have him in the room because soon all the cameras and everyone were following him instead of following me all the time."

Fourteen years Cauthen's senior at the age of thirty, Velasquez went from being a role model to being a mentor. They developed a fast friendship that did nothing to diminish their fierce competitiveness on the track. In the jocks' room, where they liked to pass the downtime in the mornings by playing spirited games of Ping-Pong, Cauthen was no match for Velasquez. On the track at Aqueduct, though, Cauthen was running away with the New York jockey standings at the expense of the defending champion.

Not long afterward, on the opening day of Belmont's 1977 spring meet, Velasquez again found himself following Cauthen, this time into the stretch of the fateful race that would end horrifically and interrupt both of their seasons. It all happened so quickly that Velasquez had no chance to react. He saw Cauthen's horse, Bay Streak, suddenly go down, and before Velasquez knew it, his own mount, Volney, smashed into Bay Streak and crashed to the turf. As it was happening, all Velasquez's mind had time to do was to invoke the patron saint of his Chepo hometown in Panama: "Aye! San Cristobal! Protect me!" Knocked unconscious, he would be unaware how lucky he was that the horse behind him narrowly missed crushing him while crashing over Volney. Velasquez and Cauthen would be rushed to the hospital with concussions and broken bones. One of the first questions Cauthen asked the emergency room doctors was about the condition of Velasquez, who was having his broken ankle and heel set in a cast before being discharged while the youngster was admitted to the hospital's pediatric ward for two days.

If not for the gruesome spill that linked them in the headlines, serendipity would have put Cauthen on Affirmed and Velasquez on Alydar right from the start of both horses' racing careers. But as fate would have it, their respective injuries precluded Cauthen from riding Affirmed's first race and Velasquez from riding Alydar's.

Not long before the spill, John Veitch had called Velasquez's agent and asked whether his client could come out to Belmont early one morning to work Alydar because the trainer already thought this was his Derby horse and he wanted the jockey's opinion. Velasquez jumped at the chance to breeze Calumet's great chestnut hope for three furlongs. Starting behind three other colts, Alydar flew right by them and, even more impressive, Velasquez felt as if his mount was doing it easily and effortlessly. Afterward, the jockey came back and told Veitch, "This is our Derby horse. I like him very much."

Velasquez started getting on his new "Derby horse" every morning at Belmont. "Before we went out on the track," he would fondly recall, "I'd let him stop and look around and watch the horses going by galloping and working. And when he was ready, he'd turn his head, open his mouth, and I'd drop a sugar in his mouth. Then he'd drop his head and we'd go to work. Every time he was being cooled off in the shedrow while I was coming back from working other horses and he heard my voice, he would drag the hot-walker around to where I was, looking for sugar."

One morning, Velasquez brought his wife, Margarita, to see his new Derby horse. "He's crazy about me," the jockey beamed to her like a proud father. As they got out of the car, Velasquez started calling out to the big colt from behind a tree near the barn. "Hey, Champ!" the jockey yelled, jumping the gun somewhat in his pet name for a horse who had yet to run a single race. Looking around but unable to locate the source of the disembodied voice, Alydar started bucking and kicking. Hearing the commotion, Veitch emerged from the barn, spotted Velasquez, and told him he'd better come from behind the trees before Alydar hurt himself.

In just a few short weeks, Velasquez felt he and the horse had already "developed a nice, close relationship," and he was looking forward to riding Alydar's first race. But the broken ankle sidelined Velasquez until just six days before Alydar's debut, by which time the mount had already gone to Eddie Maple. Velasquez could only watch, wistfully, as Maple rode Alydar in the colt's first seven races.

In the meantime, Velasquez could at least console himself by riding Alydar's older half-sister, Our Mims. With Calumet's star filly mired in a four-race losing streak going into the summer, Veitch decided to switch jockeys and put the crafty Panamanian aboard Our Mims. Velasquez rode the big bay to three major stakes wins, virtually locking up the 1977 three-year-old filly championship by Labor Day. Once Veitch decided it was to time to make a similar jockey change on Alydar, there was never any doubt whom he would tap. He called Velasquez's agent and offered the coveted mount.

Better late than never, destiny had been fulfilled: the two jockeys who were supposed to start the horses in the spring now finally would both be in the irons squaring off for the first time—in a fall showdown in the biggest juvenile race of the year, the Champagne Stakes.

*   *   *

Just as the rivalry was starting to heat up, Lou Wolfson tried to pour cold water on it. As far as he was concerned, the budding rivalry should have ended right after Affirmed outdueled Alydar by a nostril in the nail-biting Belmont Futurity. "I was satisfied that Affirmed was the better horse, and I didn't think these two good colts should keep racing against each other," he explained. So he hatched a takeover plan to purchase Alydar from Calumet and run him in different races than Affirmed. He asked Leslie Combs, the renowned syndicator who owned Spendthrift Farm, if Alydar could be bought. Combs said he would find out from the Markeys, with whom he was close friends. "Go ahead and pay any price you want to pay," Wolfson instructed Combs, "and I'll take any part of the colt you want me to." Combs called him back with bad news: the Markeys weren't interested in selling, at any price. The Affirmed-Alydar rivalry was now an unstoppable force shifting into high gear.

By the fall of 1977, not even the crustiest of old-timers could recall any rivalry this heated between two-year-olds. Scouring their memories and the record books, the closest that turf historians could come were the three 1930 showdowns between Equipoise, the dark chestnut nicknamed "The Chocolate Soldier," and Twenty Grand at the dawn of the Great Depression. Half a century after waging two of the most rousing stretch duels in the annals of racing, that pair of future Hall of Famers had nothing on Affirmed and Alydar. Never before had two such brilliant two-year-olds as Affirmed and Alydar, both clearly superior to all their contemporaries, hooked up in so many thrilling head-to-head battles.

Their fifth meeting, in the Champagne Stakes, figured to be yet another one. The richest race for two-year-olds at $134,000, the Champagne represented a step up to a mile for both rivals. But more than that, it was, for Affirmed, a chance to lock up the juvenile championship and, for Alydar, a shot at redemption.

It was a cloudy, damp mid-October day, and the track at Belmont was sloppy from a rainstorm that had passed through in the morning. Both Affirmed, once again a 6-to-5 favorite, and Alydar, a 3-to-2 second choice, were calm as their teams got them ready in the saddling stalls. After hoisting Velasquez up onto Alydar's back, Veitch gave the jockey some last-minute instructions on how to deal with Affirmed. "I don't think you can sneak up on this horse," the trainer said. "You've got to put yourself in a position where you can just overwhelm him."

At the bell, Affirmed once again broke sharply and then settled back in third while Alydar tucked in fifth. Both bided their time up the backstretch and around the turn until Darby Creek Road began to make a move, swinging around to the outside. Cauthen, too, asked Affirmed to move up, and as the leaders came out of the turn four abreast, the pace quickened. At the top of the stretch, Affirmed surged into the lead, with Darby Creek Road at his hip challenging. Affirmed had his right ear turned toward Darby Creek Road, making sure the challenger couldn't get past him. Fifty feet from the wire, both Affirmed and his rider were stunned to see Alydar, all a blur, blowing by them on the far outside. It was too late for either Affirmed or Cauthen to respond. Alydar flew on to win going away by a length and a quarter.

Despite Veitch's instructions, Velasquez had done what the trainer said couldn't be done: the jockey had indeed snuck up on Affirmed. In the middle of the stretch, Velasquez had pulled Alydar wide from the rail so that he would have room to pass the wall of four horses. Once Velasquez had a clear view to the finish line, he asked Alydar to pour it on and the colt had responded. Affirmed and Cauthen never knew what hit them. "My horse had plenty left," Cauthen would lament afterward, "but he was so busy playing games with Darby Creek Road he never even saw Alydar until it was too late." In Cauthen's mind, it was an aberration. He was still riding the best horse.

Lou Wolfson wasn't so sure. Moments after the race, he turned to Patrice and said, "Sugar, I don't know about your little guy. I don't think he's going to be the horse you think he is." Defending her pet, Patrice rattled off a list of excuses, from the muddy track to the sneak attack. Lou shook his head, unwilling to rationalize away a loss. But Patrice wasn't about to let one race change her mind. She turned to Lou and said firmly, "You just wait."

Back at the Calumet barn, Veitch was ecstatic. He was sure he had finally found the winning formula: the right jockey, the right blinkers, the right training regimen. After winning the race that had determined the two-year-old champion for each of the previous thirteen years, Alydar was now the odds-on favorite for the 1977 award without having to run another step. Veitch could have ended the season then and there. But he wanted another shot at Affirmed, who had won three out of their five meetings. Veitch wanted to even up the score and to prove that the Champagne wasn't a fluke.

After driving Alydar past Affirmed in the stretch of the Champagne Stakes, Jorge Velasquez celebrates the win with a bottle of champagne (Bob Coglianese)

Before Alydar could even be cooled out, Veitch announced that he would enter the colt in the Laurel Futurity two weeks later. "Not with the idea of helping our chance to win the championship, but to give him more experience," he explained. "He'll need all he can get next year." The trainer wanted to make sure that Affirmed was going to show up, so he threw down the gauntlet by challenging Barrera. "They're both equally good colts, but I would think that if he wants the title, he has to go to Laurel and run against us again."

When reporters relayed that challenge to Barrera's barn minutes later, Affirmed's trainer made an immediate change in plans. He had indicated beforehand that the Champagne probably would end Affirmed's 1977 campaign, but now he was ready to pick up the gauntlet.

"If he goes to Laurel, I go."

*   *   *

When Affirmed and Barrera showed up at Laurel Race Course in suburban Baltimore, Alydar and Veitch were waiting and primed. On the strength of Alydar's dominating Champagne finish, bettors had restored him to his favorite's role, at 2-to-5, with Affirmed the second choice in the four-horse field at 7-to-5. In the Laurel Futurity, the two rivals would battle not only to win a stakes race but also to determine the 1977 two-year-old championship.

Veitch was sure the added distance—the Futurity would be both colts' first race around two turns, at a mile and a sixteenth—made Alydar an even stronger choice. At the prerace press conference the day before the main event, he was so confident he was even willing to announce his strategy to Barrera and the world.

"When you're going against a good horse," Veitch proclaimed, "you don't dog 'em and wear them down. You slug 'em and hit them over the head."

Barrera shot a look at Veitch and retorted, "He's not going to come out of the back and hit me over the head no more, because I'm going to wait for him."

In the paddock on race day, after cautioning Cauthen to keep track of where Alydar was every second of the race, Barrera gave his jockey the final instructions: rate Affirmed in the early going, wait for Alydar's inevitable charge, then outduel him down the stretch.

As instructed, Cauthen settled Affirmed in second behind the leader and bided his time, while the slow-starting Alydar lingered a few lengths back. The Calumet colt gradually crept up on Affirmed along the back-stretch and, on the far turn, moved up between the two frontrunners. As the three horses swept around the turn abreast, Cauthen asked his mount to pick up the pace, pushing Affirmed to the front. Velasquez decided the time was right for Alydar to make his move, and they grabbed the lead at the top of the stretch. The two colts pulled away and battled ferociously down the stretch for the lead, Velasquez hitting Alydar left-handed on the rail and Cauthen slapping Affirmed right-handed. With a sixteenth of a mile to go, Affirmed surged and put a nose back in front. As they drove toward the wire, Affirmed inched away to win by a neck.

For Barrera, Cauthen, and the Wolfsons, it was vindication. Barrera was gracious in victory. "There is never a disgrace when one of them loses," he said. The more he would reflect on the race over the next few weeks, the more impressed he was by the heart shown by both horses. "That Laurel Futurity was one of most amazing races ever run. Anytime! Anywhere! Any country!" he would marvel. "They hook up and go at each other like a couple of fighting chickens—only there is no chicken in either of them."

That was small consolation to Veitch. While he understood that Alydar had just run his heart out, the Laurel left Veitch with a bad taste. The only way he could think of to expunge it was to run his colt again. This time, it would be in the Remsen Stakes and there would be no Affirmed. With his nemesis already finished for the year, Alydar was sure to end his season on a positive note. But Eddie Maple and Believe It, the Derby hopeful the jockey had picked up after losing his mount on Alydar, spoiled Veitch's plans by stunning the 3-to-5 favorite in the Remsen at Aqueduct on Thanksgiving weekend. Believe It, a colt Alydar had decisively beaten twice before, built a big early lead that the Calumet star's one late run couldn't overcome in his first attempt at a mile and an eighth, falling two lengths short. The four battles with Affirmed over the previous three months had obviously taken their toll. Both rivals needed a break to recharge for the upcoming road to the Derby.

*   *   *

Racing's most coveted prize—this side of the Kentucky Derby Gold Cup, at least—is the Eclipse Award. Named after the fabled unbeaten eighteenth-century British Thoroughbred whose bloodlines course through almost all modern-day racehorses, the Eclipse Awards honor the sport's leading equine as well as human performers each year. Although Affirmed obviously could not attend the black-tie Eclipse Awards Dinner in a Miami hotel ballroom shortly after New Year's, there were plenty of his human connections on hand to reap the spoils of the surprisingly strong year he had just enjoyed.

In a season when the undefeated Triple Crown winner Seattle Slew was the landslide choice for Horse of the Year, Patrice and Lou Wolfson were thrilled to accept Affirmed's own Eclipse Award—as the champion two-year-old colt, once again outdueling Alydar. Although they fell short of the Eclipse for leading owner, having finished fourth on the earnings list in a year they sold their Ocala farm to cut their losses and liabilities, the Wolfsons took pride in other awards that evidenced the resurgence of their racing stable. Thanks largely to his handling of Harbor View horses, Laz Barrera won the Eclipse Award as America's outstanding trainer for the second straight year, this time earning it by easily topping the money list with $2,715,848 in purses.

Team Affirmed's biggest winner was the smallest honoree: Steve Cauthen, fresh off the most amazing year in the annals of race riding. Cauthen had won $6,151,750 in 1977 purses to obliterate the all-time earnings record by 30 percent and to garner yet another nickname: "The Six Million Dollar Boy," an allusion to the hit TV show *The Six Million Dollar Man*. Despite being sidelined for a full month by injuries, he had won 487 races (including 23 stakes) to become the youngest jockey ever to top the national list. All of which earned Cauthen an unparalleled sweep of both Eclipse Awards for riding—one as the outstanding jockey, the other as the best apprentice. In addition, he won the Eclipse Award of Merit "for his inestimable and far-reaching contribution to Thoroughbred racing."

As the truest measure of his transcendence, Cauthen was named by *Sports Illustrated* as the magazine's 1977 Sportsman of the Year—the only horse racing figure ever so honored. Gracing his second *Sports Illustrated* cover of the year, he appeared noticeably more mature with his arms folded confidently across the flamingo-pink silks of Harbor View Farm. In a year when Reggie Jackson smashed three home runs on three straight pitches in the World Series clincher to rocket the Yankees to their first championship since 1962 and when Pelé capped his incomparable soccer career by elevating the world's most popular sport to new heights in the New World, both superstars were relegated to runners-up behind racing's wunderkind.

Proving that *Sports Illustrated*'s choice was hardly a minority view, Cauthen also was selected as the *Sporting News* Sportsman of the Year and the Associated Press Male Athlete of the Year, the only racing personality on a roster swelled for nearly half a century with the most storied of sports legends. Suddenly, people who didn't know a homestretch from a home run were anxiously watching to see what The Kid would do for an encore.

Whatever he did do in 1978 would be tied intimately with Affirmed and, by extension, Alydar. Although Affirmed had won four of their six showdowns as two-year-olds, the colts were ultimately separated by three photo finishes and a combined total of three feet. As the Winter Book favorites for the 1978 Kentucky Derby, Affirmed opened at 3-to-1 with Alydar right behind at 7-to-2. But those were just odds set by Las Vegas, and there were still miles and months of racing and trash-talking before the colts would meet in Louisville on the first Saturday in May.

Alydar and Jorge Velasquez in the post parade for the Blue Grass Stakes (Keeneland Association)

CHAPTER 10

Collision Course

LIKE A JOYFULLY ANTICIPATED GUEST WHO GREATLY OVERSTAYS HIS WEL-come, the rains in Southern California had settled in and were showing no signs of abating. Week after week in the winter of 1978, rain pelted Santa Anita Park, gushing down gutters, flooding pathways, and drowning the track. Adding to the overall gloom was a damp chill that cut through clothes, biting right to the bone.

Laz Barrera had shipped Affirmed to Santa Anita shortly after the Laurel Futurity figuring that he would get his colt away from "that big monster," Alydar. The move would allow the two horses to prep for the Kentucky Derby on opposite coasts with a full continent between them. But now, as he watched the rain pouring down off the shedrow roofs, Barrera was beginning to question the wisdom of shipping to California. When a Louisville turf writer called Barrera's barn in mid-January to check on Affirmed's progress, the trainer sighed, "He's doing well. He hasn't been training too much because we got rain here for so long and the main track has been most of the time closed." Though that particular day had been relatively dry, Barrera said it had been raining steadily for twenty-seven days and nights.

As gloomy day gave way to gloomy day, Barrera became increasingly disheartened. His colt was missing out on a lot of training. During the heaviest downpours, Affirmed would spend hours just walking the shedrow underneath the overhang. On lighter days, Barrera had him jog around the barn. When the rain would lighten up enough for the track to open, Affirmed was allowed only to take long gallops, his groom greeting him at the end with a handful of towels to dry him off so he wouldn't catch cold. On the rare dry days when the track condition permitted, Barrera would squeeze in a work between races—something he had never done before. The trainer would often come home at night waterlogged as if he "had been out in the sea."

Barrera fretted that if it didn't clear up soon, there wouldn't be enough time to get his colt ready for the Derby. And hearing about all the good weather in Florida—and Alydar's speedy progress on the sundrenched track at Hialeah—didn't help.

$$* \quad * \quad *$$

Alydar was flourishing under the bright Florida sun. After allowing the colt two weeks to rest and recuperate, John Veitch had put him to work, concentrating first on that pesky lead-change problem. It hadn't been a major issue in most of the two-year-old competitions, but with increasingly longer races, the colt's refusal to switch from his left lead to his right was sure to be a handicap—and might even be enough of a problem to give the advantage to Affirmed in the spring classics.

Most horses, like humans, tend to exhibit "handedness" to a greater or lesser degree. Just as people can be left-handed or right-handed, horses will show a preference for the left or right lead almost from the moment they are born. That becomes important in a longer race because the footfalls at the gallop are not symmetrical, and as a result the horse's body is worked a little differently depending on which lead he is on. When galloping on the left lead, the horse begins each stride with his right hind leg hitting the ground while the other three legs are in the air; the left hind leg lands next, followed by the right front leg, and then the left front leg sweeps through the air and lands, giving the appearance of "leading" the stride. The horse is briefly supported by the left front leg, which then pushes off, giving him a moment of suspension in which no leg is in contact with the ground. This means that the leading foreleg, in this case the left, ends up doing a little more work as it sends the horse airborne. The footfalls of a horse on the right lead are the mirror image of the left.

Horses can arc their bodies slightly in the direction of the lead. So a horse will negotiate left turns more easily while on the left lead—which is why racehorses will always be on the left lead going through the turns. Since the left foreleg is doing a little more work while the horse is on its left lead, jockeys will ask their mounts to pick up the right lead on the straightaway to give that left foreleg a bit of a rest.

Problems can arise when horses feel so much more confident and comfortable on one lead that they will fight to stay on it. Alydar, it turned out, was fonder of the left lead than the right. And while he had been willing to pick up the right lead during gallops and works in the morning, he had stubbornly refused to switch during his races as a two-year-old.

Veitch's solution was to start every morning during that winter at Hialeah with a session of figure eights at the gallop. The athletic colt had no problem with the exercise and was soon doing lead changes with such elegance and flair that he reminded the trainer of Baryshnikov going through his leaps and spins in a ballet. Veitch eagerly awaited the colt's next race to see how effective those morning sessions had been.

On February 11, a fit and feisty Alydar entered the starting gate at Hialeah for a seven-furlong allowance race that would serve as a warm-up for his first stakes of the season. He romped home two lengths ahead of seven others, but once again stubbornly refused to switch leads for Jorge Velasquez. It was one thing to offer up that right lead as part of a morning exercise, but quite another for the opinionated colt to deliver it in the heat of battle when competing against others. Veitch was at once soothed by the win but disheartened by the colt's stubborn refusal to listen to his jockey's cue to pick up the right lead. He hoped that as the races got longer, Alydar might grow tired on his left lead and pick up the right on his own. After all, Veitch never had a horse that didn't eventually recognize the benefit of switching in a long race.

With the win in the allowance race, the next challenge would come on March 4 in the Flamingo Stakes, where Alydar would once again tangle with Believe It, the colt who had trounced him in the Remsen back in November. When the gates banged open, Alydar made his usual slow start, sitting near the back of the eight-horse field, while Believe It grabbed the lead. At the top of the turn, Alydar came alongside Believe It and then, with a powerful surge, flew past him. With every ground-eating stride, Alydar pulled away to win by four and a half lengths in 1:47, just a fifth of a second off the stakes record and two-fifths faster than Seattle Slew had covered the same mile and an eighth the year before while prepping for his Triple Crown sweep.

With his star back in top form, Veitch paused for a few minutes to reflect after the race. "I thought going in we had a better horse than Believe It, and of course I think he's a better horse now. Affirmed, now that's a different story. We'll have to see." Veitch was hoping that moment wouldn't be coming soon. "I'd prefer not to meet him until Kentucky," the trainer said. "It's not a matter of ducking him. I would rather meet him at a mile and a quarter on the first Saturday in May. It would make a better race for both horses."

* * *

By mid-February, the California deluge had finally tapered off and Laz Barrera was able to put his colt back to work. His original plan had been to make the San Vicente Stakes on February 8 Affirmed's three-year-old debut, but with all the rain, he'd had to give that up and set his sights on a March 8 allowance race.

Though still nervous over being a month behind schedule, Barrera was relieved that he could finally put his master plan in motion. The plan had included importing to the West Coast not only Affirmed but also the colt's famous jockey. It didn't take long for Barrera to persuade Steve Cauthen to trade his headlining engagement on New York's Big Wheel for the California circuit. Shortly after Christmas, the seventeen-year-old jockey moved into an apartment with Larry Barrera, Laz's eighteen-year-old son and assistant trainer, planning to stay through the winter and spring Derby preps.

The Wolfsons, too, relocated to California, renting an apartment in Beverly Hills. Each morning they would stop by the track to visit with the trainer and to see their colt. The minute Patrice would come into view, Affirmed would turn his head to her, his entire focus on his favorite human being. The colt had developed a kind of tropism for her, leaning in to her just as a flower turns itself toward the sun. If Patrice showed up as Affirmed was being led back to his stall, the colt would pull the lead shank through his groom's hands to get close to her. Any time she stood next to him, Affirmed would reach his head over to put it in her arms, just as he had that first time as a weanling. Laz was amused by their relationship. "We're going to have to put you at the finish line," the trainer would tell Patrice with a smile. "He'll run right to you."

For his first prep race, Affirmed went into the starting gate a little taller and more muscled up than he had been in the fall. Once again, he broke alertly and Cauthen positioned him behind the leader until half-way through the race. In the stretch, the jockey asked Affirmed to move and the colt powered ahead, pulling away to a seven-length lead. But as soon as there were no other horses in sight, Affirmed lost interest and started to loaf despite Cauthen's urgings, his lead gradually shrinking to four lengths by the end of the six-and-a-half-furlong race. Cauthen was pleased, despite the laziness near the end. He could tell the colt was fit and ready to take on all comers.

As for Barrera, Affirmed's performance had swept away any lingering worries about the season's late start. "He's better now than he was as a two-year-old because he's matured some and picked up about a hundred pounds," the trainer said. "We're right on schedule now." Still, Barrera wasn't foolish enough to think his colt was invincible. As he stood by the rail ten days later watching Affirmed gallop the morning of his next race, the San Felipe Handicap, the trainer gave voice to some of his doubts. "He's a short horse," he said. "He could get beat today if somebody else becomes a tiger. I'm worried just a little bit. The San Felipe is just a small stroll in the sunshine. I'm looking down the road toward the Kentucky Derby. That is what matters. We're going to have to fight Alydar again like we did all last year. My horse, he no will meet Alydar before the Derby. But that day we put on the heavy gloves. It will be him and us. Today we lace the gloves up and spar. Later on Affirmed will be ready to say, 'Grrrr.'"

Affirmed looked splendid, coat glistening copper and gold in the California sunshine, as he took his place in the starting gate for the San Felipe. He broke alertly and once again took up a position behind the leader. As the horses hit the first turn, something on the inside, a shadow maybe, caught Affirmed's eye and he startled and then lugged out to the middle of the track, carrying two others with him. Within seconds he had settled down again, but the outward drift cost him. He'd dropped to third place behind the two leaders, Tampoy and Chance Dancer. On the backstretch, Chance Dancer took the lead and then pulled away by nearly two lengths. Finally, near the top of the stretch, with Cauthen slapping him a total of ten times with the whip, Affirmed surged on the outside, caught Chance Dancer, and poked his head out in front. Engaged now, Affirmed started to pull away. By the time he hit the wire, he was two lengths ahead. His time for the mile and one-sixteenth wasn't anything special at 1:42, but he'd shown he could come back from a deficit and win.

Back at the barn later that evening, a happier and more voluble Barrera entertained reporters' questions as he watched Juan Alaniz cool Affirmed out. "Bring him in," Barrera told the groom. "But stop him under this big light." Barrera paused for a moment to let his visitors admire the colt. "He's bright as a shined copper penny," the trainer beamed. "But when you look at him, you see spun gold. He is a magnificent horse. Smart. Real smart. In the afternoon before he run in the race, he lies down in his stall and sleeps. Only *I* walk around like a crazy man. Everyone asks, 'How is the horse?' I say he is good. Nobody ask, 'How is the man?' Me. I am slowly going crazy with worry. I don't want him to lose. Every morning I come into this barn and I look over all the stakes horses I have. Of forty horses, fifteen are stakes winners in this barn. Who else have that? Nobody. But each morning I go to Stall Nine and I look in on the spun gold first. I say, 'You look good, Mr. Gold.' He don't say nuthin'. He just look back and laugh at me. He knows he is the gold."

*   *   *

With his strong finish in the Flamingo, Alydar came into the Florida Derby on April 1 as the clear favorite. The colt had sprouted to 16.2 hands and also muscled up so he still had a balanced look, his dark umber coat gleaming in the Southern sun. As the horses approached the starting gate, Alydar was feeling good and was on his toes. Though he usually marched obediently into the gate when asked, this time he balked and the assistant starters had to link arms behind his rump and push him in. But once he had loaded, the colt was ready to go.

He broke slowly once again and settled into fourth place, with Believe It behind him. On the far turn, Alydar surged to the lead, and Believe It made his move at the same time. For an instant, Believe It pulled even at the head of the stretch, but Alydar fought back to win by two lengths in 1:47, just one-fifth of a second off the track record for a mile and an eighth. Velasquez was exuberant afterward. "He was pulling me out of the saddle down the backstretch," the jockey told reporters. "He won with a lot left. He turned it on when I asked him—a very powerful race."

Alydar's decisive win in the Florida Derby put him in the spotlight, and convinced many that he would be the one to beat in the Kentucky Derby. "Alydar is a standout right now," said Woody Stephens, Believe It's trainer. As for Affirmed, Stephens said, "He's not going to get nothing. He's been wintering in California. They had a terrible winter out there, and Barrera had to miss so many days of training with Affirmed. I don't think California horses compare with these kinds of horses. There have been a couple of horses come out of California and win the Derby, but more horses come out of Hialeah and Gulfstream." Stephens even went so far as to predict that Affirmed "may get beat" in his next race, out in California the following day.

* * *

Affirmed had been training well in the days leading up to the Santa Anita Derby on April 2. But Barrera had a big problem. Cauthen wasn't going to be able to ride the colt this time. The stewards had suspended him for "not making the proper effort to keep his mount on a straight course" in a race on March 9. He had appealed the five-day suspension and had gotten a stay that allowed him to ride while the ruling was being reviewed. That had allowed him to pilot Affirmed in the San Felipe. But on March 30 the California Horse Racing Board upheld the suspension, which meant Cauthen wouldn't be able to ride in the much more prestigious Santa Anita Derby.

Barrera needed a jockey fast. As it turned out, both Angel Cordero and Laffit Pincay were available—and their agents were both pushing hard for the mount. Barrera, not wanting to offend either of them, came up with a simple solution: they would decide the matter with a coin flip. He told Pincay's agent, George O'Bryan, to toss the coin and Cordero's agent, Tony Matos, to call it when it was in the air. Matos called "heads." When the nickel landed, it was tails—which meant that Pincay would get the mount. Matos was furious, even though he had initially agreed to the coin toss. After a heated argument with Barrera, he stormed off. Pincay, however, was elated when his agent told him about the toss. He asked for the lucky nickel to hang on to as a keepsake. He would later have it laminated and stored in a safe to be brought out only on special occasions when he wanted to tell people the story of how he got Affirmed back, if only for one race.

On the day of the Santa Anita Derby, Affirmed was, as always, calm and relaxed. As Pincay rode him out onto the track, he thought that this time the horse was perhaps a little too relaxed, too listless and lethargic to be running a race that day. Pincay turned to the pony boy and warned him to watch out. Then he took his whip and slapped the colt once on the belly. "Just to wake him up," Pincay explained. The startled colt jumped forward, now much more alert.

Apparently the technique worked. Affirmed shot out of the starting gate just a hair behind the leader. Midway up the backstretch, he surged into the lead and continued to pull away. By the time they crossed under the wire, Affirmed was eight lengths out in front of Balzac, the second-place finisher. Pincay was jubilant. "This horse has every chance to be one of the greats, like Secretariat and Sham," he told reporters. "A horse this good makes you feel like a really great jockey because they do it all so easily."

For his part, Barrera was happy that, even though he hadn't had anywhere near the sixty days he thought would be necessary to train the colt, somehow it had all worked out well. "He's ready," the trainer pronounced. "He's right where I want him to be. I only had forty-five days to get him ready for this race because of the rain, and I was worried about rushing him. But he showed today that he's the same horse he was as a two-year-old—probably better."

Barrera had originally planned to ship Affirmed east after the Santa Anita Derby, but by April, he'd changed his mind. The colt's final race would be the Hollywood Derby on April 16. That decision set the critics wailing. No horse that had prepped only in California over the past quarter-century had gone on to win the Kentucky Derby, a reporter reminded Barrera. All seven of those who'd started the season in California, including Barrera's own Bold Forbes, had gotten in at least one East Coast prep race prior to the Derby. Barrera saw the strategy as one that would minimize the amount of time his colt spent traveling. Flying east for the Wood Memorial in New York and then shipping south to Kentucky for the Derby would just be too much. Besides, Barrera said, it was clear that Affirmed liked the Hollywood Park track, having run fast there in the Juvenile the year before.

In the days following the Santa Anita Derby, everything seemed to be going according to plan, with Affirmed continuing his training in the mornings. But on April 8, as the colt finished up his morning gallop, he shied at something. He ducked out from underneath his exercise rider and bolted, tail flagging high in the air, the wrong way down the track. A panic-stricken Barrera took off after the riderless colt, lumbering in Affirmed's wake until the futility of it all struck him. "All of a sudden," he later recalled, "an idea goes through my head. 'You must be crazy,' my head says, 'because no fifty-four-year-old man can outrun Affirmed. If you catch Affirmed, you won't be catching no Affirmed, you'll be catching a donkey.'"

Affirmed running loose on the Santa Anita track after dumping his exercise rider
(Lydia Williams)

When the colt spotted the gap in the rail, he skittered off the track and down the path to the backside barns. Barrera and a search crew combed the stable area and finally spotted Affirmed at Charlie Whittingham's barn, standing directly in front of Balzac's stall—staring down the enemy he'd vanquished six days earlier. When Barrera walked up to Affirmed, the colt hung his head. "He knew he had done something wrong," the trainer recalled. "He was afraid we were going to punish him."

Throughout the winter and early spring, the Wolfsons had been reviewing tapes of Alydar's races. The colt's powerful drives to the finish line made Patrice a little nervous, though she wasn't letting on to the press. When reporters asked her what she'd learned from the tapes, she shot back, "He can run." Barrera, however, said he hadn't watched a single one of Alydar's races either on TV or on tape. "I saw enough of him last year," the trainer cracked. "I have to worry about my horse. Horses are like women. You have to worry about your wife. You can't worry about someone else's wife."

For all the worry Affirmed put Barrera through on the day of the escape, there wasn't even a scratch on the colt. On the morning of the

Hollywood Derby, he was his usual mellow self. Barrera was starting to show some wear, but that didn't stop him from holding forth on the intensifying rivalry. Standing outside his stable office that morning, he told reporters, "I hate the word 'great.' Everything must be great these days. Great, great, great! If a man walks down the road with a pumpkin and you stop him and say, 'That's a good-looking pumpkin you have,' he'll get mad at you. But if you say, 'What a great pumpkin you have there,' he'll stop and talk. I don't think there are too many great pumpkins and there are damned few great racehorses. But let me say this: Alydar is a great racehorse. Affirmed? He is far and away the smartest horse I have ever trained. The first time I saw him, I didn't look to see how big he was or how good-looking he was. My eyes went to his eyes and I said, 'There is something about you that I do not understand. You're smart.' I wasn't wrong either."

Barrera knew that Affirmed's intelligence might be the one thing that could lead to the colt's undoing. Most of the time Affirmed would push himself only when he could see his rival up close, refusing to waste energy running fast when there was no one to challenge him. Once he had passed all the other horses in a race, he'd start to ease off and loaf. Barrera was afraid that the colt's loafing might leave him prey to sneak attacks like the one practiced by Alydar and Velasquez in the Champagne. When it came time to give Cauthen his final instructions for the Hollywood, Barrera told his jockey to keep the colt focused. The trainer was hoping that Cauthen would keep Affirmed in high gear even after they'd left their rivals behind. "Don't take no chances," Barrera said. "Go to the lead and don't let nobody get ahead. Use the whip. Don't let him start fooling around when he get the lead."

Cauthen followed Barrera's directions to the letter. Affirmed sprang out of the gate immediately in front of Radar Ahead. The two colts ran head to head for the first six furlongs, with sizzling fractions: the first quarter in 22⅖ seconds, the half in 45 flat, and three quarters in 1:09⅖. The first three furlongs were so fast that Radar Ahead's jockey, fearing both colts would run out of steam before the end of the race, yelled over to Cauthen, "We still got a long way to go." The speed proved too much for Radar Ahead, who started to drop back as they went into the far turn. Driving around the turn, Affirmed opened up the lead by a length, which turned into two lengths in the stretch. He'd run a mile in 1:35. With no rivals in sight and another eighth of a mile to go, Affirmed started to slow down, even though Cauthen hit him a dozen times, just as Barrera had instructed. Though Affirmed won the race by a length and a half, he had slowed so much in the stretch that his final furlong clocked at a sluggish 13⅕.

At the postrace press conference, Cauthen talked about the colt's disposition and his need for company to make him run—and his unwillingness to speed up when there wasn't any competition, whip or no whip. "When he's hooking a horse, you don't have to hit him; he fights back then," the jockey said. "But when he's in front by himself, he sort of eases himself up. Beating the heck out of him doesn't do much good." Barrera defended his jockey, telling reporters that Cauthen had used the whip precisely as instructed. "I know what kind of horse I've got," the trainer said when asked why Cauthen had continued to hit Affirmed even after they'd taken the lead. "We didn't want to get into any trouble. We didn't want anyone to get close to us."

Affirmed and his team were now ready to head to Churchill Downs for the biggest challenge of the colt's life. On the Saturday after the Hollywood, Affirmed loaded up on a plane bound for Kentucky. It would give Barrera two weeks to get his colt adjusted to the new surroundings and the Kentucky Derby track.

*   *   *

After Alydar's win in the Florida Derby, John Veitch had to decide which race would be the colt's final Kentucky Derby prep. While the Wood Memorial at Aqueduct on April 22 had some advantages, he was leaning toward running in the Blue Grass Stakes at Keeneland Race Course on April 27 even though that was just nine days before the Derby. "It will be springtime in Kentucky, and there will be grass for him to eat," he reasoned. "In climate, it will be more similar for him at Churchill Downs."

More important to Veitch, however, was the proximity of the Blue Grass Stakes to Calumet Farm. By this time, both Lucille and Admiral Markey were in their eighties, frail and crippled by arthritis, relying on wheelchairs to get around. They hadn't been able to attend any of Alydar's races and had been relegated to catching them either on the radio or on TV. At Keeneland, though, the Markeys might have a chance to actually watch the race in person. The track's staff had offered to cordon off an area near the rail, about halfway down the homestretch, so the Markeys could be driven there and watch the race from the comfort of a car.

Veitch decided Alydar should ship to Keeneland right away so that the colt would have a chance to acclimate to the weather and the track.

Both felt at home, just a few miles down the road from Calumet. Veitch would visit the colt often during the day. Sometimes he'd just lean back against a post near Alydar's stall, taking the colt in, wondering what it was that made this horse so special, what gave him such a will to win. Over the years, Veitch had seen his share of well-conformed colts that just didn't have the heart to go into battle and claw their way to victory. This colt had something special, something you didn't often see in a racehorse, no matter how well-bred he was or how well he was put together. Maybe it was the colt's macho personality. Though Alydar knew his name and would often come to his door to beg for a lump of sugar, he wasn't a pet. He wouldn't tolerate people hugging him or hanging on him in any way. He would run anyone who tried that out of his stall. Veitch would sometimes describe him simply as "all horse."

One night, as the day of the Blue Grass drew near, Veitch stopped by the barn for his 8 P.M. check. The evenings had been chilly, so the trainer had opted to put a night blanket on Alydar to keep him warm. When Veitch looked in the stall, he saw that the colt was resting, eyes closed. Noticing that Alydar's blanket had slipped a little to one side, Veitch opened the stall's lower door, ducked under the webbing, and walked over to the colt's flank to pull the blanket straight. He had barely touched Alydar when the colt startled awake, let both hind hooves fly, and then wheeled around, lunging at the trainer with teeth bared. Veitch dove under the webbing and escaped, his heart racing but his body uninjured. As the trainer leaned on the barn wall, catching his breath, Alydar poked his head over the webbing. Recognizing Veitch, Alydar—the attack already forgotten—was now asking for a lump of sugar.

As Veitch's thumping heart slowed down, he reviewed what had just happened. The colt had probably been sound asleep when the trainer ducked into the stall. His touch had awakened Alydar, and the colt immediately had gone into defensive mode without checking first to see what was there. "That was my fault," Veitch thought. "I was stupid. I should have gotten the night watchman to come in and hold his head while I straightened out the blanket." The trainer straightened up and walked over to the colt, pulling a sugar cube out of his pocket. He opened his palm, and Alydar took the cube gratefully. All was right with his world once again.

On the day of the Blue Grass, Keeneland officials contacted the Markeys and asked if they would like to come and watch the race in person. When the couple said yes, a station wagon was sent to Calumet to collect them.

At the track, the driver pulled the car across the clubhouse lawn and angled it alongside the rail. Once it was parked, a few feet off the rail, the Markeys eased themselves out of their seats—just in time to see Alydar coming up the stretch in the post parade. Velasquez steered Alydar over to where the Markeys were standing next to the rail, she in a dark purple dress with white gloves covering her hands and wrists, he in an ascot, a tan jacket, and a brown houndstooth ivy cap.

As Velasquez pulled the colt up to a stop, a delighted Lucille, peering through thick glasses, whispered excitedly to her husband, "I can see him! I can see him!" Velasquez could hear Lucille softly say, "That's my boy, Alydar."

"Hello, Jorge," the Admiral called out.

"Hello, My Lady," Velasquez said. "How are you? How do you feel?"

Without waiting for a response, the jockey continued: "Here's your baby. Don't he look pretty?"

"He looks wonderful," the Admiral said. "So do you, Jorge."

"Thank you," Velasquez replied, reaching his left hand down to pet Alydar's side.

"Bless his heart," the Admiral said. "Bless you, boy."

With Alydar getting antsy, Velasquez asked, "Is that OK?"

"Fine," the Admiral answered. "Thank you, Jorge. Thank you very much, Jorge."

"OK," the jockey said. "See you a little later."

With that, Velasquez turned his mount back to the post parade and headed over to the starting gate while the Markeys returned to the station wagon where they could listen to the race on the car radio.

When the bell rang, Alydar stood flatfooted for a split second, then broke slowly, falling into eighth place with just one horse behind him. On the backstretch, Raymond Earl opened up a five-length lead, while Alydar moved up into fifth. When they hit the turn, Velasquez asked Alydar to kick into high gear, and the colt surged past the others and came up to challenge the leader. With a quarter-mile to go, Alydar flew to the front and opened up a six-length lead, speeding ahead as if the others were moving in slow motion behind him.

With the home crowd cheering him on, the Markeys got so caught up in the excitement that they once again left the station wagon so they could watch the stretch drive from the rail. As the big colt thundered past

Jorge Velasquez brings Alydar to the rail so Lucille and Admiral Markey, standing at the far right, can see their colt up close (Keeneland Association)

the Markeys, his lead widening with every stride, Lucille started pounding a white-gloved fist in the air and yelling, "Come on! Come on, Alydar!" When he flew across the finish line a whopping thirteen lengths in front, Lucille brought her hand down over her mouth for a second and then, as it dropped under her chin, she turned to the Admiral with a huge smile, the emotion so strong that she couldn't utter a word.

After the trophy was presented to Veitch in the winner's circle, it was brought to the Markeys' station wagon and handed to Lucille in the back seat. On the ride home to Calumet, she grasped the gold cup tightly in one hand while clasping her husband's hand in the other.

As the Markeys were excitedly savoring the win on the way home, Velasquez was putting it into perspective for reporters. "We are ready now for the big Run for the Roses," he proclaimed. A reporter asked him if Alydar was "the best one" of all the Derby hopefuls the jockey had ever ridden. "One, two, and three," Velasquez shot back. "But he's not the champion yet. He's got to beat Affirmed. And that's not easy."

PART III

CORONATION

Affirmed and Steve Cauthen in the post parade for the Kentucky Derby (Keeneland Library Featherston Collection)

CHAPTER 11

Dream Derby

MORE THAN ANY DATE CIRCLED ON THE CALENDAR EACH YEAR, "THE first Saturday in May" looms as the sports equivalent of Christmas. Long before there was such a thing as a Super Bowl or a World Series, the Kentucky Derby had forged an annual tradition as the single most anticipated sporting spectacle in America. Yet even by that standard of eager expectations building to every Derby Day since 1875, nothing in the fabled history of the nation's most cherished horse race could match the buzz elicited by this pair of chestnut colts hurtling headlong toward the first Saturday in May of 1978.

By prepping for it separately three thousand miles apart on opposite coasts, Affirmed and Alydar managed to fan the flames in each other's absence even more than they had in each other's presence the previous year when it often took a photo-finish snapshot to distinguish between them.

"I'm glad we haven't met yet this year," John Veitch declared upon Alydar's arrival at Churchill Downs. "It makes the Derby all the more exciting."

"It's good it turned out like this: the Derby is the place to settle the issue," Laz Barrera echoed. "We knew, always, that this is where we would hook up with Alydar again."

Before Affirmed and Alydar could even set foot on the same track together as three-year-olds, their rivalry was already being compared favorably to the greatest in racing lore and their Kentucky Derby showdown the most anticipated ever. In the frenzied week leading to the 104th renewal of America's most storied sports event, old-timers breathlessly recalled the great expectations they had for past Derby duels—Citation versus Coaltown in 1948, Nashua versus Swaps in 1955, Secretariat versus Sham in 1973—but even the ballyhoo for those classic confrontations paled now in comparison to Affirmed versus Alydar.

The 1978 Kentucky Derby had taken on the air of a heavyweight championship bout, replete with sportswriters hyping the battle and trainers verbally sparring like prizefighters at a weigh-in. Barrera, for one, figured that was only fitting given the fighting spirit Affirmed and Alydar had personified in their six 1977 matchups as two-year-olds. "They're both fighters," he observed. "They're like Muhammad Ali and Joe Frazier." To hardcore railbirds and casual followers alike, the rival colts' long-awaited first meeting as mature three-year-olds was the equine equivalent of the rival boxers' long-awaited first confrontation in "The Fight of the Century" pitting two unbeaten champions with legitimate claims to the world heavyweight title.

Like that 1971 Ali-Frazier showdown, this Affirmed-Alydar main event promised a classic clash of styles and personalities: the sleek front-runner with the grace of a deer and the heart of a lion versus the brawny closer with a bull's aggressiveness and a slugger's knockout punch. As if that weren't enough, this drama was rife with enough juicy subplots to intrigue the media horde descending upon Louisville: the Bluegrass hometown hero prepped back East versus the Florida carpetbagger prepped out West.

Once the pair converged on Churchill Downs, both of them having flawlessly completed their parallel four-race prep seasons, their teams of rivals could stop firing shots across the continent. Now, at long last, the dueling trainers could engage each other directly from the close range of neighboring backside barns.

Barrera had shipped Affirmed from California two weeks before the first Saturday in May, bedding him down in the very same Barn 41 stall where the trainer had readied Bold Forbes for his stunning Derby upset two years earlier. Barrera was eager to let everyone see his latest Derby horse work at Churchill so as to silence the criticism that Affirmed hadn't been anywhere near as impressive as Alydar in their respective winter and spring prep races.

On the last Saturday in April, under an early morning sky dotted with colorful hot-air balloons that signaled the liftoff of Derby Week, all stopwatches were glued to Affirmed as he worked a mile and an eighth over a sluggishly sandy track in 1:56⅖—a clocking that turned the whispers into shouts of skepticism. "He don't impress nobody," Barrera bristled, dismissing the critics. "Everybody said it was a bad work, very slow, very

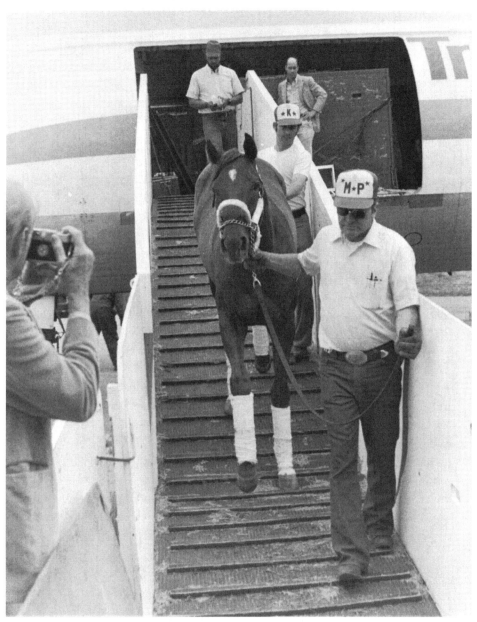

Alydar stepping off the plane in Lexington for the Derby (Keeneland Library Featherston Collection)

slow. Well, it was one of the most brilliant workouts I've seen, because I started him in a place where he would have to go around a lot of turns. He work around the turn and he went the last eighth in twelve. There are not too many horses that can do that on a very cuppy track. Nobody appreciate how good that work was."

Three days later, early on a chilly Tuesday morning, Alydar turned in a less-than-impressive work of his own, breezing four furlongs in a pedestrian 50 seconds and leaving "a cloud of doubt" in Veitch's mind over his colt's failure to extend himself. The tepid works prompted horseplayers to give more respect to two other contenders in what was shaping up as the strongest Derby field in decades: Sensitive Prince, a dangerous though green speedster with a perfect record in six career starts, and Believe It, the only horse besides Affirmed to have won a race over Alydar. For all the respect accorded those two challengers and their canny Hall of Fame trainers, however, most handicappers still envisioned the Derby developing into yet another eyeball-to-eyeball match race between Affirmed and the only horse ever to beat him.

"This is no pickin' chicken party," Barrera cautioned. As reporters smiled and scribbled furiously, the trainer went on to reel off the names of potential spoilers: Sensitive Prince, Believe It, Darby Creek Road . . . "But," he interrupted himself, "I think Affirmed has to beat Alydar, and it could be just as simple as that. I still think it's a two-horse race between Affirmed and Alydar. In any race, luck influences the outcome, but Affirmed and Alydar have always dominated their races and left the other horses far behind. A lot of people don't believe Affirmed can be rated, but they are wrong about that." He paused and shook his head. "Once you get to Kentucky, you have to listen to so much nonsense that your head gets full of bees. All I hear in Kentucky is that Affirmed cannot win the Derby because he was bred in Florida and raced in California this winter. Florida and California are part of the United States of America, aren't they? Affirmed has not been winning his races in China. Before the Derby, I am going to give Affirmed a workout that will cause the bees to go bye-bye. Watch it."

On a cold Wednesday morning three days before the Derby, Barrera and the Wolfsons climbed into the cement-block clockers' stand perched above the Churchill Downs backstretch to do just that. Hands shoved deep into the pockets of his trench coat, the trainer watched Affirmed breeze five furlongs in a lively 59 seconds, the last one in a crisp 11⅘, and nodded knowingly as he turned to Patrice and Lou. "It's a perfect work," he assured Affirmed's owners. "It does two things. First, it puts some speed into him to get him sharp. Second, the pressure comes off because the bees will stop buzzing." He paused, smiled, then confided, "The party is over. Nobody is going to beat this horse. He is, in the old Spanish expression, like a man who just got married."

Likewise emboldened by that final tune-up, Lou Wolfson stood on the backstretch afterward and made a brash prediction of his own. "If Affirmed is in front at the top of the stretch, you can put your binoculars down because Alydar won't catch him," he told reporters. "I realize that sounds presumptuous, but that's the way I analyze the race. We have examined the six meetings between Affirmed and Alydar pretty carefully, and it looks to me like Affirmed digs in when things get toughest. Up to this point in his career, Affirmed has done everything asked of him, but I couldn't call him a great horse yet because the Kentucky Derby hasn't been run. Because Affirmed and Alydar haven't met since last fall, and each has won all its starts this year, people are very decided in their opinions. Well, here's mine: The critical point will come when the horses turn for home, and I think that you will see Affirmed leading at that stage. If so, I have to believe he will win. When they cross the finish line, those two will be eight lengths ahead of the rest of the field. That's the way it was last year, and they've both improved since then, so why should it be any different?"

One day earlier, the Wolfsons had made a pilgrimage to Lexington's Spendthrift Farm so they could pay their respects to the three stallions that on those hallowed grounds had produced Saturday's leading contenders: Raise a Native, the shooting star whose career-truncating injury had precluded him from becoming Harbor View's first Derby hero, and two of his prepotent sons. The Wolfsons visited first with the feisty Raise a Native, who sired Alydar; then with Majestic Prince, who won the Derby that Lou had watched on a prison TV and sired Sensitive Prince; and finally, of course, with Exclusive Native, who sired their cherished Affirmed.

Standing outside Spendthrift's famed stallion barn, Lou couldn't help thinking back to the genesis of it all sixteen years earlier when he bought Raise a Native as a yearling and watched him blossom into Harbor View's best Derby prospect—until Affirmed. "It is a great feeling to own a champion, but it is not the same thing as racing one you have bred," he mused with the pride of a father. "I spent twenty years of my life to get this one.

I brought him into the world; I bred and raced his sire; I raised him at my farm. The feeling you get when a horse you have bred and raised has a good chance to win the Kentucky Derby—well, it is something that you just cannot go out and buy." Or, in Lou's case, sell. He had only recently turned down an $8 million offer for Affirmed. "Don't talk to me about this horse," he had told the would-be buyer. "He's not for sale at any price."

As the couple drove the seventy-five miles west from Lexington back to Louisville, Lou had plenty more time to reflect on what Affirmed had already given him. "Let me put it this way," he told reporters upon his return to Churchill Downs. "With all the problems of the world and with the frustrations and violence, this horse has reduced some of the problems for me, made me stop worrying about things I can't do much about. He has given me so many pleasing and happy moments. My outlook on life may be better because of him."

Squinting in the glare of Derby Week's media spotlight amid the endless stream of inquiring minds, the retired financier faced the inevitable questions about his past—from his corporate takeover wheeling and dealings to his legal problems and imprisonment—and handled them all with dignity and aplomb. The general press had painted this Derby as a class clash between the inherited old money of eighty-one-year-old Lucille Markey, the blue-blood queen of a Thoroughbred empire, and the self-made new money of sixty-six-year-old Louis Wolfson, the proxy-fighting giant of a financial empire. If his checkered background was often compared unkindly to the aristocratic mien of the Markeys, Lou Wolfson's dignified handling of the tough questions may have helped change his image.

As the excitement of Derby Week built, the Wolfsons, both publicity shy to the point of reclusiveness, emerged as racing's glamour couple: Lou, like a dashing leading man with his silver hair and athletic build tucked neatly into his custom-fitted suits, alongside Patrice, her sunny good looks and trim figure shown to advantage by her tailored outfits. Reserved by nature, Patrice let down her guard and charmed reporters with her engaging enthusiasm. "The Doris Day of racing," was how *Sports Illustrated* described her, "a blonde bundle of smiles and nerves." She could be found hanging around Stall 21 in Barn 41, smiling as Affirmed tossed his head at the mere sound of her familiar high-pitched voice. "You love to see a horse do that," she beamed. "I think he likes the attention. He knows he's special. I know he knows he's special. This is the kind of horse that you endeavor to breed

and train and be around. It's a dream come true to have a horse like this."
Could this, she was asked, be the horse to realize the Derby dream that had
eluded her husband as well as her late father, Hirsch Jacobs, throughout his
long Hall of Fame career as a leading trainer of nine Derby horses? "My
father would have loved this horse," Patrice said. "I think we're running the
best horse Saturday. I think he has the potential to be a great horse."

For all the quiet charisma that Patrice and Lou brought to Derby Week,
no Bluegrass outsider could possibly compete with the affection for Alydar's
owners felt by Kentuckians anticipating Calumet's return to its old glory.
In Louisville, where the storyline focused on Calumet's revival in a race the
stable had won a record eight times between 1941 and 1968, Lucille and
Gene Markey were now as conspicuous by their absence as Patrice and Lou
Wolfson were by their presence.

While the Wolfsons were busy fielding reporters' questions at Churchill Downs in the shadows of the iconic Twin Spires, the Markeys, both
too frail in their eighties to travel there for the Derby, were entertaining
the occasional newspaperman in the Trophy Room at Calumet Farm.
There, surrounded by five hundred trophies evoking the halcyon days of
the Calumet dynasty, Lucille and the Admiral sat in matching wheelchairs
and basked in Alydar's reflected glory. "The wheelchair kids," the Admiral,
nattily attired in a tweed jacket and striped turtleneck, quipped by way of
introduction at the start of one of those rare interviews.

Just as Affirmed had fanned the Wolfsons' passion for the ponies and
Lou's quest for redemption, so was Alydar rejuvenating and revitalizing the
Markeys. Friends marveled at how Alydar had "breathed life" into Lucille,
who often referred to the colt as "my baby." In their golden years, Lucille
and the Admiral were relishing this fling with the single event that inextricably defined the Calumet mystique.

Asked by an interviewer if she had ever considered getting out of the
business during the depths of Calumet's long recent slump, Lucille shook
her head emphatically. "Never," she said firmly. "I enjoy horses too much."

"She never bobbled," the Admiral confirmed, a cigar in one hand and a
glass of brandy in the other. "There was never a moment when she thought
of giving it up. It's a sport with her. Nothing commercial. She's always been
like that about horse racing."

"That's very kind, dear," Lucille said. "I hate pushers with a poison-ivy
passion."

"Have you ever had a poison-ivy salad with Roquefort, dear?" the Admiral deadpanned. "It's delightful."

Like millions of other Americans, the Markeys would be watching Saturday's Derby on television, sitting in red-leather easy chairs in their sunny living room, soaking in the prerace coverage with building apprehension, then rooting their Alydar on. "I'll be a wreck," Lucille predicted. "We're hopeful, but I'm scared to death of Sensitive Prince."

As an omen, she could literally point to the Kentucky Derby Gold Cups that Calumet had won in every previous year ending in the numeral 8: Citation's in 1948, Tim Tam's in 1958, and Forward Pass's in 1968. Reflecting on Alydar's chances in 1978, she thought for a moment and said, "I've seen the best horse lose. It can happen. Can't it, darling?"

"Yes," the Admiral nodded. "All Ben Jones would ever say is, 'I think he'll run good.' And they usually did. If the Lord smiles, we'll win the Derby."

"I don't see it that way, dear," Lucille demurred. "If the horse is good enough and doesn't get into trouble, he'll win." Then, like any snakebitten horseplayer, she hastened to add, "I think."

Either way, Alydar had already transported her back in time to Calumet's salad days. She surveyed all the gold and silver spoils of Calumet's legacy, then said to no one in particular, "I knew we'd come back—someday."

All of which made Alydar and his octogenarian owners the heavy sentimental favorites for the 104th Kentucky Derby. Owned by the queen of the Calumet dynasty, bred in the heart of the Bluegrass, saddled by a Lexington-born trainer, and racing in the familiar devil's-red and blue silks of history's surpassing stable, Alydar was Kentucky's favorite son, the hometown hero with the home-team advantage.

To be sure, the presence of Steve Cauthen—the Bluegrass State's *other* favorite son—aboard Affirmed would elicit backing from his fellow Kentuckians, as evidenced by the billboard that proudly proclaimed "Walton, Ky., Population 800—Hometown of Steve Cauthen." But not even Cauthen's homecoming for his Derby debut could offset the fact that the Florida-bred, California-raced, Floridian-owned, and Cuban-trained colt he would ride was the consummate carpetbagger. And besides, The Kid figured to have many more Kentucky Derby mounts ahead of him while time was running out on the Markeys' last best chance to reclaim Calumet's rightful place at the top for what had become a beloved Bluegrass institution. After all, Calumet was as much a part of Kentucky as aged bourbon and as much a part of the Kentucky Derby as the mint julep.

Geography, though, played only a small part in Alydar's installation as the morning-line favorite over Affirmed when the early Derby odds were set two days before the race. In making Alydar the even-money favorite and Affirmed the second choice at 7-to-5, the Derby oddsmaker, Mike Battaglia, cited factors that dealt strictly with the horses and their performances: Alydar's four prep races on the traditional road to the Derby had been more impressive than Affirmed's against weaker competition out West, and Alydar's powerful stretch-running style made him less vulnerable than Affirmed to an early speed duel and more suited to the classic distance of a mile and a quarter.

When Barrera heard those morning-line odds, he could hardly contain his shock—or his anger. He railed at Battaglia, "There's no way my horse won't be the favorite." Then he carped to the press. "I don't understand: you've got the champion two-year-old from last year, the champion trainer, and the champion jockey—and the *other* horse is the favorite?" he snorted. "Why do they make this other horse the favorite? Six times last year they ran against each other, and four times my horse beat the other one. Every time they go head and head, the other one never gets past him." He shook his head. "This is a crazy business," he sighed. "What does Affirmed have to do to make people believe in him? Everybody is saying what's wrong with this horse. Am I the only one who can see so much that's right with him?"

By the trainer's book and by the past performance charts, his horse had done everything right to establish himself as the one to beat: Affirmed had won eleven of his thirteen career starts while Alydar was just nine for fourteen; Affirmed had made history as the first horse ever to have earned $700,000 coming into the Derby; and, most persuasively, Affirmed had proved his mettle by outdueling Alydar in three of their last four head-to-head meetings to secure the two-year-old championship.

Next door in Barn 42, the morning-line favorite himself, Alydar, was relaxing while his trainer fielded questions on that very topic. A reporter mentioned the remarkable stat that if all six of their meetings were strung together, the two rivals would have raced five miles and finished less than half a length apart—with Affirmed in front. The reporter reminded the trainer that, as it was, the juvenile championship had been decided by a neck—Affirmed's neck.

"But this is a new year," Veitch interjected, smiling as he turned toward his charge. "Right, Aly?"

Alydar responded with a loud snort. "That's the sound," Veitch laughed, "of a horse that's run four good races and is ready for more."

The post position draw on Thursday would give Alydar and his backers even more ammunition to bolster their confidence. In the eleven-horse field, Alydar drew one of the coveted outside post positions that would enable him to run his race unfettered without worrying about traffic: number 10, sandwiched between the stalker Believe It in number 9 and the speedster Sensitive Prince outside in number 11. Affirmed had the bad luck to draw one of the dreaded inside post positions: number 2, with only the speedster Raymond Earl inside him on the rail.

"God gave me number two, so I guess I better be happy with it," Barrera shrugged. "It'll be perfect. Post positions don't mean nothing when you got a good horse."

At the same time in the barn next door, Veitch wasn't seeing it that way. "This gives Alydar a tremendous advantage," he told reporters. "I like where my horse is. And I love where Affirmed is, down on the inside. I think it poses a serious problem to them. They've got to make a decision. Cauthen may have to use his colt earlier than he wants in order to get position. Or he may get trapped when the speed horses begin to stop in front of him." Alydar's trainer then proceeded to speculate, in a monologue that lasted longer than the two minutes the Derby itself would take, about how Affirmed and Cauthen might run the race.

When Veitch's comments were relayed to his counterpart moments later, Barrera felt his blood boiling to the surface. "You go tell John Veitch to train his own horse and stop trying to train mine," Barrera snapped. "He should worry about his post position and let mine alone. I don't say how he's going to run his horse or what's going to happen to him. I don't care. He can run any way he wants. I never make any comment about nobody else's horse. It surprises me that a young man like him—and I got a lot of respect for him—makes this kind of comment. That makes me mad. The only thing I say all my life is Alydar is a great horse, a *helluva* horse, and a horse you have to run your eyeballs out to beat. But he got a job to do, and I got mine to do. That's babyish to guess what will happen in a race. The year

Bold Forbes won, some nut threw a smoke bomb on the track. Did anyone guess that would happen? Once those gates open, nobody in America can tell what's gonna happen."

Until then, of course, nobody in America could resist predicting what was going to happen in this most analyzed of all races—both trainers included. As reporters relayed their fighting words back and forth, Barrera and Veitch sounded like two grandmasters trading chess moves . . .

Veitch: "Last year, we weren't going a mile and a quarter the time Affirmed beat us. Now he's going to be playing our game."

Barrera: "You don't have to tell me Alydar is a great horse, but the longest we ran against him—a mile and a sixteenth—we beat him."

Veitch: "Velasquez will be a few lengths behind Cauthen and outside him, where he can see what Affirmed is doing and then try to burst past him when it's time."

Barrera: "Yeah, but he don't got no jet plane that can blow by my horse. Affirmed will take the lead at about the head of the stretch, then Alydar will start to come at him, and it should be a helluva Derby."

Veitch: "May the best horse win."

Barrera: "Yeah, may the best horse win—*again*."

For the time being, Barrera may have had the last word, if not the last laugh. On Friday morning, as Veitch prepared to take Alydar onto the track for his customary three-furlong blowout the day before a race, the Calumet trainer smiled confidently and quipped, "When he gets back to his stall, I'll have wall-sized pictures of Affirmed hanging in there and signs saying, 'Kill! Kill! Kill!'"

After Alydar breezed the three furlongs in 37⅖, much slower than Veitch had wanted, the workouts were done and all that was left was to wait, to talk, to analyze, and to wonder. Heading into his first Derby, Veitch couldn't help but second-guess whether he had done everything right. He sat on a cot in Barn 42 and wondered if perhaps he should have worked Alydar harder at Churchill after his romp in the Blue Grass Stakes. He wondered whether he had sufficiently matched wits with three of racing's shrewdest trainers: Barrera, who had turned in the training job of the decade by transforming the sprinter Bold Forbes into the 1976 Derby and Belmont winner; Woody Stephens, another Derby-winning veteran who primed Believe It with an impressive Wood Memorial prep; and Allen Jerkens, who had earned his nickname as "The Giant Killer" for slaying

Secretariat, Kelso, and Forego with longshots and was now taking dead aim at Alydar and Affirmed with Sensitive Prince. Training against that collection of grand old masters and magicians, the thirty-two-old Veitch's winning brand of self-deprecating humor was going to come in handy.

For his part, Barrera wasn't worrying about any trainer but himself. "In racing, everybody trains everybody else's horse," he said. "I train my own and let people say whatever they want. You can do anything with Affirmed. On the afternoons of his races, he goes to sleep in a stall when all the other horses are up and about and getting themselves on edge. Affirmed is his own main man. He knows himself, and by now I think I know him. I think we haven't seen how good he is yet because you can only tell when another horse challenges him—and no one has challenged him yet this year. Affirmed needs a horse like Alydar to make him run. Yes, it's a confrontation."

Not everyone saw it that way, however, especially the Kentucky hardboots. It wasn't just that more horseplayers, horsemen, and handicappers were picking Alydar to win the showdown; it was that some of them didn't even think Affirmed was the second-best horse in the field. Among the doubters were two of America's most respected turf writers: Bill Nack, covering his last Derby for *Newsday* before moving on to *Sports Illustrated*, picked Affirmed to finish fourth; and Andrew Beyer, the *Washington Post* columnist who invented the revolutionary handicapping tool known as the "Beyer Speed Figures," picked Affirmed to finish fifth. For the record, Beyer's speed figures, comparing performances adjusted for varying distances and track conditions, favored Alydar over Affirmed by just one point. Woody Stephens, Believe It's trainer, didn't even see it that close. "I don't know about Affirmed," he scoffed. "He kind of looks like he's all legs this year."

Others wondered aloud about Affirmed's jockey, whether Steve Cauthen could handle the pressure in his very first Kentucky Derby. Early one morning in the stable area, a reporter asked Barrera what the trainer would deem the stupidest question in a week full of them: "Are you worried about entrusting your Derby horse to an eighteen-year-old who has never ridden in this race before?"

"Worried? You kidding?" Barrera shot back. "Maybe some people still don't understand. Steve Cauthen is no eighteen-year-old. He's an old man. Sometimes he makes me believe in reincarnation. Maybe he had another life, where he was a leading rider for fifty years. That's how much he knows about his business. Maybe Steve is the thousand-year-old man. Maybe he came to us as a gift from some other planet—in a flying sausage."

When the laughter had died down from Barrera's malapropism, there was no denying among the assembled press that Cauthen seemed as immune to the Derby pressure as he had been to the great expectations produced the year before by his unprecedented rise to fame. On Thursday evening, just three days after his eighteenth birthday and two days before the race he had been dreaming of his whole life, Cauthen returned to his home state, arriving in neither "a flying sausage" nor a Superman cape. He may no longer have been the nation's leading jockey, but the $1.8 million he had earned through the first four months of the year left him only slightly behind his record-smashing pace of 1977.

After spending the winter and early spring babysitting Affirmed in California, Cauthen had kept his mind occupied through much of Derby Week by riding races at Aqueduct. But once he arrived in Kentucky, there was no escaping the magnitude of the moment at hand. Early Friday morning, when he was driven up to Barn 41 for a meeting with Barrera and the Wolfsons, dozens of reporters were waiting to barrage him with questions. He gave them cryptic one-word or one-sentence answers, terse as always. His nonchalance notwithstanding, his feelings belied his words. From the first Derby he attended at the age of three, Cauthen had spent many a first Saturday in May on the backstretch at Churchill Downs, caught up in the excitement as a spectator cheering the wins of Majestic Prince in 1969, Secretariat in 1973, Bold Forbes in 1976. Now he was back at the site of his very first race as a jockey—a last-place finish—to ride in the Kentucky Derby for the first time. The most important thing, he figured, was to stay calm. "I gotta make it like just another race," he told himself.

Cauthen lacked the experience of his friend and counterpart Jorge Velasquez. Alydar's jockey had ridden in the Derby four times, twice finishing as high as third. The Derby, Velasquez admitted, was the one race that made him shake, the one race that made it hard to sleep well the night before.

For Cauthen, who seemed as serene and unflappable as ever, that would not be a problem. On the eve of the biggest race of his life, Cauthen spent the night in a sleeping bag on the floor of a hotel room crowded with family because, as his fifteen-year-old brother Doug put it with a shrug, "it was his turn." The Kid slept, as he would report after his father had nudged him awake the next morning, "like a baby."

*   *   *

Derby Day dawned cool and spectacularly clear. The gates opened at 8 A.M., and the early arrivals began flooding through the turnstiles and filling the Churchill Downs grandstand and infield well in advance of the 11:30 first race on the card. Throughout the morning and early afternoon, the festive crowd would swell to 131,004, the third-largest ever to see a Derby. Fans streamed to the betting windows from the moment they opened at 11 A.M. By late afternoon, they would bet more money on the featured eighth race than any other race in the annals of the American turf: over $4.4 million, the vast majority of it on Alydar and Affirmed. Wagering with their hearts as well as their wallets, the bettors made Alydar—the pride of Kentucky and Calumet—the 6-to-5 favorite, with Affirmed the solid second choice at 9-to-5, followed by Sensitive Prince at 9-to-2 and Believe It at 15-to-2.

Veitch would spend the day trying to read a book and watch TV—anything to keep from second-guessing himself. When reporters asked in mid-afternoon if he had any second thoughts, he answered, "Well, they're not second thoughts, but you do question yourself: Have I done too much? Have I done too little? Is Alydar fit enough to go a mile and a quarter?"

To which Barrera could only smile knowingly in the barn next door. "Thinking is only going to send you to the crazy house," he said. "It is too late to do that. Nothing more I can do. It's out of my hands. I was nervous the whole week. Monday, I'm nervous. Friday, I'm nervous. Not today. I relax now. Today, I feel my job is done. I think I train him perfectly. My horse will never be as ready as he is today. He's game. He fight. Out there, on the racetrack, he give you the last thing he has inside of him."

As he spoke, perspiring lightly in the lazy midday sun, Barrera's hands rested in the pants pockets of his light suit, the only one that still fit since diabetes had forced him onto a diet. The Derby was less than two hours away. He could hear the muffled roar of the festive crowd cheering from the track half a mile away.

Around 5 P.M., the horses, grooms, and trainers started for the paddock, walking between the barns and out the gate leading to the track. They congregated in the chute at the head of the backstretch where track staff organized the eleven horses so they could begin their march to the paddock in order of post position. The horses began walking clockwise in single file around the clubhouse turn, and as they neared the stands along the homestretch, fans began to rhythmically chant: "Al-ee-dar, Al-ee-dar, Al-ee-dar . . ." As the crowd's chant grew louder and louder, Veitch could feel his heart swell with pride and a mix of joy and anticipation.

About halfway up the stretch, the horses turned left, leaving the track and heading into the tunnel that would take them under the grandstand to the paddock. Affirmed, led by Juan Alaniz, and Alydar, led by Clyde Sparks, circled the ring and entered their saddling stalls, where the trainers and jockeys' valets tacked them up. As the girths were pulled tight, the riders began to descend from the jocks' room upstairs in the clubhouse. Then came the traditional call that signaled the start of everything: "Riders up!"

Barrera's final instructions to Cauthen were the same as the trainer had already divulged to Howard Cosell and more than twenty-two million Americans glued to the telecast: take him out briskly and safely, then tuck him in behind the two speed horses likely to set the pace; make sure that no other horse can box him in and allow Alydar to sneak past on the outside. Veitch's final instructions to Velasquez were more succinct: good luck and just stay out of trouble. All the talk finally done, each jockey was lifted into his saddle.

The horses went back through the tunnel and, within seconds, emerged into the bright sunlight and onto the track. Each of them, with the exception of Alydar, was greeted by the stable pony that would accompany him throughout the post parade. As they walked down the stretch past the clubhouse, the brass band struck up the sentimental favorite that brings goose bumps to natives and visitors alike: "My Old Kentucky Home." The song resonated with Cauthen especially, evoking memories of his Bluegrass roots. He allowed himself to soak it in as he evaluated Affirmed's mood. Despite the crowds and all the noise, the colt walked along with his neck and head lowered, quiet and relaxed as if he were just heading back to the barn after a morning jog. Alydar pranced along by himself, neck arched, as the horses paraded back up the long homestretch. For a few seconds, Cauthen allowed Affirmed to canter alongside the pony as they made their way back toward the starting gate at the head of the stretch.

One by one, the eleven colts were loaded into their stalls in their post order. Affirmed, the number 2 horse, slipped right in as always. Alydar, the number 10 horse, swung his haunches sideways at the sight of the gate and then had to be straightened out and pushed into his stall by two assistant starters. Within seconds of the door shutting behind the final horse, the bell clanged.

*   *   *

When the doors sprang open at exactly 5:41, Raymond Earl, the 117-to-1 speedball on the rail just inside of Affirmed, shot to the lead as expected. Affirmed broke briskly and tucked himself next to the pacesetter's flank, galloping along comfortably. Alydar broke slowly, and though that had become a habit, the colt felt a little different under Velasquez this time. The jockey could tell that his mount was keyed up and was off the bit as they dropped to the back of the pack.

As the field thundered past the teeming grandstand, Cauthen glanced to his right looking for Sensitive Prince, the speed horse who was angling in from the far outside post. Passing under the wire for the first time a quarter mile into the race, Affirmed and his rider felt Sensitive Prince pressing in on the right flank, and the two Raise a Native grandsons were soon galloping side by side. Within a few strides, Sensitive Prince surged ahead to challenge Raymond Earl. Cauthen, hearing Barrera's voice in his ear warning him not to get caught up in an early speed duel, eased Affirmed back and away from the rail as the other two took off. "Let them go," the jockey told himself as he steadied Affirmed in third. The two frontrunners were setting a sizzling pace, with Raymond Earl blazing the opening quarter in 22⅗ seconds and Sensitive Prince, who snatched the lead coming out of the clubhouse turn, burning up the half-mile in a suicidal 45⅗—two seconds faster than Secretariat's record-smashing pace in the 1973 Derby.

Flying up the backstretch, Sensitive Prince opened two lengths on the fading Raymond Earl while Affirmed cruised along in third, relaxing some six lengths off the pace—right where Cauthen and Barrera wanted him. With Affirmed sitting pretty on the backstretch, Cauthen started to look for Alydar. But neither the dark chestnut colt nor the bright devil's-red silks were anywhere to be seen. Alydar was running fully seventeen lengths behind the leaders in ninth place, farther back than anyone could have imagined. Velasquez had been trying to help the colt find his stride, but Alydar was too tense. The jockey urged him on at first with only his voice, clucking to the colt. When that didn't work, Velasquez tried slapping him on the shoulder with the whip. Though Alydar did move up a little, he still wouldn't pick up the bit and Velasquez was worrying that the leaders might be too far ahead for even Alydar's patented big move to catch them.

As Sensitive Prince strung the field through three quarters in 1:10⅘, Affirmed and Cauthen continued to bide their time in third place, four lengths back. Moving through the final turn, Cauthen realized that the two pacesetters were running out of gas and that he was going to pass them without even having to ask Affirmed to speed up. Eddie Maple, who had been sitting quietly in fourth on Believe It, also noticed that the two leaders were starting to flag and figured it was time to make his move. Affirmed sensed someone coming on the outside even before Believe It reached his flank and, his right ear rotating back toward the challenger, started to surge on his own. He flew past Raymond Earl and then Sensitive Prince to take the lead, with Believe It drafting.

Affirmed and Believe It, moving as a team, rounded the turn running head to head. Sweeping into the stretch, with a quarter mile to go, Believe It poked his head out in front. Affirmed rolled an eye back at his challenger and surged past him, opening a two-length lead. With Believe It disposed of, Cauthen started looking back for Alydar, surprised to find no devil's red in sight. The Calumet colt, who had been slowly moving up around the turn, was now in fourth place but still a full five lengths back.

Safely out in front, Affirmed started pricking his ears forward, as he always did when he had no competition and was losing interest in the race. There was still three-sixteenths of a mile ahead of them, and Cauthen knew he couldn't let his guard down: Alydar was still lurking back there somewhere, threatening to unleash his powerful kick. Cauthen didn't want a repeat of the Champagne, so he tapped Affirmed to wake him up and remind him that the race wasn't over yet.

They continued to cruise along, and then suddenly, as they passed the eighth pole, Cauthen heard a roar from the crowd. It got louder with every stride. He looked around and saw Alydar four lengths back, closing fast on the outside. For the first time, Velasquez felt the colt in his hands. Alydar had taken the bit and was accelerating.

Down the stretch they came, Alydar gaining with every stride. Velasquez slapped his horse half a dozen times, and Alydar shot past Believe It into second and set his sights on Affirmed. But no matter how fast he drove, there wasn't enough track left to catch his nemesis and hook him in another eyeball-to-eyeball duel.

Affirmed swept under the wire with Alydar a length and a half in his wake. He had won the race with a time of 2:01⅕, equaling the fifth-fastest in Derby history though still almost two seconds slower than Secretariat's stakes record of 1:59⅖.

Slowing Affirmed down to a walk, Cauthen looked up at the screaming fans and did something he had never done before. He reached up, grabbed his cap, and doffed it to the crowd. Then he turned Affirmed toward the winner's circle.

Up in the Wolfsons' clubhouse box, Barrera slumped into his seat without a word, emotionally drained. Patrice took her husband's hand and excitedly said, "Let's go down to the winner's circle."

"Oh, Sugar," Lou said, "can't you take care of this for us?"

"No! You have to come. You've got to do it for the scrapbook. Do it for history."

Lou finally relented, and they began to make their way down through the gathering throng to the winner's circle. With Lou clearing a path for her, Patrice was the first to pop through the police cordon. A few feet behind her, Lou strode toward the horse and rider. As they watched, the traditional garland of roses was draped across Affirmed's withers. Cauthen hopped off his mount, and Patrice gave him a big hug. Minutes later, during the trophy presentation, Cauthen was introduced to the crowd by Governor Julian Carroll as "the pride of Kentucky." Cauthen took the microphone and said, "It was tremendous. I didn't realize how good it feels until after the race—but it's something else."

*　　*　　*

With Laz Barrera holding forth, the postrace press conference in the clubhouse would be almost as entertaining as the race itself. Reporters peppered the trainer with questions.

Can Affirmed be caught by Alydar in a longer race?

"No, no, no, no, no, no, no," he replied, causing the press box to explode with laughter. "We can go five miles, and it's going to be the same result. Excuses is enough."

What if Alydar had moved earlier?

"No! Alydar move with him early, and we beat him. He move from the middle, we beat him. He move from the back, and we beat him. I don't want to hear no more excuses no more."

How do you think your horse handled everything?

"If you take a look the whole week at the horse, he look like he just come from the beauty parlor. He was all nice and shining here. And nothing bothers him. The way he won today, he was just playing out there."

Were you disappointed with the time of 2:01?

"When you get one hundred and eighty thousand dollars to win a race, how can you be disappointed in time?"

Could you compare Affirmed with Secretariat?

"I got an opinion, and it'll be proved the day we find a horse that can make him run fast. And we still don't know how good this horse is gonna be until some horse makes him run fast."

Seated nearby, Cauthen nonchalantly chewed on his gum. When it was his turn to face the questions, he answered them with his usual brevity.

Asked if Affirmed could have run faster, Cauthen responded, "My horse wasn't all out at the finish. At the wire, I had a lot of horse left."

A reporter asked, "Do you think he could have run a better race, Steve?"

Cauthen stared at his inquisitor with disbelief. "What do you want?" he replied softly. "He just won the Kentucky Derby."

Reporters turned to Barrera to ask his opinion of how Cauthen rode in his first Derby.

"Steve Cauthen rode that horse perfect," Barrera said. "He rode like he rode this race one hundred years ago and came back with all that experience to ride this one at eighteen years old. Do you believe in renaissance?"

Not long after he got the last laugh in the press box with his malapropism, Barrera found himself in the director's room at Churchill Downs, surrounded by celebrants carrying roses and glasses of champagne. He was still mulling over the meaning of "renaissance" and the phenomenon of reincarnation. "People say that Steve Cauthen is eighteen years old," the trainer, leaning forward in his chair with his hands clasped, was telling a reporter. "For a while, I believed things like that. But the more I watch him ride, the more I start to think other things. He must be at least one hundred years old. And maybe he don't come from Walton, Kentucky, at all. One night when all the racing world was sleeping, a small flying saucer landed out in the desert somewhere and he got off it. He came to the United States from wherever it was with the coolness of Georgie Woolf, the old Iceman; and the talent of The Master, Eddie Arcaro; and there was some Shoemaker, too. Stevie stands by the spaceship and waits three minutes. Horses come from everywhere toward the spaceship. They come out of California and Chicago and New York. And they line up and say, 'Stevie, come be my jockey.' Stevie doesn't say anything for a few minutes, then waves his hand for silence. 'Horses,' he says, 'I will get to you all eventually. Be patient. I am looking for a special horse, one that can win the Kentucky Derby. You there, big chestnut horse, what is your name?' This horse says, 'Affirmed.' And Stevie says, 'Affirmed, I choose you to be my first Derby winner. We will win in 1978 before a huge crowd, and I will put up a ride that people will talk about for years to come.' And, of course, Stevie do it."

With no press conference for the losing team, Cauthen's counterpart had retreated to the Churchill Downs jockeys' quarters. After the formal press conference, Cauthen would attempt to escape there as well, only to be trailed by a swarm of reporters. As The Kid fielded a steady stream of questions, Velasquez ducked into the shower area with Maple, who had ridden Believe It to a third-place finish five lengths behind Affirmed, and the two vanquished jockeys compared notes.

"Well," Maple sighed as he soaped his head, "you beat me again."

"Yeah," Velasquez laughed, "and *he* beat *me* again."

Emerging from the shower, Velasquez turned serious as he replayed the race for reporters. "My horse had a tough time with the track; the track was too hard for him," the jockey said, alluding to Churchill's practice of rolling the dirt strip right before the race to make the surface tightly packed and fast. "I never had the problems with him like I had today. He just couldn't handle the track in the beginning. That's why he dropped back so far. Running was not on his mind. He didn't start running until the last eighth of a mile."

John Veitch had spent the last hour or so at the barn. After checking on Alydar one last time, he called Calumet to discuss the race with the Markeys. Before the trainer had a chance to say anything, the Admiral jumped in and said, "John, don't worry about a thing. He got himself too far out of it and couldn't make it up."

Veitch then told the Markeys that he might have an explanation for Alydar's lackluster performance. "When we brought Alydar back to the barn, his eye was swollen shut," the trainer said. "Something, a clod of dirt or a stone, hit him in the eye during the race. We had the vet look at it. It's swollen, but it will be fine in a couple of days. There's no damage to the eye itself."

Lucille paused for a second and then responded, "Have you told anyone about this?"

"No," Veitch replied.

"Then don't," she said. "I don't want anyone to think we are looking for an excuse. That's not something Calumet does. We'll go right on to the Preakness."

"Yes, ma'am, we will."

The next morning at Barn 41, Barrera was once again fielding questions from reporters while Affirmed pulled mouthfuls of breakfast out of his hay net. One reporter mentioned that Velasquez had said after the race that Alydar was having trouble getting hold of the track in the early going. Barrera shrugged and said, "I don't know. Might be right. Velasquez is a good rider. But if he don't get hold of the track, he don't finish second either. The only trouble he got, he can not get hold of Affirmed."

Next door at Barn 42, Veitch was philosophical as he talked about Alydar's loss. "He ran a good race, but he just got beat," Veitch said. "Nobody likes to lose, but people take things differently. I think you have to take victory in stride and you can't get screwed up if you get beaten—because you lose more than you win. Life goes on. Affirmed was the best horse in the Derby. Whether he will be the best in the Preakness and Belmont, nobody knows. We'll have to wait and see. But Alydar will try Affirmed again in both races."

Over at Affirmed's barn, Barrera was grumbling about the lack of respect for what his colt had accomplished. Affirmed had now beaten Alydar five out of seven times, capped by the previous day's decisive win in what many call America's greatest sports event. Barrera couldn't understand why everyone was still mentioning Alydar in the same breath as Affirmed.

"Does that mean the war is over?" a reporter asked him.

"The war is over a long time ago," Barrera replied firmly. "The time my horse convinced me was the Laurel Futurity. They went seven furlongs head and head, and you know what happened."

Now Barrera couldn't wait to go back to Maryland so Affirmed could prove it again, this time in the Preakness Stakes. On the Monday after the Derby, as he celebrated his fifty-fourth birthday, Barrera packed up and loaded his horse on a van headed for his barn at Belmont Park—the first step on the road to the Preakness.

Affirmed and Steve Cauthen leaving the saddling area before the Preakness (Lydia Williams)

CHAPTER 12

Affirmation

THE MORNING OF THE PREAKNESS, LAZ BARRERA WAS SITTING IN FRONT of the Stakes Barn whiling away the hours chatting with the occasional reporter who would drop by to get an update on Affirmed. As the trainer sat on his metal folding chair near his colt's stall in the barn where all the Preakness horses were stabled, Affirmed could often be caught dozing peacefully inside, head hanging low. "See," Barrera said to a visitor, "he like an old man, nodding off." Barrera turned and gestured down the long line of stalls. "See down at the other end of the barn?" he said, taking a moment to point out the differences between Affirmed and his archrival. "Alydar is being walked around. He's nervous and been walking for forty-five minutes or more. Affirmed, he no walk; he does a doze. Me, I cannot doze. I like to sit here and talk to people who stop by. The days of big races are long ones. You come to the barn at six in the morning, and if you win, you don't leave until nine o'clock at night. But you sit here long enough, you might learn something."

The trainer knew that Affirmed's ability to relax—and doze—could turn out to be the ultimate secret weapon. "This colt will relax and run wherever we want him," he said. "Affirmed is a very smart racehorse. You can do anything with him. If a band came around the barn, he would dance."

The week leading up to the Preakness had been a quiet one for Affirmed. It was clear that the Derby had taken a toll on the colt. He was noticeably leaner than he'd been before that race and Barrera's response was to rest him, giving him only as much work as was needed to keep him fit. The colt had worked only once at Belmont Park, breezing a mile in 1:40⅕ exactly a week prior to the Preakness, before shipping to Baltimore on Sunday. After resting for four days at Pimlico, he had been breezed half a mile through fog that was so dense the clockers couldn't time him. But Barrera knew just how fast his colt had covered the distance. He explained to a reporter, "We couldn't see anything, but I said, 'Here come my horse.' 'You crazy,' they told me. But I could hear him. The other horses were all 'thumpety-ump, thumpety-ump.' My horse, you could only hear 'thrrip, thrrip, thrrip.' He hits the ground and gets out of there so quick. Very light." The next day, the only exercise the colt got was walking under the cover of the shedrow overhang for about an hour.

Barrera had been fielding an assortment of questions from reporters all week. One day, he was asked if Lou Wolfson would be open to selling a part interest in Affirmed. The trainer snorted, then smiled and said, "No. Mr. Wolfson loves Affirmed so much that if he could have the horse in his bedroom, that's where Affirmed would be right now."

While Barrera was resting his horse, John Veitch took the opposite tack. Alydar had come out of the Derby fit and in good flesh, and Veitch wanted to use the days at Pimlico to make sure his horse was comfortable with his surroundings and the track surface. He worked the colt on his usual schedule, putting in a blistering six-furlong work of 1:10⅖ over a sloppy track on the Monday before the race and a sizzling three-furlong blowout in 35 seconds as the final tune-up on Friday.

After the Derby, there had been plenty of people offering postrace analysis and advice. In fact, Veitch told reporters that some three hundred fans had written to Calumet with suggestions on how to beat Affirmed in the Preakness. Not all the letters and telegrams were kind. "One fellow wrote that we ought to send Velasquez back to Panama and keep the Canal," Veitch said.

The trainer didn't need the three hundred letters to recognize that Alydar would have to run a completely different race at Pimlico. The Preakness, a sixteenth of a mile shorter than the Derby, was thought to favor early speed and would thus give a frontrunner like Affirmed a tactical advantage. But Veitch insisted that the length of the race wouldn't matter: Alydar would just unleash his big move earlier and that would be the end of Affirmed. "We beat Affirmed twice last year by flying past him with a big move," he said. "This year my colt is bigger and stronger. I feel he can wear Affirmed down in the stretch drive. If Alydar can look Affirmed in the eye, I think we can win."

Before the Derby, Veitch had told Velasquez not to be any more than three lengths behind Affirmed. Alydar's problems with the track surface at Churchill Downs had made it impossible to follow those instructions. Veitch was hoping that this time, on a softer surface, Alydar wouldn't fall so far behind and would move up on the turn to home. "We don't want to be more than three or four lengths out of it at the three-eighths pole," he told Velasquez. "I think Affirmed will go to the front and Cauthen will try to control the race while saving his horse as much as possible. You know your horse. Ride your race. Get position and come charging."

As race day wore on, Barrera became increasingly agitated. It was already mid-afternoon, and he hadn't seen his jockey all day. Though Cauthen had arrived at Pimlico in the morning, he'd been lying low in hopes of avoiding the media mob. And in the afternoon, he was too busy riding races to stop by the Stakes Barn to have a conversation with Barrera. "I'm mad at Stevie," Barrera grumbled to reporters. "He hasn't even called me yet. I wanted him out in the barn this morning so we could discuss how the race might be run. He should have been here last night. Instead, he come today. When you go out in the paddock to saddle the horse for the race, there isn't enough time to talk."

At 5 P.M., the horses were called to the paddock. Only one runner from the Derby was bold enough to take another shot at the two stars: Believe It. Joining him this time were Noon Time Spender, Indigo Star, Dax S., and Track Reward, a colt trained by Barrera's son Albert.

Track Reward was originally slated to be shipped to Chicago for the Illinois Derby, but at the last minute his owner had decided to give the Preakness a shot. "I have to do what's right for my horse and his owner," the younger Barrera explained. "I could have shipped the horse to the Illinois Derby where there's loads of purse money, but the owner would have had to pay two thousand dollars to fly him there, two thousand dollars to enter him, and two thousand dollars to bring him back to New York. That's a big investment to run a horse in a big field on a small track. And if he loses, his record shows he got beat by no great ones. In the Preakness, at least we might lose to class." The elder Barrera tried not to let his disappointment show. "What he'd really rather do is win in Illinois than lose to me here," Laz said. "But maybe that's not the choice he had. I hope Albert gets a piece of it."

As miffed as Laz was by his twenty-three-year-old son's presence in the Preakness, he was much angrier at the absence of the eighteen-year-old jockey he had come to view as a surrogate son. Because Cauthen hadn't stopped by the barn, Barrera wouldn't see him until Affirmed was already being tacked up for the Preakness. The jockey strode into the infield paddock just as Barrera was girthing up the colt. That meant the trainer would only have a few minutes to discuss race tactics with him. Once Barrera had given his final instructions and hoisted Cauthen into the saddle, horse and rider made their way to the track for the post parade to the strains of "Maryland, My Maryland."

As Cauthen warmed up his mount with a short canter at the side of the stable pony, he was startled by a sudden roar of the crowd. He looked around and saw Alydar blasting off in a high-spirited gallop toward the starting gate. It was clear that Alydar was fit and raring to go.

Lou and Patrice Wolfson leaving the saddling area to watch the race (Lydia Williams)

* * *

For the big rematch, a record 81,261 fans had packed Pimlico's historic wooden grandstand, clubhouse, and infield—the largest crowd that had ever witnessed a sporting event in Maryland—in anticipation of a stirring stretch showdown in the 103rd running of the Preakness Stakes.

In the 107-year history of America's second-oldest racetrack (behind Saratoga), the only time there had been this level of electric excitement was for the celebrated match race between Seabiscuit and War Admiral exactly forty years earlier. As post time drew near on this sun-drenched afternoon of May 20, 1978, the fans flocked to the betting windows to make Affirmed the clear favorite at 1-to-2, with Alydar the solid second choice at 6-to-5.

When the starting gate banged open, Track Reward and Affirmed sprang out in front. Coming up to the clubhouse turn, the two were running together stride for stride, with Believe It third on the rail and Alydar five lengths back in sixth. Cauthen was happy that the pace was slow but irked that Track Reward was so close. The jockey knew that Affirmed would not be able to relax with another colt running right next to him. Glancing over at Track Reward, Cauthen thought, "Fine, either go by me and get the lead or I'll go by and get the lead." Halfway round the turn, with the two leaders still side by side, Cauthen decided enough was enough and asked Affirmed for a little more pace, and they scooted ahead of the other colt.

As soon as Affirmed took the lead, he relaxed once again, waiting for a challenge. Alydar was still at the back of the pack moving sluggishly, despite having broken sharper than usual. Velasquez, not wanting a replay of the Derby, immediately started to urge his mount to pick up the pace. This time Alydar responded, and as they rounded the turn, he started to move up from fifth place.

As the leaders straightened down the backstretch, Affirmed pulled away by nearly a length, while Alydar was flying past horses on the outside. As they came around the stretch turn, Affirmed was still in front, now with Noon Time Spender just behind him on the outside. Approaching the homestretch, Affirmed's left ear rotated back as Eddie Maple urged Believe It to challenge along the rail. Suddenly Affirmed's right ear swiveled back and the crowd grew louder. Cauthen snuck a quick look back over his right shoulder and saw that Alydar was charging up.

As they hit the stretch with three-sixteenths of a mile to go, Alydar drew closer. Cauthen was ready for the challenge. He knew he still had plenty of horse underneath him. Velasquez switched his whip to the left side and slapped Alydar twice on the hip, in an attempt to get the big colt to pop onto the right lead. He was hoping that the left-handed whip might jolt Alydar into making the switch. But the colt refused.

Cauthen felt a huge acceleration as Affirmed met the challenge, and the two colts drew away from the rest of the field at the sixteenth pole. The crowd roared its appreciation for the duel that everyone had been denied in the Derby. As the two colts thundered down the stretch toward the wire, Cauthen felt they were flying. Velasquez switched his whip to the right hand and slapped his colt repeatedly, urging him on. As they powered forward and Alydar got his nostrils even with Affirmed's throatlatch, Velasquez was sure they'd caught their rival this time. But Cauthen tapped Affirmed up, slapping him repeatedly on the right hip. Affirmed surged once again, and Alydar's head dropped back to Affirmed's withers. Alydar made a final lunge, but Affirmed wouldn't be passed. As they flew across the finish line, Affirmed was still a neck ahead.

Affirmed had captured the Preakness the same way he always won the close ones from Alydar: by simply refusing to let his rival pass.

The pulsating stretch duel made an afterthought of everyone else in the field, leaving third-place finisher Believe It seven and a half lengths back. And it made a footnote of the winning time: 1:54⅖, the same clocking as Triple Crown winners Secretariat and Seattle Slew had recorded in their blazing Preakness wins.

As Affirmed stood gazing at the crowds around him in the winner's circle and posing for photos, a blanket of black-eyed Susans was draped over his withers. Pimlico's general manager marveled at what he had just seen. "I don't know when you'll ever again see two three-year-olds like this in the same year," Chick Lang told reporters. "Honest, both of them, one hundred percent honest, running their hearts out at one another. When somebody asks what a Thoroughbred is, you can describe it in two words: Affirmed and Alydar."

Minutes later, as the winning team was making its way from the winner's circle up to the press box, Cauthen was ushered into the elevator and Barrera was left behind to wait for the car to come back—which in twenty minutes never happened. Feelings obviously hurt, the trainer groused to a reporter nearby, "Steve Cauthen is the only hero in this damned game. The day before the race, Maple was here, Velasquez was here, all the jockeys were here—except Cauthen. I had about two seconds to talk to him before the race. I work all week here and he's the prima donna."

While Barrera was stuck downstairs waiting for the elevator that would never return, Cauthen was answering reporters' questions in the press box. One wanted to know if the jockey and the trainer had discussed strategy before the Preakness. "I haven't really talked to him since the Kentucky Derby," Cauthen replied. "I just read what he says in the papers. We both know the horse, and there's nothing for us to say."

The jockey then went on to describe his trip in the race. "We broke well," he started. "I thought Believe It would set the pace but he didn't, so we took the lead and just waited for Alydar. Jorge came to us in the stretch and set his horse down for a drive. I set my horse down and hit him about six times, and my horse beat his horse. That's all there was to it. The last few jumps they might have gained a few inches, but I wasn't really worried."

Alydar galloping out right after the Preakness stretch duel (Lydia Williams)

Over at the jockeys' room, the vanquished poured out their tales of woe.

"Coming to the three-sixteenths pole, I thought I was going by him," Velasquez said. "But when I got to Affirmed, he just took off again." Velasquez shrugged in resignation. "I don't know," he said, "I got about a head away from him—I never got by him—and Affirmed picked it up. He's a tough sonuvabitch. Coming to the sixteenth pole, my horse started digging in some more. He tried to get by him, and I thought he was getting to him and he could win. But the other horse took off again. He tried, but he couldn't get by him. Beat by a neck."

Eddie Maple, Believe It's jockey, was even more discouraged. "Horses like Alydar and my horse aren't losing because we're running out of gas," Maple said. "It's just that when anybody challenges Affirmed the way we did in the Derby and the way Alydar did today, he comes up with more horsepower. He didn't run away from the opposition the way Secretariat did, but he's at the head of a class of very fine horses."

For John Veitch, a day that had started out bright and full of hope was now gloomy. Sitting on the wooden fence outside the Stakes Barn, Veitch talked to reporters about Alydar, the race, and the future. "Do I think that Affirmed has broken Alydar's heart because he has beaten him six out of the eight times the two have met?" he said in answer to a question. "No. Not with a horse like Alydar. He's just too good. This Preakness was an exceptional race, and Alydar got beaten only by a neck. In racing, necks have a way of changing around from one week to the next, and three weeks from now in the Belmont, Alydar could have his neck in front. There isn't a thing in the world for Alydar to be ashamed of."

Woody Stephens wasn't quite as copacetic. He spent a few minutes summing up his thoughts on competing against Affirmed and Alydar. "I tried them in the Derby and the Preakness, and that's enough for me," he said. "I'm going to wherever they ain't. In the Derby, Believe It was beaten by less than three lengths. In the Preakness, it was nearly eight. So long, Affirmed. Bye-bye, Alydar."

Renowned cartoonist Peb's caricature of the traditional painting of the weathervane above the winner's circle minutes after the Preakness (Keeneland Library Peb Collection)

Alydar and Affirmed parading around the walking ring in the Belmont paddock (Bob Coglianese)

CHAPTER 13

Dueling for the Crown Jewel

IF WINNING THE KENTUCKY DERBY HAS ALWAYS BEEN THE DREAM OF every breeder, owner, trainer, and jockey, then going on to sweep the Triple Crown is the impossible dream—the one goal they dare not let themselves even fantasize about until it's within reach. Now that Affirmed's Derby and Preakness triumphs had made a Triple Crown possible, he and his human connections were knocking on the door of the most exclusive club in all of sports. Initiation into it was so rigorous that only ten Thoroughbreds had thus far managed to capture all three jewels of the crown he was chasing.

All that stood between Affirmed and immortality now were the Belmont Stakes, the grueling mile-and-a-half marathon revered as "The Test of the Champion," and Alydar, the formidable stretch runner still stalking his nemesis with the stubborn obsessiveness of Ahab pursuing Moby-Dick.

The intensity of their surpassing rivalry made this Triple Crown quest transcendent. In the anxious days leading to the 1978 Belmont Stakes, Laz Barrera nervously paced Barn 47 pondering how much heart and soul had gone into Affirmed's unlikely charge up the mountain—and how much more would be demanded to crest it.

"Affirmed and Alydar are going at each other for the ninth time," the trainer marveled during Belmont Week with a shake of his head. "Nine times! Muhammad Ali and Joe Frazier only went three times. If somebody beat somebody six times out of eight, wouldn't you think the other somebody would feel that was enough? Not Alydar. Here he comes again, and they are going to fight it out down the stretch."

No sooner had Affirmed survived their head-to-head slugfest down the Pimlico stretch than speculation turned to his chances of capturing the third jewel. His figured to be a much tougher challenge than any of history's ten Triple Crown winners overcame, if only because none of them ever had to face a foe as forbidding as Alydar every stride of the way. By the time those ten champions had dispatched all comers in the Derby and Preakness, the Belmont constituted little more than a coronation. All of them went on to claim their crowning glory with ease, dusting overmatched opponents and waltzing blithely down the Belmont stretch: Citation romping by eight lengths, Count Fleet by twenty-five lengths, Secretariat by an astounding thirty-one lengths. The pretenders they vanquished were anonymous before and forgotten after. If Affirmed were to join their exclusive ranks, rest assured everyone would remember the name of the archrival he had to outslug to get there.

That's why Barrera had to reach beyond the racetrack to find a metaphor in the boxing ring—and he was hardly alone in comparing the equine rivalry to the three-match blood feud waged by Ali and Frazier. Like those two legendary champions fighting for a heavyweight crown only one could wear, Affirmed and Alydar inspired Barrera to make fists whenever he talked about their stretch showdowns. Less than three years since Ali had outlasted Frazier in "The Thrilla in Manila" to cap an epic trilogy that held the whole world in its thrall, Affirmed and Alydar were promising to put an exclamation point on a classic trilogy of their own. Newspapers hyped the 110th running of the Belmont Stakes as if it were a heavyweight title bout pitting the reigning champion Affirmed against the relentless challenger Alydar.

Even before the two equine heavyweights could ship to New York for the sport's most anticipated showdown since Seabiscuit's 1938 match race against War Admiral, the venerated sportswriter Red Smith had already extended the riveting rivalry to the ring in his *New York Times* column headlined "A Tale of Two Horses." Pounding away in the Pimlico press box on the afternoon of the Preakness, Smith compared Affirmed and Alydar to a pair of prizefighters who had famously squared off twenty times more than half a century earlier. "The score is now 6–2 in favor of Affirmed but the game is far from over," Smith began. "Not since Jack Britton and Ted (Kid) Lewis made slugging each other their life work has there been a rivalry in sports to captivate the public like the continuing duel between the winner of the Kentucky Derby and the Preakness and his indefatigable pursuer, Alydar." After ticking off history's greatest individual and team sports rivalries, Smith concluded by matter-of-factly declaring, "None of these was a patch on the saga of Affirmed and Alydar."

The climactic chapter in their spellbinding saga was elevating the Belmont Stakes to a stature beyond anything in its 111-year history as the oldest of the three spring classics. Most years, as soon as there was no hope for a Triple Crown, the world beyond racing's diehard fans lost interest in what the Bluegrass hardboots dismissively called "the eighth race at Belmont." Even in those years when a Triple Crown was on the line, the Belmont Stakes still lacked the Kentucky Derby's gravitas. In part, that was because the prominence of the Triple Crown as the surest stamp of Thoroughbred greatness was itself a relatively recent phenomenon, dating back only two or three decades.

Back in 1919, when Sir Barton became the first to sweep the Derby, Preakness, and Belmont, there was no such thing as a Triple Crown. It wasn't until Gallant Fox repeated the feat in 1930 that the eminent turf writer Charles Hatton, inspired by the old Victorian tradition of the English Triple Crown, started applying the term to America's premier races for three-year-olds. Hatton's "triple crown" may not yet have merited capital letters when it was achieved by Omaha in 1935 and War Admiral in 1937, but the pithy term and the achievement it ennobled would gain traction and popularity through the sport's golden decade—thanks to the stirring sweeps by Whirlaway in 1941, Count Fleet in 1943, Assault in 1946, and Citation in 1948. By the time racing officials formally embraced the title in the 1950s and retroactively feted those first eight Triple Crown winners, there ironically were no more to honor. The Triple Crown's alluring mystique only grew during a quarter-century drought when the task proved too tough for every Thoroughbred including the great Gray Ghost, Native Dancer. By 1973, when Secretariat ended the twenty-five-year wait in the most dominating and spectacular way imaginable, the Triple Crown had become revered as the most daunting and demanding challenge in sports.

The fact that Affirmed now stood on the verge of joining 1977 Triple Crown champion Seattle Slew as history's first back-to-back winners did nothing to diminish that distinction. On the contrary, Affirmed's unlikely quest, coming on the heels of Slew's coronation as the first undefeated horse to sweep the series, only added to the romanticism of what had become racing's true holy grail—and to the pressure on everyone involved in the campaign.

For the interminable three weeks between the Preakness and the Belmont, the palpable pressure on Affirmed's connections was intensifying to a fever pitch. To Patrice Wolfson, it was nothing short of "excruciating." To Laz Barrera, it was even more wrenching than that.

"It's bad, very tough," the trainer would lament to anyone who'd listen. "It's tough on your stomach, your mind, your nerves. You say you should look in the mirror laughing in the morning, but you don't. You can't. On Belmont Day, my ulcer will bother me again and my blood pressure will go up. And when I get up early in the morning and look in the mirror, I'll say, 'Lazaro, you are having a big year. You should be proud. Laz, why aren't you smiling?'"

His big year already boasted two jewels of the Triple Crown and more than $2 million in purse earnings, twice as much as any other trainer in America. The horse responsible for that was already a millionaire in his own right, his Preakness earnings making him the youngest ever to achieve that distinction. But the closer they got to the Triple Crown, the more it weighed on the trainer. "It's so hard you begin to think it's impossible," he sighed.

Tossing and turning, Barrera could hardly get a wink of sleep. He would wake up with a start in the middle of the night, reach for the phone, and call Barn 47. "Is Affirmed alright?" he'd ask the night watchman. "Is he lying down? Good. Leave him alone." Then Barrera would lie back down himself, envying Affirmed's ability to sleep through anything.

Affirmed, calm and relaxed as ever, may have been in better shape than his anxious trainer, but the normally trim colt had lost nearly a hundred pounds from his pre-Derby weight. His saving grace may have been that the California rains, which had delayed his winter conditioning and washed away fifteen days of training, now looked like a blessing in disguise. The forced hiatus might have left him a bit fresher for the grueling Triple Crown campaign of three tough races—over three different tracks and three different distances—in the span of just five weeks. The grinding demands of that hard road had taken their toll on the eight predecessors that had won the first two legs only to falter badly in the Belmont. "What beat most of those horses when they lost the Triple Crown in the Belmont was soundness," Barrera reminded the skeptics, pointing especially to the three most recent failures over the previous decade. "Forward Pass wasn't sound when he lost, Majestic Prince wasn't sound when he lost, and Canonero wasn't sound when he lost. Affirmed, my friends, is sound."

That begged the question of how much the sapping stretch duel at Pimlico might have taken out of Affirmed. When Patrice would stop by Belmont to check on him, she couldn't help worrying that he was noticeably lighter than he had been for the Preakness. With her constant inquiries and concerns over Affirmed's condition, she drove both the trainer and her husband so crazy that Lou quipped, "Affirmed, Affirmed, Affirmed—that's all she's ever talking about. I'll be so glad when this Triple Crown is over."

Barrera had enough concerns of his own over how Affirmed was holding his flesh, how the streamlined colt couldn't afford to lose another pound. In the wake of the Preakness, the trainer was careful to simply relax Affirmed with long, leisurely gallops. When the colt breezed a mile in 1:40⅕ a week and a half before the Belmont, Barrera was happy to report that "he went the last quarter in twenty-five and change—and wasn't breathing hard." In his final work on the Wednesday before the race, Affirmed breezed a leisurely five furlongs in 1:01 without any urging from his exercise rider. "The big thing is," Barrera explained, "you want him relaxed when he gonna go a mile and a half." The trainer felt satisfied that Affirmed was indeed relaxed and girded for battle.

As for the race strategy, Barrera wasn't about to change any of the tactics that had won him the first two legs of the Triple Crown. "You win, you cannot change anything," he said. "The loser has to change."

* * *

Less than twenty-four hours after Alydar's heartbreaking loss in the Preakness, John Veitch was judging a yearling show at Timonium Race Track outside Baltimore. As people walked up hoping to console him, nearly everyone offered a variation on the same theme: "Alydar is such a great horse, but he can't get by Affirmed. It must be frustrating, but I guess you have to keep trying." The losing trainer could only shake hands politely, nod knowingly, and smile wanly.

The previous evening, shortly after Affirmed had won the Preakness by a neck, Veitch had been asked whether there were any steps he planned to take to help Alydar overcome his nemesis.

"Yeah," Veitch cracked, "put a longer neck on him."

Now, as he drove back to New York from Timonium on Sunday night, the trainer began to think seriously about what changes he could make to help Alydar finally catch his white whale. "I've got to try something," he thought. "I know that Alydar can beat Affirmed. He did it twice, and both times were at Belmont Park."

As the miles passed by, Veitch plotted his first change. "I'm going to take the blinkers off Alydar in the Belmont, and maybe that will help," he told himself. "He's a professional horse and he doesn't need them anymore.

And he might relax better without them—and that's important in a mile-and-a-half race. I think if I take them off, Alydar will be more alert and able to use his speed to get closer to Affirmed early."

He had learned that training trick from his father, Syl Veitch, who had taken the blinkers off Count Fleet's son Counterpoint to win the 1951 Belmont. The same strategy worked for the younger Veitch in 1977 when he had taken them off Alydar's half-sister Our Mims to win the female equivalent of the Belmont, the Coaching Club American Oaks. He had actually considered removing Alydar's blinkers during the prep season, but four straight wins convinced him not to tamper with what was working. Now that Alydar had lost two in a row, Veitch was convinced it was time to remove the semi-cups his colt had worn in each of his past twelve starts. "People are going to say it's a desperation move, but I've got to do something," he thought. "I'm leaving myself wide open to criticism if Alydar runs a bad race with the blinkers off. Also, if he beats Affirmed with the blinkers off, everyone will say, 'Why didn't you take them off earlier? You could have won the Triple Crown!'"

The blinker decision out of the way, Veitch pondered other tweaks he could make to give his horse that little edge he would need to get past Affirmed. The trainer had already resigned himself to the fact that he couldn't get Alydar to change leads in a race—a disadvantage that Eddie Arcaro had spotlighted in his commentary during ABC's telecasts of both the Derby and the Preakness and that was sure to become magnified around Belmont's massive mile-and-a-half oval.

If Alydar couldn't be persuaded to switch leads, Veitch might be able to make up for it with a bigger change. Having failed to overtake Affirmed in three straight stretch runs, Veitch figured it might be a good time to change his race strategy. He needed to rewrite the script that had always placed Affirmed on the lead off the turn and Alydar charging from behind down the stretch, usually with too little too late. So Veitch resolved to engage earlier with Affirmed. Just how much earlier was something he wouldn't decide until it was time to give the final jockey instructions to Jorge Velasquez.

Only once before had the runner-up in both the Derby and Preakness spoiled a Triple Crown bid by turning the tables in the Belmont. That was in 1969 when Arts and Letters, coincidentally trained by Veitch's mentor Elliott Burch, avenged narrow losses in the first two legs with a decisive Belmont win over an ailing Majestic Prince. Four years later Sham, the

Derby and Preakness runner-up to Secretariat, tried to reprise the spoiler role by engaging his nemesis in a Belmont speed duel that ultimately left him exhausted, staggering home last more than forty-five lengths behind the freshly anointed Triple Crown winner.

Determined to prove that Alydar was no Sham, Veitch resolved to sharpen his workhorse for the Belmont with the type of hard training the colt thrived on. A week and a half before the race, on the same morning Affirmed had breezed a mile, Alydar went a full mile-and-a-half lap in 2:43⅗ with Velasquez up. The Monday before the race, Alydar breezed six furlongs in 1:12⅗. That Friday, he did his usual day-before-a-race blowout through an early morning fog, covering the three furlongs on a sloppy track in a sharp 35 seconds. He appeared fit and primed, the first two classics having sapped not a pound from his strapping frame.

His mental state was another matter, especially after the two defeats that must have taken their toll on his fighting spirit, if not his muscular horseflesh. He had now lost five Grade I stakes races to Affirmed by a combined total of less than six yards, a demoralizing three of those defeats in photo finishes. In the wake of the narrow Preakness loss, reporters repeatedly asked Veitch whether Alydar's heart had been broken.

"Alydar doesn't go back to his stall and hang his head," the trainer responded. "He isn't sitting there in his stall saying to himself, 'Affirmed has caved my head in six times and now I've got to tangle with him again on Saturday and try to keep him from winning the Triple Crown.' He doesn't sit there like some football player and say, 'Oh damn, I gotta go out there Saturday against Affirmed and bang heads.' Racehorses aren't like human athletes; horses don't psych themselves out. I don't think Alydar will even be able to identify Affirmed as the horse who has been beating him when he sees him on the track Saturday. In fact, Alydar probably thought he won the Preakness. He didn't watch the rerun on the tube. Actually, we turned his television set off so he wouldn't hear all the negative comments. He's mad, though—he misses the cartoons."

*   *   *

The frenzy of anticipation building to this climactic showdown between Affirmed and Alydar on Saturday, June 10, evoked the kind of hype previously reserved for the most fabled of match races: Man o' War versus Sir Barton, Seabiscuit versus War Admiral, Swaps versus Nashua, and, freshest and rawest in everyone's memory, Foolish Pleasure versus Ruffian on the same Belmont track only three years earlier.

Of course, the way the 110th Belmont Stakes was shaping up, no one would have been surprised if it actually became a match race. Going into Belmont Week, it appeared only two other horses besides Alydar would dare even try Affirmed with the Triple Crown at stake. "After they fight one time with Affirmed, they don't come back again," Barrera said. "Believe It made a run at him in the Derby, but he don't fight him in the Preakness. None of them fight him again. Except Alydar." What was more, the one-two punch of an Affirmed-Alydar exacta scared off trainers who might have tried one of them again but figured that there would be no chance to beat both of them running virtually as a team. "Right now," Barrera said early in the week, "people are saying the Belmont will have only four starters. That could be right, but people have very short memories. Go back one year to Seattle Lou. Everybody says nobody will run against him, but seven horses fell out of the trees and ran against him." Without pausing to acknowledge the sportswriters' smiling reaction to his malapropism of Seattle Slew's name, he continued, "Third-place money in the Belmont is bigger than for the Derby and Preakness. I'll believe there will be four starters when the starters are named. But if there are only four, you have a jockey's race more than a horse race."

When the starters were named on Thursday, there were actually five: Affirmed, Alydar, Darby Creek Road, Noon Time Spender, and Judge Advocate. Not that the three longshots were anything more than historical footnotes fighting it out for show money. "It's only been two horses so far," Barrera said. "All the time, since last year, it's only been two: Affirmed and Alydar. Nothing has changed."

No matter how many or how few horses showed up Saturday, everybody was characterizing the Belmont as a pure match race. For all intents and purposes, it was.

A student of history who devoured serious nonfiction in his spare time, Veitch figured he had better verse himself in the rich tradition of the great match races. He could start by watching a replay of the first horse race ever caught on motion picture film: "The Race of the Century" between Man o' War and Sir Barton in 1920. Emboldened by winning the first Triple Crown the year before, Sir Barton had exploded from the start under his jockey's whip, but Man o' War responded quickly by grabbing the bit and the lead. Putting an exclamation point on his incomparable career, Man o'

War proceeded to literally run the horseshoes off Sir Barton, romping home seven lengths in front and smashing the track record by six seconds despite being actually rated down the stretch.

Though Sir Barton's bold attempt to steal the race at the start had no chance against history's greatest Thoroughbred, Seabiscuit's similar strategy worked to perfection in his 1938 duel with Man o' War's most famous son, 1937 Triple Crown winner War Admiral. When they finally squared off in their anxiously anticipated match race after a year of false starts, Seabiscuit, the crowd-pleasing stretch runner, stunned War Admiral, a dominating frontrunner like his father, by darting to the lead at the drop of the flag and at the crack of the jockey's whip. Grabbing the momentum with George "The Iceman" Woolf slapping away, Seabiscuit repelled War Admiral's furious drive and drew off down the stretch for a commanding four-length upset with a Pimlico track record in what was hailed the greatest match race ever run.

Of all the match races that ever captured the nation's imagination, none carried more relevance for the 1978 Belmont than Swaps-Nashua because that one, like Affirmed-Alydar, was actually a rematch race. Three months after Swaps had upset him in the 1955 Kentucky Derby by grabbing the lead early and hanging on down the stretch, Nashua was determined to turn the tables in a showdown that drew a TV audience estimated at fifty million. This time it was Nashua, normally a stalking stretch runner, who shocked everyone by getting the jump on Swaps, a confirmed pacesetter. With Arcaro whipping furiously and whooping loudly at the break from the gate, Nashua instantly grabbed the lead and stunningly romped home six and a half lengths in front.

Suffice it to say, history had taught Veitch that there was one way to win a match race: get the jump, set the tone, control the intensity of the pace, and force your rival to come get you. "The theory is that the horse in front has the advantage," Veitch explained one sunny morning in the stable area early Belmont Week. "He who sets the pace controls the race."

In their eight career meetings, that had always been Affirmed, who dictated the terms of any race and controlled the pace from the front whether he was actually on the lead or simply stalking the speed horses. In a match race, that style would give Affirmed, a versatile runner with natural speed and an arsenal of tactical options, an advantage over Alydar, a one-dimensional stretch runner notorious for breaking slow and charging late with a powerful kick. With a classic one-run horse like his, Veitch knew he had to tread a fine line: taking the fight to Affirmed earlier, but not expending Alydar's one big move too soon and sapping his finishing kick.

"What we do will depend on what happens when they come out of the gate," Veitch said. "I don't think Affirmed's speed is as much of an advantage this time as it was in the Derby and Preakness. If he uses it early, he'll have to coast the rest of the way. He's not going to get much chance to coast with Alydar behind him. Alydar will be Affirmed's shadow. I'll tell you this: the first time Affirmed takes back and slows down the pace, he's going to be looking at Alydar from behind."

To which Barrera countered, "Pace makes the race, and I can't see nobody in front but Affirmed. Stevie can do whatever he pleases in front—go as slow or fast as he wants. I don't know what Alydar will do. Maybe he's going to dingdong it with Affirmed and go head to head from the gate. But that isn't his style. Maybe when you lose six out of eight, you change your style. One thing I do know: at some point, Affirmed and Alydar are going to be head to head. Heck, aren't they always?"

In the end, down the stretch where everyone was expecting to see the two archrivals running eyeball to eyeball, it would all depend on which one was stronger and tougher over the longer distance that makes this race "the great unknown" for all the entrants. Veitch still saw the distance as Alydar's big advantage. Belmont's sweeping turns and interminable homestretch seemed custom-made for Alydar's long-striding running style and hard-charging finishing kick. Not only did he have the size edge in the tale of the tape, but Alydar had been bred for distance. His half-sister Our Mims had proven their pedigree by winning the Coaching Club American Oaks, the only race for fillies at a mile and a half, the previous summer over the same Belmont track.

"The Belmont Stakes will be a test of strength and stamina," Veitch noted. "Our strong point is stamina and strength over a distance of ground, and I think my horse is strong enough to wear that other one down over a mile and a half. We are going to try to grind Affirmed down over the final five furlongs. I'm sure they'll drag each other quite a ways. But Alydar is going to beat Affirmed, I think."

"Anybody who thinks Affirmed can't run a distance is crazy," Barrera countered, smiling as he recalled how he had transformed the sprinter Bold Forbes into the 1976 Belmont winner. "If Bold Forbes can go a mile and a half, this one certainly can. This horse can run five miles; he is no stopper. Native Dancer put a lot of class into these two colts, but I tell you this: as long as Affirmed can see Alydar, he can play with him, like a cat play with a mouse."

* * *

If those tactical mind games were likely to make this Belmont more of a jockey's race than usual, then it would thrust Steve Cauthen and Jorge Velasquez even further into the spotlight. This race, more than any other, might depend on the split-second decisions the two jockeys would have to make based on the positions of their mounts and the fractional times at each pole. As they raced against each other on lesser specimens every afternoon at Belmont Park for the three weeks leading to the big showdown, that aspect of the rivalry between the riders was heating up too.

Velasquez, usually easygoing, mild-mannered, and good-humored, was running on a short fuse in the face of criticism over Alydar's Derby and Preakness trips. When Belmont's spring meet began right after the Preakness, Velasquez had vowed to show all the critics that he was indeed "number one." He was running away with the jockey standings by racking up more winners than the next three riders combined—among them Cauthen, who for five shutout days was mired in the longest slump of his career. One day about a week before the Belmont, all the pent-up frustration finally boiled over.

"I'm tired of all that crap I've been taking," Velasquez snapped to reporters. "I'm going to keep winning and winning to make people realize that in the Derby and Preakness it wasn't the kid beating me—it was the horse. For a week after the Derby, the people got on my tail. They booed me after every ride, no matter what the odds on my horse. The week after the Preakness, the same crap. I'm a professional; usually things like that don't bother me. But it gets to the point you can't take it no more."

Velasquez went out of his way to make it clear that his anger wasn't directed at Cauthen, but rather at all the horseplayers who assumed that The Kid had outridden him in both the Derby and Preakness. "He's a nice kid; we get along beautiful," Velasquez said. "It's not anything against Cauthen. It's the public I'm mad at. He's the leading rider for one year and they think he's God. When the kid wins a hundred-thousand-dollar race, it's a big headline; I've won a lot of them and my name is always buried in the fine print. I've been one of the leading riders for twelve years. My record speaks for itself. Now I'm going to show the public who is boss around here."

Velasquez had reigned as the leading rider four of his nine years on the New York circuit, holding the annual record of 299 winners that Cauthen shattered with his 433 in 1977. Along with Velasquez's records, Cauthen had stolen the spotlight as America's cover boy. After the Derby, *Sports Illustrated* featured The Kid on its cover for the third time in fourteen months, this time riding Affirmed down the Churchill Downs homestretch with Alydar and Velasquez not even visible in the frame. After the Preakness, Cauthen smiled out from the cover of *Time* magazine, with a victory cigar clenched between his teeth and a knowing look well beyond his years.

Now, with Cauthen on the verge of becoming the youngest jockey ever to win a Triple Crown, Velasquez was burning to prove himself in the national spotlight of the Belmont Stakes, a race he had ridden six times without finishing better than third. But to do that, he would have to out-ride Cauthen, whose flawless trips in his first Derby and first Preakness had made him an even bigger superstar than he'd been as everyone's 1977 Sportsman of the Year.

If the pressure was getting to The Kid, his cool, calm demeanor wasn't betraying it. The controversy surrounding his failure to confer with Barrera until minutes before the Preakness had quickly blown over. The morning after the race, Barrera had said, "I don't want this to happen again. I'm not mad at Stevie. He's a great boy and I feel like his second father, but we have to work as a team. I love him like my own son. I will sit down and talk to him like a father." With that "father-son" talk out of the way, there was plenty of time now for trainer-jockey strategizing.

To the eighteen-year-old rider, the interregnum between the Preakness and the Belmont would feel like "the longest three weeks of my life." Though racing's wunderkind had grown accustomed to being stalked by swarms of reporters, this was something else again. A record flood of requests for Belmont press credentials inundated the New York Racing Association, drawing reporters from as far away as Japan and Australia. While Derby Week had traditionally attracted a media circus long before there was such a thing as Super Bowl Week, the anticipation of Affirmed battling Alydar for the Triple Crown kicked it up another notch during Belmont Week. The media mob got so unwieldy in the days leading to the Belmont that reporters would actually follow Cauthen into the restroom. As far as The Kid and everyone else were concerned, Belmont Day and post time for the eighth race couldn't come fast enough.

*　　*　　*

On the eve of the Belmont, Barrera was standing in front of Barn 47 under the shedrow overhang in front of Affirmed's stall when Red Smith wondered aloud, "Did you ever have a smarter horse, Laz?"

"Not like this one," the trainer told the columnist.

Barrera then mentioned the only two races Affirmed had lost in his fifteen lifetime starts—both to Alydar, both by decisive margins, both right here at Belmont. In the last one, the Champagne Stakes eight months earlier, Alydar had streaked past on the outside while Affirmed was preoccupied fighting for the lead with two other horses. "He knows better now," Barrera said, explaining how Affirmed had learned to alert his jockey to the threat of a charging contender. "Watch his ears in the stretch." The trainer made horns with his forefingers and waggled them alternately back and forth. "A horse comes up on the outside? 'Hey, Stevie!'" he said, pointing the right finger back. "A horse on the left? 'Stevie, look!'" he said, pointing the left finger back.

For all Affirmed had accomplished with his intelligence and athleticism, Barrera was miffed that many handicappers were still picking Alydar over Affirmed. Bill Nack spoke for many of his fellow turf writers when he wrote: "I picked Alydar in the Derby and Preakness, and was wrong both times. But this is a mile and a half, a test of strength, and it is too late to abandon him now."

On the eve of the big race, everyone's emotions were spent, fuses short, nerves frayed. But not Affirmed's. The colt was still enjoying his long naps, oblivious to the battle to come.

Late that night, as Affirmed rested in his stall, a TV camera crew climbed into the rafters of Barn 47. A cameraman sat on top of Barrera's barn office ceiling, shooting down on Affirmed as he slept, hoping to get some footage of the colt as he woke up. Barrera had instructed the two night watchmen to call him if anyone or anything was disturbing Affirmed. Upon seeing the TV crew, one of the watchmen called to tell Barrera about the cameraman up in the rafters. The trainer was furious. He bounded out of bed, flew down to the barn, and chased the TV people away. The next morning, Barrera reported there was no problem: "The horse slept perfect. Only *I* didn't."

Alydar and Affirmed dueling down the stretch in the Belmont Stakes (Bob Coglianese)

CHAPTER 14

Crowning Glory

Dawn broke over Belmont Park on Saturday, June 10, as serenely as it did any other perfect spring morning on western Long Island. Affirmed and Alydar were resting peacefully in the stalls they had come to call home, going through their normal routines as if this were any other race day. Laz Barrera and John Veitch had gotten to their respective barns before 6 A.M. as usual, going through their own regular race-day routines and settling in for the twelve-hour wait until the call to post for the featured eighth race. Only this time, the wait would seem more interminable and the sense of urgency more palpable than ever—especially for Barrera as he anxiously prepared to send Affirmed into battle for the final jewel of the Triple Crown.

From the moment the gates opened at 8:30 A.M., there was already a buzz of excitement building in anticipation of the 110th running of the Belmont Stakes. By the first race at 1:30 P.M., with the sun straight up in the blue sky and temperatures rising into the seventies, the largest racetrack grandstand in America was filling up with eager fans. By mid-afternoon, 65,417 of them had passed through the turnstiles, making this one of the biggest crowds in Belmont history. By late afternoon, the anticipation was crackling like electricity through the grandstand and clubhouse.

Expecting a jam-packed stadium, Belmont Park officials opted for the first time to open all 512 pari-mutuel windows to accommodate the flocks of bettors who would wager more than $1.2 million on the featured race—the vast majority of it, predictably, riding on either Affirmed or Alydar. Another $1.3 million would be wagered at Off-Track Betting parlors by New Yorkers who'd watch the race on TV like millions of others across America. The bettors at Belmont ultimately would send Affirmed to the post as the odds-on favorite at 3-to-5, with Alydar the solid second choice at even money.

The objects of all the betting and bustle had spent the long day separated by three-quarters of a mile—Affirmed at Barrera's Barn 47 on the hill all the way on the easternmost tip of the sprawling grounds, Alydar at the circular Calumet barn down near the horse tunnel leading to the paddock behind the ivy-covered clubhouse—before they would come together for what promised to be a mile-and-a-half duel to the finish.

The call to the paddock finally came at 5 P.M. Patrice and Lou Wolfson stood on the grass in front of the saddling stalls and looked back at the crowd overflowing the paddock stands that surround the walking ring. Thousands of fans jostled each other, straining to get a peek at the two chestnuts as they finished their journey down the path from the barns to the paddock.

The crowd let out whoops of encouragement when they spotted Alydar being led in by groom Clyde Sparks. A banner, made up in the devil's-red and blue colors of Calumet, was raised. It read: ALYDAR, FORGET THE PAST. TODAY IS YOUR DAY.

Moments later, a burst of applause greeted Affirmed as groom Juan Alaniz led him into the paddock. The ovation followed Affirmed like a wave around the walking ring all the way to the saddling stalls. Patrice couldn't help but remember that maiden race at Belmont a year earlier when Affirmed came prancing in, so beautiful, his mane blowing in the wind. Today, her heart was pounding and the colt was walking into the paddock so calm and poised. Patrice smiled when she saw Steve Cauthen making his way over to the stalls, the accompanying applause exceeding even the ovations accorded the two colts.

In Affirmed's stall, Laz Barrera took a few seconds to give final instructions to his jockey. Send Affirmed up from the start and position him on the inside, the trainer said. And then, "Any time Alydar goes for the lead, you go right with him. You go with him wherever he wants to go."

Over in Alydar's stall, John Veitch was taking the opportunity to give Jorge Velasquez his final instructions. Stay closer and take the fight to him earlier, the trainer said.

"Riders up!" the paddock judge's voice boomed.

Alaniz led Affirmed out for Cauthen to mount. Barrera gripped the jockey's shin and hoisted him up into the saddle. Cauthen took a few seconds to undo the first few of Affirmed's braids, so that he'd have some mane to grab on to when they bounded out of the starting gate. Patrice looked at the colt and his young rider, marveling at their composure, wondering how they and Lou could seem so calm while she and Laz felt like they were on the verge of a nervous breakdown.

Veitch likewise popped his jockey up onto Alydar's back. As the two colts then made their way around the walking ring, the crowd gave them one last round of applause to send them off from the paddock. From inside the racetrack, the familiar staccato of the bugler playing the Call to Post could be heard. As if on cue, Affirmed and Alydar were joined by the other three colts as they marched through the tunnel that would take them under the grandstand to the track.

As the five horses spilled onto Belmont's homestretch and into the sunshine, the band struck up the opening chords of "The Sidewalks of New York." Cauthen was happy to be greeted by the same stable pony and pony boy that had met them before. Trying to make it seem like just another race, the jockey chatted up the pony boy as usual. Then Cauthen said he wanted to limber Affirmed up, and they took off at a slow gallop. Meanwhile, Alydar, without a pony as usual, seemed strong and ready as Velasquez galloped him toward the starting gate.

As the colts loaded, Alydar once again balked at entering his stall, so full of himself that he had to be pushed into the gate. Once Alydar had settled into the number 2 post right outside of Darby Creek Road, Affirmed quietly slipped into the number 3 stall and then waited patiently as Judge Advocate and Noon Time Spender were loaded. Before the bell could shatter the silence, Judge Advocate broke through the gate. The false start only heightened the tension. As soon as Judge Advocate was reloaded into number 4, they were ready again.

It was exactly 5:43 P.M., but nobody in Belmont Park was looking at a clock or a watch.

*   *   *

The crowd takes a collective breath and stares at the starting gate in silent anticipation.

The bell clangs and Affirmed shoots to the front as expected. This time Alydar also breaks sharply, his head at Affirmed's left shoulder, while Judge Advocate settles in on Affirmed's right flank. Coming into the first turn, Affirmed has the lead by half a length, with Judge Advocate on the outside in second. Alydar is on the rail in third, with Noon Time Spender in fourth.

Cauthen looks back and can see the devil's-red silks on his left skimming along the rail. He drifts over a little to the outside, hoping that this will relax his horse and, maybe, tempt Velasquez to move up on the inside. Cauthen knows that Alydar doesn't like to be on the rail. Besides, if Alydar moves up on the inside, he could get trapped behind the leaders, who are bunched tightly together.

Velasquez guesses what Cauthen is up to and refuses to take the bait. He pulls his horse off the rail and swings around to the outside of Affirmed and Judge Advocate.

As they move into the turn, Affirmed is going along easily in a hand ride. The pace is leisurely and the time is slow. Judge Advocate tucks into second by a head. Velasquez knows that the only way he can win this race is to join the battle early. He moves alongside the leaders and then starts to move past Judge Advocate. Affirmed's right ear swivels back toward his rival.

The first quarter has been a slow 25 seconds. Velasquez is annoyed at the sluggish pace. "C'mon, Stevie, how can you go slow there?" he thinks. "Let's put the pressure on. This is a mile and a half. Let's see who's who in America."

They move to the backstretch and Affirmed is out in front by a length. He's gone through the opening half mile in a plodding 50 seconds, a time slower than all but three leaders in the race's 110-year history. Velasquez decides it's time to start pushing Affirmed. He doesn't want Cauthen saving his mount's strength for the homestretch.

Cauthen hears a roar building from the distant crowd and knows that Alydar is moving up. Within a few strides, Alydar cruises alongside Affirmed. With nearly a full mile still to run, the battle has been joined.

"Now we've got a speed duel beginning to develop," the track announcer, Chic Anderson, excitedly yells into his microphone.

Cauthen looks over at Velasquez and Alydar. He knows Affirmed can relax even with another horse right next to him, pushing. He thinks, "OK, let's look at each other for a while. I'm not going to let you push me too much. I'm not ready to go yet."

Velasquez sees that his plan hasn't worked. But he's fine with where he is for now. "We'll just sit alongside him and give him some competition, and make him run for his money," he thinks.

With seven-eighths of a mile to go, Affirmed and Alydar are now running as a team. They are just heads apart as they glide down the backstretch, having opened six lengths on Noon Time Spender and Judge Advocate, with Darby Creek Road still trailing in last place.

The crowd is standing on tiptoes, straining to see which colt is in front and screaming for their favorite to win. In the Wolfsons' box, Patrice tries to watch the race through her binoculars, but she can't hold them still enough because her hands are trembling so violently. She can barely breathe.

As Affirmed and Alydar cruise down the backstretch, the pace is speeding up but still on the slow side. Three quarters have gone by in 1:14. "Go ahead if you want to, buddy," Cauthen thinks as he looks over at Velasquez. But Alydar doesn't speed up. "Fine, we can play cat and mouse if you like," Cauthen says to himself.

The two colts move as one into the far turn, with Affirmed just a head in front. Alydar challenges again on the outside, but Affirmed fights back and maintains his slight lead. Now Alydar's nose is at Affirmed's ears. They pick up the pace as they power through the turn, covering the fourth quarter in a mere 23⅖ seconds and the next one in 24⅕, taking them through the first mile and a quarter in 2:01⅗.

At the head of the stretch, Affirmed and Alydar pour it on, leaving the rest of the field far behind. Affirmed still is leading by a head, but Cauthen senses that his mount is tiring. He knows Affirmed will not give up, but he's not as sure that the colt will be able to keep his head in front. "It's all or nothing today," Cauthen says to himself.

Velasquez asks for more and Alydar surges, pushing his head in front. "I got him this time," Velasquez tells himself.

Up in the grandstand, Veitch can tell that Alydar is in front of Affirmed for the first time all year and hisses a barely audible *"Got 'im!"*

Chic Anderson is now screaming his calls: "The two are heads apart. And Alydar's got a lead! Alydar put a head in front right in the middle of the stretch!"

Fans are now standing on their seats, jumping up and down. The grandstand is swaying as if it's been rocked by an earthquake. In the Wolfsons' box, Patrice can barely keep her balance with the shaking of the stands. Barrera's wife, Carmen, looks over and sees that with every passing second Laz's fingers are gripping his binoculars tighter. She's worried about her husband's heart. Lou alone has an air of calmness as he stares through his binoculars and watches Affirmed in the toughest battle of his life.

"It's Alydar, and Affirmed battling back along the inside!" Anderson is telling the crowd. "We'll test these two to the wire!"

The two colts fly down the homestretch, each struggling to take the lead. With an eighth of a mile to go, Affirmed once again pokes his head past Alydar's.

The crescendoing roar of the crowd is so loud that no one can even hear the announcer's calls.

At the sixteenth pole, Velasquez moves his colt to the left and crowds Affirmed. The jockey is thinking that if he comes close enough, he can force Cauthen to pass his whip from his right hand to his left: there's a chance that Affirmed's rider will bobble the switch and drop his whip.

But Cauthen passes the whip smoothly, and as he starts to slap his horse on the left hip, he tells himself, "It's now or never." Cauthen knows there's a chance that Affirmed's surprise at being hit on the left side for the first time will spur him to give just a little more.

Affirmed surges forward, pushing his nose in front. Cauthen keeps urging him with the left-handed whip while Velasquez whales away on Alydar's right side.

Alydar desperately challenges again, but Affirmed stubbornly digs in and refuses to let him pass. They sprint nearly dead even through the frantic final strides, straining and driving, their heads bobbing in unison all the way to the finish line.

As they cross under the wire, it's too close for the frenzied crowd to tell who has won the race as the PHOTO FINISH sign flashes.

But Cauthen knows. He stands in his stirrups and raises his left arm, his fingers still clutching the whip, in triumph. A few strides past the finish line, he looks up at the crowd and waves in exultation.

Whether it was the surprise of the hit on his left side or just pure heart that drove Affirmed forward to victory, no one will ever know.

As the two jockeys begin to pull up their mounts, Velasquez yells over to Cauthen: "Stevie, congratulations."

"Georgie, thank you," Cauthen yells back. "It ain't been easy."

Velasquez reaches down and pets Alydar on the withers. "Champ, you gave it a good try," he says to the colt. "You're still my champ."

Up in the grandstand, Patrice's legs have become so wobbly from the excitement that she falls back into Lou's arms. When she rights herself, she turns to Barrera and gives him a big hug. Like everyone else in Belmont Park, they hold their breath waiting for the finish line photo to be read. Finally, the PHOTO FINISH sign is replaced by Affirmed's number 3. The crowd immediately roars in appreciation.

The picture of the photo finish makes it official and freezes the historic moment: Affirmed's head reaching toward the wire and Alydar straining to catch up, his nose just past Affirmed's throatlatch. Affirmed has won by a head—and a short head at that, just inches.

*　　*　　*

As soon as everyone could catch their breath, the Wolfsons and Barreras, their hearts still racing and palms still sweaty, started making their way down to the winner's circle to join Affirmed and Cauthen. As they walked through the bedlam, they hadn't yet absorbed the magnitude of what Affirmed had just accomplished: winning the Triple Crown in the most thrilling way imaginable.

After Cauthen slowed his mount to a walk, he steered Affirmed toward the winner's circle in Belmont's infield. As Affirmed's connections looked on, the traditional blanket of carnations was draped over the colt's withers. A mob of photographers started snapping the obligatory win shots. As the minutes passed, the adrenaline rush from the race dissipated and Affirmed's neck started to droop. Soon, his head was down by his knees. He was so tired and so spent, a warrior who had left everything he had to give on the track. Barrera saw it and said, "Enough. No more pictures."

Barrera immediately sent Affirmed back toward the stable area with Alaniz, and everyone else made their way to the trophy presentation. As Governor Hugh Carey presented the August Belmont Memorial Cup to the Wolfsons, a jubilant Patrice hugged Cauthen, bussed Barrera on the cheek, and blew kisses to friends in the crowd.

Affirmed beating Alydar to the Belmont finish line by a head (Bob Coglianese)

By now, the significance of what their horse had just accomplished was starting to sink in. They had won not just the Belmont Stakes, but also the Triple Crown. Affirmed had become only the eleventh horse ever to sweep the Kentucky Derby, the Preakness, and the Belmont. It had been by far the hardest-earned Triple Crown in history. After racing Alydar for four miles in three showdowns over five grueling weeks, Affirmed had won the Triple Crown by a combined total of less than two lengths—easily the smallest margin of any of the eleven champions to accomplish the feat. And he had capped it off by capturing the final jewel by just a head for a Belmont coronation that all ten of his predecessors had measured in lengths.

While the winners celebrated, John Veitch walked quietly back toward the Calumet barn. As he passed by the stands, he heard a voice call out, "Hey, Veitch, you know what Alydar needs?"

The man, wielding a king-sized beer, was obviously drunk. Though Veitch would normally have just walked on without responding, he was so distracted by the emotions sparked by the race that, unthinking, he looked up and said, "What?"

"Laz Barrera!" the man shouted back with a smirk.

Veitch turned away shaking his head, wondering why on this day of all days he would have responded to a drunken fan.

As he made his way back to the stable area, his horse was in the test barn where blood and urine samples must be taken on the first three finishers after all races. Affirmed and Alydar were trudging, one behind the other, around the walking circle.

Meanwhile, Cauthen had made a beeline to the jockeys' room to change silks and prepare for the next race. As he entered the room, the valets—most of them veteran racetrackers three times his age—began cheering and applauding, then stepped forward one by one to offer handshakes and backslaps.

Cauthen looked across the room, spotted Velasquez, and walked over to him. The two riders threw their arms around each other, no hint of expression crossing either Cauthen's pink-cheeked baby face or Velasquez's worldly and wispy-mustached countenance. Cauthen spoke the only words that passed between them. "A helluva race," he said. Velasquez nodded.

Then they watched a TV replay of the race, Cauthen in silence and Velasquez in animated Spanish repartee with Angel Cordero, who had finished a distant third on Darby Creek Road.

Afterward, the two rival riders walked to opposite sides of the jocks' room, Cauthen followed by a horde of poised pens and microphones, Velasquez by himself. Cauthen reached for a Coke and, as he popped it open, said, "I can't believe it. What can you say after winning a race like that?"

As the jockey changed from the flamingo-pink silks of Harbor View to the green and gold ones he would wear in the ninth race, he fielded questions from the army of reporters. As always, his responses were terse, delivered with his usual subdued expression.

How does it feel to be the youngest jockey ever to win the Triple Crown?

"Feels very good."

What about the duel at the finish?

"Oh, it was a real horse race alright."

Then he excused himself to get back to work.

As he rushed to the paddock for the ninth race, he spotted his father and veered toward him. Cauthen grabbed and hugged his father, his excitement finally bubbling over. "Dad," he blurted, "we did it. We just won the Triple Crown. The whole Triple Crown!"

It was, for the kid, a rare public display of emotion, one that was short-lived because he needed to rush off to the next race. Riding a favorite named Thousand Nights in a claiming race, the jockey finished a well-beaten second to Romanticize, a horse owned by Harbor View and trained by Barrera. When a steward's inquiry disqualified Romanticize, Cauthen was awarded his fourth win of the day.

A short time later, now dressed in a leisure suit, Cauthen stood in the stands of the now-empty racetrack, a *Daily Racing Form* tucked under his arm, answering more questions from reporters about the only race that mattered. "I wasn't worried about any other horse in the race," he said. "I knew Alydar would come up and we would fight it out. I didn't think we'd have to fight it out for a mile, but with Affirmed and Alydar it always seems to turn out that they fight for every inch. He had the lead on us, briefly. Affirmed fought back, and I guess we got ahead of him about twenty yards from the wire."

Standing next to the jockey, Barrera nodded. "Steve gave Affirmed a perfect ride," the trainer said. "I think he deserve a kiss, so I give him one after the race."

The race had gone exactly as Barrera had planned, from the way his jockey kept Alydar close to the way his colt dug in and fought for every inch of ground. "As long as my horse sees Alydar, he don't let him get in front of him," Barrera said. "He don't let *nobody* get in front of him. It is very hard to pass Affirmed because he don't like to let anything get ahead. In the stretch Affirmed put his head in front, and I guarantee you that if they run around again, another mile and a half, his head still be in front."

But it was a hard-fought and nerve-racking duel, Barrera added, giving Alydar his due. "I'll say this: Alydar is a great horse too. He fights like a tiger. I think as long as I live, I never see two horses like these ones. Horses going head and head for so long, fighting it out to the wire. I suffered a lot through the last three-eighths of a mile. That last eighth of a mile was terrible and wonderful for me to have to watch."

For Veitch, it was terrible and excruciating. Alydar had become the most infamous runner-up in all of sports. He had earned the dubious distinction of being the only horse ever to finish second in all three Triple Crown races. If he had run the same three races without Affirmed, Alydar would have swept the series by a combined margin of twenty-two and a quarter lengths—more than every other actual Triple Crown winner except Secretariat and Count Fleet.

"What can I say? The other horse is *that* much better," Veitch said, holding his hands inches apart. "That's all. But he keeps beating us. It was a helluva horse race and we got beat. I'm proud of my horse, and we'll be back to try Affirmed again. We'll get him sometime, somewhere."

When he returned to the stable area, Veitch found Alydar already cooled out and grazing on the grass in the late-afternoon sun. As Veitch grabbed the halter, Alydar picked his head up and started nuzzling the trainer like the pet he never was before. The trainer looked his horse in the eyes and told him, "You won't remember this day and probably won't remember me, but I will never forget you."

Nor would he ever forget this private moment between a horseman and a horse who had both shown the world how to lose with grace. Even in this most crushing of defeats, Veitch remained a model of good sportsmanship, his dry sense of humor intact through it all.

Later on back at the Calumet barn, leaning over a railing with the sun setting in the distance, the trainer was waxing philosophical. "If you don't know how to lose, you'd better not play this game," he told a reporter. "You lose many more than you win. You can't be hysterical. I did the very best I could. And Alydar ran great. Maybe they should charge extra for the thrills. But if you don't get used to accepting defeat, it will drive you crazy. I learned from my father that you should lose the same way you win. And I think you show more class in the way you act when you lose than when you win." He shrugged. "You live in hopes, you die in despair," he mused. "That's why I'm not much for carrying around disappointments. I'm just looking forward to tomorrow."

With that, Veitch excused himself to the reporter, saying he had a pressing engagement with a Jack Daniel's on the rocks. But before he left to drown his sorrow at a cocktail party, he went over to Alydar's stall, leaned forward, and whispered into the colt's ear: "We'll always be friends."

*   *   *

No sooner had the sweat dried on the shiny coats of the two chestnuts than their Belmont duel was immortalized in ink as "The Greatest Horse Race Ever Run." Typing away in the afterglow of the breathtaking battle, turf writers were proclaiming it the most dramatic and most sublime confrontation of two horses ever seen on a racetrack. If such heavily hyped sports events—from match races to Super Bowls to heavyweight title bouts—rarely ever live up to their ballyhooed buildups, this one had somehow managed to actually exceed expectations.

For all its wrenching drama, The Greatest Race Ever was merely the fitting climax of what had already been acknowledged as The Greatest Rivalry Ever. The race had simply taken the rivalry to another level. Affirmed's Triple Crown triumph, Bill Nack wrote in his *Newsday* column, was "kind of a sidelight to the larger and more dramatic show—the greatest rivalry in racing history." The rivalry, Bill Leggett declared in his *Sports Illustrated* race story, "transcends what is supposedly racing's greatest show, the Triple Crown." After all, the Triple Crown had now been won eleven times—thrice in the past five years alone and an unprecedented twice in successive springs—but this kind of rivalry and this kind of race come along maybe once in an eternity.

Affirmed and Alydar had outdone not only themselves but also all their forerunners. In the late-afternoon sun of June 10, their surpassing duel had turned everyone and everything into historical footnotes.

From the moment they hit the wire, the duelists had made a footnote out of the impressive time. Despite the slow early going, which precluded any challenge to Secretariat's Belmont record of 2:24 flat, Affirmed's winning time of 2:26⅘ was still the third-fastest in the race's history. Never before had the Belmont seen a faster closing half-mile (49⅖) or a faster closing mile (1:36⅘)—a remarkable pace coming as it did at the end of a mile-and-a-half marathon. Those closing fractional splits would remain as unapproachable as Secretariat's record final time. "If Secretariat's Belmont victory was the single greatest performance ever seen on a racetrack," wrote Nack, who had authored that legendary Thoroughbred's definitive biography, "then just five years later the same race was the setting for the greatest horse race of modern times."

Like Secretariat had done in winning his Belmont by an astounding thirty-one lengths, Affirmed and Alydar's electrifying duel made footnotes out of the also-rans in their Belmont. The closest pursuers, Darby Creek Road and Judge Advocate, were so far back entering the stretch that their trainers, Lou Rondinello and John Russell, would later both sheepishly admit that they had swung their binoculars from their own colts to the two superhorses locked in battle on the lead and had gotten caught up, like everyone else, watching the desperate duel to the finish. Only after Affirmed and Alydar had swept under the wire as a team did the two trainers return their gaze to their own colts, with plenty of time to catch Darby Creek Road straggling home third more than thirteen lengths back and Judge Advocate fourth another eight lengths back.

Old-timers dug deep into their memory banks and racing manuals trying to find a race as gripping and rousing as this one. The consensus choice had been the 1962 Travers Stakes when Jaipur and Ridan dueled so close that no one could tell whose nose was in front throughout the mile-and-a-quarter race or even at the wire—until the finish line photo separated them by Jaipur's flaring nostril. But now, even that race paled alongside this duel in which two sublime rivals pushed each other to the breaking point with the Triple Crown at stake. "The sum total of the parts made this the greatest race I've ever seen," said New York Racing Association executive Pat Lynch, a former turf writer who had been watching races for five decades. "There was this enormous rivalry, and there has never been one like it before. Head and head from the top of the far turn to the wire. The only thing like this was the Hatfields and McCoys. They'll be plunking guitars about this race for years to come."

In the stable area at Belmont, they already were.

"Gosh, what a race," gushed Billy Turner, who one year earlier had trained Seattle Slew to a Triple Crown win so dominating that jockey Jean Cruguet was standing in his stirrups and triumphantly waving his whip-clenching right arm through the final twenty yards of the Belmont stretch run. "They are some pair. Three crucial races, with so much at stake, and they ran them so close together. Win, lose, or draw, there was enough glory for both of them."

"When people think about the Belmont Stakes of 1978," echoed Hall of Fame trainer Phil Johnson, "they will say they saw it and will never forget it. That's fine. I'll remember it another way. Affirmed and Alydar really started fighting each other last August in the Hopeful at Saratoga. That's when racetrackers started thinking of the two horses as something special. The way Laz Barrera trained Affirmed and John Veitch trained Alydar is beyond belief. Anyone who expects that two horses can run in the Kentucky Derby and Preakness and then come back in the Belmont and run head to head for the final mile is expecting too much. But they did it, didn't they? I don't know how they did it."

After a horse race that could easily have been mistaken for a knock-down-drag-'em-out prizefight, the Ali-Frazier analogy never seemed more apt. Affirmed and Alydar had just capped their epic Triple Crown trilogy with the equine equivalent of Ali-Frazier III. Like The Thrilla in Manila three years earlier, this thriller in New York would be seared in the collective memory for its breathtaking drama and breathless climax: Alydar poking his nose ahead evoked Frazier wresting the momentum from Ali; Affirmed reaching deep down to reclaim the lead evoked Ali rallying back; the two colts' final frantic drive to the wire evoked the two boxers savagely battling on until the fight was stopped with both seated in exhaustion. In the same manner Ali had retained his heavyweight crown, Affirmed earned his Triple Crown by surviving a grueling war of attrition that tested each rival's will, resilience, and heart.

Woody Stephens, the Hall of Fame trainer who had turned himself into a Triple Crown spectator after futile third-place finishes in the Derby and Preakness, was still catching his breath after watching Affirmed and Alydar slug it out like Ali and Frazier all the way down the Belmont stretch when he spoke for hardened horsemen everywhere. "Been around racing fifty years, and I've seen dawn come up over a lot of tracks," said the sixty-four-year-old Stephens. "People will tell you about the great races between Citation and Noor out in California in the early '50s, and the race between Ridan and Jaipur in the Travers at Saratoga in 1962. Great races. But

Affirmed and Alydar in the Belmont? Probably the best horse race that's ever been run. I'll look at it again and again anytime I'm fortunate enough to get the chance. I'll raise a glass to 'em while I'm watchin' the replays and, damn, I'll root: 'Come on, Affirmed! Come on, Alydar! Come on, Cauthen! Come on, Velasquez!'"

Stephens paused, as if savoring the stretch duel all over again in his mind's eye. "Whatever it is that these two horses have cannot be bought or manufactured," he said finally. "It's the greatest act horse racing has ever had. I hope it never ends."

Affirmed leading Alydar in the Travers Stakes at Saratoga (Bob Coglianese)

CHAPTER 15

The Anticlimax

THE MORNING AFTER THE GREATEST RACE EVER RUN, LAZ BARRERA AND John Veitch were back at work in the Belmont Park stable area. The two magnificent animals in their charge were resting peacefully in their stalls, but for the two trainers, the previous day's adrenaline high had waned and given way to a vaguely empty sensation.

The previous night, after a victory dinner with family, Barrera had gone home and watched a tape of the race. "Watching the rerun gave me a migraine headache," he complained to reporters dropping by Barn 47. "I had to keep an ice pack to my head most of the night." He also had spent most of the night swilling Maalox. "But lemme tell you," he said, "if Alydar keeps running against Affirmed, John Veitch is gonna wind up with an ulcer bigger than I got."

Down at the Calumet barn, Veitch had been keeping busy since dawn. Now, with a gaggle of reporters surrounding him, the trainer was standing, one foot propped on the bumper of his yellow Jaguar, talking about the future and how he couldn't wait for Round 10 of history's greatest rivalry—and yet another shot at Affirmed. "I think I can beat him," he said between bites of a Fudgsicle. "We were in front at the eighth pole and there's no reason we can't be in front again—at the wire next time."

The Greatest Race Ever Run may have anointed Affirmed as the eleventh Triple Crown winner and cemented the entwined legacy of the two archrivals, but it did not settle the debate over which horse was better. As far as Alydar's supporters were concerned, the rivalry was just heating up. They were impatiently waiting for the beginning of the next chapter in a compelling saga that was still gaining momentum.

The next big race where the two colts were likely to meet up was the Travers Stakes on August 19, a date both trainers had already circled on their calendars. America's oldest stakes, dating back to 1864, the Travers has always been the marquee race of Saratoga's August meet. Reverentially called "The Mid-Summer Derby," it's where the top three-year-olds that have battled it out in the Kentucky Derby and the other two spring classics vie as more mature and more seasoned combatants in what some call "the fourth leg of the Triple Crown." The promise of another Affirmed-Alydar showdown, coming in the afterglow of their surpassing duel in the Belmont, was raising the excitement and expectation for the 109th Travers Stakes beyond anything in the history of America's most storied racetrack. What could these rivals possibly do for an encore?

* * *

When Belmont Park closed for the season, Barrera vanned his stable of thirty horses up to Saratoga, lodging his charges in the barns near the Oklahoma Track, which was the site of the very first races at Saratoga back in 1863. When the current track was built on the other side of Union Avenue in 1864, the Oklahoma was kept as a training track where it would be used mostly for jogs and gallops. Some trainers, Barrera among them, preferred to be stabled in the barns around the Oklahoma because it put them a little off the beaten path.

Patrice and Lou Wolfson had driven up to Saratoga Springs to catch the monthlong meet and, once again, had rented a house close to the racetrack. Just as they had the year before, the couple stopped by to visit with Affirmed each morning so that Patrice could give him his hugs. Lou would stand back, a smile playing on his lips, as he watched his wife cuddle with the colt. Lou never got too close. He didn't need to snuggle with his star. His joy was simply in watching Affirmed run.

The colt had been recuperating from the grueling Triple Crown campaign ever since the Belmont Stakes, his only exercise consisting of jogs and leisurely gallops. Now, in addition to the gallops on the Oklahoma, there would be a work or two on the main track at Saratoga to sharpen him for the Jim Dandy Stakes on August 8, which would be his prep for the Travers.

The Markeys had already been in Saratoga Springs for a month by the time the Wolfsons arrived. As they became older and more frail, Lucille and the Admiral switched from vacationing in Europe to summering in

Saratoga at their twenty-five-acre estate just off East Avenue. The big mansion had amenities that made it easier for the older couple, like an elevator that allowed them to avoid walking up and down stairs. The property had the added advantage of being near the storied racetrack dubbed "The Spa."

John Veitch had vanned the twenty-four Calumet horses up to Saratoga when Belmont had closed for the season. When he met up with the Markeys, they handed him an envelope. Inside were two letters, one addressed to Admiral Markey and the other to Veitch himself, both written by Lou Wolfson and dated June 14, 1978, four days after the Belmont Stakes. Wolfson had wanted to let Veitch and the Markeys know how highly he regarded them as competitors and how much he appreciated their commitment to racing.

To the Admiral, he wrote: "I want to take this opportunity to express to you and Mrs. Markey my sincere feelings and congratulate you on raising and running this great three-year-old, Alydar, which has, along with Affirmed, brought new life, interest, and pleasure to millions of people, many of whom have never had an interest in racing before." He went on to give their trainer a pat on the back. "The conduct of your young trainer, John Veitch, has been outstanding. He is not only a good horseman, but also a perfect gentleman."

The second letter was shorter, but carried similar sentiments. Addressed to Veitch, it read: "I'm very sorry I did not have the opportunity after the Belmont Stakes to congratulate you on the great job you did with Alydar. I thought the Belmont Stakes was one of the most exciting races in the history of the sport."

Though Alydar had shown little sign of wear after the Belmont, Veitch wanted to let him rest until the Saratoga meet. But the colt was revved up following the race, and with each passing day he got harder and harder to handle, bucking and rearing as he was led around the barn. So the trainer decided to enter him in a race to take some of the edge off. After looking at what was available, Veitch chose the Arlington Classic on July 22 in Chicago. Alydar was in peak form and raring to go. The colt, who came in as the 1-to-20 favorite, stalked off the pace until the final turn, when he took off like a rocket, flying by his competitors to win by a full thirteen lengths. With that as a warm-up, the next race would be the Whitney Stakes at Saratoga on August 5. Though the race was open to horses of any age and a Barrera star, J. O. Tobin, was entered, Veitch was confident that his colt would prevail.

Saratoga was the one track where the Markeys and their racehorses lived in close proximity. Taking advantage of that, the couple visited the barn regularly. When they'd arrive, Veitch would set up lawn chairs for the Markeys and give them a private little horse show, pulling out the colts and fillies one by one so that Lucille could see them up close. When Alydar was brought out, she would dig out a lump of sugar, carefully place it on her flattened, white-gloved palm, and hold it out to her "baby." He'd hungrily snatch it from her hand, suck it to the back of his mouth, and crunch it with relish in his powerful molars, licking his lips when it was all gone.

One day as Veitch was running through his show-and-tell, a barn cat hopped up onto Lucille's lap, startling her so much that she tipped over backward in her lawn chair. Veitch was horrified to see the frail old lady hit the ground. But Lucille just got up, dusted herself off as if nothing had happened, and asked for the show to continue.

Though the Markeys were able to stop by the barns to visit their horses, they still couldn't watch any of them run in person. Saratoga just wasn't set up for wheelchairs, and the logistics were too difficult to allow the Markeys to get up into the stands. So on the first Saturday in August, when Alydar entered the starting gate for the nine-furlong Whitney, the couple was listening on the radio.

At the bell, Alydar broke sharply, but fell back to sixth, thirteen lengths behind the leaders by the time the field hit the first turn. He was relaxed and galloped easily at the back of the pack until the final turn, when he took off like a shot, flying by everything in front of him with stunning speed to win by ten lengths. Veitch smiled to himself, pleased with the colt's two wins. Everything was going according to plan. This time, he was sure they would catch Affirmed, and Alydar would be vindicated.

Veitch knew all about the veracity of Saratoga's nickname "The Grave-yard of Champions." It was there, in the 1930 Travers Stakes, that Gallant Fox, as the odds-on favorite fresh off his Triple Crown sweep, lost by eight lengths to a 100-to-1 longshot named Jim Dandy. And it was there, in the 1973 Whitney, that Secretariat, as the 1-to-10 favorite fresh off the thirty-one-length Belmont romp that capped his Triple Crown coronation, was upset by an unknown longshot named Onion. Now Veitch was taking aim at the champion who'd won the latest Triple Crown at Alydar's expense.

The day after the Whitney, Affirmed was out on the main track putting in a fast work to tune up for his Travers prep race. Barrera was happy to see the colt breezing easily with his last quarter in a little over 22 seconds. After two months off, his colt was ready for a challenge.

As Affirmed and his groom made their way back to the barn, a photographer caught up with them and asked if he could shoot a picture. Affirmed and Juan Alaniz paused for the photo. The colt seemed to know he was the subject of all the attention, standing a little taller and turning his head to the left like a model trying to show off her best side. Watching her colt, Patrice told a reporter, "He's almost human." Then she regaled the reporter with the story of Affirmed's escape at Santa Anita. "He was dodging other horses and his trainer, Laz Barrera, was chasing him, and it was only later that we all thought, 'What chance does a man have to catch a racehorse?'" Patrice said with a smile at the memory. "But Affirmed wasn't hurt, and when we got him back, Juan said in a severe tone, 'Bad boy.' Affirmed dropped his head. He knows what 'bad boy' means. He doesn't like being called 'bad boy.'"

Two days later, Affirmed was in the starting gate waiting for the bell that would signal the start of the Jim Dandy Stakes. When it clanged, he broke with his usual sharpness, but then fell to the back of the pack. Barrera, who was sitting next to Patrice in the Wolfsons' box, jumped up, a look of concern spreading across his face. "My God," Barrera said, "what's happened? Did he break down? What's the matter?"

Barrera continued to stand, watching as Sensitive Prince took the lead and Affirmed dawdled down the track a full twelve lengths behind the leaders. It was clear now that the horse was OK, just not running his usual race. Patrice wondered if there was any way her boy would be able to catch up. She knew that Sensitive Prince had dangerous speed and was now far out in front. She also knew that his trainer, Allen Jerkens, had played the spoiler at Saratoga before, upsetting Secretariat with Onion.

Coming off the final turn, Affirmed seemed to suddenly find his stride. The afterburners flashed on and he began to run down Sensitive Prince, who by this time was still a good eight lengths out in front. With each stride, Affirmed closed on Sensitive Prince as they thundered down the homestretch, but the distance between the two colts seemed insurmountable. At the eighth pole, Affirmed was still four lengths behind Sensitive Prince. Then, at the sixteenth pole, Affirmed seemed to explode, rocketing toward Sensitive Prince, who now looked as if he were running in slow motion. By the time they hit the wire, Affirmed was half a length in front, having run the last furlong in just 11 seconds. Barrera let out a sigh of relief and dropped back into his seat, exhausted. It had been an amazing race, he thought, almost as thrilling as the Belmont. And it had also shown that the colt was ready for battle.

As the day of the Travers grew near, the excitement continued to build. One day as the Markeys' car rolled up Broadway, the crowds walking along the street recognized the silver Rolls-Royce and started rhythmically chanting "Al-ee-dar, Al-ee-dar, Al-ee-dar . . ."

Lucille smiled.

*   *   *

At the track in the days leading to the Travers, the tension was getting on Barrera's nerves. He was tired of hearing Veitch predict Affirmed's imminent defeat.

"Won't this ever end?" Barrera snapped one morning at the stable. "He always come back and fight again. The record is seven wins for Affirmed and two for Alydar. If this was boxing, he wouldn't get no more shots at the title. For a young man who is supposed to be a good trainer, Veitch certainly say some stupid things. He always say he has a new way to beat Affirmed. What new way? Seven out of nine, and four losses in a row to Affirmed, don't show me any new way."

Part of what was making Barrera so bristly was the possible loss of his jockey. Steve Cauthen had been injured in a spill at Saratoga ten days before the Travers, and his knee still had not recovered. Although his agent assured Barrera that the jockey would be fine by the time the big race rolled around, the trainer could see that Cauthen was still limping and protecting the joint. Several days before the Travers, Barrera put a call in to Laffit Pincay's agent. When he got Tony Matos on the phone, Barrera asked if Pincay would be willing to be his backup jockey. No problem, Matos had said. In the end, Cauthen's knee didn't heal and Pincay got the mount.

The day of the Travers dawned with the usual morning mist, but the moisture soon burned off to reveal blue skies and pleasant temperatures. The two colts were relaxing peacefully in their stalls as their trainers and jockeys geared up mentally for the long-anticipated battle.

With the infield open to the public, a record crowd of 50,122 jammed itself into The Spa—almost 15,000 more than had ever seen a race at America's oldest track. An hour before post time, fans were standing four-deep behind the paddock's white fence eagerly awaiting the arrival of the two archrivals. Affirmed walked in first, and the crowd burst into applause. After the longshots Shake Shake Shake and Nasty and Bold entered to silence, Alydar strutted in last and was greeted by another round of applause. The differences between the two favorites couldn't be missed: Alydar was even more mature-looking, taller, heavier, and more muscled than he had been two months earlier, while Affirmed still had a sleek, trim, deerlike appearance.

As they made their way to the track, the tote board flashed the same final odds as the Belmont: Affirmed favored at 3-to-5, with Alydar second choice at even money. The four colts loaded into the starting gate, Affirmed in the number 3 post position with Alydar just to his outside.

At the bell, the two favorites broke sharply, just behind Nasty and Bold on the rail with Shake Shake Shake, ridden by Angel Cordero, right next to him in second. Shake Shake Shake soon took the lead, with Affirmed and Alydar close behind. As they moved into the turn, Shake Shake Shake continued to lead, with Affirmed on his outside. Alydar had now dropped back to last on the outside.

Alydar started moving up on the outside and was soon in third as they made their way down the backstretch. Cordero's 20-to-1 longshot started to drift to the outside, taking Affirmed with him all the way to the middle of the track, opening space along the rail. Velasquez guided Alydar behind the leaders toward the rail. When Pincay heard the crowd, he looked over his shoulder and spotted the devil's-red silks coming up on the inside. He tapped Affirmed up. As they powered past Shake Shake Shake, Pincay asked his colt to move over toward the rail. Alydar, meanwhile, had passed Shake Shake Shake on the inside and was also moving up.

But by now Affirmed was coming toward the rail fast, closing the hole. As Affirmed's haunches swept toward Alydar's head, Velasquez took his colt back sharply, yanking on the reins and pulling him to the outside as the crowd let out a collective gasp. Startled, Alydar lost his momentum for a few seconds, dropping back about five lengths. But then he found his stride again and made another run at Affirmed, this time on the outside as they came around the final turn.

As they hit the stretch, Velasquez slapped his colt twice on the left hip and this time Alydar switched to the right lead. The two colts thundered down the stretch, both jockeys slapping their mounts to encourage them forward. But Alydar was once again denied. Affirmed was a length and three quarters in front as they crossed under the wire.

The tote board showed Affirmed in first place, but his number was blinking and an INQUIRY sign had been posted. The stewards pulled the video that had been shot from the tower and scrutinized it, trying to figure out exactly what had happened.

Waiting for the verdict in the Wolfsons' box, Barrera seethed. He was sure that there had been some sort of conspiracy between Velasquez and Cordero, who had opened up the hole on the rail by allowing his colt to drift out and, in turn, pushing Affirmed into the center of the track. Barrera was hot and wanted to go up and complain to the stewards. He insisted that Velasquez had to have seen Affirmed coming over but pushed up along the rail anyway, endangering both colts. The jockey never should have taken that chance, Barrera fumed. Lou Wolfson realized there was nothing to be done at this point. The most important thing was that neither horse had been hurt. He tried to calm Barrera down, finally telling him, "Let's drop it."

For his part, Veitch was angry at Pincay for a move that he saw as putting Alydar's life at risk. When Velasquez had yanked his colt back, hoping to quickly go around Affirmed, it had looked, from where Veitch stood in the grandstand, as if Alydar might have broken down.

Moments later, the stewards made their decision: Affirmed was disqualified and his number was placed second on the tote board while Alydar's was moved up to first. The crowd that had been cheering just a short time before began to boo.

Alydar was ridden over to the winner's circle. Veitch accepted the trophy for the Markeys and quickly left to check on his horse. Back at the barn, Veitch noticed that Alydar had a bruise on his right leg and cuts on both front legs. He was incensed. "Pincay should get thirty days on bread and water," he snapped. "I think he blew the race and panicked. There is no place on a racetrack for any rider who does that."

Barrera sat in the Wolfsons' box, still seething as he watched the next race. He was so angry that he couldn't let go of what had happened in the Travers. "Alydar don't got no business to be in there on the rail if he don't know Cordero was going to open up the inside for him," Barrera sputtered. "My horse was head and head with Cordero's horse, and all of a sudden Cordero's horse took my horse out and left the rail to Alydar."

An hour and a half after the race, Velasquez came over to the Calumet barn to celebrate, carrying a bottle of champagne. But for Veitch, the win was tainted, the victory hollow. This wasn't how he wanted to beat Affirmed. There would be no party afterward—and the bottle of champagne was never drunk. It sat in front of the barn unopened.

When everyone had left, Velasquez walked over to Alydar's stall to commiserate. "We're going to get him next time," he told the colt. "It's a shame we couldn't have done it on our own. You were going to beat him. This is the worst way for the thing, between you and Affirmed."

The Travers took what had been a gentlemanly competition and turned it into an ugly brawl. In the aftermath of the race, each camp took potshots at the other. Reporters speculated that there had, indeed, been some sort of prearrangement between Velasquez and Cordero to set up Pincay and Affirmed. Bill Nack summed it up for many of them. "I believe he was set up because Angel and Jorge were very good friends," *Sports Illustrated*'s turf writer said later in a TV interview. "I used to see them at dinner at night at Saratoga, and they were the best of buddies. And Pincay was a California guy. These guys were New York guys. And I'm sure that Angel told Jorge, I've got no chance and I'll just make room for you and I'll do whatever I can for you."

When a reporter told Veitch that Barrera had blamed the incident on Velasquez for putting Alydar on the rail, Veitch was incensed. "That's chicken," he snapped. "Who the hell is Barrera to say that Velasquez couldn't go to the inside? Does he own the racetrack?"

Fed up, Barrera vowed to keep his colt away from Veitch's: "I don't plan to run no more against Alydar."

* * *

In time, the hard feelings between the Affirmed and Alydar camps would soften, and the controversial ending of the Travers would be overshadowed by the memory of the nine previous meetings that had brought out the best in both colts. They would never race against each other again, but their riveting rivalry would live on forever in the mind's eye.

EPILOGUE

Where Have You Gone, Affirmed and Alydar?

THE YEAR AFTER AFFIRMED HAD OUTDUELED ALYDAR TO CAPTURE THE Triple Crown in the most electrifying fashion imaginable, Laz Barrera was entertaining a turf writer at his home just a few furlongs from Santa Anita Park. When the *Daily Racing Form* columnist asked if he could see the trainer's Triple Crown trophy, Barrera smiled wryly. "You wanna see my Triple Crown trophy?" he said. "I'll *show* you my Triple Crown trophy." With a flourish, Barrera unbuttoned his shirt, pulled it open, and showed off a seventy-two-stitch scar bisecting his chest. He considered the scar— resulting from bypass surgery after a massive heart attack early in 1979—a memento of all the stress and pressure from the previous year's grueling classic confrontations.

From the peak of the Belmont Stakes coronation, 1978 had not ended well for Affirmed, Laz Barrera, or Steve Cauthen. In his September return to Belmont Park following the Travers disqualification, Affirmed took on Seattle Slew in a historic showdown pitting two Triple Crown winners against each other for the first time ever. Though the fans made Affirmed the heavy favorite, he finished an exhausted second, a galling three lengths behind Slew.

In their nationally televised rematch back at Belmont a month later in the Jockey Club Gold Cup, Affirmed ran up against even worse luck after hooking Slew in a speed duel right out of the gate. Both Triple Crown winners were roaring side by side through the clubhouse turn when, suddenly, Cauthen's saddle slipped forward onto Affirmed's withers. With the jockey unable to balance himself or control his mount, Affirmed flew down the backstretch with Slew at a suicidal clip for a mile-and-a-half marathon. Spent, Affirmed faded to fifth and trudged home through the mud nineteen lengths behind Slew, who himself was overtaken by Exceller to lose by a nose. For Affirmed, it was an ignominious comedown from that spring's crowning glory.

Despite the disappointing denouement to the season, Team Affirmed cleaned up at the 1978 Eclipse Awards: Affirmed winning as Horse of the Year and champion three-year-old, Barrera as outstanding trainer for the third straight season, and the Wolfsons' Harbor View Farm as leading owner and leading breeder for the first time ever.

Affirmed and his connections returned to the track the following January determined to avenge the three-race losing streak and to reaffirm his worthiness as a great champion. After two more demoralizing defeats, Barrera knew he needed to make a big change. With Cauthen mired in an unfathomable 110-race losing streak—a shocking fall from grace that mirrored Affirmed's—Barrera decided to give the mount to Laffit Pincay, the veteran jockey who had filled in twice before.

Affirmed, responding to Pincay's more dominant riding style, promptly ran off with the Strub Stakes by ten lengths and the Santa Anita Handicap by four and a half. The Santa Anita celebration was shortened, however, when Barrera had to be whisked from the winner's circle to the hospital, suffering the heart attack that would require triple-bypass surgery. Less than three months later, remarkably, he was back to saddle Affirmed for two straight impressive wins in handicap races. Burdened with a backbreaking 132 pounds, Affirmed was at his gritty best in the Hollywood Gold Cup as he vanquished challengers carrying 12 to 20 fewer pounds.

By the time Affirmed shipped east late that summer for his triumphal return to Belmont, Alydar had already run the last race of his career. Just three weeks after the Travers, Alydar's 1978 season was cut short by a fractured coffin bone. He came back the following year looking burlier and more intimidating than ever, but he was no longer the same force of nature. He lost four in a row, managed to win a minor stakes, and then struggled to a woeful third in the Suburban Handicap at Belmont on the Fourth of July. Two weeks later, after sustaining a hairline sesamoid fracture, Alydar was retired from a racing career in which he had won fourteen of his twenty-six starts and $957,195 in purses. He returned to Calumet Farm to stand at stud without the kind of hero's welcome that had greeted the likes of Whirlaway and Citation.

In stark contrast, much fanfare welcomed Affirmed back to Belmont Park later that summer. The golden chestnut struck the New York fans as more muscled up, mature, and substantial than he had been the year before. As a four-year-old, his head had dried out to give it a fine, chiseled appearance, while his neck remained slender, shapely, and elegant. A model of consistency on the track, he ran with the precision of a stopwatch and the grace of Barrera's favorite two-legged athlete. "If Affirmed was a baseball player, he'd be Joe DiMaggio," the trainer liked to say. "DiMaggio made everything look easy; he was a perfect ballplayer. Affirmed does the same thing: you never know how hard he is trying." Affirmed certainly made it look easy that summer in New York, first trouncing 1979 Belmont Stakes winner Coastal in the Woodward and then taking on a challenger even more daunting than Alydar.

In what would be hyped as "The Race of the Century," Affirmed faced a summit showdown with Spectacular Bid, the steel-gray colt who had been on the verge of his own Triple Crown coronation until stepping on a safety pin the morning of the Belmont and getting upset by Coastal. Affirmed, carrying five more pounds than Spectacular Bid in the Jockey Club Gold Cup that October, rocketed right to the lead and then dared the younger stretch runner to pass him. Time and again around Belmont's mile-and-a-half oval, Spectacular Bid would discover what Alydar had known all too well. Four times Spectacular Bid challenged for the lead, and each time Affirmed dug in, surged forward, and drew away on his own without any urging from Pincay. Then when Coastal suddenly came charging up to the front on the stretch turn, Affirmed looked him in the eye, too, and promptly snatched back the lead. With Spectacular Bid unleashing a desperation drive down the stretch, Pincay finally went to the whip and Affirmed responded, stretching out and pulling away over the last hundred yards to win by a widening three-quarters of a length.

On the very track where his career had begun in total obscurity and peaked with the Triple Crown coronation in the glare of a national TV spotlight, Affirmed now had fittingly clinched his second straight Horse of the Year title to join the likes of Secretariat, Kelso, and Forego as the only repeat winners since World War II. More than that, the superb triumph had burnished Affirmed's reputation as one of the most tenacious, resourceful, and consistent warriors ever to grace a racetrack. "Look at him," Barrera marveled as he entered Affirmed's stall to say goodnight after the Gold

Cup. "It look like he don't even run. He knows he's a champion. No horse can look like that and not be a champion."

Two weeks later, on the eve of what was to be Affirmed's farewell race, Barrera made a surprising announcement: the richest Thoroughbred of all time would never compete again. Rather than run Affirmed as scheduled in an Aqueduct stakes on a grass surface he disdained, Lou Wolfson had taken Barrera's advice to retire the champion colt while still completely sound.

For the record, Affirmed had won twenty-two of his twenty-nine races—including seven of his ten meetings with Alydar—and an unprecedented $2,393,818 in purses. Now, the first horse ever to win $2 million would stand at stud, having been syndicated the year before for a record $14.4 million. But not before enjoying one last curtain call. Parading down the Aqueduct stretch on "Affirmed Day" two weeks later, he would take his final bows: walking and jogging in front of the stands to a fitting ovation, pausing now and then to strike a pose for photographers, holding his head a little higher as if to improve the camera angle on his familiar white-striped face. "It's like saying goodbye to someone in your family," Barrera lamented, brushing away a tear. "Watching over this horse was like being with a person you love: seven days a week you worry, going to the barn every morning for three years. I'm going to miss him."

So would Patrice Wolfson. A few days after the public farewell, it was time for her to privately say goodbye before her special pet was loaded on a plane to start his new career as a stud horse. It was going to be a tough transition for both Patrice and Lou. For the past three years, they had traveled with their colt from coast to coast, following his races and visiting with him most days. Now he was going to Kentucky, far from where they lived. "We'll get down there every once in a while," Patrice said as they stood in front of Affirmed's Belmont stall. "I think they're trying to wean me away from him right now."

Lou stood behind Patrice with his hand on her shoulder while Affirmed curled his neck around so he could once again bury his head in her arms.

"I'm gonna miss you, big boy," Patrice said, her voice starting to crack. "I'm gonna miss you."

Then, as she stroked his face, she planted a kiss on his forehead.

*　*　*

Arriving at Spendthrift, Affirmed settled into the farm's famed stallion barn and bedded down in the stall right next door to his sire, Exclusive Native, who in turn lived adjacent to his own sire, Raise a Native. Like his father and grandfather, Affirmed now earned his living in Spendthrift's bustling breeding shed, the very building where both he and Alydar had been conceived.

Over the next few years, though, the Spendthrift breeding empire would crumble financially and Affirmed would have to look for new digs. Out of loyalty to Spendthrift boss Leslie Combs, Lou Wolfson had initially resisted the temptation to follow the lead of Seattle Slew's owners and move Affirmed to greener bluegrass pastures. All this despite the fact that Lou had been given an open invitation to move Affirmed to—of all places—the hallowed home of Alydar, Calumet Farm.

Though hesitant to abandon the sinking Spendthrift, Lou was lured by the romantic notion of Affirmed and Alydar renewing their rivalry in the same Bluegrass breeding shed. "It really would be something to see those two horses side by side again," Lou mused to a go-between.

A year later, with Spendthrift now in freefall, Lou finally agreed to transfer Affirmed to nearby Calumet Farm. On October 10, 1986, Affirmed strode out of the van and joined Alydar in Calumet's opulent stallion barn.

As eleven-year-olds, the two chestnut archrivals lived in adjoining stalls, separated by a concrete wall trimmed in oak. Though they couldn't see one another, each could hear the other rustling through his straw, crunching his oats, and sucking down his water. Outside the barn, they got to see quite a bit of each other during the day—while grazing in their nearby three-acre paddocks, while nickering at the broodmares that were vanned in for servicing, while being led to and from the breeding shed. Their differences in temperament could now be seen in greater relief: Affirmed remained the more tractable and sociable of the pair, while Alydar was more aloof with a bit of a nasty streak.

The breeding shed was where Alydar's fans had hoped their star could finally claim a measure of redemption and revenge. They'd never given up the idea that Alydar was the better horse, even after watching their darling get beaten time and again. If he couldn't best his nemesis on the track, perhaps he could prove his superiority through his progeny.

By the time Affirmed joined him at Calumet, it looked like the Alydar adherents were getting their wish. Alydar—more regally bred than his nemesis as the son of Raise a Native and Calumet's foundation dam—already ranked as one of America's most prepotent sires. His yearlings were bringing in an average of $500,000 at auction, almost double what Affirmed's brought. Among active sires ranked according to the average earnings of their progeny in the mid-1980s, Alydar was second behind Seattle Slew while Affirmed wasn't even in the top sixty-five stallions on the list. Alydar's stakes winners were rolling out as if they were coming off an assembly line, leading some to compare him to the greatest of all Calumet sires, Bull Lea.

Alydar's first foal crop featured two $1 million earners, including Althea, the 1983 Eclipse Award winner as champion two-year-old filly. His second foal crop boasted Turkoman, the 1986 Eclipse winner as champion older horse while running his earnings past the $2 million mark. By the time his fourth foal crop had produced Alysheba, Alydar could spend the spring classics living vicariously through the progeny he was stamping with his own strapping size, powerful stride, and regal look.

In the 1987 Kentucky Derby, Alysheba accomplished something his sire had been denied by Affirmed: capturing America's marquee race. After repeating in the Preakness, all that stood between Alysheba and the Triple Crown were the Belmont and Bet Twice, the fierce rival he had outdueled in the first two legs just like Affirmed had Alydar nine years earlier. The difference was that Bet Twice rebounded to spoil the party, winning the Belmont by fourteen lengths while Alysheba faded to a sorry fourth. Alysheba would go on to win the 1988 Breeders' Cup Classic, the Eclipse Award as Horse of the Year, and a record $6,679,242 in career earnings.

By the time Alysheba was retired, Alydar had produced a talent every bit as good: Easy Goer. In 1989, with Sunday Silence poised to become the twelfth Triple Crown winner, Easy Goer accomplished something his sire couldn't against Affirmed: turning the tables after close seconds in the first two legs. Playing the spoiler in the Belmont, Easy Goer trounced his nemesis by eight lengths in a time bettered only by Secretariat's record and then went on to amass $4,873,770 in career earnings.

Alydar's boosters could now brag that their star had finally risen above Affirmed, who as a sire hadn't yet produced anything remotely as successful on the track as himself. Alydar may have gotten his redemption in the breeding shed as a prepotent sire, but it would come at a cost.

*   *   *

In the wake of Lucille Markey's death at the age of eighty-five in 1982, two years after the Admiral's passing, everything that she feared for Calumet Farm came to pass—and then some.

Under the terms of Warren Wright's will, Calumet had been Lucille's to run as long as she lived and then was to pass to their only son. But since Warren Wright Jr. had died in the midst of the Affirmed-Alydar Triple Crown campaign, the farm had passed to his heirs: his wife, Bertha, and their four children. That's how control of Calumet wound up in the hands of their daughter Cindy's husband, J. T. Lundy.

Lundy, a good ol' boy with extravagant plans for Calumet, immediately began to take out huge loans to restore and update the farm as well as to purchase new, expensive racing stock. Starting with a $13.2 million loan in 1983, he quickly added to that debt with a $20 million mortgage on the farm and another $25 million in loans from Lexington banks. Two years later, he borrowed another $50 million. By 1990, the banks were starting to get nervous. One, First City Bank, called in its $15 million loan in October of that year. Lundy was told that if he didn't pay off the loan by the following February 28, the bank would foreclose on Calumet, taking everything including the horses. By this time, the farm was bleeding money at a rate of $1 million per month. It didn't look like there was any way out.

But then, on a chilly night in November, Alydar was discovered in his stall with his right hind leg broken, the bone exposed and hanging by skin and tendons. Though veterinarians tried to save his life, Alydar was eventually put down. Which meant that Lundy would be able to collect on the almost $40 million insurance policy that he'd taken out on the prize stallion.

Many were suspicious, wondering how Alydar could have sustained such a severe break while in his stall. As it turns out, that wasn't the first time Alydar had a suspicious brush with death. In the early 1980s, he had become severely ill and seemed on the verge of dying until an astute vet diagnosed lead poisoning. Lundy told the *Los Angeles Times* that the horse must have been gorging himself on paint chips that had blown off the barn roof.

The notion that someone might fatally injure a horse for insurance money wasn't so farfetched. In the early 1990s, Americans learned about "The Sandman," a horse hitman who, for the right sum of money, would sometimes fake an accident or electrocute a horse, leaving vets to usually diagnose colic as the cause of death. When he testified in court, The Sandman admitted to breaking the hind leg of one horse with a crowbar and killing fourteen others through electrocution so the owners could collect insurance money.

Though the insurance money from Alydar's death may have temporarily staved off disaster, Calumet Farm soon went bankrupt. Lundy would be prosecuted and later sent to jail for his financial wheeling and dealing. But the death of Alydar at the age of fifteen would remain controversial, an unsolved mystery.

*　　*　　*

Late in the summer of 1991, in the wake of Alydar's death and Calumet's collapse into chaos, the Wolfsons decided to relocate Affirmed to nearby Jonabell Farm. Affirmed would stand at stud there until his death at the age of twenty-six in 2001, when he was humanely put down after months of continued pain from laminitis that set in after surgery to repair a dislocated pastern joint.

Laz Barrera, to whom the Wolfsons had generously given the rights to breed one mare to Affirmed every year for life, had paid occasional visits to him at Spendthrift and Calumet. But in 1991, just a few months before Affirmed relocated to Jonabell, Barrera died at sixty-six due to heart failure. For all his success as the first trainer ever to win four straight Eclipse Awards, Barrera would be remembered for what he deemed the best training job of his career: guiding Affirmed to the Triple Crown.

On December 30, 2007—the Wolfsons' thirty-fifth wedding anniversary—Lou passed away at the age of ninety-five following a protracted struggle with Alzheimer's disease, during which Patrice faithfully cared for him through what she called the "long, sweet goodbye." Obituaries in newspapers across the country identified Louis Wolfson, in headlines and leads, as both a controversial financial wizard *and* a Triple Crown winner. Though his star chestnut's success could never erase the conviction that had besmirched his reputation, racing in general and the Triple Crown in particular had indeed granted Lou the redemption he desired. "On the back of Affirmed, he was resurrected," eulogized Steve Wolfson, the eldest of his three sons to follow him into racing. "It was a great bringing together of a family, seeing him rise to the top again. He had lost his name, which meant more to him than anything in the world, and never stopped trying to prove his innocence. Affirmed brought him back. Affirmed and his offspring took Dad to a world where he felt good about life again."

In the end, Lou Wolfson's legacy as a sportsman would extend beyond breeding, owning, and campaigning the grittiest of all Triple Crown winners.

Starting in the 1960s, he had tirelessly tried to reform a racing industry he saw as stagnating, taking on the patrician establishment that had never allowed him into its club. Again in the 1980s, following his remarkable comeback and successful second act in racing, he issued blistering reports advocating reforms to save the sport he loved. Among his recommendations were standardized drug testing, improvement of backside working conditions, and establishment of a national organization to oversee all segments of the racing industry. No one will ever know whether his prescient suggestions would have stopped the eventual erosion of the sport, but as time went on, he would look more and more like a visionary who had foreseen racing's decline.

It would take decades before the declining sport would see the wisdom of Wolfson's recommendations. Spurred by an alarming spate of doping scandals and racehorse deaths, Congress in 2020 passed the Horseracing Safety and Integrity Act, which created an authority to enforce a national set of health and safety rules that would be applied to every participant and track. By the spring of 2023, the authority's safety and antidoping programs were both up and running.

Lou's passing left Patrice as the keeper of the flame for Affirmed's legacy. Likewise had Lucille Markey's earlier passing left John Veitch to carry the torch for Alydar's memory right up until his own death in 2023 at seventy-seven. A year after Alydar became the only horse to place second in all three legs of the Triple Crown, Veitch had gotten a share of redemption when Davona Dale—Calumet's next and last star—won the Triple Tiara, the filly equivalent of the Triple Crown. Forced out of Calumet by Lundy three years later, Veitch went on to become a successful trainer for the Galbreaths' Darby Dan Farm. Following his retirement from training in 2003, he was elected to the Hall of Fame, joining his father, Syl Veitch, as well as Laz Barrera.

As for the rivalry itself between Affirmed and Alydar, the keepers of the flame remain the jockeys who rode them through their Triple Crown campaign: Steve Cauthen and Jorge Velasquez.

Battling a long slump and weight gain after losing his mount on Affirmed, Cauthen left the United States in the spring of 1979 just before his nineteenth birthday to ride in England. Bouncing back in a country where a jockey's weight is less of an issue, he won on his very first mount and a month later rode a longshot to victory in his debut English Triple Crown race. He soon mastered the rugged European turf courses and became a star jockey, winning three British riding titles. Though he never rode in another American Triple Crown race, he twice won the Epsom Derby—the English precursor of the Kentucky Derby—and became the first jockey ever to complete the international grand slam of derbies by adding the Irish and the French. He continued to win major stakes around the world until he retired in 1992 at the ripe old age of thirty-two. Cauthen, to whom the Wolfsons had given one free breeding to Affirmed for each of the Triple Crown wins, soon returned to Kentucky and settled down near his boyhood home on a three-hundred-acre horse farm, where he owns and operates his own Thoroughbred breeding business.

For all that came before and after, Steve Cauthen's name would forever be inextricably bound with that of the mount he deemed the greatest he ever rode. Likewise did Jorge Velasquez, who captured the 1981 Kentucky Derby and Preakness aboard Pleasant Colony, consider Alydar the best mount of his thirty-seven-year career—and Affirmed his toughest nemesis. At the National Racing Museum and Hall of Fame just a furlong from historic Saratoga Race Course, visitors to the "Affirmed, In Front" exhibit commemorating his Triple Crown triumph are greeted by a banner immortalizing the words that a heartbroken Velasquez uttered minutes after the 1978 Belmont in praise of the victor: "This is a great horse . . . as great as Secretariat, Native Dancer, or any of the other great horses."

Cauthen and Velasquez never raced each other again on their favorite mounts, but they will always have Belmont. On the thirty-fourth anniversary of that stirring duel, the two Hall of Fame jockeys returned to Belmont Park to team up at a signing session commemorating their rides on Affirmed and Alydar. At that and other public appearances, Cauthen and Velasquez once again find themselves side by side—now to autograph the moving photos of their gripping Belmont stretch duel, to relive that glorious spring of 1978, and to reminisce with fans and with each other about the greatest rivalry in the history of horse racing.

*   *   *

At the turn of the millennium, when the *Blood-Horse* magazine polled experts to select the "Top 100 Racehorses of the 20th Century," Affirmed placed twelfth on a definitive list predictably topped by the consensus trifecta of Man o' War in first, Secretariat second, and Citation third (with Native Dancer seventh and Alydar twenty-seventh). With each passing year sans another Triple Crown winner through the first decade and a half of the current century, Affirmed's stature only continued to grow.

In 2003, when Derby-Preakness winner Funny Cide failed to close the deal in the Belmont, the Triple Crown drought had reached twenty-five years—assuring that it would surpass the record quarter-century between the runaway sweeps by Citation in 1948 and Secretariat in 1973. By 2013, when Derby winner Orb had his Triple Crown dreams dashed in the Preakness by a horse named Oxbow carrying the black and gold silks of a reconstituted Calumet Farm rather than the familiar devil's red and blue of the long-gone Calumet dynasty, the dry spell had reached thirty-five years and parched racing fans wondered if it would ever end.

Each year like clockwork on the first Saturday in May, fans and pundits continued to reiterate the same burning question: Would this finally be the year that the Derby winner went on to sweep the Triple Crown for the first time since Affirmed in 1978? And when the same answer invariably came back after the Preakness or Belmont, they'd wax nostalgic at the memory of that magical spring when Affirmed outdueled Alydar for all three jewels—and wonder how much longer it would be before another champion duplicated a feat most Americans were too young to remember ever having been accomplished.

At the time of Affirmed's Triple Crown, ironically, railbirds and turf writers were starting to get a bit blasé, what with Seattle Slew and Secretariat each having won it over the previous five years. With the 1970s destined to go down as "The Decade of Champions," Affirmed was the Triple Crown winner that got the shortest shrift. Affirmed, with his deceptive elegance and silky smoothness, didn't have the majestic Secretariat's explosive power or the magnetic Seattle Slew's electrifying speed. Nor did Affirmed, with his fighting spirit and indomitable will to win, overwhelm the competition as Secretariat and Slew had done. But what ultimately distinguishes Affirmed was his dominance over an indefatigable rival of comparable ability who made him prove his mettle every step of the way—as a true champion winning the hardest-earned Triple Crown with by far the narrowest combined margin of victory ever. As Laz Barrera was quick to point out, "Affirmed is greater than Secretariat, or any Triple Crown winner, because only Affirmed had to face Alydar."

Lou Wolfson was, at first, more cautious in his appraisal. Minutes after Affirmed had outdueled Alydar in the Belmont, Lou was asked if he would characterize his golden chestnut as a "great" racehorse. "Yes, a great three-year-old, and so is Alydar," came his qualified response. "But I want to see him run at four before I call him great overall."

The grace and grit that Affirmed demonstrated as a four-year-old—winning the last seven races of his career impressively under burdensome handicap weights and running away with his second straight Horse of the Year title in a landslide—convinced Lou that the colt was indeed worthy of the distinction "great." What's more, Affirmed had finally won over the skeptics who had never accorded him the level of respect he deserved. From the moment he was born as a one-in-thirty-thousand longshot in his 1975 foal crop until he died as a once-in-a-lifetime champion, Affirmed was always the Rodney Dangerfield of Thoroughbreds: too plebian in his pedigree, too scrawny as a baby, too slight as a Derby hopeful, even too streamlined as a Triple Crown winner.

"Affirmed never got the bouquets he deserved," Bill Nack, who had famously picked Alydar to win each of their Triple Crown confrontations, wrote twenty-three years later in a *Sports Illustrated* appreciation eulogizing the victor. "Indeed, the more regally bred Alydar, a product of the finest racing blood at the storied Calumet Farm, was always the more popular of the duo. But Affirmed made an indelible mark on the sport, and in his own unforgettable way—from the eighth pole to the wire in the Belmont Stakes—he crowned his decade as the richest and most competitive in the history of horse racing."

For thirty-seven years, Affirmed would reign as "the last Triple Crown winner." Although American Pharoah usurped that title by finally ending the long interregnum in 2015 with his rousing Belmont coronation, nothing could diminish Affirmed's enduring legacy as history's longest-reigning Triple Crown winner.

If it took the passage of time and the thirty-seven-year absence of any Triple Crown successors to give Affirmed his just due as a racehorse, more years would need to pass before he could likewise finally get some respect as a sire.

By the time Alysheba and Easy Goer took their star turns in the late 1980s, their sire, Alydar, had been widely declared the winner in the breeding shed sweepstakes over Affirmed. Of course, Alydar's superiority there could be explained by many factors, not the least of which was that he had gotten, right from the start, the very best mares because many old-time breeders were convinced that he had the stronger pedigree and was therefore likelier to be the more prepotent sire. Another factor in his favor: he hadn't been syndicated. Like Secretariat before him, Affirmed was experiencing the downside of syndication. He would, for the most part, only get mares from those who had bought lifetime breeding rights—and if those mares didn't cross well, there wasn't much to be done.

But as the years passed, Affirmed's stock as a stud started to rise. In the end, the two colts were once again separated by the barest of margins: Alydar with 11 percent stakes winners versus Affirmed with 10 percent. The late 1980s and early '90s brought such stars as Affirmed Success, Zoman, and Peteski, each of whom won more than $1 million on the track. The homebred foal that brought the most joy to the Wolfsons was Flawlessly, who was born in 1988. Lou and Patrice campaigned their Affirmed daughter for five years during which she earned $2,572,536, two consecutive Eclipse Awards as turf champion, and a place in the Hall of Fame. As it turned out, Affirmed had yet another thing in common with Secretariat: both ended up excellent broodmare sires.

*　　*　　*

In the years since Affirmed outdueled Alydar for the Triple Crown, The Sport of Kings changed in ways that make it far less likely that any such rivalry could ever occur again.

Most important may have been the seismic shift in how horse racing is run from the breeding shed all the way through the Triple Crown classics. What used to be known as "the racing game" has now become little more than the racing business.

The beginning of the end came when breeders shifted their focus from the winner's circle to the sales ring as auction prices blew through the roof in the 1980s. Instead of breeding for competition, people now were planning matings that would produce attractive and early maturing yearlings with hot pedigrees. Those expensive prospects couldn't be turned out to roughhouse in the pasture because they might incur a blemish that would detract from their value. As a result, they wouldn't get a chance to toughen up for competition or to build the dense bones that can only come from pounding across a field.

Over the last few decades, the horses themselves have changed and become much more fragile. Today's Thoroughbred racehorses are decidedly less sound, less rugged, and less durable than their ancestors from the sport's golden ages. Comparing today's racehorses to Raise a Native, one can't help but notice how spindly many of their legs look against the abundant bone in his. Small wonder that there are so many breakdowns on the track today with such fine-boned contenders. Selecting solely for speed, breeders apparently have lost sight of the importance of power and durability.

Whereas the Wolfsons and the Markeys had been in it primarily for the sport, many of today's owners predicate every decision on how much money a horse can make. Thoroughbred stars are often retired early because owners want to start collecting stud fees as soon as possible. Compare the twenty-nine lifetime starts that Affirmed made over three years to the eleven races that his successor American Pharoah ran before ending what was by far the shortest career of any Triple Crown winner. That is, it was the shortest only until three years later, when Justify's entire undefeated career spanned a total of six races over a whirlwind 112 days. The only one of history's thirteen Triple Crown winners never to race before turning three, Justify introduced to racing lexicon the controversial basketball concept of "one and done" in which the biggest college stars turn pro right after their freshman year. As Bob Baffert, trainer of both American Pharoah and Justify, quipped, "I'm like a basketball coach: one and done, two and done."

What made them retire so early was the explosion in stud-fee prices. American Pharoah's breeding rights were sold for $30 million after his three-year-old season and Justify's for $60 million right after his Triple Crown. With numbers like those, the last thing owners want their meal ticket to do is bang heads with a rival that could compromise their colt's earning power.

All of which explains why there will never be another rivalry quite like Affirmed versus Alydar. The two best Thoroughbreds ever to come along in the same foal crop grew up to confront each other six times as two-year-olds for the juvenile championship, then four more times as three-year-olds in the sport's most important races. Now, in an era when most of the top horses run fewer than ten races over their entire careers, it's unfathomable that any rivals will ever go head to head as often as Affirmed and Alydar, let alone battle as closely and as fiercely as they did.

The names Affirmed and Alydar remain inextricably intertwined, as tightly bonded by battle as Ali and Frazier or David and Goliath. Less than half a century since Affirmed outfought Alydar for the Triple Crown, their rivalry has reached mythic proportions. It's not just that the rivalry transcended even the Triple Crown and the sport—it's that it brought out the best in each rival, in their human connections, and in all of us.

And that's why we love Affirmed and Alydar. We're nostalgic for a purer, simpler time when sportsmen and sportswomen cared more about the finish line than the bottom line. Affirmed outdueling Alydar for the Triple Crown marks June 10, 1978, as the end of an epoch, the turning point for the sport, the crowning glory of racing's last golden age.

Nothing could ever top that peak—not for the two horses, not for their humans, not for the sport they ennobled. Both of the colts would flash before our eyes on the track and be retired to stud as four-year-olds; both of the farms and their racing stables would fade completely from view; and The Sport of Kings itself would lose much of the luster that had made it once America's most popular pastime.

But none of that can dim the enduring image of Affirmed and Alydar dueling in the late-afternoon sun on a perfect spring day in New York: a pair of burnished chestnuts galloping nose to nose down the stretch, driving and bobbing all the way to the wire.

APPENDIX I

Affirmed vs. Alydar: The Showdowns

LONG BEFORE AFFIRMED AND ALYDAR SQUARED OFF FOR THE TENTH AND last time, their showdowns had taken on the air of match races. In all but the first of their ten meetings, they finished 1-2. Since no rivalry in racing history could compare for the number, intensity, closeness, and high stakes of their duels, those matchups were promoted by the press like heavyweight title bouts. In the afterglow of their epic 1978 Triple Crown trilogy, newspapers across the country used the same boxing lingo to hype their next match: "Round 10." Following is a round-by-round account of their rivalry—the first six meetings to settle the two-year-old championship, the last four to decide the Triple Crown and three-year-old supremacy.

ROUND 1

1977 YOUTHFUL STAKES

JUNE 15, 1977   BELMONT PARK   5½ FURLONGS

HORSE	JOCKEY	ODDS	PP	ST	¼	⅜	STR	FIN	MARGIN
Affirmed	Cordero	3.40–1	1	1	2	2	1	1	Won by a neck
Alydar	Maple	1.80–1	7	9	9	9	5	5	6¾ lengths behind

Race result: Affirmed first in 1:05 over fast track for $22,665 winner's share of purse

Rivalry record: Affirmed 1, Alydar 0

ROUND 2

1977 GREAT AMERICAN STAKES

JULY 6, 1977   BELMONT PARK   5½ FURLONGS

HORSE	JOCKEY	ODDS	PP	ST	¼	⅜	STR	FIN	MARGIN
Alydar	Maple	0.80–1	7	7	4	1	1	1	Won by 3½ lengths
Affirmed	Cordero	4.60–1	1	1	1	2	2	2	2nd, 3½ lengths behind

Race result: Alydar first in 1:03⅗ over fast track for $22,095 winner's share of purse

Rivalry record: Affirmed 1, Alydar 1

ROUND 3

1977 HOPEFUL STAKES

AUGUST 27, 1977   SARATOGA RACE COURSE   6 FURLONGS

HORSE	JOCKEY	ODDS	PP	ST	¼	½	STR	FIN	MARGIN
Affirmed	Cauthen	2.30–1	4	1	3	2	1	1	Won by ½ length
Alydar	Maple	1.00–1	1	4	4	4	2	2	2nd, ½ length behind

Race result: Affirmed first in stakes-record 1:15⅖ over fast track for $48,105 winner's share of purse

Rivalry record: Affirmed 2, Alydar 1

ROUND 4

1977 FUTURITY STAKES

SEPTEMBER 10, 1977   BELMONT PARK   7 FURLONGS

HORSE	JOCKEY	ODDS	PP	ST	¼	½	STR	FIN	MARGIN
Affirmed	Cauthen	1.20–1	2	2	2	1	2	1	Won by a nose
Alydar	Maple	1.50–1	1	5	3	2	1	2	2nd, a nose behind

Race result: Affirmed first in 1:21⅗ over good track for $63,570 winner's share of purse

Rivalry record: Affirmed 3, Alydar 1

ROUND 5

1977 CHAMPAGNE STAKES

OCTOBER 15, 1977   BELMONT PARK   1 MILE

HORSE	JOCKEY	ODDS	PP	ST	¼	½	¾	STR	FIN	MARGIN
Alydar	Velasquez	1.50–1	1	5	5	4	5	4	1	Won by 1¼ lengths
Affirmed	Cauthen	1.20–1	5	2	3	3	1	1	2	2nd, 1¼ lengths behind

Race result: Alydar first in 1:36⅗ over muddy track for $80,400 winner's share of purse

Rivalry record: Affirmed 3, Alydar 2

ROUND 6

1977 LAUREL FUTURITY

OCTOBER 29, 1977   LAUREL RACE COURSE   1 1/16 MILES

HORSE	JOCKEY	ODDS	PP	ST	¼	½	¾	STR	FIN	MARGIN
Affirmed	Cauthen	1.40–1	3	2	2	2	2	1	1	Won by a neck
Alydar	Velasquez	0.40–1	1	4	3	3	1	2	2	2nd, a neck behind

Race result: Affirmed first in 1:44⅕ over fast track for $82,290 winner's share of purse—and two-year-old championship

Rivalry record: Affirmed 4, Alydar 2

ROUND 7
1978 KENTUCKY DERBY

MAY 6, 1978   CHURCHILL DOWNS   1¼ MILES

HORSE	JOCKEY	ODDS	PP	¼	½	¾	1	STR	FIN	MARGIN
Affirmed	Cauthen	1.80–1	2	2	3	3	2	1	1	Won by 1½ lengths
Alydar	Velasquez	1.20–1	10	9	9	8	4	3	2	2nd, 1½ lengths behind

Race result: Affirmed first in 2:01⅕ over fast track for $186,900 winner's share of purse—and first jewel of Triple Crown

Rivalry record: Affirmed 5, Alydar 2

ROUND 8
1978 PREAKNESS STAKES

MAY 20, 1978   PIMLICO RACE COURSE   1³⁄₁₆ MILES

HORSE	JOCKEY	ODDS	PP	ST	¼	½	¾	STR	FIN	MARGIN
Affirmed	Cauthen	0.50–1	6	1	2	1	1	1	1	Won by a neck
Alydar	Velasquez	1.80–1	3	2	6	6	4	2	2	2nd, a neck behind

Race result: Affirmed first in 1:54⅖ over fast track for $136,200 winner's share of purse—and second jewel of Triple Crown

Rivalry record: Affirmed 6, Alydar 2

ROUND 9
1978 BELMONT STAKES

JUNE 10, 1978 BELMONT PARK 1½ MILES

HORSE	JOCKEY	ODDS	PP	¼	½	¾	1	STR	FIN	MARGIN
Affirmed	Cauthen	0.60–1	3	1	1	1	1	1	1	Won by a head
Alydar	Velasquez	1.10–1	2	3	2	2	2	2	2	2nd, a head behind

Race result: Affirmed first in 2:26⅘ over fast track for $110,580 winner's share of purse—and final jewel of Triple Crown

Rivalry record: Affirmed 7, Alydar 2

ROUND 10
1978 TRAVERS STAKES

AUGUST 19, 1978 SARATOGA RACE COURSE 1¼ MILES

HORSE	JOCKEY	ODDS	PP	¼	½	¾	1	STR	FIN	MARGIN
Affirmed	Pincay	1.80–1	2	2	3	3	2	1	1	1st by 1¾ lengths, Lost by DQ
Alydar	Velasquez	1.20–1	10	9	9	8	4	3	2	2nd, Won by DQ

Race result: Alydar awarded $62,880 winner's share of purse through DQ of Affirmed, who had finished first in 2:02 over fast track

Rivalry record: Affirmed 7, Alydar 3

Charting the Classics:
The 1978 Triple Crown

1978 KENTUCKY DERBY OFFICIAL CHART

EIGHTH RACE
Churchill
MAY 6, 1978

1 ¼ MILES. (1.59⅖) 104th running THE KENTUCKY DERBY. $125,000 Added 3-year-olds. By subscription of $100 which covers nomination for both The Kentucky Derby and Derby Trial. All nomination fees to Derby Winner. $4,000 to pass the entry box Thursday, May 4, $3,500 additional to start, $125,000 added, of which $30,000 to second, $15,000 to third, $7,500 to fourth, $100,000 guaranteed to winner (to be divided euqally in the event of a dead heat.) Weight 126 lbs. Starters to be named through the entry box Thursday, May 4, at time of closing. The maximum number of starters for The Kentucky Derby will be limited to twenty. In the event more than twenty entries pass through the entry box at the usual time of closing, the twenty starters will be determined at that time with preference given to those that have accumulated the highest lifetime earnings. For those that enter and are eliminated under this condition, the nomination fee and the fee to pass through the entry box, will be refunded. The owner of the winner to receive a gold trophy. Closed with 319 nominations.

Value of race $239,400, value to winner $186,900, second $30,000, third $15,000, fourth $7,500. Mutuel pool $4,425,828.

Last Raced	Horse	Eqt.	A.Wt	PP	¼	½	¾	1	Str	Fin	Jockey	Odds $1
16Apr78 ^{8}Hol^{1}	Affirmed		3 126	2	2^{hd}	$3^{2\frac{1}{2}}$	$3^{1\frac{1}{2}}$	2^{3}	1^{2}	$1^{1\frac{1}{2}}$	Cauthen S	1.80
27Apr78 ^{7}Kee^{1}	Alydar	b	3 126	10	9^{hd}	9^{5}	8^{hd}	4^{hd}	3^{3}	$2^{1\frac{1}{4}}$	Velasquez J	1.20
22Apr78 ^{8}Aqu^{1}	Believe It		3 126	9	$4^{\frac{1}{2}}$	$4^{\frac{1}{2}}$	5^{3}	1^{hd}	2^{2}	$3^{4\frac{1}{4}}$	Maple E	7.40
22Apr78 ^{8}Aqu^{2}	Darby Creek Road	b	3 126	7	$7^{\frac{1}{2}}$	7^{2}	7^{2}	$5^{\frac{1}{2}}$	4^{2}	$4^{2\frac{1}{4}}$	Brumfield D	33.00
29Apr78 ^{7}CD^{2}	Esops Foibles	b	3 126	3	$5^{1\frac{1}{2}}$	5^{4}	4^{1}	6^{3}	5^{3}	$5^{5\frac{1}{4}}$	McCarron C J	49.70
18Apr78 ^{7}Kee^{1}	Sensitive Prince		3 126	11	$3^{2\frac{1}{2}}$	$1^{1\frac{1}{2}}$	1^{2}	$3^{1\frac{1}{2}}$	6^{3}	$6^{\frac{1}{2}}$	Solomone M	4.50
22Apr78 ^{9}GP^{6}	Dr. Valeri	b	3 126	8	11	11	10^{4}	10^{5}	$7^{1\frac{1}{2}}$	$7^{3\frac{1}{4}}$	Riera R Jr	96.10
29Apr78 ^{7}CD^{3}	Hoist the Silver		3 126	5	8^{2}	$8^{\frac{1}{2}}$	9^{5}	7^{3}	8^{5}	8^{7}	Depass R	123.70
19Apr78 ^{8}Kee^{1}	Chief of Dixieland	b	3 126	6	6^{3}	6^{2}	$6^{\frac{1}{2}}$	9^{1}	9^{1}	9^{1}	Rini A	121.70
27Apr78 ^{7}Kee^{2}	Raymond Earl		3 126	1	1^{2}	2^{4}	2^{2}	8^{1}	10^{2}	10^{2}	Baird R L	117.10
27Apr78 ^{7}Kee^{6}	Special Honor	b	3 126	4	10^{3}	$10^{\frac{1}{2}}$	11	11	11	11	Nicolo P	177.10

OFF AT 5:41 EDT. Start good for all but SPECIAL HONOR, Won driving. Time, :22⅗, :45⅗, 1:10⅘, 1:35⅘, 2:01⅕ Track fast.

$2 Mutuel Prices:				
	2–AFFIRMED	5.60	2.80	2.60
	10–ALYDAR		2.60	2.40
	9–BELIEVE IT			2.80

Ch. c, by Exclusive Native—Won't Tell You, by Crafty Admiral. Trainer Barrera Lazaro S. Bred by Harbor View Farm (Fla).

AFFIRMED away alertly but held in reserve for six furlongs, moved up boldly along outside thereafter to take command on second turn, relinquished the lead momentarily a quarter mile out but responded to a rousing ride to regain command in upper stretch and was fully extended to hold ALYDAR safe. The latter, under snug restraint early, commenced to advance from the outside after six furlongs, continued wide into the stretch, swerved in to bump with BELIEVE IT in closing sixteenth and finished strongly when straightened.BELIEVE IT reserved off the early pace, moved up with a bold rush while bearing out on second turn to gain command momentarily a quarter mile away, continued wide while lacking a further response and was bumped by ALYDAR in the closing stages. DARBY CREEK ROAD lacked speed and hung after making a rally on the final bend. ESOPS FOIBLES faltered after making a mild bid on the second turn. SENSITIVE PRINCE sent to the fore on rounding the first turn, continued to make a swift pace while along the inside to final bend where he gave way suddenly. DR. VALERI was without speed. CHIEF OF DIXIELAND was bumped about before going a quarter mile. RAYMOND EARL showed brief early speed and tired badly. SPECIAL HONOR reared at the start.

Owners— 1, Harbor View Farm; 2, Calumet Farm; 3, Hickory Tree Stable; 4, Phillips J W; 5, Frankel J; 6, Top the Marc Stable; 7, Renzi V & R; 8, Dasso-Golob-Levinson-Solomon; 9, Dixie Jake Inc; 10, Lehmann R N; 11, Gaston Linda T & Haynes A D.

Trainers— 1, Barrera Lazaro S; 2, Veitch John M; 3, Stephens Woodford C; 4, Rondinello Thomas L; 5, Rettele Loren; 6, Jerkens H Allen; 7, Perez Aurelio M; 8, Fischer Richard J; 9, Morreale Jake; 10, Adams W E Smiley; 11, McCann Edward T.

1978 PREAKNESS STAKES OFFICIAL CHART

EIGHTH RACE
Pimlico
MAY 20, 1978

1 $\frac{3}{16}$ MILES. (1.54) 103rd Running PREAKNESS. $150,000 Added. 3-year-olds by subscription of $100 each, this fee to accompany the nomination. $1,000 to pass the entry box, starters to pay $1,000 additional. All eligibility, entrance and starting fees to the winner, with $150,000 added, of which $30,000 to second, $15,000 to third and $7,500 to fourth. Weight 126 lbs. Starters to be named through the entry box Thursday, May 18, two days before the race by the usual time of closing. A replica of the Woodlawn Vase will be presented to the winning owner to remain his or her personal property. Closed Wednesday, February 15, 1978 with 247 nominations.
Value of race $188,700, value to winner $136,200, second $30,000, third $15,000, fourth $7,500. Mutuel pool $1,335,965, Minus place pool $17,998.60, Minus show pool $17,914.65. Exacta Pool $262,946.

Last Raced	Horse	Eqt.	A.	Wt	PP	St	¼	½	¾	Str	Fin	Jockey	Odds $1
6May78 ^{8}CD^{1}	Affirmed		3	126	6	1	2^{1}	1^{1}	1^{1}	$1^{\frac{1}{2}}$	1^{nk}	Cauthen S	.50
6May78 ^{8}CD^{2}	Alydar	b	3	126	3	2	6^{2}	6^{4}	$4^{1\frac{1}{2}}$	$2^{1\frac{1}{2}}$	$2^{7\frac{1}{2}}$	Velasquez J	1.80
6May78 ^{8}CD^{3}	Believe It		3	126	2	5	3^{1}	3^{2}	3^{hd}	$3^{3\frac{1}{2}}$	$3^{2\frac{1}{2}}$	Maple E	6.70
6May78 ^{8}Pim^{8}	Noon Time Spender	b	3	126	1	7	$5^{2\frac{1}{2}}$	$4^{\frac{1}{2}}$	2^{1}	4^{5}	4^{8}	Hinojosa H	80.80
6May78 ^{8}Pim^{5}	Indigo Star	b	3	126	7	3	$4^{\frac{1}{2}}$	5^{1}	$6^{2\frac{1}{2}}$	5^{6}	5^{6}	Fitzgerald R	89.80
12May78 ^{5}Pim^{1}	Dax S.	b	3	126	5	4	7	7	7	6^{1}	6^{4}	Kurtz J	93.30
14May78 ^{8}Aqu^{5}	Track Reward		3	126	4	6	1^{hd}	2^{1}	5^{2}	7	7	Gonzalez B	88.70

OFF AT 5:41 EDT. Start good, Won driving. Time, :23⅗, :47⅗, 1:11⅘, 1:36⅕, 1:54⅖ Track fast.

$2 Mutuel Prices:

6-AFFIRMED	3.00	2.10	2.10
3-ALYDAR		2.10	2.10
2-BELIEVE IT			2.10

$2 EXACTA 6-3 PAID $4.00.

Ch. c, by Exclusive Native—Won't Tell You, by Crafty Admiral. Trainer Barrera Lazaro S. Bred by Harbor View Farm (Fla).

AFFIRMED, taken under light restraint after breaking alertly, quickly joined TRACK REWARD from the outside, gained the advantage leaving the first turn, made the pace under clever rating, responded gamely to rousing when challenged by ALYDAR in the upper stretch and turned back that rival under brisk handling. ALYDAR, under restraint and allowed to settle early, advanced willingly outside of horses in backstretch, engaged AFFIRMED well out from the rail approaching the stretch to nearly reach even terms then couldn't get to that rival when set down in a steady drive. BELIEVE IT saved ground under a snug hold while maintaining a good striking position, came around TRACK REWARD when that rival began to retire on the final turn then quickly regained the rail and couldn't stay with the top pair when the real test came. NOON TIME SPENDER, saving ground while not far back, eased outside of horses in backstretch and steadily gained ground, loomed boldly on the final turn and weakened in the drive. INDIGO STAR had good early speed and gave way readily on the final turn. DAX S. showed little. TRACK REWARD was quickly sent up to join for the lead soon after the start, saved ground while prompting the pace into the last bend and gave way readily.

Owners— 1, Harbor View Farm; 2, Calumet Farm; 3, Hickory Tree Stable; 4, Miami Lakes Ranch; 5, Procopio R F; 6, Scherr N; 7, Aisquith Stable.

Trainers— 1, Barrera Lazaro S; 2, Veitch John M; 3, Stephens Woodford C; 4, Arcodia Antonio; 5, Leatherbury King T; 6, Gross Mel W; 7, Barrera Albert S.

1978 BELMONT STAKES OFFICIAL CHART

EIGHTH RACE
Belmont
JUNE 10, 1978

1 ½ MILES. (2.24) 110th running THE BELMONT. $150,000 Added. 3-year-olds. By subscription of $100 each to accompany the nominations; $500 to pass the entry box; $1,000 to start. A supplementary nomination may be made of $2,500 on Wednesday, June 7 plus an additional $10,000 to start, with $150,000 added, of which 60% to the winner, 22% to second, 12% to third and 6% to fourth. Colts and Geldings, weights, 126 lbs. Fillies, 121 lbs. Starters to be named at the closina time of entries. Thursdav. June 8. The winnina owner will be presented with the August Belmont Memorial Cup to be retained for one year, as well as a trophy for permanent possession and trophies will be presented to the winning trainer and jockey. (Closed Wednesday, February 15, 1978 with 268 nominatons.)

Value of race $184,300, value to winner $110,580, second $40,546, third $22,116, fourth $11,058. Mutuel pool $1,186,662, OTB pool $1,389,646.

Last Raced	Horse	Eqt.A.Wt	PP	¼	½	1	1¼	Str	Fin	Jockey	Odds $1
20May78 ^{8}Pim^1	Affirmed	3 126	3	1^1	1^1	$1^{\frac{1}{2}}$	1^{hd}	1^{hd}	1^{hd}	Cauthen S	.60
20May78 ^{8}Pim^2	Alydar	3 126	2	$3^{1\frac{1}{2}}$	2^1	2^5	2^8	2^{12}	2^{13}	Velasquez J	1.10
28May78 ^{8}Bel^2	Darby Creek Road	3 126	1	5	5	5	$3^{1\frac{1}{2}}$	3^4	$3^{7\frac{3}{4}}$	Cordero A Jr	9.90
22May78 ^{5}Aqu^9	Judge Advocate	3 126	4	$2^{1\frac{1}{2}}$	$3^{2\frac{1}{2}}$	4^3	5	4^{hd}	$4^{1\frac{1}{4}}$	Fell J	30.10
29May78 ^{8}Mth^2	Noon Time Spender	b 3 126	5	4^1	4^3	$3^{\frac{1}{2}}$	4^{hd}	5	5	Hernandez R	38.40

OFF AT 5:43, EDT. Start good, Won driving. Time, :25, :50, 1:14, 1:37$\frac{2}{5}$, 2:01$\frac{3}{5}$, 2:26$\frac{4}{5}$, Track fast.

$2 Mutuel Prices:

3-(C)-AFFIRMED	3.20	2.10	—
2-(B)-ALYDAR		2.20	—
1-(A)-DARBY CREEK ROAD		—	—

(No Show Wagering)

Ch. c, by Exclusive Native—Won't Tell You, by Crafty Admiral. Trainer Barrera Lazaro S. Bred by Harbor View Farm (Fla).

AFFIRMED went right to the front and was rated along on the lead while remaining well out from the rail. He responded readily when challenged by ALYDAR soon after entering the backstretch, held a narrow advantage into the stretch while continuing to save ground and was under left-handed urging to prevail in a determined effort. ALYDAR, away in good order, saved ground to the first turn. He came out to go after AFFIRMED with seven furlongs remaining, raced with that rival to the stretch, reached almost even terms with AFFIRMED near the three-sixteenths pole but wasn't good enough in a stiff drive. DARBY CREEK ROAD, unhurried while being outrun early, moved around horses while rallying on the far turn but lacked a further response. JUDGE ADVOCATE broke through before the start and was finished at the far turn. NOON TIME SPENDER raced within striking distance for a mile and gave way.

Owners— 1, Harbor View Farm; 2, Calumet Farm; 3, Phillips J W; 4, Phipps O; 5, Miami Lakes Ranch.

Trainers— 1, Barrera Lazaro S; 2, Veitch John M; 3, Rondinello Thomas L; 4, Russell John W; 5, Arcodia Antonio.

Dueling Careers:
Racing Records of the Rivals

AFFIRMED'S RACING RECORD

Racing Daily Form

Affirmed

ch. c. 1975, by Exclusive Native (Raise a Native)–Won't Tell You, by Crafty Admiral

Lifetime record: 29 22 5 1 $2,393,818

Own.– Harbor View Farm
Br.– Harbor View Farm (Fla)
Tr.– Lazaro S. Barrera

6Oct79- 8Bel	fst 1½	:49 1:13^{1} 2:02^{2} 2:27^{2}	3↑ J C Gold Cup-G1	3	2	1½	1^{hd}	1½	1¾	Pincay L Jr	126	*.60	83-21	Affirmed126¾Spectacular Bid121^{3}Coastal121^{31}	Driving	4
22Sep79- 8Bel	sly 1¼	:47^{3} 1:11^{4} 1:36^{1} 2:01^{3}	3↑ Woodward-G1	2	2	2^{4}	1½	1^{3}	12½	Pincay L Jr	126	*.40	92-15	Affirmed1262½Coastal1203¾Czaravich1208½	Ridden out	5
29Aug79- 0Bel	sly 1	:22^{2} :45 1:09^{2} 1:34	3↑ Alw 30000	3	1	1½	1^{1}	1^{2}	1^{6}	Pincay L Jr	122	-	98-15	Affirmed122^{6}Island Sultan115^{14}Prefontaine117	Ridden out	3
	No wagering. Exhibition race run between 7th and 8th races															
24Jun79- 8Hol	fst 1¼	:45^{3} 1:09^{3} 1:34^{1} 1:58^{2}	3↑ Hol Gold Cup-G1	1	2	1^{hd}	1^{hd}	1^{hd}	1¾	Pincay L Jr	132	*.30	99-13	Affirmed132¾Sirlad120^{4}Text119^{5}	Driving	10
20May79- 8Hol	fst 1$\frac{1}{16}$	:22^{2} :44^{4} 1:09^{1} 1:41^{1}	3↑ Californian-G1	2	1	1^{1}	1^{1}	1^{2}	1^{5}	Pincay L Jr	130	*.30	89-16	Affirmed130^{5}Syncopate114^{4}Harry's Love117¾	Driving	8
4Mar79- 8SA	fst 1¼	:46^{2} 1:10^{1} 1:34^{1} 1:58^{3}	4↑ S Anita H-G1	3	2	2^{1}	1½	1^{4}	14½	Pincay L Jr	128	*1.30	103-09	Affirmed1284½Tiller127^{3}[DH]PaintedWagon115	Speed to spare	8
4Feb79- 8SA	gd 1¼	:47 1:10^{4} 1:35^{3} 2:01	C H Strub-G1	8	2	3^{1}	1^{1}	1^{2}	1^{10}	Pincay L Jr	126	*.90	91-17	Affirmed126^{10}Johnny's Image115^{4}Quip115^{7}	Handily	9
20Jan79- 8SA	gd 1⅛	:45^{3} 1:09^{3} 1:35 1:48	San Fernando-G2	4	3	49½	57½	33½	22¾	Cauthen S	126	*.50	88-14	Radar Ahead1232¾Affirmed126^{nk}Little Reb120^{4}	Drifted out	8
7Jan79- 8SA	fst 7f	:22^{2} :45 1:08^{3} 1:21	Malibu-G2	2	1	3^{2}	32½	32½	32¼	Cauthen S	126	*.30	96-13	LittleReb1202¼RadarAhed123^{hd}Affrmd126^{3}	Hemmed in to str	5
14Oct78- 8Bel	sly 1½	:45^{1} 1:09^{2} 2:01^{4} 2:27^{1}	3↑ J C Gold Cup-G1	2	2	2^{hd}	3^{7}	4^{15}	518¾	Cauthen S	121	2.20e	65-13	Exceller126^{no}Seattle Slew126^{14}Great Contractor1264¾		6
	Saddle slipped															
16Sep78- 8Bel	fst 1⅛	:47 1:10^{1} 1:33^{3} 1:45^{4}	3↑ Marlboro Cup H-G1	1	2	22½	22½	2^{3}	2^{3}	Cauthen S	124	*.50	95-12	SeattleSlew128^{3}Affirmed124^{5}NastyandBold118^{4}	No excuse	6
19Aug78- 8Sar	fst 1¼	:48 1:11^{3} 1:36^{4} 2:02	Travers-G1	3	2	2^{hd}	11½	1^{2}	11¾	Pincay L Jr	126	*.70	91-14	[D]Affirmed1261¾Alydar1263¾NastyandBold126^{15}	Came over	4
	Disqualified and placed second															
8Aug78- 8Sar	gd 1⅛	:46^{3} 1:10^{1} 1:35 1:47^{4}	Jim Dandy-G3	4	2	2^{8}	2^{7}	2^{4}	1½	Cauthen S	128	*.05	96-04	Affirmed128½SensitivePrince119^{20}Addison1146½	Going away	5
10Jun78- 8Bel	fst 1½	:50 1:14 2:01^{3} 2:26^{4}	Belmont-G1	3	1	1^{1}	1^{hd}	1^{hd}	1^{hd}	Cauthen S	126	*.60	86-11	Affirmed126^{hd}Alydar126^{13}Darby Creek Road1267¾	Driving	5
20May78- 8Pim	fst 1$\frac{3}{16}$	:47^{3} 1:11^{4} 1:36^{1} 1:54^{2}	Preakness-G1	6	2	1^{1}	1^{1}	1½	1^{nk}	Cauthen S	126	*.50	98-12	Affirmed126^{nk}Alydar1267½Believe It1262½	Brisk handling	7
6May78- 8CD	fst 1¼	:45^{3} 1:10^{4} 1:35^{4} 2:01^{1}	Ky Derby-G1	2	2	35½	2^{hd}	1^{2}	11½	Cauthen S	126	1.80	91-12	Affirmed1261½Alydar1261¼Believe It1264¼	Fully extended	11
16Apr78- 8Hol	fst 1⅛	:45 1:09^{2} 1:35 1:48^{1}	Hol Derby-G1	2	1	1^{hd}	1^{1}	12½	1^{2}	Cauthen S	122	*.30	91-17	Affirmed122^{2}Think Snow122^{3}Radar Ahead122^{2}	Driving	9
2Apr78- 8SA	fst 1⅛	:45^{4} 1:09^{4} 1:35^{3} 1:48	S Anita Derby-G1	7	2	1^{1}	11½	13½	1^{8}	Pincay L Jr	120	*.30	92-16	Affirmed120^{8}Balzac120^{1}Think Snow1202½	Handily	12
18Mar78- 8SA	fst 1$\frac{1}{16}$	:24^{1} :48^{2} 1:12 1:42^{3}	San Felipe-G2	4	2	2^{1}	2^{hd}	1^{hd}	1^{2}	Cauthen S	126	*.30	89-17	Affirmed126^{2}Chance Dancer117^{6}Tampoy1181½	Driving	6
8Mar78- 6SA	fst 6½f	:21^{3} :44^{2} 1:09 1:15^{3}	Alw 30000	4	1	43½	11½	1^{4}	1^{5}	Cauthen S	124	*.20	92-16	Affirmed124^{5}Spotted Charger114½Don F.114^{hd}	Easily	5
29Oct77- 8Lrl	fst 1$\frac{1}{16}$	:24 :48^{4} 1:13^{3} 1:44^{1}	Lrl Futurity-G1	3	2	2^{1}	2^{hd}	1^{hd}	1^{nk}	Cauthen S	122	1.40	92-27	Affirmed122^{nk}Alydar122^{10}StardeNskr122^{27}	Long,hard drive	4
15Oct77- 6Bel	my 1	:24^{2} :48^{1} 1:12^{2} 1:36^{3}	Champagne-G1	5	3	3^{2}	1^{hd}	1½	21¼	Cauthen S	122	*1.20	84-17	Alydar1221¼Affirmed1221¼Darby Creek Road1221½	2nd best	6
10Sep77- 8Bel	gd 7f	:23^{3} :46^{3} 1:09^{4} 1:21^{3}	Futurity-G1	2	2	2½	1^{hd}	2^{hd}	1no	Cauthen S	122	*1.20	94-10	Affirmed122^{no}Alydar122^{11}NastyandBold122^{hd}	Strong drive	5
27Aug77- 8Sar	fst 6½f	:22^{4} :45^{1} 1:09^{1} 1:15^{2}	Hopeful-G1	4	1	3^{2}	2^{hd}	1^{hd}	1½	Cauthen S	122	2.30	98-11	Affirmed122½Alydar1222½RegalandRoyal122^{hd}	Good handling	5
17Aug77- 8Sar	fst 6f	:21^{4} :44^{3} 1:09^{3}	Sanford-G2	3	2	35½	4^{3}	2½	12¾	Cauthen S	124	*1.30	92-15	Affirmed1242¾TltUp122^{hd}JtDplomcy124^{nk}	Driving,very wide	6
23Jly77- 5Hol	fst 6f	:21^{3} :44^{2} :56^{2} 1:09^{1}	Juv Champ (Div 1) 104k	6	3	1^{hd}	1½	1^{4}	1^{7}	Pincay L Jr	122	*.40	93-15	Affirmed122^{7}He's Dewan122^{6}Esops Foibles122¾	Easily	8
6Jly77- 8Bel	fst 5½f	:22^{2} :45^{4} :57^{2} 1:03^{3}	Great American 36k	1	1	1^{1}	2^{hd}	21½	23½	Cordero A Jr	122	4.60	93-16	Alydar1173½Affirmed122^{2}Going Investor122^{4}	No match	7
15Jun77- 8Bel	fst 5½f	:22^{2} :45^{3} :58^{2} 1:05	©Youthful 37k	1	1	2½	2½	1^{hd}	1^{nk}	Cordero A Jr	119	3.40	90-17	Affirmed119^{nk}Wood Native119½Sensitive Nose1192½	Driving	11
24May77- 4Bel	fst 5½f	:23 :47^{2} :59^{3} 1:06	Md Sp Wt	10	1	1½	11½	1^{2}	14½	Gonzalez B	117	14.30	85-21	Affirmed1174½Innocuous1223½Gymnast122^{2}	Ridden out	10

ALYDAR'S RACING RECORD

Daily Racing Form

Alydar ch. c. 1975, by Raise a Native (Native Dancer)–Sweet Tooth, by On–and–On

Lifetime record: 26 14 9 1 $957,195

Own.– Calumet Farm

Br.– Calumet Farm (Ky)

Tr.– John M. Veitch

4Jly79- 8Bel	fst 1¼	$:49^{2}\ 1{:}13^{3}\ 1{:}37^{1}\ 2{:}01^{3}$	3↑ Suburban H-G1	4	3	36½	2hd	3½	31¼	Fell J	126		*.60	91-16	StateDinner118½MistrBr120¾Alydr126½	Weakened 5
17Jun79- 8Bel	sly 1⅛	$:46\ 1{:}09\ 1{:}33^{3}\ 1{:}46^{3}$	3↑ Nassau County H-G3	1	2	21½	2½	11½	13¾	Fell J	124		*.40	94-06	Alydar1243¾Nasty and Bold11614Sorry Lookin113	In hand 3
28May79- 8Bel	fst 1	$:22^{4}\ :45\ 1{:}09^{1}\ 1{:}34$	3↑ Metropolitan H-G1	9	3	3½	32	66½	612	Velasquez J	126		*.40	86-16	State Dinner1153Dr. Patches1183¼Sorry Lookin1131½	Tired 9
5May79- 8Aqu	fst 7f	$:22^{4}\ :45^{1}\ 1{:}09^{1}\ 1{:}21^{4}$	3↑ Carter H-G2	2	3	35½	38½	36	2nk	Velasquez J	126		1.50	92-25	StardeNaskra122nkAlydr1263¾SnstvPrnc1266¾	Finished fast 6
13Apr79- 9OP	fst 1 1/16	$:24^{1}\ :48^{1}\ 1{:}13\ 1{:}43^{3}$	4↑ Oaklawn H-G2	2	5	3nk	2½	3½	2no	Velasquez J	127		*.30	90-19	SanJuanHill114noAlydar127¾ALetrtoHrry1257	Lost the nod 7
31Mar79- 5Hia	fst 7f	$:23^{3}\ :46^{2}\ 1{:}10^{3}\ 1{:}22^{2}$	4↑ Alw 13000	5	2	31½	3½	12	17	Velasquez J	114		*.10	91-17	Alydar1147Fort Prevel1224Jachal II1091¼	Much the best 6
19Aug78- 8Sar	fst 1¼	$:48\ 1{:}11^{3}\ 1{:}36^{4}\ 2{:}02$	Travers-G1	4	4	32	21½	22	21¾	Velaquez J	126		1.00	89-14	D Affirmed1261¾Alydar1263¾Nasty and Bold12615	Taken up 4
	Placed first through disqualification															
5Aug78- 8Sar	fst 1⅛	$:46^{3}\ 1{:}10^{2}\ 1{:}35^{1}\ 1{:}47^{2}$	3↑ Whitney H-G2	9	7	613	45½	14	110	Velasquez J	123		*.70	98-09	Alydar12310Buckaroo112hdFather Hogan114nk	Hand ride 9
22Jly78- 8AP	fst 1¼	$:47^{4}\ 1{:}11^{1}\ 1{:}35^{3}\ 2{:}00^{2}$	Arl Classic-G2	3	3	23½	15	18	113	Fell J	126		*.05	95-19	Alydar12613ChiefofDixieland1141GordieH.1145	Much best 5
10Jun78- 8Bel	fst 1½	$:50\ 1{:}14\ 2{:}01^{3}\ 2{:}26^{4}$	Belmont-G1	2	3	21	2hd	2hd	2hd	Velasquez J	126		1.10	86-11	Affirmed126hdAlydar12613Darby Creek Road1267¾	Game try 5
20May78- 8Pim	fst 1 3/16	$:47^{3}\ 1{:}11^{4}\ 1{:}36^{1}\ 1{:}54^{2}$	Preakness-G1	3	6	65½	42	2½	2nk	Velasquez J	126	b	1.80	98-12	Affirmed126nkAlydar1267½Believe It1262½	Game effort 7
6May78- 8CD	fst 1¼	$:45^{3}\ 1{:}10^{4}\ 1{:}35^{4}\ 2{:}01^{1}$	Ky Derby-G1	10	9	917	44½	34	21½	Velasquez J	126	b	*1.20	89-12	Affirmed1261½Alydar1261¼Believe It1264¼	Closed fast 11
27Apr78- 7Kee	gd 1⅛	$:47^{1}\ 1{:}11^{2}\ 1{:}37^{2}\ 1{:}49^{3}$	Blue Grass-G1	9	6	611	47	16	113	Velasquez J	121	b	*.10	89-19	Alydar12113Raymond Earl121noGo Forth1211¾	Ridden out 9
1Apr78- 9GP	fst 1⅛	$:47^{1}\ 1{:}11^{1}\ 1{:}35^{2}\ 1{:}47$	Florida Derby-G1	6	4	21	1½	1hd	12	Velasquez J	122	b	*.20	99-10	Alydar1222Believe It1227½Dr. Valeri122nk	Handily 7
4Mar78- 9Hia	fst 1⅛	$:45^{3}\ 1{:}09^{4}\ 1{:}35\ 1{:}47$	Flamingo-G1	6	6	65	31	12	14½	Velasquez J	122	b	*.90e	97-05	Alydar1224½NoonTimeSpender1221Dr.Valeri122nk	Ridden out 8
11Feb78- 5Hia	fst 7f	$:23^{4}\ :46^{4}\ 1{:}10^{3}\ 1{:}22^{1}$	Alw 14000	5	8	54	53½	2hd	12	Velasquez J	122	b	*.30	92-13	Alydr1222NoonTimeSpendr1195½LaVoyagus109nk	Ridden out 8
26Nov77- 8Aqu	sly 1⅛	$:47^{1}\ 1{:}11^{2}\ 1{:}35^{1}\ 1{:}47^{4}$	Remsen-G2	5	4	49	45½	35	22	Velasquez J	122	b	*.60	94-13	Believe It1222Alydar1221¼Quadratic1166	2nd best 5
29Oct77- 8Lrl	fst 1 1/16	$:24\ :48^{4}\ 1{:}13^{3}\ 1{:}44^{1}$	Lrl Futurity-G1	1	3	31	1hd	2hd	2nk	Velasquez J	122	b	*.40	92-27	Affirmed122nkAlydr12210StrdNskr12227	Steadied,sharp try 4
15Oct77- 6Bel	my 1	$:24^{2}\ :48^{1}\ 1{:}12^{2}\ 1{:}36^{3}$	Champagne-G1	1	5	42	52¾	41½	11¼	Velasquez J	122	b	1.50	85-17	Alydar1221¼Affirmed1221¼DarbyCreekRoad1221½	Ridden out 6
10Sep77- 8Bel	gd 7f	$:23^{3}\ :46^{3}\ 1{:}09^{4}\ 1{:}21^{3}$	Futurity-G1	1	5	32½	2hd	1hd	2no	Maple E	122	b	1.50	94-10	Affirmd122noAlydr12211NstyndBold122hd	Short lead,missed 5
27Aug77- 8Sar	fst 6½f	$:22^{4}\ :45^{1}\ 1{:}09^{1}\ 1{:}15^{2}$	Hopeful-G1	1	4	44	4¾	2hd	2½	Maple E	122	b	*1.00	97-11	Affirmed122½Alydar1222½RegalandRoyl122hd	Steadied early 5
13Aug77- 8Mth	sly 6f	$:22^{2}\ :45^{3}\ 1{:}10^{3}$	Sapling-G1	4	5	34	23	2hd	12½	Maple E	122	b	*.60	87-17	Alydr1222½NoonTimeSpendr1224½DominantRulr122no	Easily 5
27Jly77- 8Bel	fst 6f	$:23\ :45^{4}\ 1{:}10$	Tremont 36k	4	4	33	31½	11	11¼	Maple E	124		*.40	92-16	Alydar1241¼Believe It1173¾Jet Diplomacy1245½	Ridden out 5
6Jly77- 8Bel	fst 5½f	$:22^{2}\ :45^{4}\ :57^{2}\ 1{:}03^{3}$	Great American 36k	7	7	42½	1hd	11½	13½	Maple E	117		*.80	97-16	Alydar1173½Affirmed1222Going Investor1224	Ridden out 7
24Jun77- 4Bel	fst 5½f	$:22^{4}\ :46^{1}\ :58^{1}\ 1{:}04^{1}$	Md Sp Wt	9	8	63¾	1hd	12	16¾	Maple E	122		*2.10	94-20	Alydar1226¾Believe It1221Sauce Boat1173½	Handily 10
15Jun77- 8Bel	fst 5½f	$:22^{2}\ :45^{3}\ :58^{2}\ 1{:}05$	©Youthful 37k	7	9	912	911	510	55	Maple E	115		*1.80	85-17	Affirmed119nkWoodNative119½SenstvNos1192½	In close turn 11

APPENDIX IV

Family Trees:
Pedigree Charts of the Rivals

THE FOLLOWING PEDIGREE CHARTS FOR AFFIRMED AND ALYDAR GO BACK four generations. For each generation, the sires are listed on the top side and the dams on the bottom side (followed by their birth years).

AFFIRMED'S PEDIGREE

AFFIRMED 1975			
EXCLUSIVE NATIVE 1965	RAISE A NATIVE 1961	NATIVE DANCER 1950	POLYNESIAN 1942
			GEISHA 1943
		RAISE YOU 1946	CASE ACE 1934
			LADY GLORY 1934
	EXCLUSIVE 1953	SHUT OUT 1939	EQUIPOISE 1928
			GOOSE EGG 1927
		GOOD EXAMPLE 1944	PILATE 1928
			PARADE GIRL 1933
WON'T TELL YOU 1962	CRAFTY ADMIRAL 1948	FIGHTING FOX 1935	SIR GALLAHAD 1920
			MARGUERITE 1920
		ADMIRAL'S LADY 1942	WAR ADMIRAL 1934
			BOOLA BROOK 1937
	SCARLET RIBBON 1957	VOLCANIC 1945	AMBROSE LIGHT 1933
			HOT SUPPER 1939
		NATIVE VALOR 1948	MAHMOUD 1933
			NATIVE GAL 1939

ALYDAR'S PEDIGREE

ALYDAR 1975			
RAISE A NATIVE 1961	NATIVE DANCER 1950	POLYNESIAN 1942	UNBREAKABLE 1935
			BLACK POLLY 1936
		GEISHA 1943	DISCOVERY 1931
			MIYAKO 1935
	RAISE YOU 1946	CASE ACE 1934	TEDDY 1913
			SWEETHEART 1920
		LADY GLORY 1934	AMERICAN FLAG 1922
			BELOVED 1927
SWEET TOOTH 1965	ON-AND-ON 1956	NASRULLAH 1940	NEARCO 1935
			MUMTAZ BEGUM 1932
		TWO LEA 1946	BULL LEA 1935
			TWO BOB 1933
	PLUM CAKE 1958	PONDER 1946	PENSIVE 1941
			MISS RUSHIN 1942
		REAL DELIGHT 1949	BULL LEA 1935
			BLUE DELIGHT 1938

APPENDIX V

Tale of the Tape: How They Measured Up

AFFIRMED	VS.	ALYDAR
February 21, 1975	BIRTHDATE	March 23, 1975
Ocala, Florida	BIRTHPLACE	Lexington, Kentucky
Chestnut (golden)	COLOR	Chestnut (liver)
16.1 hands	HEIGHT*	16.1½ hands
74½ inches	GIRTH*	74½ inches
48 inches	SHOULDER TO HIP*	47 inches
57 inches	BUTTOCK TO GROUND*	56½ inches
15 inches	SHOULDER TO SHOULDER*	16 inches
1,100 pounds	WEIGHT**	1,300 pounds
29	RACES	26
22-5-1	W-P-S RECORD	14-9-1
7-3	HEAD-TO-HEAD RECORD	3-7
$2,393,818	PURSE EARNINGS	$957,195
Hall of Fame (1980) 1978 Horse of the Year 1979 Horse of the Year 1977 2-Year-Old Champ 1978 3-Year-Old Champ 1979 Older Male Champ	HONORS	Hall of Fame (1989) 1990 Leading Sire
Reigned as "the last Triple Crown winner" (1978) for a record 37 years	CLAIM TO FAME	The only horse to place second in all three Triple Crown races

* All measurements taken in September 1978 when both were mature three-year-olds.

** Both weights are Triple Crown estimates from *New Orleans Times-Picayune*.

ACKNOWLEDGMENTS

IT WOULD NOT HAVE BEEN POSSIBLE TO BRING TO LIFE THE STORY OF Affirmed and Alydar's riveting rivalry without the help of those who played an intimate part in it.

First and foremost, we are deeply indebted to Patrice Wolfson and John Veitch, who graciously opened their lives to us and provided insights we couldn't have found anywhere else. They were extremely generous with their time, each of them setting aside an hour every week to chat and reminisce. We will miss those weekly conversations.

Though we didn't talk as often with Steve Cauthen, he made himself ever available with details that illuminated his relationship with Affirmed and put us in the saddle from start to finish. He patiently entertained questions he must have heard countless times before, and thoughtfully addressed the ones he hadn't.

His fellow jockeys Laffit Pincay Jr. and Eddie Maple also provided us with insights into the distinct characters of the two horses. Others who shared their perspectives and memories included Melvin James, Henry Manne, Austin Mittler, John Williams, and Steve Wolfson, who generously shared indispensable insights into his father's life.

For helping us transport readers back to the time and place of the Affirmed-Alydar showdowns, we'd like to acknowledge the journalists who wrote the first draft of history—particularly the likes of Joe Hirsch, Bill Leggett, Bill Nack, and Red Smith. We must also thank the librarians who dug out hard-to-find clips from their archives: Cathy Schenck at the Keeneland Library and Paul Wilder at the Harness Racing Museum & Hall of Fame.

The Keeneland Library, the nation's foremost repository of racing history, made it possible for us to add numerous photos to this revised edition. Our thanks go to Keeneland librarian Kelly Coffman for providing those images as well as to photographers Lydia Williams and Barbara Livingston for providing other pictures. Special thanks go to Adam Coglianese, track photographer for the New York Racing Association, for providing photos taken by his father, Bob—from the spectacular shot that graces this edition's cover to several interior pictures.

We'd also like to thank NYRA's Jon Forbes for his assistance; *Daily Racing Form* senior editor Irwin Cohen for providing the official charts for Affirmed, Alydar, and their Triple Crown showdowns; and Tammy Gantt at the Florida Thoroughbred Breeders' and Owners' Association for helping us track down some elusive sources. And thanks to Jim Gluckson of the Breeders' Cup for his help and his memories of the single event that inspired him to become a racing executive: witnessing the 1978 Belmont duel from a seat twenty yards from the finish line.

The starting line for this book dates back to the response from Jane Dystel, our stellar literary agent, to our proposal for horse racing as a subject for a follow-up to our first collaboration (*The Concussion Crisis: Anatomy of a Silent Epidemic*): "Horses are a great idea. Get me something with horses in it!" A constant source of encouragement as always, she championed this project from the moment we first floated the idea, and she found a welcoming home for it in 2012.

We were lucky to find an editor who, as an avid horsewoman on the side, felt this book "was meant just for me": Abby Zidle, now executive editor at the Gallery Books division of Simon & Schuster, enthusiastically helped mold the manuscript with a nurturing touch and encouraged our efforts to present the horses with personalities as distinct as those of their human connections.

Because we had to compress all the research, reporting, and writing into nine months, however, the original 2014 hardcover edition felt a bit rushed. So when the rights reverted to us in 2022, we went looking for a publishing house that might give us the chance to revise and update it into this new paperback edition.

We were extremely fortunate to find all that and more at the Eclipse Press imprint of Globe Pequot. We couldn't have anticipated the enthusiasm with which Brittany Stoner, our acquisitions editor, and the whole Eclipse Press team have embraced this book. In guiding this project every step of the way, Brittany has been a delight to work with. Ditto the rest of the Eclipse Press team, from the graphic designers to the production editors to the marketing folks. We feel honored to have joined the Eclipse Press equestrian team and its stable of authors.

Finally, we'd like to thank our families for their support throughout the grueling race to the wire and beyond to this revised edition—especially Mariela, who despite her youth understood that Mom had homework of her own.

SOURCES

INTERVIEWS
Personal interviews were conducted with the following: Steve Cauthen, John Jacobs, Melvin James, Henry Manne, Eddie Maple, Austin Mittler, Laffit Pincay Jr., John Veitch, John Williams, Patrice Wolfson, Steve Wolfson.

BOOKS
Auerbach, Ann Hagedorn. *Wild Ride: The Rise and Tragic Fall of Calumet Farm, Inc., America's Premier Racing Dynasty.* New York: Henry Holt, 1994.

Axthelm, Pete. *The Kid.* New York: Bantam, 1978.

Blood-Horse Publications Staff. *Horse Racing's Greatest Rivalries.* Lexington, KY: Eclipse Press, 2008.

Bolus, Jim. *Remembering the Derby.* Gretna, LA: Pelican, 1994.

Bowen, Edward L. *Legacies of the Turf: A Century of Great Thoroughbred Breeders (Vol. I).* Lexington, KY: Eclipse Press, 2003.

———. *Legacies of the Turf: A Century of Great Thoroughbred Breeders (Vol. II).* Lexington, KY: Eclipse Press, 2003.

———. *Masters of the Turf: Ten Trainers Who Dominated Horse Racing's Golden Age.* Lexington, KY: Eclipse Press, 2007.

Boyd, Eva Jolene. *Native Dancer.* Lexington, KY: Eclipse Press, 2000.

Capps, Timothy T. *Affirmed and Alydar: Racing's Greatest Rivalry.* Lexington, KY: Eclipse Press, 2007.

Daily Racing Form. *The American Racing Manual* (editions 1961, 1964, 1965, 1977, 1978, 1979). Lexington, KY: Daily Racing Form, 1961, 1964, 1965, 1977, 1978, 1979.

———. *Champions: The Lives, Times, and Past Performances of America's Greatest Thoroughbreds.* New York: Daily Racing Form Press, 2005.

Drager, Martin. *The Most Glorious Crown: The Story of America's Triple Crown Thoroughbreds from Sir Barton to Affirmed.* Chicago: Triumph Books, 2005.

Eisenberg, John. *Native Dancer: The Grey Ghost, Hero of a Golden Age.* New York: Warner Books, 2003.

Englade, Ken. *Hot Blood: The Millionairess, the Money, and the Horse Murders.* New York: St. Martin's, 1996.

Flake, Carol, and Henry Horenstein. *Thoroughbred Kingdoms: Breeding Farms of the American Racehorse.* Boston: Bulfinch/Little Brown, 1990.

Henriques, Diana B. *The White Sharks of Wall Street: Thomas Mellon Evans and the Original Corporate Raiders.* New York: Scribner, 2000.

Hervey, John. *Racing in America: 1922–1936.* New York: The Jockey Club, 1937.

Hirsch, Joe, and Gene Plowden. *In the Winner's Circle: The Jones Boys of Calumet Farm.* New York: Mason & Lipscomb, 1974.

Karr, David. *Fight for Control.* New York: Ballantine, 1956.

Leerhsen, Charles. *Crazy Good: The True Story of Dan Patch.* New York: Simon & Schuster, 2008.

Leicester, Charles. *Bloodstock Breeding.* London: Allen, 1957.

Loy, Myrna, and James Kotsilibas-Davis. *Myrna Loy: Being and Becoming.* New York: Knopf, 1987.

Marchman, Judy, and Tom Hall. *The Calumet Collection: A History of the Calumet Trophies.* Lexington, KY: Eclipse Press, 2002.

Marshall, Mary. *Great Breeders and Their Methods: Leslie Combs II and Spendthrift Farm.* Neenah, WI: Russell Meerdink, 2008.

Palmer, Joe H. *This Was Racing.* New York: Barnes, 1953.

Reeves, Richard Stone (portraits and commentary) and Jim Bolus (text). *Royal Blood: Fifty Years of Classic Thoroughbreds.* Lexington, KY: The Blood-Horse.

Robertson, William H. P. *The History of Thoroughbred Racing in America.* New York: Bonanza Books, 1964.

Shogan, Robert. *A Question of Judgment: The Fortas Case and the Struggle for the Supreme Court.* New York: Bobbs-Merrill, 1972.

Simon, Mary. *Racing Through the Century: The Story of Thoroughbred Racing in America.* Irvine, CA: BowTie Press, 2002.

Sobel, Robert. *Dangerous Dreamers: The Financial Innovators from Charles Merrill to Michael Milken.* New York: Wiley, 1994.

Sports Illustrated. *Classic Rivalries: The Most Memorable Matchups in Sports History.* New York: Sports Illustrated Books, 2003.

Winn, Matt J., with Frank G. Menke. *Down the Stretch: The Story of Colonel Matt J. Winn.* New York: Smith & Durrell, 1945.

MAGAZINE ARTICLES

Axthelm, Pete. *Sports Illustrated.* January 23, 1967: "Building an Empire on Horses Ready to Run."

Bauer, Hambla. *Saturday Evening Post.* June 16, 1945: "Plain Ben Jones"; September 11, 1948: "Boss of Calumet Farm."

Beech, Mark. *Sports Illustrated.* July 7, 2003: "Jorge Velasquez, Jockey."

Blagden, Nellie. *People.* March 7, 1977: "Success Hasn't Spoiled Kid-Whiz Steve Cauthen, but Growing Up Might."

Brean, Herbert. *Life.* November 22, 1954: "It's Easier to Make a Million Than a Hundred Thousand."

Deford, Frank. *Sports Illustrated.* December 19, 1977: "When All the World Is Young"; April 23, 1984: "Riding Horses Is the Pleasure of His Life."

Hammer, Richard. *Fortune.* September 1961: "Why Things Went Sour for Louis Wolfson."

Hirsch, Joe. *Sports Illustrated.* February 27, 1961: "Louis Wolfson at the Stable Door."

Holland, Gerald. *Sports Illustrated.* March 17, 1958: "Say Hello to Jimmy Jones"; June 26, 1961: "Sex, Slaughter and Smoke!"

Hollandsworth, Skip. *Texas Monthly.* June 2001: "The Killing of Alydar."

Kalter, Suzy. *People.* May 4, 1981: "In Racing, Blood Tells, and at 21, Laz Barrera's Son Larry Is Already Running for the Roses."

Lambert, William. *Life.* May 9, 1969: "The Justice . . . and the Stock Manipulator."

Leggett, William. *Sports Illustrated.* May 6, 1957: "Colossal Calumet"; February 5, 1962: "The Latin Invasion"; April 26, 1976: "Fast Ride on the Puerto Rican Rolls-Royce"; May 10, 1976: "The Look of Eagles"; June 14, 1976: "Putting the Beans on the Fire"; January 2, 1977: "That Baby Face Will Fool You"; March 7, 1977: "This Could Be the Start"; July 4, 1977: "He Looked a Tiger in the Teeth"; September 5, 1977: "A Fine Way to Affirm His Worth"; October 24, 1977: "Eeny Meeny Miney Mo"; March 6, 1978: "It's Tough Playing Favorites"; March 27, 1978: "Golden Horse of the West"; April 17, 1978: "The Derby Is Old Hat at Calumet"; May 8, 1978: "It's the Rosiest Derby in Years"; May 15, 1978: "Reaffirmation at the Downs"; May 29, 1978: "A Firm Bid for the Triple Crown"; June 12, 1978: "Why Isn't This Man Smiling?"; June 19, 1978: "The Race of a Lifetime"; August 14, 1978: "They Shook the Rafters at Saratoga"; August 28, 1978: "Close Encounter of the Worst Kind"; July 2, 1979: "The Richest of Them All"; September 17, 1979: "A Simply Spectacular Shoe-in for the Bid"; October 1, 1979: "The Horse Did All the Talking."

Lidz, Franz. *Sports Illustrated.* December 1, 1997: "Breeder Goes the Distance."

Life. November 1, 1948: "Life Visits Calumet Farm"; September 6, 1954: "Young Threat to an Old Pro"; October 26, 1959: "The First Lady of Racing."

Look. May 3, 1955: "The Private Life of a Self-made Millionaire."

Looney, Douglas S. *Sports Illustrated.* June 19, 1978: "More Than a Runner-up."

Mann, Jack. *Sports Illustrated.* March 21, 1966: "Tradin' Platers Is Mr. Van's Game."

Markey, Gene. *Sports Illustrated.* April 28, 1958: "My New Kentucky Home."

Martin, Harold H. *Saturday Evening Post.* July 24, 1954: "Florida's Fabulous Junkman."

Minor, Audax. *New Yorker.* "The Race Track" (department). September 30, 1950; April 4, 1953; April 30, 1960; October 19, 1963; February 21, 1970; March 29, 1976; February 14, 1977; October 24, 1977; December 19, 1977.

Nack, William. *Sports Illustrated.* October 15, 1979: "Glorious Affirmation in the Gold Cup"; October 29, 1979: "No Sweat for Laffit"; June 1, 1981: "Scaling the Heights at Long Last"; June 8, 1987: "Old Foes, New Race"; June 15, 1992: "Welcome Back, Kid"; November 16, 1992: "Questions about Alydar"; January 22, 2001: "A Scion of the Times."

Nack, William, and Lester Munson. *Sports Illustrated.* November 16, 1992: "Blood Money."

Palmer, Joe H. *Packard Sports Library.* Volume 10, 1952: "Thoroughbred Racing's Calumet Farm."

Phillips, B. J. *Time.* May 29, 1978: "Cauthen: A Born Winner."

Plummer, Bill. *People.* May 3, 1993: "Home Boy."

Reed, William F. *Sports Illustrated.* June 5, 1978: "A Frontrunner Launches a Comeback"; September 2, 1991: "Clouds over Calumet Farm."

Time. October 26, 1936: "Pigeons to Platers"; May 30, 1949: "Devil Red and Plain Ben"; February 9, 1953: "Florida's Big Dealer"; October 25, 1954: "Wolfson at Work"; July 25, 1955: "Challenge to Management"; October 8, 1956: "Retreat"; November 10,

1958: "Charity Begins"; April 11, 1960: "Head of the Horse Factory"; September 30, 1966: "The Woes of Wolfson"; December 8, 1967: "Downed Eagle"; May 2, 1969: "Exit for Wolfson"; January 31, 1977: "King of the 'Bug Boys'"; May 15, 1978: "The Kid Becomes a Man"; May 29, 1978: "'A Nice Quiet Life'"; June 19, 1978: "Claiming Their Triple Crown."

Tower, Whitney. *Sports Illustrated.* March 19, 1956: "Ladies' Year"; July 27, 1959: "Bargain Hunting for Horseflesh"; September 5, 1960: "Hot in the Hopeful"; October 21, 1963: "A Do-It-Yourself Guide to the 2-Year-Olds"; March 4, 1958: "Calumet Is Back with a Wicked-Running Colt"; July 21, 1969: "Cousin Leslie Goes to Market"; April 27, 1970: "Pick 'em with a Pin—and Don't Give Up on the Office Pool"; May 25, 1970: "A Preakness with Personality."

Wahl, Grant. *Sports Illustrated.* June 16, 1997: "Jockey Steve Cauthen."

Weinberger, Alan M. *Hofstra Law Review.* Volume 39: 645–81, 2011: "What's in a Name?— The Tale of Louis Wolfson's Affirmed."

Yardley, Jonathan. *Sports Illustrated.* August 21, 1978: "Steve Cauthen, Only 18 and Riding High, Already Has His Own Boswell."

TURF PERIODICALS

Turf periodicals most heavily relied on: *Blood-Horse, Daily Racing Form, Morning Telegraph, Thoroughbred Times.* Other turf periodicals used as resources: *Backstretch, Canadian Horse, Harness Horse, Hoof Beats, Horse Breeder, Horse Review, Post Time USA, Trotter and Pacer.*

In addition to news stories from the turf periodicals listed above, the following feature articles and columns were most helpful:

Glass, Margaret. *Canadian Horse.* September 1953: "The Calumet Story."

Gocher, W. H. *Trotter and Pacer.* December 8, 1927: "The Rise of Calumet Farm."

Goldberg, Ryan. *Daily Racing Form.* December 19, 2009: "Panama: Cradle of Jockeys"; March 10, 2012: "Hatton Provides Window into Racing's Golden Age"; August 22, 2013: "'Affirmed and Alydar's Travers Showdown Still Rouses Emotions."

Haskin, Steve. *Blood-Horse.* 2003: "The Greatest Rivalry."

Hirsch, Joe. *Daily Racing Form.* 1978: "Calumet No. 1 in Derby's History," "John Veitch Plays a Major Role in Calumet's Return to Glory"; May 6, 1978: "Favor Alydar over Affirmed in $239,400 Kentucky Derby."

Horse Review. September 17, 1924: "Calumet Stock Farm"; September 2, 1931: "William Monroe Wright."

Hovdey, Jay. *Daily Racing Form.* January 13, 2001: "Affirmed: A Champion in Every Way"; May 30, 2003: "After a Lost Decade, a Return to the Winner's Circle for a Trainer"; June 5, 2003: "Affirmed-Alydar Rivalry Still Inspires"; June 3, 2004: "Crowning Moments: The Last Time"; February 2, 2007: "A Day Spent with Two Legends"; June 8, 2007: "Affirmed Set the Bar High"; January 1, 2008: "A Life of Drama on and off the Track"; April 1, 2008: "Before Crown Run, Affirmed Ruled the West"; May 30, 2008: "Reliving Racing's Ultimate Rivalry"; June 1, 2012: "Triple Crown History Laid to Rest."

McFarland, Cynthia. *Thoroughbred Times.* April 30, 2011: "The Last Triple Crown Winner."

Nagler, Barney. *Daily Racing Form.* 1978: "Velasquez Close to Goal in Life."

Oakford, Glenye Cain. *Daily Racing Form.* June 3, 2004: "Crowning Moments: The Owners"; December 31, 2007: "Affirmed Owner Louis Wolfson Dead at 95."

Paulick, Ray. *Blood-Horse*. September 27, 2005: "Greatness Affirmed."

Shuff, Jesse. *Trotter and Pacer*. December 22, 1928: "Kentucky Kernels."

Shulman, Lenny. *Blood-Horse*. April 26, 2008: "Back in the Saddle."

Stevens, Gene. *Post Time USA*. February 2008: "There Will Never Be Another Like Lou Wolfson."

White, Henry Ten Eyck. *Trotter and Pacer*. June 16, 1927: "W. M. Wright and Calumet Farm's Greatness."

White, Tom. *Hoof Beats*. June 1978: "William Monroe Wright: Improver of the Breed."

Wolfson, Patrice. *Blood-Horse*. April 22, 2008: "Affirmed Career."

Wolfson, Steve. *Backstretch*. November/December 2000: "Louis Wolfson," Part I; January/February 2001: "Louis Wolfson," Part II.

———. *Thoroughbred Times*. April 24, 2004: "Parke's Patience a Classic for All Time"; June 7, 2012: "Connections of Affirmed Could Get Company in Exclusive Club."

NEWSPAPERS

Daily newspapers most heavily relied on for archived news stories and features: *Chicago Tribune, Los Angeles Times, New York Times, Newsday*. Other sources of news stories: Associated Press, *Cincinnati Enquirer, Florida Times-Union, Lexington Herald-Leader*, Maysville (KY) *Ledger Independent, Miami Daily News, Miami Herald, Milwaukee Journal, New Orleans Times-Picayune, Ocala Star-Banner, Philadelphia Inquirer, Sarasota Herald-Tribune, Seattle Times, St. Louis Post Dispatch, St. Petersburg Times, South Florida Sun-Sentinel*, Toronto *Globe and Mail*, United Press International, *USA Today, Wall Street Journal, Washington Post, Washington Times*.

In addition to daily news stories from the newspapers listed above, the following in-depth feature articles and columns were most helpful:

Bauer, Hambla. *Miami Daily News*. December 29, 1950: "Warren Wright, Noted Horseman, Dies Here."

Blackford, Linda B. *Lexington Herald-Leader*. April 27, 2008: "Two Great Horses, One Great Rivalry."

Brenner, Anita. *New York Times*. August 10, 1941: "Whirlaway: Problem Horse."

Cady, Steve. *New York Times*. February 14, 1970: "Hirsch Jacobs, Leading Trainer, Is Dead"; February 20, 1977: "Here Comes 'The Kid'!"; May 1, 1978: "Royal Confrontation: Alydar vs. Affirmed in Kentucky Derby"; June 5, 1978: "The Man Behind Steve Cauthen"; July 8, 1978: "No Commercials for Affirmed"; December 15, 1979: "A Team That Is Worth $100 Million"; May 31, 1987: "Affirmed and Alydar Ran into Our Hearts."

Carfango, Jacalyn. *Seattle Times*. March 29, 1992: "The Rise and Fall of Calumet Farm."

Christine, Bill. *Los Angeles Times*. March 2, 1985: "John Veitch Knows He Has a Good Thing Going"; June 8, 1989: "After the Storm"; April 26, 1991: "Triple Crown Trainer Laz Barrera Dies at 66"; June 5, 1997: "A Kid and His Horse . . . 19 Years Later."

Comerford, Ed. *Newsday*. September 23, 1969: "The Panama Jockeys," Part I; September 24, 1969: "The Panama Jockeys," Part II; February 14, 1970: "$2 Bettors Will Miss Hirsch Jacobs Most"; January 22, 1977: "Cauthen's Good, and So Is His Agent"; April 30, 1978: "On the Road to the Kentucky Derby"; June 4, 1978: "Laz and the Kid."

Condon, David. *Chicago Tribune*. May 5, 1978: "Calumet Farm in a Class by Itself"; May 7, 1978: "Barrera Had Derby Win Planned."

Crist, Steven. *New York Times.* November 3, 1980: "Down in Kentucky's Bluegrass Country, the Breed Is Changing"; May 24, 1987: "The Legacy of Alydar Heads for Biggest Test."

Drape, Joe. *New York Times.* January 22, 2001: "Affirmed and Alydar, and Sport at Its Noblest"; May 4, 2023: "First, a Run for the Roses. Then, a Dash to the Breeding Shed."; May 7, 2023: "At Churchill Downs, Humans Failed the Horses Again"; May 30, 2023: "Horse Regulators Hold Emergency Meeting to Investigate Horse Deaths."

Durso, Joseph. *New York Times.* November 27, 1977: "Superkid: Man of the Year"; April 30, 1991: "Fondness and Grief Run Deep for Laz Barrera."

Dwyre, Bill. *Los Angeles Times.* June 3, 2008: "Affirmed-Alydar Duel Still Sets the Standard."

Fichtner, Margaria. *Miami Herald.* December 2, 1990: "Calumet Farm's Horses—and Its Doyenne—Ruled Racing."

Finney, Peter. New Orleans *Times-Picayune.* June 11, 2011: "Affirmed, Alydar Lifted Triple Crown to New Heights."

Hiers, Fred. Ocala *Star-Banner.* June 1, 2008: "Trainer Tells Tales of Affirmed's Roots."

Isaacs, Stan. *Newsday.* April 20, 1970: "Personality: The Spirit of Hirsch Jacobs"; February 5, 1978: "Steve Cauthen: The $6-Million Boy."

James, Brant. *St. Petersburg Times.* June 4, 2003: "Looking Back at a Legend."

Layden, Tim. *Newsday.* June 2, 1993: "At 18 He Rode Affirmed to the Triple Crown, but Now Steve Cauthen Is out to Pasture."

Lexington Herald-Leader. February 21, 1929: "Calumet Farm Stallions."

Lipsyte, Robert. *New York Times.* June 6, 1970: "Get out with Jacobs."

Los Angeles Times. April 29, 1985: "The Rivalry."

Manne, Henry G. *Wall Street Journal.* January 18, 2008: "The Original Corporate Raider."

Milbert, Neil. *Chicago Tribune.* June 8, 1978: "In a Crazy Sport, Barrera Fits In"; April 26, 1991: "Laz Barrera's Brilliance Spoke Volumes."

Murray, Jim. *Los Angeles Times.* February 19, 1988: "Sticking His Neck Out Just Wasn't Enough"; March 11, 1990: "He's the Perfect Trainer for the Perfect Race Horse"; May 2, 1991: "Prince Lost to Sport of Kings."

Nack, Bill. *Newsday.* May 13, 1976: "A Biter and a Stall-Walker Team up for the Preakness"; June 6, 1976: "A Test This Champion Couldn't Flunk"; May 26, 1977: "Moment of Fear Relived"; March 7, 1978: "Alydar out of Gate First in the Race for the Derby"; April 23, 1978: "'78 Kentucky Derby a Family Affair"; May 2, 1978: "This Is the Derby of the Magicians"; May 4, 1978: "He Got the One Job He Wanted"; May 6, 1978: "In the Finest Tradition"; May 7, 1978: "Laz Barrera Played It Perfectly"; May 18, 1978: "The Most Memorable of the 3"; May 21, 1978: "2 Honest Thoroughbreds"; May 20, 1978: "Alydar Appears to Be More Fit for This Outing"; June 10, 1978: "A Vote for Alydar in a Match Race"; June 11, 1978: "It Was a Match Race for All Time"; August 20, 1978: "Winners, Losers—They're All Sore"; September 9, 1978: "Burden of Proof Finally Rests on Seattle Slew"; September 17, 1978: "Best Horse Flies Like an Airplane."

New York Times. January 3, 1955: "Today's Giants in Finance."

Newhan, Ross. *Los Angeles Times.* February 4, 1977: "Barrera: Long Way from Destructo to Bold Forbes"; February 6, 1977: "Riding High at 16."

Patton, Janet. *Lexington Herald-Leader.* April 29, 2012: "Field of Dreams: At Spendthrift, It All Begins in the Breeding Shed."

Povich, Shirley. *Washington Post.* May 21, 1978: "Alydar Peaks Too Soon—in Post Parade."

Robards, Terry. *New York Times.* October 3, 1967: "Wolfson and the Law"; October 7, 1967: "U.S. Court Denies Bid for New Trial by Louis Wolfson"; November 29, 1967: "Wolfson Gets Year and a Fine"; June 21, 1968: "Financier Tells of Wolfson Deal"; June 1, 1969: "Charitable Wolfson: It Began at Home."

Schmidt, Neil. *Cincinnati Enquirer.* April 28, 2003: "The Kid Still Has Dreams."

Smith, Red. *New York Times.* April 19, 1976: "Be Bold, Be Bold, Be Not Too Bold"; May 2, 1976: "A Rose for Senor Baeza"; May 17, 1976: "'Nice and Quiet and Relaxed'"; June 6, 1976: "Latins from Manhattan"; June 7, 1976: "God Did a Hell of a Job, Too"; May 28, 1977: "Steve Cauthen Didn't Milk His Spill"; June 29, 1977: "The Day Young Steve Grew Up"; August 15, 1977: "What They Talk about at Saratoga"; March 24, 1978: "He Was Named for Aly, Darling"; April 3, 1978: "A Colt Built for Two"; April 4, 1978: "Affirmed Affirms His Derby Class"; May 1, 1978: "Native Dancer and the Derby"; May 5, 1978: "The Barn Where It All Began"; May 6, 1978: "Spendthrift Farm Mob"; May 7, 1978: "Cauthen's Hundred Years"; May 8, 1978: "So Now the Score Is 5–2"; May 20, 1978: "The Preakness: What They Say"; May 21, 1978: "Cauthen on Preakness: 'My Horse Beat Him'"; May 22, 1978: "A Tale of Two Horses"; June 10, 1978: "Man Here Loves His Horse"; June 11, 1978: "L. Barrera, Oracle"; June 12, 1978: "Barrera and Match Races"; August 7, 1978: "Laz Barrera, Yankee Fan"; March 18, 1979: "Alydar and His Friends"; October 24, 1979: "For the Champion, an Easy Gallop"; May 3, 1980: "Three Who Wear the Triple Crown."

Surface, William. *Chicago Tribune.* July 3, 1960: "Winningest Gal at the Tracks."

Talley, Rick. *Chicago Tribune.* May 23, 1978: "Alydar Would Have Won—with Cauthen Aboard"; June 11, 1978: "Cauthen Says It All: 'A Helluva Race.'"

Terry, Dickson. *St. Louis Post-Dispatch.* June 27, 1948: "Behind Citation, Ben Jones and Crack Calumet Stable Is Modest Millionaire Wright."

Winfrey, Carey. *New York Times.* May 5, 1978: "2 Octogenarians Look to Derby for a Ninth Hurrah."

INTERNET

Websites used for source material and background: affirmedtriplecrown.com, americanclassicpedigrees.com, belmontstakes.com, bloodhorse.com, cbsnews.com, drf.com, drf.uky.edu, espn.com, es.redskins.com, hisaus.org, horseracingnation.com, jockeyclub.com, kentuckyderby.com, ntra.com, nytimes.com, paulickreport.com, racingmuseum.org, si.com, tampabaydowns.com, thoroughbredtimes.com.

VIDEO

Various from ABC, CBS, ESPN, NBC, and NRYA, plus the Affirmed documentary *One of a Kind.*

INDEX

Page references for figures are *italicized*.

ABC racing telecasts, 236
Abshire, Lonnie, 145
Affectionately (horse), 93, 95, 96, 166
Affiliate (horse), 166
Affirmed (horse):
  Alydar compared with, 24–25, 113, 130,
    138, 187, 192, 207–9, 222–23, 226,
    241, 256–59, 275–76
  Alydar's rivalry with, 1–6, 24, 134–39,
    163–68, 173, 174–75, 178–79, 181,
    187, 188–89, 192, 196, 199–219,
    221–29, *230*, 231–43, 245–59, 269,
    275, 279–85, 283–85, *287–96*, *305–6*
  in Belmont Futurity Stakes, 166–67
  in Belmont Stakes, 228, *230*, 231–43,
    244, 245–51, *252*, 252–59, 261–62,
    263, 266, 267, 271, 280, 281, 282,
    296
  bloodlines of, 3, 5–6, 24–25, 157–58,
    302
  braiding of, 136, 249
  breeding of, 3, 18, 24–25, 87–88, 282
  California training period of, 183–84,
    186–93, 200, 202, 211, 234
  in Champagne Stakes, 174, 175–76, *177*,
    178, 192, 215, 243
  coat color of, 5, 129
  as colt, 113–15, 136
  death of, 278, 282
  disqualification of, 268–69, 271
  Eclipse Awards won by, 179, 272, 273,
    282
  escape of, 190–91, *191*, 265

  farewell "Affirmed Day" for, 174
  final race of, 173–74
  as foal, 101–2
  as four-year-old, 273, 282, 285
  in Great American Stakes, 137–38, 139,
    164
  in Hollywood Derby, 190–93
  in Hollywood Gold Cup, 272
  in Hopeful Stakes, 5–6, 139, 140, 161,
    163–66, 258
  as Horse of the Year, 272, 273, 282
  in Jim Dandy Stakes, 262, 265–66
  in Jockey Club Gold Cup, 271–72, 273
  jockeys for, 2, 6, 136, 138–41, 159–61,
    178–79, 180, 186, 189–90, 206, 211,
    226–27, 241–42, 266
  in Juvenile Championship, 138–39, 190
  in Kentucky Derby, 136, 164, 167,
    179, 181, 183, 184, 187, 196, *198*,
    199–219, 222–23, 227, 231, 232, 233,
    236–37, 238, 239, 241–43, 252, 258,
    262, *294*
  in Laurel Futurity Stakes, 178–79, 183,
    219
  legacy of, 6, 261, 279–85
  maiden race of, 129–30, *131*, 159–60,
    246, 273
  naps of, 113–14, 210, 221, 234, 243
  odds on, 129, 164, 178, 181, 207, 210,
    212, 225, 245–46, 267
  Patrice Wolfson's relationship with, 101–
    2, 114, 115, 129–30, 136, 140, 161,
    164–65, 167, 176, 186, 191, 202–3,

204–5, 216, 233, 234–35, 246, 247,
    249, 250, 251, 262, 265, 274, 279
photographs of, *131, 162, 177, 191, 198,*
    220, 230, 244, 252, 260, 265, 274
physical appearance of, 3, 5, 161, 221,
    234–35, 267, 272, 273–74, 282,
    305–6
in Preakness Stakes, 219, *220,* 221–28,
    231–32, 233, 234, 235, 236, 237, 238,
    240, 241, *252,* 258, *295*
racing record of, 1–2, 279–85, *287–299*
racing strategy for, 135–36, 167, 178,
    213–16, 235, 242, 246
reputation of, 130, 179, 192, 212,
    256–59, 261–62, 272, 274
retirement of, 273–76
in San Felipe Handicap, 187–88, 189
in Sanford Stakes, 139, 140, 160, 161,
    164
in Santa Anita Derby, 189–90
in Santa Anita Handicap, 272
speed of, 3, 6, 138–39, 161, 192–93, 217,
    248–49, 256–57
statistical charts for, *287–99, 305–6*
in Strub Stakes, 272
as stud stallion, 274–76, 278, 282–83
temperament of, 2, 3, 6, 114, 129–30,
    191–92, 200, 213, 265, 275
as three-year-old, 186, 199, 226, 262,
    284
trainer for, 2, 113–15, *116,* 117–30, *131,*
    135–36, 138–41, 167, 180, 183–84,
    186–93, 199–200, 207–9, 221–24,
    272
in Travers Stakes, *260,* 262–69, 271
as two-year-old, 129–30, 164, 175, 187,
    207, 284
for two-year-old championship, 175,
    207, 284
weight of, 234, *306*
Wolfsons as owners of, 138, 140, 161,
    165, 179, 180, 186, 191, 202–5, 216,
    222, *224,* 234–35, 246, 247, 250, 251,
    262, 265, 268, 274, 275, 278, 279,
    280, 281–82, 284
in Woodward Stakes, 273
as weanling, 101–2

in Youthful Stakes, 134–36
Affirmed Success (horse), 283
Aga Khan, 42, 71
Alabama Stakes, 140
Alaniz, Juan, 135–36, 188, 213, 246, 251, 265
Ali, Muhammad, 1, 3, 4, 168, 200, 231, 232,
    258, 284
Althea (horse), 276
Alydar (horse):
    Affirmed compared with, 24–25, 113,
        130, 138, 187, 192, 207–9, 222–23,
        226, 241, 256–59, 275–76
    Affirmed's rivalry with, 1–6, 24, 134–39,
        163–68, 173, 174–75, 178–79, 181,
        187, 188–89, 192, 196, 199–219,
        221–29, *230,* 231–43, 245–59, 269,
        275, 279–85, 283–85, *287–96, 305–6*
    in Arlington Classic, 263
    in Belmont Futurity Stakes, 166–68
    in Belmont Stakes, 228, *230,* 231–43,
        244, 245–51, *252,* 252–59, 261–62,
        263, 267, 280, 281, *296*
    blinkers worn by, 139, 176, *182,* 235–36
    bloodlines of, 3, 5–6, 24–25, 87–88, *303*
    in Blue Grass Stakes, *182,* 193–96, *196,*
        209
    breeding of, 2, 24–25, 87–88
    in Champagne Stakes, 174–76, *177,* 178,
        192, 215, 243
    coat color of, 5
    as colt, 109–13, 194
    death of, 277–78
    earnings of, 272
    in Flamingo Stakes, 185, 188
    in Florida Derby, 188, 193
    Florida training period of, 184–85,
        188–89
    as foal, 102–3,
    as four-year-old, 272, 285
    in Great American Stakes, 137–38, 139,
        164
    in Hopeful Stakes, 5–6, 139, 164–66, 258
    injuries suffered by, 268, 272, 277–78
    jockeys for, 2, 133–35, 139, 166–67,
        168–74, 185, 195–96, 213–14,
        241–42

in Kentucky Derby, 135, 138, 167, 174,
181, 188, 196, 199–200, *201*, 202–19,
223, 232, 236, 240, 241–42, 243, 258,
262, 241, 258, *294*
in Laurel Futurity, 179–79
legacy of, 6, 261, 284–85
maiden race of, 133–37, *137*
Markeys as owners of, 134, 135, 137, 175,
193–96, *196*, 204, 205–6, 218–19,
262–64, 266, 268, 276, 279, 284
naming of, 109–10
odds on, 178, 179, 181, 207, 210, 212,
225, 243, 245–46, 263
as "one-run horse," 135, 239–40
photographs of, *100, 132, 137, 177, 182,*
196, 201, 227, 230, 244, 252, 260
physical appearance of, 3, 5, 138, 164,
183, 188, 222, 237, 272, *305–6*
in Preakness Stakes, 219, 221–27, *227,*
228, 232, 235, 236–37, 238, 240,
241–42, 243, 258, *295*
racing record of, 1–2, 272, *287–299*
racing strategy for, 135, 235–37, 239–40,
246
in Remsen Stakes, 179, 185
reputation of, 2, 5–6, 130, 133–35, 164,
256–59, 261–62
retirement of, 272–73
running style of, 3, 5, 133–35, 237–40
in Sapling Stakes, 139, 164
speed of, 133–34, 237, 248–51, 256–57
statistical charts for, *287–99, 305–6*
as stud stallion, 272, 275–76, 282–83
in Suburban Handicap, 272
switching leads by, 166–67, 184–85, 226,
236, 267
temperament of, 3, 5–6, 174, 194, 200,
247, 255–56, 275
as three-year-old, 199–200, 226, 262,
284
training of, 109–13, 133–35, 166–67,
168, 184–85
in Travers Stakes, *260*, 262–69, 272
in Tremont Stakes, 139
as two-year-old, 164, 175, 184, 207, 284
for two-year-old championship, 175,
207, 284

weight of, 5, 237, 272, *306*
in Whitney Stakes, 263–64
as yearling, 109–13
in Youthful Stakes, 134–36
Aly Khan, 54, 110
Alysheba (horse), 276, 282
American Derby, *15*
American Motors, 10, 68, 79
American Pharoah (horse), 4, 282, 284
Anderson, Chic, 248–50
Aqueduct Racetrack, 14, 88, 91–95, 125,
151–53, 155, 160, 172–73, 179, 193,
211, 274
Arcaro, Eddie, 44–46, 48–49, 150, 152, 157,
169, 217, 236, 239
Arlington Classic, 16, 263
Arlington Park, 39–40, 149
Armed (horse), 48, 91
Arruza, Carlos, 122
"The Art of Race Riding" (Arcaro), 169
Arts and Letters (horse), 17, 236
Assault (horse), 48, 91, 233
Associated Press, 181
Atkinson, Ted, 149–50
August Belmont Memorial Cup, 251
Avery, Sewell, 66–67
Axthelm, Pete, 156

Baeza, Braulio, 143, 151, 170, 171
Baffert, Bob, 284
Balzac (horse), 190, 191
Barrera, Alberto "Albert," 122, 128, 223
Barrera, Carmen Miramontes, 122, 123,
250
Barrera, Lazaro, Jr., "Larry," 122, 128, 186
Barrera, Lazaro Sosa "Laz," 2, 114–15,
116, 117–30, *131*, 132–41, 159–61,
166, 167–68, 178–79, 180, 183–84,
186–93, 199–200, 202, 207–14,
216–19, 221–24, 226–27, 231–35,
238, 240–43, 245–47, 250–51, 253–
54, 258, 261–66, 268–69, 271–74,
278–79, 281
Barrera, Luis, 127–28, 130
Barrera, Willie, 115, 127
Battaglia, Mike, 207
Bay Streak (horse), 157, 173

Believe It (horse), 139, 179, 185–86, 188, 202, 208–10, 212, 215, 218, 223, 225–28, 238

Belmont Futurity Stakes, 166–67, 175

Belmont Park, 13, 90, 105–6, 115, 125, 127, 129, *131*, 133, *137*, 157, 166, 219, *230*, 221, 235, 241, *244*, 245–47, 251, *252*, 257, 261–62, 271, 273, 280

Belmont Stakes, 1–2, 17, 46, 76, 86, 96, 104, 126, 140, 157, *230*, 231–43, *244*, 245–52, *252*, 253–59, 261–63, 271, 273, 276, 280–82, 285

Belwin (horse), 32

Bet Twice (horse), 276

Beyer, Andrew, 210

Beyer Speed Figures, 210

Bieber, Isidor, 89–91, 94, 96, 97

Bieber-Jacobs Stable, 94, 96, 97

Blenheim II (horse), 42

Block, Charlie, 70

Blood-Horse, 280

Blue Delight (horse), 23

Blue Grass Stakes, 44, *182*, 193–96, *196*, 209

Bold Forbes (horse), 124–28, 148, 159–60, 190, 200, 209, 211, 240

Booth, Albie, 61

Breeders' Cup Classic, 276

Britton, Jack, 232

Brumfield, Don, 151

Buck Mountain (horse), 136

Bull Lea (horse), 39–40, 47–49, 56–57, 76, 83, 85, 88, 276

Burch, Elliott, 104–5, 236

Butazolidin, 86

Cain Hoy Stable, 72–73

California Horse Racing Board, 189

Calumet Baking Powder Co., 27–33, 49–50

Calumet Butler (horse), 34, 37–38

Calumet Farm, 2, 5, 10, 22–25, 30, 32–35, 38–57, *78*, 82–88, 102–3, 106–10, 193–94, 196, 205–7, 272, 275–78, 281–82

Campbell, Eddie, 151

Cannonade (horse), 148

Canonero (horse), 234

Capital Transit, 63, 65–66

Carey, Hugh, 251

Carroll, Julian, 216

Carson, Johnny, 156

Castro, Fidel, 122

Cauthen, Doug, 211

Cauthen, Myra Bischoff, 143–44, 149

Cauthen, Ronald "Tex," 143–52, 254

Cauthen, Steve, 2, 6, 141, *142*, 143–61, *162*, 164–67, 172–73, 176, 178–79, 180–81, 186–87, 189, 192–93, *198*, 205, 206, 208, 209, 210–11, 213–18, *220*, 223–27, 241–42, 246–51, 253–54, 259, 266, 271, 272, 279–80

Century Gold (horse), 97

Champagne Stakes, 72, 76, 174–76, *177*, 178, 192, 215, 243

Chance Dancer (horse), 187

Chateaugay (horse), 143

Churchill Downs, 24, 36, 41, 44–46, 49, 85, 95, 125, 143, 148–49, 151–52, 193, *198*, 199–219, 222, 241

Chris Evert (horse), 172

Cinnamon, Melvin, 102–3, 106–9

Citation (horse), 14, 22, 48–49, *50*, 71, 86, 91, 125, 140, 199, 206, 232–33, 258, 272, 280–81

Claiborne Farm, 69, 88

Coaching Club American Oaks, 236, 240

Coaltown (horse), 48–49, 140, 199

Coastal (horse), 273

Comaneci, Nadia, 154

Combs, Leslie, II, 19, 54–55, 72–74, 84, 175, 275

Confidential, 67

Continental Enterprises, Inc., 79–81

Cordero, Angel, Jr., 126, 128, 130, 136, 138, 140, 148, 151–55, 158, 160, 172, 189, 253, 267–69

Cornell, Reggie, 103, 107–8

Cosell, Howard, 213

Counterpoint (horse), 104, 236

Count Fleet (horse), 72, 232–33, 236, 255

Crab Grass (horse), 158

Crafty Admiral (horse), 18, 97, 121

Cruguet, Jean, 257

Daily Racing Form, 130, 152–53, 156, 254, 271
Dancer's Image (horse), 86
Darby Creek Road (horse), 140, 165, 176, 202, 238, 247, 249, 253, 257
Davona Dale (horse), 279
Dax S. (horse), 223
Destructo (horse), 123
DiMaggio, Joe, 3, 65, 80, 120, 273
Dolce, Emil, 123–24
Donnagal (horse), 119
Dustwhirl (horse), 42, 51

Easy Goer (horse), 276, 282
Eclipse (horse), 1, 179
Eclipse Awards, 158, 179–80, 272, 276, 278, 283
Eglin Federal Prison Camp, 81, 96
English Triple Crown, 233
Epsom Derby, 280
Escudero, Rafael, 124
ESPN, 4
Exceller (horse), 272
exercise riders, 12, 111, 129, 144, 148, 160, 190, 235
Exclusive Native (horse), 16–22, 24, 82, 98, 203, 274–75

Fairland Farm, 31–32
Feller, Bob "Rapid Robert," 154
First City Bank, 277
Fitzsimmons, Jim "Sunny Jim," 48, 69
Flamingo Stakes, 43, 75, 185, 188
Flawlessly (horse), 283
Florida Derby, 188, 193
Florida Pipe and Supply, 61–63
Foolish Pleasure (horse), 238
Forego (horse), 161, 210, 273
Fortas, Abe, 81–82
Fortune, 68
Forward Pass (horse), 85–86, 108, 206, 234
Francis S. (horse), 72
Frazier, Joe, 1, 3, 4, 168, 200, 231, 232, 258, 284
Funny Cide (horse), 281

Galbreaths' Darby Dan Farm, 279
Gallant Fox (horse), 37, 48, 233, 264
General Foods Corp., 33
Gerbert, Elkin, 68, 79
Glendora G (horse), 30–32
Gonzalez, Bernie, 129–30, *131*, 160
Goodman, Lenny, 151–52, 155, 158–60
Grand Circuit, 32
Great American Stakes, 137–39, 164
Great Depression, 33, 62, 66, 89, 175
Gretzky, Wayne, 156
Grid Iron Hero, 123
grooms, 12–13, 20–21, 104–5, 110–11, 114, 119–20, 122–23, 129–30, 134–35, 167, 183, 186, 188, 212, 246, 265
Guggenheim, Harry F., 11, 19, 72

Hail To Reason (horse), 92–93, 95–96, 165
Hall of Fame. *See* National Racing Museum and Hall of Fame
Hambletonian Stake, 33–34, 38
Happy Valley Farm, 82
Harbor View Farm, 11–17, 70–77, 82, 88, 97, 101–2, 113–14, 124–25, 128, 136, 157, 180, 203, 253–54, 272
harness racing, 28, 30, 32–35, 37
Hatton, Charles, 14, 233
Hawthorne Racetrack, 150
Herbager (horse), 88, 103
Hertz, John D., 34–35, 37
Hialeah Park, 12–13, 43, 52, 56, 70, 73–76, 95, 107–12, 114, 118, 127–28, 184–85, 189
High Echelon (horse), 96
Hill Gail (horse), 56
Hindoo (horse), 14
Hipódromo de las Américas, 120
Hipódromo Presidente Remón, 168–69
Hirsch, Joe, 14, 130
Hirsch, Max, 69
Hollywood Derby, 190, 192–93
Hollywood Gold Cup, 272
Hollywood Park, 122–23, 138, 166, 190
Honest Pleasure (horse), 125, 148
Hooper, Fred, 71, 170–71
Hopefully On (horse), 88

Hopeful Stakes, 5–6, 93, 139–41, 161, 163–66, 258
Horsemen's Benevolent and Protective Association (HBPA), 94
Horse of the Year, 19, 47–49, 76, 95, 104, 161, 272–73, 276, 282
Horseracing Safety and Integrity Act, 279
Howard, Charles, 71

Indigo Star (horse), 223
Iron Liege (horse), 57

Jackson, Reggie, 180
Jacobs, Ethel, 88, 91, 93, 96
Jacobs, Hirsch, 14, 17, 88–97, 118–19, 124, 127, 205
Jacobs, John, 93, 95–96
Jaipur (horse), 257–58
James, Melvin, 114
Jerkens, Allen, 209–10, 265
Jet Diplomacy (horse), 139, 161
Jim Dandy (horse), 264
Jim Dandy Stakes, 262, 265–66
Jockey Club, 93–94, 112
Jockey Club Gold Cup, 271–73
jockeys:
    agents for, 151
    as "apprentice jockeys," 129, 148–52, 156–60, 169–70, 172, 180
    licenses for, 148, 169
    weight made by, 71, 145–46, 151, 279
    See also Arcaro, Eddie; Cauthen, Steve; Maple, Eddie; Pincay, Laffitt, Jr.; Velasquez, Jorge
Johnson, Phil, 258
Jonabell Farm, 278
Jones, Ben "Plain Ben," 40–41, 41, 42–46, 48–49, 56–57, 82–83, 85, 90, 93, 103, 206
Jones, Jimmy, 43, 56, 73, 82–84
J. O. Tobin (horse), 263
Judge Advocate (horse), 238, 247–49, 257
Justice Department, U.S., 80
Justify (horse), 4, 284
Juvenile Championship (race), 138–39, 190
juvenile championship (annual title), 93, 175, 208, 284

Keeneland Race Course, 193–96, 196
Keeneland sales auctions, 9–10, 35, 70, 72, 94, 97, 115
Kelso (horse), 210, 273
Kentucky Derby, 1, 5–6, 11–12, 14, 17–18, 22–24, 34–36, 39–41, 43–46, 47, 47–49, 56–57, 71–72, 74–75, 82, 85–86, 93, 95, 108–9, 125–26, 135–36, 138, 140, 143, 147–48, 155, 159, 163–64, 166–67, 173–74, 179, 181, 183–84, 186–90, 193, 196, 198, 199–200, 201, 202–19, 221–23, 225–28, 231–34, 236–43, 252, 258, 276, 280–82
Kentucky Derby Gold Cup, 35, 46, 56, 86, 179, 206
Kentucky Derby Trial, 44
The Kid (Axthelm), 156
King, Hal, 122
King of Swat (horse), 149

Lamarr, Hedy, 53, 67
Lang, Chick, 226
Latonia Race Course, 144–46, 148
Laurel Futurity, 178–79, 183, 219
Lawrin (horse), 40, 45
Lazar, Swifty, 156
Leggett, Bill, 256
Lewis, Ted "Kid," 232
Life, 65, 81
Little Miracle (horse), 157–58
Los Angeles Times, 277
Loy, Myrna, 53–54
Lundy, J. T., 277–79

McMahon, Dick, 34, 38–39
Majestic Prince (horse), 17–18, 203, 211, 234, 236
Manne, Henry, 81
Man o' War (horse), 1, 5, 14, 36–37, 44, 48–49, 90, 155, 164, 166, 237–39, 280
Maple, Eddie, 134–35, 137–39, 165–67, 174, 179, 215, 218, 225–26, 228
Markey, Gene "Admiral," 52–57, 85–86, 103–4, 107–10, 133, 135, 137, 175, 193–96, 196, 204–6, 218, 262–64, 266, 276, 284

Markey, Lucille:
    as Alydar owner, 134–35, 137, 193–96, *196*, 204–6, 218–19, 262–64, 266, 276
    background of, 2, 22, 51–55
    as Calumet Farm owner, 22–24, 25, 41–42, 46, 52–57, 83–88, 175
    first marriage of, 23, *26*, 37, 50–53, 54–56
    as horse breeder, 22–26, 39, 49–50, 56–57, 83–85, 102–3
    and naming of Calumet racehorses, 51, 109–10
    purse earnings of, 22, 37–38, 46–50, 56, 57, 83, 86–87, 109, 205
    reputation of, 22–24, 85–88
    second marriage of, 52–57
    trainers hired by, 39–45, 48–49, 56–57, 83–85, 90, 93, 103–13, 206
    wealth of, 22–23, 54–55, 57, 276–77
    Wolfson compared with, 24–25, 57, 72, 73, 75, 82
Marquette, Pére, 28
Martens, George, 158
Matos, Tony, 189, 266
Mellon, Paul, 68, 104
Merritt-Chapman & Scott, 65–68, 72–73, 79, 80–81
Molter, Willie, 120
Monmouth Park, 14–16, 85, 140
Montgomery Ward, 10, 66–68, 79
Moreno, Bolivar, 169
Morning Telegraph, 14, 92
El Mundo, 119
Murray, Jim, 117, 118

Nack, Bill, 106, 209, 243, 256–57, 269, 282
Nashua (horse), 19, 69, 73, 165, 199, 237, 239
Nashua Motel, 19–20, 22
Nasrullah (horse), 69, 71
Nasty and Bold (horse), 267
National Racing Museum and Hall of Fame, 2, 69, 71, 84, 95, 103, 149, 151, 175, 202, 205, 258, 279, 280, 283
Native Dancer (horse), 3, 5, 9–12, 14, *15*, 123, 125–26, 164, 233, 241, 280
Native Heritage (horse), 97–98

Navarro, Ramon, 170–71
Nearly on Time (horse), 160–61
Newsday, 210, 256
New York Racing Association, 94, 242, 257
New York Times, 68, 80, 232
New York State's "Big Wheel," 153, 157, 160, 171–72, 186
New York Yankees, 2, 3, 4, 23, 117, 120, 180
Noon Time Spender (horse), 223, 225, 238, 247–49
Noor (horse), 71–72, 258
Núñez, Jorge, 120

O'Bryan, George, 140, 189
Ocala Stud, 74
O'Farrell, Joe, 74–76
Off-Track Betting (OTB), 130, 153, 245
Oklahoma Track (Saratoga), 262
Omaha (horse), 48, 233
On-and-On (horse), 87–88
Onion (horse), 264–65
Orb (horse), 281
Oriental Park, 118–19, 127–28
Our Mims (horse), 88, 140, 174, 236, 240
Our Native (horse), 18
Oxbow (horse), 281

Palmer, Joe, 39
Palmieri, Edmund L., 80–81
pari-mutuel wagering, 36, 129, 245–46
Parke, Burley, 10–15, 70–73, 124
Parke, Ivan, 71, 124
Peb (Pierre Bellocq), *229*
Pelé, 180
Penney, J. C., 62
People, 157
Personality (horse), 95–96
Peter Manning (horse), 31
Peteski (horse), 283
Phalanx (horse), 104
Pimlico Race Course, 92, 126, 221–228, *229*
Pincay, Laffit, Jr., 138–40, 151, 155, 160, 171–72, 189–90, 266–69, 272–73
Pleasant Colony (horse), 280
Plum Cake (horse), 88
Poole, George, 85

Preakness Stakes, 1, 17–18, 46, 49, 86,
    95–96, 126, 219, *220*, 221–24, *224*,
    225–27, *227*, 228, *229*, 231–38,
    240–44, 252, 258, 276, 280–81

Quarter Horses, 71

racing, horse:
    antigambling laws and, 36
    blinkers used in, 45, 95, 125, 139, 176,
        235–36
    claimers in, 18, 89–91, 94, 97, 118, 123,
        149, 153, 158, 254
    deaths of Thoroughbreds in, 75, 279
    disqualifications in, 86, 254, 268, 271
    furlongs in, 112
    handicap division of, 90–91, 96, 97, 123,
        160–61, 187, 272, 282
    handicapping in, 125, 126, 155, 164,
        202, 210, 243
    harness vs. flat and, 28, 34–38
    "hundred-grander" stakes in, 125, 140,
        167
    leg injuries and breakdowns of
        Thoroughbreds in, 14–15, 16, 17, 30,
        93, 103, 108, 109, 111, 112, 126, 140,
        203, 272, 277, 278
    morning works in, 12–14, 43, 45, 93,
        119, 122, 125, 129, 134, 137, 138,
        156, 164, 200, 202, 209
    photo finishes in, 1, 167, 171, 181, 199,
        237, 250–51, 257
    popularity of, 28, 35–37, 153–56,
        180–81, 242, 285
    racing licenses for, 98
    as "Sport of Kings," 1, 2, 3, 5, 22–23,
        36–37, 50, 91, 283, 285
    stakes races in, 164
    Standardbred trotters in, 28, 31–38
    whips used in, 146–47, 149, 150, 152,
        156, 169, 187, 189, 192, 193, 214,
        225, 238, 250, 259, 273
Radar Ahead (horse), 192
Raise a Native (horse), *8*, 9–20, 22, 24,
    75–76, 82, 88, 97–98, 103, 135–36,
    158, 203, 214, 276, 284
Raise You (horse), 11

Raymond Earl (horse), 196, 208, 214–15
Red Pipe (horse), 149
Reigh Count (horse), 34–35
Remsen Stakes, 179, 185
Rice, Ewell, 108–9
Rice, Grantland, 44
Ridan (horse), 257–58
Rittmaster, Alex, 68
River Downs Racetrack, 146–47, 149–52
Robards, Terry, 80
Robertson, A. G., 70
Rokeby Stables, 104–6
Roman Brother (horse), 76, 115
Romanticize (horse), 254
Rondinello, Lou, 257
Rose, Carl, 74
Rose, Charlie, 111
Rough Sea (horse), 167
Roving Minstrel (horse), *58*, 72, 75
Royal Patrice (horse), 96
Rubirosa, Porfiro, 122
Ruffian (horse), 238
Runyon, Damon, 89, 91, 153
Russell, John, 257

"The Sandman," 277
San Felipe Handicap, 187, 189
Sanford Stakes, 16, 139–40, 160–61, 164
Santa Anita Derby, 188–90
Santa Anita Handicap, 272
Santa Anita Park, *50*, 76, 128–29, 155–56,
    183–84, 190–91, *191*, 265, 271–72
San Vicente Stakes, 186
Sapling Stakes, 14, 139, 164
Saratoga Special Stakes, 140
Saratoga Race Course, 5–6, 16, *26*, 56,
    92–93, 95–96, 139–40, 151, 160–61,
    162, 163–66, 225, 258, *260*, 262–69,
    280
Saratoga Yearling Sale, 11–12, 35, 47, 75
Saturday Evening Post, 65
Seabiscuit (horse), 47, 71, 91, 225, 232, 237,
    239
Seattle Slew (horse), 157, 180, 185, 226,
    233, 238, 271–72, 275–76, 281
Secretariat (horse), 1, 5, 18, 155, 164, 190,
    199–200, 209–11, 214, 216–17,

226, 228, 232–33, 236–37, 256–57, 264–65, 273, 276, 280–81, 283
Securities Act of 1933, 79–80
Securities and Exchange Commission (SEC), 16, 68, 79–80
Sensitive Prince (horse), 202–3, 206, 208–10, 212, 214–15, 265
Shake Shake Shake (horse), 267
Sham (horse), 18, 190, 199–200, 236–37
Shoemaker, Willie, 150–51, 154–55, 171–72, 217
Sinatra, Frank, 64, 72
Sir Barton (horse), 233, 237–39
The Six Million Dollar Man, 180
Slade (horse), 144–45
Smith, Red, 163, 233, 243
Snyder, Larry, 146, 150
Sobel, Robert, 81
Sparks, Clyde, 111, 134, 213, 246
Spectacular Bid (horse), 273
Spendthrift Farm, 16–21, *21*, 22, 24, 54, 69, 72–73, 84, 88, 175, 203, 274–75, 278
Sporting News, 181
Sports Illustrated, 2, 92, 117, 154, 169, 180–81, 204, 210, 242, 256, 269, 282
Stage Door Johnny (horse), 86
Stakes Barn (Preakness), 221, 223, 228
stallions, Thoroughbred:
  barns for, 19–20, *21*, 22, 33, 203, 274–75
  stud fees for, 16, 47, 284
  syndication of, 17, 19–20, 73, 88, 274, 283
  See also Bull Lea, Exclusive Native, Nashua, Raise a Native
Standardbreds, 28, 31–32, 34–35, 38–39
Stengel, Casey, 117, 118
Stephens, Woody, 139, 188–89, 209–10, 228, 258–59
And Steve Cauthen Sings Too (album), 156
Straight Deal (horse), 96, 101
Strub Stakes, 272
Stymie (horse), 90–91, 102, 124
Stymie Manor, 91
Suburban Handicap, 272
Sunday Silence (horse), 276
Supreme Court, U.S., 81–82
Swaps (horse), 73, 199, 237, 239
Sweet Tooth (horse), 23–24, 88, 102–3, 109

Taliaffero, Chuck, 153
Tampoy (horse), 187
Teddy (horse), 18, 97–98
Thoroughbreds:
  auctions of, 10, 11–12, 19, 35, 47, 72, 74, 75, 76, 82, 94, 275–76, 283
  breeding fees for, 16, 17, 19, 47, 20, 56, 274, 282–83, 284
  drugging of, 36, 86, 279
  insurance on, 277–78
  vs. Standardbreds, 28, 31–32, 34–35, 38–39
  See also specific racehorses
Thousand Nights (horse), 254
Tilt Up (horse), 161, 165
Time, 10, 67, 242
Timonium Race Track, 235
Tim Tam (horse), 57, 85, 206
Tinajero (horse), 124
Tizol, Estéban Rodríguez, 125
The Tonight Show, 154
Track Reward (horse), 223, 225
trainers. *See* Barrera, Lazaro; Jacobs, Hirsch; Jones, Ben; Parke, Burley; Veitch, John
Travers Stakes, 257–58, *260*, 262, 264, 266–69
Tremont Stakes, 139
Triple Crown, 1–6, 17, 22, 37, 46–49, 57, 71–72, 86, 91, 95, 127–28, 157, 180, 185, 226, 231–39, 242, 245, 251–58, 261–62, 264, 271, 273, 276–85
  See also Belmont Stakes; Kentucky Derby; Preakness Stakes
Triple Tiara, 172, 279
Trophy Room (Calumet), 85, 205
Tropical Park, 43–44, 76
Turkoman (horse), 276
Turner, Billy, 257–58
Turn To Turia (horse), 108
Twilight Tear (horse), 48

Upset (horse), 166

Vanderbilt, Alfred G., 123
Veitch, John, 2, *100*, 103–9, *132*, 133–40, 164, 166–68, 173–74, 175–76, 178–

79, 184–86, 193–94, 196, 199, 202,
207–10, 212, 213, 218–19, 222–23,
228, 235–37, 238–40, 245, 246, 249,
252–53, 255–56, 258, 261, 263–64,
266, 268–69, 279
Veitch, Silas, 103
Veitch, Sylvester, 103–13, 105, 106, 107,
236, 279
Velasquez, Francisca, 168, 169–70
Velasquez, Jorge, 2, 133–34, 153, 154, 155,
157, 161, 168–174, 175–76, 177,
179, 182, 185, 188, 192, 195, 196,
196, 209, 211, 213, 214, 215, 218,
219, 222, 223, 225–26, 228, 235, 237,
241–42, 246, 247, 248–51, 253, 259,
267–69, 279, 280
Velasquez, Margarita, 174
Volney (horse), 173

War Admiral (horse), 225, 232, 233, 237, 239
Warner, Albert, 69
Washington Post, 64, 210
Washington Times-Herald, 53
Wheatley Stable, 76
Whirlaway (horse), 22, 41–46, 47, 47, 48,
51, 57, 164, 233, 272
Whitney, Cornelius Vanderbilt, 11, 72, 104,
105
Whitney, Searle, 105
Whitney Stakes, 160–61, 263, 264
Whittingham, Charlie, 117, 191
Widener, George D., 104, 105
Winfrey, Bill, 123, 126
Winter Book, 72, 75, 181
Wolfson, Florence, 65, 81, 95
Wolfson, Gary, 82, 97
Wolfson, Louis:
   as Affirmed owner, 138, 140, 161, 165,
   179, 180, 186, 191, 202–5, 216, 222,
   224, 234–35, 246, 247, 250, 251, 262,
   268, 274, 275, 278–79, 281–82, 283
   background of, 2, 10, 59–69, 75
   betting by, 69, 70
   first marriage of, 65, 81, 95
   as Harbor View Farm owner, 10–11, 16,
   58, 70, 72–73, 75, 76–77, 82, 88, 97,
   101, 124, 203, 272

   as horse breeder, 9–22, 24–25, 57, 69–73,
   75–76, 88–98, 101–2, 165
   imprisonment of, 2, 17, 81–82, 88, 96
   Jacobs as mentor of, 88–97, 118, 124
   Markey compared with, 24–25, 57, 72,
   73, 75, 82
   purse earnings of, 11, 70, 72, 76–77,
   180
   reputation of, 2, 10, 25, 57, 66–69,
   76–77, 81–82, 88, 96, 204, 278
   SEC investigation of, 16, 68–69, 79–82
   second marriage of, 17–18, 95–98, 124,
   224
   takeover deals by, 10, 59–69, 72–73, 76,
   79–82, 278
   trainers hired by, 10–15, 70–72, 118,
   123–25
   wealth of, 10, 64, 65, 69–70, 72–73, 75
Wolfson, Morris, 59–60, 61
Wolfson, Patrice Jacobs, 17–18, 88, 91–98,
101–2, 114, 115, 124, 129–130,
135, 136, 138, 140, 161, 164, 165,
166, 167, 176, 180, 186, 191, 202–3,
204–5, 216, 224, 233, 234–35, 246,
247, 249, 250, 251, 262, 265, 274,
278, 279, 283
Wolfson, Sam, 59–60, 61
Wolfson, Steve, 82, 97, 278
Wolfson Family Foundation, 64, 81
Won't Tell You (horse), 18, 20–21, 24, 97,
98, 101–2, 113, 115, 121, 158
Wood Memorial Stakes, 72, 95, 125, 190,
193, 209
Wood Native (horse), 136
Woodward Stakes, 273
Woolf, George, 217, 239
Wright, Bertha, 87, 277
Wright, Orville and Wilbur, 27
Wright, Warren, Jr., 51, 52, 87, 277
Wright, Warren, Sr., 22, 23, 26, 28–53, 54,
55, 56, 83, 85, 87, 103, 277
Wright, William Monroe, 27–35, 37, 49

Ycaza, Manny, 170
Youthful Stakes, 134, 135–37, 138

Zoman (horse), 283

ABOUT THE AUTHORS

Linda Carroll and **David Rosner** are experienced journalists who have co-authored three acclaimed nonfiction books. They won the Dr. Tony Ryan Award, which annually fetes the best book about Thoroughbred racing with a $10,000 prize, in 2018 for *Out of the Clouds: The Unlikely Horseman and the Unwanted Colt Who Conquered the Sport of Kings.*

Carroll is a Peabody Award–winning writer who covers health and medicine for NBC News and whose articles have appeared in the *New York Times* and other prestigious publications. An accomplished equestrian who owns and operates Fiery Run Farm in New Jersey, she brings three decades of experience in breeding, training, and showing her Arabian and Oldenburg sport horses. Her herd also includes a Thoroughbred racehorse turned broodmare whose sire is two-time Breeders' Cup Classic champion Tiznow and whose pedigree (like Affirmed's and Alydar's) traces back through Native Dancer and Raise a Native.

Rosner has worked as a sportswriter and editor whose articles have appeared in major metro newspapers and national magazines. While on staff at *Newsday*, he earned national Associated Press Sports Editors awards for event coverage and investigative reporting. As a cub reporter there, he was introduced to turf writing when his first bylined stories chronicled the harrowing 1977 Belmont Park spill that hospitalized wunderkind jockey Steve Cauthen on the eve of Affirmed's maiden race and delayed the teen phenom's debut as the colt's regular rider for three months.